A READER'S GUIDE TO
FINNEGANS WAKE

Richard Fallis, *Series Editor*

A READER'S GUIDE TO FINNEGANS WAKE

by William York Tindall

Syracuse University Press

First Syracuse University Press Edition 1996

97 98 99 00 01   6 5 4 3 2

Originally published in 1969. Published by arrangement with Farrar, Straus and Giroux.

Excerpts from the following books are reprinted by permission of the Viking Press, Inc. and Faber & Faber Ltd.: *Finnegans Wake* by James Joyce, Copyright 1939 by James Joyce, © 1967 by George Joyce and Lucia Joyce; *Letters of James Joyce,* edited by Stuart Gilbert, Copyright © 1957, 1966 by the Viking Press, Inc.; *Letters of James Joyce,* Volumes II and III, edited by Richard Ellman, Copyright © 1966 by F. Lionel Monro, as Administrator of the Estate of James Joyce.

Designed by Herb Johnson

The paper used in the publication meets the minimum requirements of American National Standard for Information Science—Permanence of Paper for Printed Library Materials, ANSI Z39.48-1984. ∞™

Library of Congress Cataloging-in-Publication Data

Tindall, William York, 1903–
A reader's guide to Finnegans wake / by William York Tindall.
p.   cm. — (Irish studies)
Originally published: New York : Farrar, Straus and Giroux,
[1969] , in series: [The Reader's guide series].
Includes bibliographical references and index.
ISBN 0-8156-0385-1 (alk. paper)
1. Joyce, James, 1882–1941. Finnegans wake. 2. Ireland—In
literature. I. Title. II. Series: Irish studies (Syracuse, N.Y.)
PR6019.09F5938   1996
823'.912—dc20   96-7653

To Celia

CONTENTS

A READER'S GUIDE TO
FINNEGANS WAKE

INTRODUCTION

Finnegans Wake is about anybody, anywhere, anytime or, as Joyce puts it (598.1),[1] about "Every those personal place objects . . . where soevers." At present or thereabouts the whereabouts of anybody in particular—or somebody—is Chapelizod at the western edge of Dublin on the river Liffey. This "Great Sommboddy within the Omniboss" (415.17)—he keeps a pub now—is commonly known by his initials, H.C.E., which stand for H. C. Earwicker or, when he is less individual, for "Here Comes Everybody" or, when altogether up-to-date, for "Heinz cans everywhere" or, at other times and higher places, for "Haroun Childeric Eggeberth." Indeed, the "bynames" of this "humile, commune and ensectuous" man, at one "timecoloured place" or another, are various: Adam, Christ, Caesar, Genghis Khan, Cromwell, Wellington, Guinness, Finnegan, and "Ogelthorpe or some other ginkus." When less particular, he is a Russian general. It is difficult, therefore, to "idendifine the individuone" (51.6); for H.C.E. is "homogenius" entirely. In Dublin they identify him with the hill of Howth, the Wellington Monument, and the Magazine in Phoenix Park. But here and anywhere else—Dublin is anywhere—H.C.E. is a faller, like Adam; like Jesus, a riser; and like Tim Finnegan, the Master Builder, a

[1] My parenthetical page and line references apply to every edition of the *Wake,* English, American, hard cover or paperback. References to *Ulysses* are to the new American edition (1961).

To make a line-marker, place a sheet of paper on any page of the *Wake.* Make a mark on the margin of your sheet for each line of the page and number your marks by fives.

waker at his wake. Like the Phoenix too—Phoenix Park fronts
the back of the pub—except that this bird is singular and H.C.E.
plural. From his ashes and the debris of his battles rise children,
cities, and books.

His wife, Anna, has a hand in these. Anna Earwicker, commonly known by the initials A.L.P. (Anna Livia Plurabelle), is
any woman or "annyma"—Anima. If H.C.E. is our father, she
is our Great Mother. He creates and falls. Picking his pieces up,
and renewing them, she wakes him at his wake. As he is the hill
in Joyce's familial geography, so she is the river—of life and
time. Among her signs are the delta or triangle, the female O,
and Mrs. Bloom's "yes." This "wee" (or *oui*) girl is Eve, Mary,
Isis, any woman you can think of, and a *poule*—at once a river-
pool, a whore, and a little hen.

Mr. and Mrs. Earwicker have three children, twin sons and a
daughter, who are as general as their parents. Known as Shem
and Shaun, Jerry and Kevin, Mutt and Jeff, the two boys are as
equal and opposite as the ant and the grasshopper or time and
space. The contention of these rivals—*rivae* are the banks of a
river—represents all wars and debates of man's history. Isabel,
the daughter, or Iseult la Belle—Chapelizod is the Chapel of
Iseult—is every girl, call her what you will: Nuvoletta, Margareena or Miss Butys Pott. There she sits at her mirror, admiring
herself, while father and sons admire her; for the boys are as
"ensectuous" as their old man. (A virgin, says Pussy Galore, is a
girl who can run faster than her brother, father or uncle.) The
tensions within this family are all the tensions of history. Family
process is historical process with all its quarrels, agreements,
loves, and hates. The sons, uniting like Brutus and Cassius, kill
the father and take his place. Daughter, taking mother's place,
will be replaced by her daughter as the new father by new sons,
and so on, indefinitely. Rise and fall and rise again, sleeping and
waking, death and resurrection, sin and redemption, conflict and
appeasement, and, above all, time itself—*saecula saeculorum*—
are the matter of Joyce's essay on man.

In Earwicker's local-universal household at Chapelizod are
Kate, the maid of all work, and Joe, the handyman. Kate, the

more important of these, is old A.L.P. as Isabel is young A.L.P.
Like the White Goddess, A.L.P. has three aspects, young, old,
and middling. But the seven members of the household are not
the only people around. There are twelve men, customers of
Earwicker's pub, gossips, jurors at his trial, and mourners at his
wake. There are four old men, Matthew, Mark, Luke, and John,
or, taken together, Mamalujo. These snoopers are judges and
historians, authors of the gospels and of Irish annals. (The
twelve and the four seem embodiments of Earwicker's guilt and
his conscience.) In the vicinity are twenty-eight girls, friends of
Isabel, the twenty-ninth. These twenty-eight Floras or rainbow
girls are extensions of Isabel, the leap-year girl, but all twenty-
nine are extensions of A.L.P. In the Park, Dublin's Eden, are
two girls and three soldiers, involved somehow in Earwicker's
sin. The two temptresses seem A.L.P. and Isabel. The triumvirate seems Earwicker and his sons; for, as A.L.P. observes,
"There were three men in him" (113.14), as in A.L.P. there are
three women. Since Earwicker's family is the heart of secular
process and since secular process is the subject of the book, it is
not surprising that the two girls and the three soldiers, projections of the family, make more than two-hundred appearances,
according to my count. Down by the river are two washerwomen
who, gossiping about A.L.P. and H.C.E., make his private linen
public. These old girls seem tree and stone on the banks of the
river or, as rivals on the banks, aspects of Shem and Shaun. In
short, the people of the *Wake,* all thousand and one of them, are
members or projections of the family, aspects of H.C.E. and
A.L.P., who, in a sense, are the only people of the *Wake* and in
the world. In the beginning in the Garden were Adam and Eve,
our first parents; near the end near Phoenix Park are H.C.E. and
A.L.P., "our forced payrents" (576.27).

A book about two people, here and everywhere, who, though
not themselves every time, are constant, demands suitable
method and shape. Joyce was equal to these demands; for, leading a "doublin existents" (578.14), he was of three minds: analogical, verbal, and shaping. Take the first of these first. It may
be that Adam, Noah, and Finn MacCool are Earwicker's names

now and again; but Adam, Noah, and Finn MacCool are also analogies or parallels that, bringing other times, other places, other men to mind, make particulars general. So too, in their way, the hill, the giant, and the Eucharist; for H.C.E. is also *Hoc corpus est*. By such analogies Joyce made his modern Dubliner a citizen of everywhere else all the time. Analogy was nothing new for Joyce. The Dublin of *Dubliners* is crowded with counterparts. Saluting Thoth or Hermes Trismegistus, the god of correspondences, in *A Portrait of the Artist,* Joyce enlarged Stephen, who, by the aid of correspondences, left the class of elements at Clongowes Wood College at Sallins, County Kildare, Ireland, for Europe, the world, the universe. Stephen, whose capital sin is pride, finds analogies for himself in Byron, Napoleon, the Count of Monte Cristo, Daedalus, Icarus, Lucifer, Jesus, and God. In *Ulysses,* Joyce, a proud man too, found Bloom an analogy for himself and analogies for Bloom in Ulysses, Jesus, Elijah, Sinbad, Moses, and a host of others. Take Moses—and it's news I'm telling you: buying a pork kidney at the shop of Moses Dlugacz, Bloom takes from the counter an advertisement for reclaiming Palestine. As Moses Dlugacz gives Bloom, a chosen person, this Pisgah sight of the Promised Land, so Bloom, becoming Moses and pointing to Molly's window, will give Stephen, a chosen person, a Pisgah sight of a Promised Land more "melonsmellonous" than Dlugacz's fruity "Agendath Netaim." As Moses Dlugacz to Bloom, so Moses Bloom to Stephen. Making a pork butcher of Moses Dlugacz, one of Joyce's students at Trieste and an ordained rabbi, must be accounted a private joke—a gargoyle on the fabric of analogies and reciprocal correspondences.

We can agree that Joyce had an analogical mind; but this mind, among the greatest this side Mozart (I would not love Joyce half so much, loved I not Mozart more), this mind, this great mind, I say, was verbal more—more than Mozart's, that is, and more than analogical. Another "lord of language," Joyce used words for all they are worth, and this, since words rival figures among man's inventions, is a great deal. He controlled all styles from the "scrupulous meanness" of *Dubliners* to the accurate richness of *Ulysses.* As for the *Wake:* the words of this work are a kind of play, a master's play. Playing with everyone, everywhere, at every time, at the same time, like a juggler with eleven balls in the air, requires a language that plays with many things at once. For this purpose "the pun," if I may quote myself, "is mightier than the word." In the *Wake* the Dublin talk of a triple thinker handles more than "two thinks at a time" (583.7). At once efficient and funny, his words, the charged composites of his "puntomine" (587.8), also serve a comic purpose. Not only his essay on man, the *Wake* is his human comedy.

There are puns, now and again, in *Ulysses.* Thinking of food as he encounters Parnell's brother, who is thinking perhaps of dead Parnell, Bloom says, "Poached eyes on ghost." Emerging from context to enrich it, this happy condensation says what George Eliot, indifferent to words, would have needed a page for. Consider Father Coffey's "Namine. Jacobs Vobiscuits." "Namine," fitting the holy occasion, includes *namen, nomen, numine, lumine.* "Jacobs Vobiscuits," combining Jacob's Biscuits (made in Dublin), *Pax vobiscum,* and the Eucharist, recalls the biscuit tin or ciborium of the Cyclops episode. From such Homeric origins, maybe, the witty habit of the *Wake.* "Alcohoran" (20.9–10), an agreement of disagreements like a seventeenth-century conceit, makes Alcoran compatible with incompatible alcohol. "In the buginning is the woid" (378.29), a variation on St. John's "In the beginning was the Word," confuses Genesis and God with a bug—Earwicker is an earwig— who keeps an inn in modern Dublin, and the void with the word, in Brooklyn perhaps. However funny, this verbal play is serious; for the creative word of the beginning was Joyce's end.

Not only a "punman," Joyce was a "punsil shapner" (98.30). He wrote his puns in sharpened pencil—as the manuscript of the *Wake* in the British Museum proves—and, arranging them, gave them shape. His "mundballs [mouth-and-world balls] of the ephemerids" (416.23) have all the "earmarks of design" (66.1)—"As Great Shapesphere puns it" (295.3–4). Like God and Shakespeare, the lord of language of the Globe theater, Joyce possessed the shaping spirit. A Master Builder, above giddiness, he built a second and solider tower of "Babbel" (199.31) from the debris of the first. Out of that confusion of tongues a loftier confusion.

For his construction, whether tower or sphere—these, after all, are only metaphors, inviting mixture—the shaper needed a frame, both framework and frame of reference. He built *Ulysses* on the narrative frame of Homer. The *Wake* required frame of another sort, philosophical this time, from Vico and Bruno, who proved as congenial and useful as Homer had and no less amusing.

Giambattista Vico's *La Scienza Nuova* (1725. *The New Science,* translated by Thomas Bergin and Max Fisch, Ithaca, Cornell, 1948) is a philosophy of history. After studying languages, myths, fables, and histories—with special attention to Homer and Livy—Vico concluded that man's history, created by man under the laws of divine providence, proceeds cyclically through three ages, the divine, heroic, and human. After a *ricorso* or period of reflux, the cycle begins again, *saecula saeculorum.* The idea of temporal cycling was neither new nor extravagant. As Vergil's Messianic eclogue shows, they had the idea in classical times, and in our time Yeats commended a system of gyres in his *Vision* and in many poems, "Two Songs from a Play," for example, and "Sailing to Byzantium." Cycling had become attractive again after disenchantment with the idea of linear progress.

Vico's divine age—Eden, Egypt, and the fabulous darkness after Rome's fall—produces religion and the family. His heroic age, an aristocratic period of lords and vassals, wars and duels, produces marriage. The human age, which produces cities, laws, civil obedience, and, eventually, popular government, is distinguished by burial. (Sequences of religion, marriage, and burial throughout the *Wake* indicate Vico's ages.) After the government of the people, by the people, and for the people, destroying itself, perishes from the earth, a period of confusion, the *ricorso,* stirs things up. From their confusion, "like the phoenix, they rise again"—or, as Joyce puts it, "the Phoenican [Finnegan the

Phoenix] wakes" (608.32). Each of Vico's three ages has a special language or way of communicating. The mute primitives of the divine age—like so many Mutts and Jutes—communicate by grunts, gestures, hieroglyphs, coats of arms, and fables. The imaginative men of the heroic age create alphabets, metaphors, and proverbs—*La vache qui rit n'amasse pas mousse.* The plebs of the human age take to vulgar speech on the one hand, and on the other to abstract discourse—that, for example, of instructions for making out your income tax. (To Vico's ways of communicating, all of which appear in the *Wake,* Joyce added radio and television.) Vico's recurrent cycle, at once repetitious and various—like the *Wake* itself—starts with a bang. God, the thunderer, thunders, and fearful men, retiring to caves, establish religions and families. Divine thunder, which drives man to these extremes, is both man's fall and his rise or, at least, its beginning; for his *culpa* is *felix.* There are ten Viconian thunders in *Finnegans Wake.*

Joyce found Vico agreeable because, like Yeats, whose system of gyres Joyce liked, he liked cycles. *Ulysses* is full of them. Bloom goes out in the morning, comes home at night, and will go out again in the morning. Mrs. Bloom's monologue rolls, like the earth, from "yes" to "yes." And so on, Joyce implies, through "cycles of cycles of generations" (*Ulysses,* 414). He liked Vico's emphasis upon language, fable, myth, Homer, family, and city. That, by happy coincidence, Dublin has a Vico Road, two circular roads, and a park named Phoenix could not displease a Dubliner. Neither a philosopher of history nor a convert to Vico, this family man from Dublin took from Vico what seemed agreeable to his design. Adapting his philosopher, Joyce gave more emphasis than Vico had to thunder and giants; and, giving more than Viconian importance to the *ricorso,* made four ages of Vico's three. "I would not pay overmuch attention to these theories"—those of Vico and Bruno—Joyce says in a letter (I, 241), "beyond using them for all they are worth." What they were worth to him, besides the convenience of a frame, was a parallel that, enlarging Earwicker's family process and making it general, placed and replaced it in time. Not Vico's system but Earwicker's family is central. Yet the *Wake* is crowded with references to Vico.

As Homer's story, freely adapted, determines the three-part structure of *Ulysses* and the sequence of chapters, so Vico's system, freely adapted, determines the four-part structure of the *Wake* and the sequence of its chapters. Part I is Vico's divine age, Part II his heroic age, Part III his human age, and Part IV an enlarged *ricorso*. The seventeen chapters also follow this sequence. Chapter I of Part I is a divine age, Chapter II a heroic age, and so on—wheels within a wheel. The eight chapters of Part I represent two Viconian wheels within, and affected by, the general divinity of the part. The eight chapters of Parts II and III—four chapters in each—represent two cycles within, and affected by, their heroic and human contexts. Chapter XVI of Part III, for example, though a *ricorso,* is a *ricorso* within a human age, hence different in character from Chapter IV of Part I, a *ricorso* in a divine age. Part IV, the general *ricorso,* has one chapter, which, though a *ricorso,* is by position in the sequence another divine age or its herald. Each of the parts and chapters, whatever the age it celebrates, contains elements of the other ages. Chapter I of Part I, a divine age within a divine age, displays the city which arises in the human age.

Despite this cycling, Joyce's hieroglyph for the *Wake* and its title is a square, its sides, no doubt, the quadrants, a little squashed, of Vico's wheel. From so great an inventor as Joyce a square wheel, bumping along, is not surprising: "It's a wheel, I tell the world. *And* it's all *square*" (*Letters,* I, 251). Bloom tried in vain to square the circle. Joyce, more ingenious than Bloom, has circled the square. Sometimes his hieroglyph for the *Wake* is a cube, though Shapesphere's product must be a sphere. As Joyce, squaring the circle, circled the square, so he cubed the sphere or sphered the cube, by incubation.

Giordano Bruno and Nicholas of Cusa, his predecessor, provided the reciprocating engine Joyce needed to bump his spherical cube along. Bruno of Nola—by good fortune Dublin has a bookshop called Browne and Nolan—commended discord and concord. Anticipating Hegel, he advanced a dialectical process within a closed system of moving and changing parts, each of which interpenetrates its opposite; for "all is in all"—as in the *Wake*. Yet, from opposition identity, and from the conflict of contraries their coincidence. In God all contraries are united. His concordant maximum includes all discordant minimums. Blake, in *The Marriage of Heaven and Hell,* one of Joyce's favorite books, agrees, on the whole, with Bruno: "Without contraries is no progress. Attraction and Repulsion, Reason and Energy, Love and Hate, are necessary to Human existence. From these contraries spring what the religious call Good and Evil." Bruno's philosophy, says Joyce, putting it neatly (*Letters,* I, 226), "is a kind of dualism—every power in nature must evolve an opposite in order to realise itself and opposition brings reunion." Maybe he got his quarreling twins from Bruno, without whose intrusion one son to replace the father might have seemed sufficient. Maybe Shem is Bruno's thesis, Shaun his antithesis, and godlike H.C.E., in whom these contraries coincide, their synthesis. Anyway, before and after taking father's place, the equal and opposite twins agree. H.C.E., their compound, must fall to pieces before being recompounded, and so on, we may be certain, to no certain end.

The frame supplied by Vico and Bruno is only a working part in the great arrangement. Within the frame or on it, among all the machinery, materials must be disposed according to one aesthetic rule or another. Sometimes Joyce, as if another Cicero, disposed his matter in classical shape: introduction, statement, elaboration with variation, and conclusion. This shape might do for ordering a chapter generally, but each of the matters within it is so closely involved with others that the disposition of such intricacy became "a bewildering business. . . . Complications to right of me, complications to left of me, complex on the page before me, perplex in the pen beside me, duplex in the meandering eyes of me, stuplex on the face that reads me" (*Letters,* I, 222). He listened to his hair growing white. Yet, coming through in great shape, he made a thing than which nothing is shaplier.

Motifs or themes, weaving the thing together, proved a help.

These particulars, carrying meaning from place to place and, as they reappear, acquiring new meanings from new contexts, were nothing new to Joyce. In "The Dead," the motif of snow, structural and significant at once, linking part to part and gathering a little from each, accumulates and, at the end, presents all the meanings of the story it has helped to shape. The motifs announced on the first two pages of *A Portrait of the Artist*—road, cow, flower, water, girl, bird—prove, as they recur, changing with the contexts they enrich and unite, no less serviceable. *Ulysses* is a greater complex of such motifs. Tea, soap, potato, Plumtree, Macintosh, and the Eucharist are familiar; but rocks may be unfamiliar enough to detain us. Molly's "O, rocks!" bringing both Gibraltar and Howth to mind, is echoed by the ancient mariner's "I'm tired of all them rocks in the sea." But these are no more than peaks in an elaborate range that begins in the Proteus episode, where rocks are the only deniers of external and internal flux. The dog pisses on one, Stephen on another, but rocks receive two other, equally important, creations from flux. Preparing for his oration from Scylla, a considerable rock, Stephen, a wandering rock, writes a poem on a lesser rock than Scylla and on another lays his snot. "O, rocks!" says Molly after a similar discourse. But Bloom's discourse on metempsychosis, a matter of flux, lacks the solidity of my discourse on rocks, which invites a watery syllable.

Motifs from *Ulysses* reappear in the *Wake:* tea, Eucharist, and soap, the hunt and the race. But there are more, old and new. Some are phrases or verbal tags: *felix culpa,* Dublin's motto, the Angelus, and "sin sin" or "fin fin" for the fall from the Magazine wall. Some are personal surrogates: the Prankquean, the two girls and the three soldiers. Some are actual people: Swift and Isaac Butt. Some are concentrates of the *Wake* itself: the letter dug by the hen from the dump—another motif —in the Park. Others, such as drawers, conceal and reveal Joyce's obsessions. In the great design of repetition with variation that the *Wake* shares with life, these motifs, more than devices or connective threads, become the fabric itself or, at least, important figures in it. A pattern of letter, drawers, Prankquean, dump, Swift, and the rest, the *Wake* is what it has been woven of.

It seems an arabesque—the elaborate decoration of something so simple that it evades us. This simple text, like that on some pages of the Book of Kells, is lost in the design. Like the illuminator of these pages, Joyce had a mediaeval mind. Virtuosity was a defect of his mediaeval virtue. But such decoration is a kind of play and all art is play of a kind. As for kind: let us try—try perhaps in vain—to see what kind of thing the *Wake* is before resuming these tries at its structure.

Is this arabesque of motifs a novel? Many novels have structure, some have motifs, and a few, arabesques; but none of these is essential. A novel—if we can forget Nathalie Sarraute—is a narrative with characters who, however general their implication, are individuals. *Ulysses* is a novel. It may be that Bloom has splendid parallels: Jesus, Odysseus, and Moses. It may be that Bloom, pursuing his daily odyssey, is "Everyman or Noman," but he is also Mr. Bloom of Dublin in 1904, a man so peculiar that when he is around Dubliners say, "There's Bloom" —not, "Jesus Christ! There's Moses Odysseus." But Earwicker is as different from Bloom as the *Wake* from *Ulysses*. Though the *Wake,* like the Tower of Babel and the Arabian Nights, has "one thousand and one stories, all told" (5.28–29), it has little story to tell. Such as it is, the story told, emerging from a thousand and one other stories of sin, encounter or fall, begins in Chapter IX with children playing at evening in the street in front of the pub. In Chapter X, having gone in for supper, they study their lessons upstairs while downstairs, in Chapter XI, Earwicker serves drinks to his customers and, after closing time, falls to the floor, drunk. And so to bed in Chapter XVI, to make love of a sort till cockcrow. Not much of a story, to be sure, for a book so enormous. And who is Earwicker? Bloom may suggest Everyman or Noman, but Earwicker—if that is his name— is a "general omnibus character" (444.2), Everyman entirely or, in Danish, "enver a man" (582.12). His wife, as far from individual, is every woman; his daughter, every young girl; and his sons, whatever peculiarities they owe to Joyce and his friends, are types: the introvert and the extrovert, the artist and the man of affairs. A work that, though swarming with people, lacks individuals—a work that, though composed of stories, has no story to speak of, is not a novel in the accepted sense of the eighteenth century or the nineteenth. Indeed, far from the fictional habit of these times and our own, the *Wake* goes for method—or so it seems—to *The Romance of the Rose* and *Everyman,* a method of allegorical generality that persisted more or less until Ben Jonson substituted every man in his individual humour for Everyman. For all its concrete particulars, its *haecceitas* or Scotian thisness, Joyce's pre-Jonsonian abstraction of humanity yields "someone imparticular who will somewherise for the whole" (602.7). Even Earwicker's sin, perhaps every sin of every man, is "imparticular." Schooled by old Aquinas and unable to forget his lessons, Joyce devoted the *Wake* to *quidditas* or Thomistic whatness—the whatness of mankind.

What the *Wake* is not is easier to determine than what it is. That this structure "of quibble and of quiddity" is not a novel we may be sure. But it could be a fiction in the sense (from *fingere,* fiction's root) of something made. Indeed, it may be the "Supreme Fiction" that Wallace Stevens, distantly apprehending, made notes toward; for, like the great fiction he approached, the *Wake* is an abstract thing that changes and gives pleasure. An abstraction from nature, a fiction is unnatural. A departure from nature and its violation, any artifice is false or, as Joyce put it, a fraud, a fake or a forgery. Faithful to Daedalus, the Cretan artificer or smith, Stephen, setting up his "smithy," resolves to become a forger. Jim the Penman, one of Shem's originals, was a notorious forger. (In a letter, III, 157, Joyce called himself "James the Punman.") Shem, an "ambitrickster" (423.6), is Shaun's "fakesimilar" (484.34–35); the substance of H.C.E., a created abstraction, is "fraudstuff" (7.13); and the *Wake,* an elegant edifice, is "the hoax that joke bilked" (511.34). A fiction, then, in both senses of the word—something made and something faked—the *Wake,* a thing of words, is a thing like nothing else, an arrangement to which no rules or categories apply. A thing in itself suggests autonomy, but a thing of words cannot be autonomous; for words, however important in themselves, are referential. The *Wake* is an arrangement of references with all the appearance of autonomy. A violation of nature, the *Wake* is a fake like God's world, a violation of nothing. It is not for nothing that, in her letter to Bloom, Martha confused world and word. The *Wake,* a greater confusion, is a world of words.

As if made according to Stephen's aesthetic formula, the *Wake,* "selfbounded and selfcontained," has "wholeness." The relation of part to part within this whole is what Stephen, following St. Thomas, called "harmony"; and from this harmonious whole the "radiance" or whatness that we must try to apprehend. However referential to our concerns—living, dying, and all betwixt and between—the *Wake,* "selfbounded and selfcontained," is a closed system: "no body present here which was not there before. Only is order othered. Nought is nulled. *Fuitfiat!*" (613.13–14) It is a "grand continuum [universe], overlorded by fate [Vico] and interlarded with accidence [accident and the inflections of words, 472.30–31]." Relativity rules Joyce's time-space continuum as it rules Einstein's. Like God's world without end, the *Wake* seems "whorled without aimed" (272.4–5). But if we think so, we are deceived—defrauded by Joyce's fraudstuff.

As God's world, created by the Word, is an endless arrangement and rearrangement of ninety-six elements—give or take a couple—so Joyce's closed system is an endless arrangement and rearrangement of a thousand and one elements that, whatever their multiplicity, are limited in number. In the *Wake,* as in the world, we get the same things over and over, the same things repeated with variety, to be sure, but nevertheless the same old things. The two girls and the three soldiers, Buckley, the Cad, and the Prankquean plague Earwicker again and again. The hen is always scratching that letter from the dump. Swift is always around in one capacity or another. Like these substantial motifs, subordinate shapes recur: battles, debates, quizzes, riddles, academic lectures, advertisements, fables, parodies, reversals, lyrics, ruminations, "quashed quotatoes, messes of mottage"

(183.22), and Rabelaisian catalogues of the kind that bore and divert us in the Cyclops episode—all these bits, pieces, and little shapes arranged and rearranged as if in the circle of a kaleidoscope that we keep an ear to.

Ear and eye, contraries that come to terms at last—Shem's ear, Shaun's eye—bring us by recirculation to music and the movies, two forms that the *Wake* is more or less akin to. It may be that the *Wake* is a thing like nothing else, but it owes a thing or two to other things. For his structure—to return to this— Joyce found hints in these two arts, the one devoted to eye, the other to ear. Nothing surprising here; for the *Wake*, whatever its quarreling ingredients, is a place, like Earwicker's person, where things coincide.

"All art," says Walter Pater in his essay on Giorgione, *"constantly aspires towards the condition of music,"* where matter and form are one. The *Wake* all but achieves what other works distantly aspire towards. From the time of *Chamber Music,* Joyce had music in mind. For the Sirens episode he made a structure of sound, sequence, and motif that, if not music itself, is music's parody. What kept him from music was words; for, unlike the notes of a scale, words—not only sounds and, when in sequence, rhythms—are referential. Program music of a sort is what they are condemned to. Joyce referred to the *Wake* as a "suite" (*Letters,* I, 250; III, 157), but, limited by the nature of letters, all Finnegan gets is "the finnecies of poetry wed music" (377.16–17). Nevertheless, like Eliot in *The Waste Land,* Joyce did approach what I. A. Richards called the "music of ideas"—a music of words in which ideas play second fiddle. Plainly, Joyce's variations on a theme owe something to classical music and his motifs owe even more to Wagner (see *Letters,* II, 214); but more important than these are structures which, now and again, seem less like the rhetorical pattern of Cicero than like overture, statement of theme, elaboration, variation, cadenza, and coda or, as if the opus were an opera, like solo, recitative, and duet. Chapter I, more than a formal oration, is as good an example as any of musical structure. Joyce knew his Wagner, the librettos of Lorenzo Da Ponte, and a little about

fugues; but his taste, inclining to the opera and the ballads of the nineteenth century, was imperfect. *Martha* and "The Croppy Boy" were his delight; and Bach, in the *Wake,* seems no more than the occasion for puns—so, for the matter of that, is everything else—yet in the *Wake,* as in a cantata by Bach, several things going on at once prove agreeable to the intelligent ear.

The ignorant eye delights in movies. Nothing ignorant about Joyce's ailing eye, but, like that of a "flickerflapper" (266.31), it delighted in flickers too. Joyce established a cinema in Dublin and, when he could see, saw movies in Paris. He discussed the art of film with Sergei Eisenstein, D. W. Griffith's disciple. The structure of the *Wake* is evidence of this addiction. But long before that, in the first chapter of *A Portrait,* and in the Cyclops episode, Joyce arranged his matters in a way that suggests Griffith's montage, the movie-maker's art of putting unrelated things side by side. The placing of matters throughout the *Wake* seems a kind of montage by juxtaposition as the puns seem montage by superimposition. Joyce refers to "monthage" (223.8), an art of timing and placing, calls the *Wake* his "newseryreel" (489.35), and, rolling "away the reel world" (64.25), invents scenarios, the best of them on Daddy Browning and Peaches. There are references to *Mr. Deeds, My Man Godfrey, The Birth of a Nation,* and to actors in the films. Joyce is so plainly of the company of "cinemen" (6.18)—a spicy company—that to say more here seems as uncalled for as casting perils before Pauline.

Not only like music and the movies in structure—like them in a way but neither one nor the other—the *Wake* is put together like a long poem, *The Waste Land* again, of parts placed side by side without transition, parts in a variety of rhythms, shapes, and tones. Like the parts and the whole of such a poem the parts and whole of the *Wake* evade immediate understanding. Calling this kind of poem a "superior amusement," Eliot implied perhaps that working it out is an amusement for superior people. The *Wake* is certainly an amusement for people like ourselves; but, however like a poem, the *Wake,* a thing of its own kind, is not a poem exactly. The *Wake* is the *Wake,* and, as Gertrude

Stein, had she not detested Joyce, might have added, is the *Wake*.

But the *Wake*—a complicated thing the *Wake*—is a dream, a dream that owes much of its structure and deportment to the obsessive repetition and absurdity of nightmare, our relief from the cares that, as Longfellow says, "infest the day." Long interest in dream brought Joyce to the construction of his "nightmaze" (411.8) or "dromo of todos" (598.2), his dream of all on a running track for all. Several of the early epiphanies record his dreams. The little boy of "The Sisters" has a disturbing dream of Father Flynn. Three crucial dreams condense and reveal the political, religious, and domestic horrors of *A Portrait;* and in *Ulysses,* Stephen dreams of mother and Bloom, Bloom of Molly. The Circe episode with its shifting identities and dark uncertainties, is a kind of dream. The *Wake,* a more elaborate dream, develops from these.

In Freud, whose books on wit and dream the *Wake* includes, Joyce found the condensation, displacement, and symbol-making that, revealing our deepest concerns, hide them from dreamers. (The incest that rules Earwicker's night ruled Freud's days.) Puns, sometimes the products of Freud's dream, come straight from the witty unconscious by day and night alike. Confirming Joyce's verbal inclination, Freud may have shown its appropriateness for the work in progress. But "Jabberwocky," Lewis Carroll's dream poem, which Joyce did not discover until 1927 or 1928, when he was deep in the *Wake,* gave further encouragement. This poem and Humpty Dumpty's explication seem guides to verbal method: all those "portmanteau" words of the *Wake* and slipping words for "feeling aslip" (597.12).

Ulysses tells all of man's waking life and mind. But the sleeping half of life—"la nuit de son être" (*Letters,* II, 432)—is no less important. It was to reveal " 'the dark night of the soul' " that Joyce wrote the *Wake* or so he says (*Letters,* I, 258; III, 146): "One great part of every human existence is passed in a state which cannot be rendered sensible by the use of wideawake language, cutanddry grammar and goahead plot." Question: can a work with so many intrusions of music, poetry, and the movies, besides the philosophies of Vico and Bruno, be an authentic dream, convincing enough to suspend our disbelief? Certainly, the form of some chapters, Ciceronian or musical, seems alien to dream. But within these designs are shifts, confusions, and uncertainties that seem dream's very stuff. Not a literal dream maybe—for other considerations get in the way—the *Wake* seems a verbal formula for the effect of dreaming, a conscious arrangement of dream materials for "feeling aslip." A master of words and forms, Joyce found suitable words for this effect and a suitable form. Such a form, allowing "artful disorder" (126.9) and the advantages of waking and sleeping at once, proved a convenience—just what he needed for the revelation of mankind. He must have agreed with Banquo:

> The instruments of darkness tell us truths,
> Win us with honest trifles. . . .

But as the verbal and formal trifles of dream and all its instruments of darkness conceal from the dreamer the truths they reveal to the analyst, so the *Wake,* with its trifling instruments, conceals its revelations about man from reader and analyst alike. The obscurity of the *Wake* can be thought of as the work of Freud's dream-work with its censorship. Awake at the *Wake,* we enjoy the benefits of sleep. "You mean to see," we say, "we have been hadding a sound night's sleep?" (597.1–2)

Problem: if the *Wake* is a dream, who is the dreamer? Our first guess is H.C.E., but are Sanskrit and Finnish within his linguistic capacity; does his learning include Vico, Stephen's nightmare of history, and the *Annals of the Four Masters?* But if Earwicker, more than a simple publican of Dublin, is everybody everywhere at all times, he could be the great "Sommboddy" we are after. The *Wake,* then, would be the dream of Everyman or, since Joyce saw himself in this capacity, of James Joyce, a collective consciousness drawing upon the collective unconscious.

Joyce's dream, differing in respect of this from most nightmares of history, is funny. Of that we may be sure, sure too that serious thinking about life need not be solemn or, as readers of George Eliot would prefer, earnest. "Life," said Gay, "is a jest," and gaiety is the *Wake*'s mark—its Matthew and Tristan too. Never earnest or solemn, Joyce seriously worked up to such gaiety by stages. *A Portrait*, however serious, is lightened by irony. *Ulysses,* however dark some passages, is a comedy. The *Wake,* says a friend of mine, is a farce—"the farce of dustiny" (162.2–3) perhaps, that Joyce's Verdi wrote when, aware of "the weight of old fletch," yet not dismayed, he saw coming to dust its destiny. Surely, the *Wake* abounds in farcical materials: clowns from comic strip, vaudeville, music hall, and circus. "Forced to farce" (374.11) with such "clownsillies" (537.35), we too may find the *Wake* another hilarious fake by "jamey-mock farceson" (423.1)—"God guard his . . . comicsong-book soul" (380.23–24). But farce is a category of drama, and, except for dream maybe, the *Wake* evades categories. There's "lots of fun at Finnegan's wake," says the poet in his ballad of Tim Finnegan. Taking my clue from this, distrusting categories as I distrust earnestness, I content myself with calling the *Wake* a very funny book.

As obscure as it is funny; and what keeps us from the fun of words is partly words themselves. Joyce puns in many languages, which, however justifiable by the consideration that Everybody's language must be every language, puzzle readers less linguistically competent than he. I, for instance, with no language but English to speak of or with, find the going rough. But there are dictionaries in the library; at a considerable university, such as mine, there is bound to be someone around with Sanskrit; and, having lived awhile, one gets to know a Gael or two with Gaelic and a Jew or two with Hebrew and, maybe, a little Arabic. Making a nuisance of myself, I pumped Italian, Russian, Breton, Telugu, Estonian, Volapuk, and the like, from friends and, sometimes, acquaintances. But whatever the Breton and Telugu, words from such languages are rarely essential; for the *Wake* is "basically English" (116.26) and Webster's dictionary, preferably the second edition, is our handiest guide. When other tongues intrude, they are commonly commoner than Bantu, Tagalog or Maori: Latin, French, German, Italian, Gaelic, and Danish mostly, with a few tags from Russian,

Czech, Finnish, and Hebrew that Joyce picked up from friends and, sometimes, acquaintances. Joyce had no more than a smattering of Spanish and classical Greek, yet the "dromo of todos" that we noticed awhile back is classical Greek and Spanish.

Allusions are another part of our difficulty. The general frame of the *Wake* may be Vico and Bruno, but the frames within which Joyce always worked were Ireland, the Church of Rome, and himself. To follow him we must have some acquaintance with these. His allusions to Irish history and to places in Dublin force us to read that troubled history and to visit Dublin or, at least, to consult a map of the city. His allusions to the Church and its rites—the Angelus, the cardinal virtues, and the sacraments—force us, if not Catholic, to go to Catholics for assurance or to get a Missal. His allusions to himself and his works demand considerable acquaintance with these. Privacies abound—the private joke on Moses Dlugacz is a good example —and such obsessive privacies as drawers, urination, and defecation that, clamoring for display throughout his life, Joyce was compelled to make public, in a private way, but public nevertheless. "His own image" to a man of genius, says Stephen—his own image, the bad accepted along with the good, is "all in all" and "the standard of all experience." Earwicker and Shem, like Bloom and Stephen before them, are projections, more or less, of Joyce; and A.L.P., like Mrs. Bloom and Gretta before her, is a projection of Nora.

Having mastered Ireland, the Church, and Joyce, we face another difficulty: his imperfect, scattered, and peculiar learning, allusions to which may escape us unless we get to work. He knew and referred to all the popular songs in the world, the neglected plays of Dion Boucicault, the Bible (unfamiliar to some nowadays), and the Egyptian Book of the Dead. Allusions to Parnell, who serves as parallel in the matters of father and son, betrayal, sin, gossip, and fall, send us to Parnell's biography. In his capacities of dean, writer, and old man with two girls, Swift, serving as parallel to Shaun, Shem or Earwicker, sends us to a consultation of his life and works. Sheridan Le Fanu's *House by the Churchyard,* no longer in print and missing

from most libraries, is referred to again and again. Local interest
—for this novel deals with Chapelizod and Phoenix Park—is
Joyce's excuse and our trouble. Communication, then, is as
much the problem here as identity; but since everybody in the
day of Samuel Beckett worries about communication and identity, we should feel at home and, if puzzled now and again,
blame the day we live in. Remember that the letter, scratched by
hen from dump and the *Wake*'s epitome, repels all efforts to
decipher it and, though addressed to someone and competently
carried, never reaches its destination.

Joyce prepares us by uncertainties about identity and communication and by all those clowns, swapping hats and falling off
ladders, for the day of Beckett, but these two writers are no
closer than father and son. Joyce lived in a world where accepted frames—Vico, Ireland, the Church—gave meaning to
particulars. The particulars of his reluctant disciple, who lives in
a contingent world, a mess without frames, are meaningless particulars. In Joyce's framed world a banana or a bicycle, taking
meaning from the frame around it, becomes "Havvah-ban-
Annah" (38.30) or a "bisexycle" (115.16). The unframed bananas or bicycles of Beckett are bananas or bicycles and nothing
more. Everything in the *Wake* has meaning, definite, limited by
frame or immediate context, and discoverable. Our problem is
to discover the meaning of particulars that, we may be sure, are
limited and meaningful. Our danger, a carelessness of Joyce's
limits, is too much ingenuity. As Joyce differs from his follower,
so he differs from his predecessors, the symbolists of France.
Their particulars—except for a swan or two or an albatross—
are as indefinitely suggestive as Macintosh in *Ulysses*. He is an
exception. In the *Wake,* frames and context rule indefiniteness
out. We deal, I say again, with definite things awaiting the discovery they resist. Beckett is absurd in the senses of contrary to
reason and beyond it. Joyce, in his rational world, is absurd in
the sense of funny.

The *Wake,* a world within this world, has its "sameold game-
bold adomic structure" (615.6)—a structure persisting from
Adam to H.C.E. or from the atom, which, as inquiry proves, is a

little nothing whirling around little or nothing. What is true of hydrogen is true of Adam, H.C.E., and the rest of us, whose experience of the *Wake* must parody our experience of the world it parodies. A form for the feeling of encountering the world, the *Wake* displays in three layers the stages of this daily encounter. Some things in *Wake* and world alike are immediately evident. Some things, resisting our first attempts, may be understood with a little effort. But other things, whatever our efforts, baffle us. To the pleasures of easy or difficult discovery Joyce added the pain of frustration. With this effect in mind he inserted passages, beyond common readers, in uncommon tongues—passages that, like some of the things in nature, have a meaning that escapes us. Deliberately, he inserted little puzzles (*Letters,* I, 228, 250). Suppose we solve one or two of what he called his "ninetynine-angular" mysteries. There are always more. Best not to worry about them; for they are an intended part of our experience and his effect. Joyce meant the *Wake,* like the world around it, to be inexhaustible. "Every talk," but this one, "has his stay" (597.19). What man, after such knowledge, would leave the *Wake* for a book he could get to the bottom of? No bottom here, as elsewhere falling Hopkins found, but always more and more; and, supposing a bottom, in the *Wake* there would be drawers to hide it.

The Supreme Fiction, says Wallace Stevens, "Must Give Pleasure." To the pleasure of puzzling some things out, Joyce added the pleasures of texture, feeling, and tone. The *Wake* is the most genial book in the world, formal and gay as Mozart at his saddest. Gaiety is balanced, here as there, by the equanimity of acceptance. Here too are pleasures of shape, wit, and playing with words—a verbal brilliance like nothing before or since. And from this play, as serious a matter as chess or bridge, emerges the pleasure of insight; for the radiance of the *Wake,* a vision of reality, is the condition of man and the triumph of life. All the truth and beauty of aesthetic Stephen's desire are here: truth from the most pleasing relations of the intelligible—and, sometimes, of the unintelligible; beauty from the most pleasing relations of the sensible.

So great the impact of *Ulysses* and the *Wake* that they mark a literary divide: before Joyce and after Joyce. Later writers face the problem of accommodating themselves to A.J., the new era, a more spacious time than Beckett's day. Some, with cries of dismay, retreat to the ways of an earlier time, B.J. (I have C. P. Snow and F. R. Leavis in mind.) Some, like Beckett, at once accepting and rejecting Joyce, come up with variations. Others, like John Lennon, the literate Beatle, combine acceptance with misunderstanding. Anyway, "letters have never been quite their old selves again" (112.24–27) since the hen, scratching that letter up, "looked at literature."

On first looking into Joyce's *Wake*—long ago when, as *Work in Progress,* it was coming out in the magazine *transition*—I too was dismayed; for I had expected another *Ulysses*. It was not until the fable of the Ondt and the Gracehoper appeared that I found the thing readable; and not until the publication of the *Wake* in 1939 that I found it good. In 1940, to learn more about it, I gathered a little group of graduate students at Columbia in the belief that a committee, reading the text, talking it over, and bringing to it a variety of languages and learning, might do more with the book than I alone, with small learning and less Greek. Since then this committee—like one of C. P. Snow's in one way, unlike it in another—has met, mostly in the springtime; and what I know about the *Wake,* or much of it, comes from these co-operations. (Eventually the committee became a class, known today as English G 6545 y.) A teacher taught, I was lucky in my teachers. James Gilvarry taught me almost everything about Dublin; Nat Halper taught me something about almost everything; Dounia Christiani supplied Danish, Raymond Porter, Gaelic, and others other things and other tongues. Such lessons encouraged me to read the *Wake* myself, alone, in the silence of my room. What I am telling you, then, is what I have picked up in committee or brown study through almost thirty years.

Besides Webster's dictionary the books that, writing my book, I found most useful were Clive Hart's *Concordance,* which locates almost every word, David Hayman's *A First-Draft Ver-*

sion, which shows what the *Wake* was like before Joyce complicated it, and Dounia Christiani's *Scandinavian Elements.* Writing my book, I did not consult critical commentaries on the *Wake;* for my object, not to say again what others have said, was to say what I and my committee have to say. This book is not a summary of its predecessors or their replacement but their supplement. There are nine-and-sixty ways of looking at the *Wake* and all of them are right, in part at least—wrong too, in part. I kept away from Campbell and Robinson's *Skeleton Key,* which helped me long ago, until I was through with my job. Reopening it then, I found that these pioneers, Campbell and Robinson, say many things that I do not and, on the other hand, that I say many things that they do not. "The hoax that joke bilked," like God's house, has many "dimmansions" (367.27. Cf. *Ulysses,* 394).

Insofar as I am a critic, I am a text man, concerned less with Joyce than with what he wrote. Once somebody, reprinting something of mine in his anthology of critical types, called me a formalist. Perhaps. But categories discourage me, and formalist is a dirty word in Russia.

Reading my book over, I find it hard going. The clutter of page and line references that I thought, and still think, useful gets in the way of easy reading. But this book, not for that, is for consultation—to hold in one hand with the *Wake* in the other, while the eye, as at a tennis match, moves to and fro. Not for the dozen or so experts in the *Wake,* this book is designed "for the uniformication of young persons" (529.7–8)—making them as uniform and busy as ants—and others older who have something to learn.

Necessarily I have been selective in my survey of the *Wake;* for a book so small on a book so large has room for high spots alone. Running down the page, I picked those words and paragraphs that, in my opinion, are essential for knowing what is going on. If one had world enough and wit, and the capacity, one could write a book on each chapter of the *Wake.* Things that I leave out are left out for lack of space at times, but at other times for lack of knowledge. After all, what authority on the *Wake* knows the half of it? Which half is the critical question. At the end of each of my chapters, in a kind of dump, I consider matters omitted for the sake of neatness from the body of the chapter.

Looking over my chapters and their dumps, I found repetition here and there—as in the *Wake* itself; but, though my work is of another kind, I decided to do nothing about the repetitions for this reason. Some readers, intent, let us say, on Chapter XIV of the *Wake,* may consult my book for Chapter XIV alone. Ignorant of what I say in Chapter XIII, and unaware that I say it again in Chapter XIV, they will need what might bother a reader of the book from beginning to end. If there is such a reader, I count on his absence of mind.

Besides James Gilvarry, Nathan Halper, Dounia Christiani, and Raymond Porter—all members of the committee—I am indebted to many, some co-operating members, others not. Patrick Henchy, Director of the National Library in Dublin, patiently answered questions about Ireland, the Church, and Gaelic; Eugene Sheehy, Reference Librarian of Columbia, looked things up for me; and colleagues, whom I bothered incessantly, always helped: Gilbert Highet (Latin), Elliott Dobbie (Breton, modern Greek, Esperanto, Sanskrit, and other tongues), William Nelson (sixteenth century and Russian), Joseph Mazzeo (Italian), William Jackson (German), and James Clifford (eighteenth century). Fritz Senn, Kevin Sullivan, Maurice Wohlgelernter, Edmund Epstein, Daniel Penham, and Frances Steloff supplied great things of several kinds. I am grateful to all my students, three recent ones especially: David Phillips, my authority on the letter *Shin;* Setsuko Ohara, my authority on Japanese and Telugu; and Sister Eileen Campion Kennedy, a doer of good deeds and one of my most reliable authorities on holiness.

Maybe what I have been trying to say about this four-ring circus is that it is a form for the feeling of being alive and kicking. Expect nothing deep in my attempt upon this form; for—to echo Jane Austen's young lady at Bath—I do not write well enough to be unintelligible.

PART ONE

CHAPTER I · 3-29

CHAPTER I is a place where Joyce presents—or, to be accurate, offers—themes and characters, both mistaken by the innocent reader who, to take what is offered, must reread the chapter after reading the book. Then he may find that a major concern of the introductory chapter—and, indeed, of the book —is time, process, the fall and rise of man, conflict and its litter, and the creation from litter of children, cities, and books. History parodies family tensions. Historically, in the first chapter we occupy Vico's divine age, but matters from the heroic and human ages intrude; for, in history, as in nature, the seed contains the tree—root and branch. Not a narrative, though made in part of narratives, this chapter is a formal arrangement, closer to music than to the novel. After an overture of seven pages, the chapter rises to three climactic movements, the stories of Waterloo, Mutt and Jute, and the Prankquean, and ends quietly in lower key with an address to the dead. The interludes that separate these parts are almost as important as the parts. All—interludes and parts alike—are centered in the family: father, sons, daughter, mother, and their troubled interactions. As for characters, most are around, hiding however. H. C. Earwicker, the father, hidden under initials that we know nothing about yet, appears as Finnegan, Wellington, or Van Hoother. Anna, Kate, Shem, Shaun, Joe, and Isabel are no less elusive. A variety of tones, rhythms, and diction suited to the characters may help their identification; but even such clues are lost in the general gaiety. Less decorous than Mrs. Bloom's monologue—and funnier, this chapter would have détained the censor in 1939 had he been able to read it.

The first sentence is the second half of the last; for, since the *Wake* is circular, end meets beginning. As if the opening line of an epic, this half-sentence begins the *Wake* "in medios loquos" (398.8), and, like most of Joyce's beginnings, tells all—to all who can hear what they are told. "Riverrun," the first word, is the central word of the book; for Anna Livia's Liffey, the feminine creative principle, is the river of time and life. The Liffey flows past the church of Adam and Eve (reversed here to imply temptation, fall, and renewal) and into Dublin Bay, where, after circulating down to Bray, it circulates up to Howth, the northern extremity of the Bay. "Eve and Adam's" unites Dublin with Eden and one time with another. "Howth Castle and Environs," as the initials show, is H. C. Earwicker; for, as she is the river, he is hill and castle. Locally, "vicus" (Latin for lane or vicinity) is the Vico Road along the shore of Dublin Bay. Historically, "vicus" is Giambattista Vico, the philosopher of "recirculation." "Commodius" is more difficult. Possibly a reference to Commodus (mentioned 157.26), "commodius" is probably a reference to commode or chamber pot, a suitable container for "riverrun." As *Ulysses* ends with Mrs. Bloom's pot, so *Finnegans Wake* begins with A.L.P.'s. But this pot is of philosophical interest as well. A commode is a jordan (a rivery word) and the first name of Bruno is Giordano. With Giambattista, Giordano presides over the circulating river and all process. In this commodious, alliterative fragment, therefore, Joyce has introduced his two principal characters, his two principal philosophers, and his theme.

The rest of the first page, even denser than this, says this: at the time of Adam and Eve the following seven things had "not yet" happened—seven perhaps because of the seven days of creation. (The days are separated by colons or periods.) 1. Sir Tristram is not only Tristan who comes from Armorica (Brittany) to get Isolde in "Europe Minor" (Ireland), but Sir Almeric Tristram St. Lawrence, Earl of Howth, who, across the "scraggy isthmus" of Sutton, presided over Howth Castle and environs. "Passencore," not yet in French, vies with German "wielderfight" (*wiederfechten*). "Violer d'amores" is Tristan as violator of Mark's love and a musical instrument with seven strings. But the radiant word is "penisolate," which carries Wellington's Peninsular War, the Wellington Monument, the lonely penis, and the lonely pen. Both twins, Shem and Shaun, are involved: Tristan-Shaun longs for Isolde and Shem is a lonely penman. 2. Old Dublin is repeated in the New World ("North Armorica") by Dublin, Georgia, founded by a man named Sawyer on the Oconee river in Laurens County. "Topsawyer's rocks" must be shamrocks; but topsawyer is Tom Sawyer, who, with Huck Finn, his bottomsawyer twin, is sawing up a log. If the log is father, Mark-H.C.E., they are making Mark twain. 3. "Mishe mishe" (myself or I am, in Gaelic) is what Shem the artist says—the creative voice from the fire. But practical Shaun says "tauftauf" (German baptize) and "thuartpeatrick" (you are Peter, the stone, St. Patrick, and Swift, tricky Dean of St. Patrick's, near the peat ricks). 4. The heart of this sentence is Jacob fooling Isaac and Esau with false hair, venison, and kids (Genesis, 27). "Bland" combines blind (Isaac), blond (Finn), and blend; for father is a blend of his opposing sons. "Buttended" superimposes Irish politics: young Parnell (a kid and a cad or cadet) displaced old Isaac Butt in Parliament as leader of the Home Rule Party. Cad or young son versus father is one of the principal themes of the *Wake*. 5. Not only venison and very soon, "venissoon" is also Swift's Vanessa, echoed by "vanessy" in the sentence before us and by "sosie sesthers." Stella and Vanessa, introducing the theme of two girls and an older man, were both named Esther, and "sosie" is French for a person resembling another. "Nathanjoe" is Jonathan (Swift) backwards; "twone" is a union of opposites. 6. Brewing and distilling proceed in Dublin, the brewing of Guinness, the distilling by "Jhem or Shen," Shaun and Shem or John Jameson & Son. "Arc" and rainbow refer to Noah, a drunk. The "regginbrow," according to Joyce himself, is an eyebrow on the face of the waters. Germanic "ringsome" refers to Wagner's ring. 7. Adam's fall and Vico's thunder are embodied in a word of a hundred letters, the

first of ten thunders in the *Wake*. This one is composed of words
for noise and thunder (tonner-thunn) and for defecation.
"Konnbronn" refers to General Pierre Cambronne and
"merde," his word. *Le mot de* Cambronne becomes a theme.
Other falls follow Adam's—and Cambronne's: those of stocks
in Wall Street, of Humpty Dumpty from his wall, and of Finnegan, the bricklayer, from his. Old Parr is an old man of the
seventeenth century, but parr is the first stage of the developing
salmon. "The knock out in the park" is Knock Gate, an incident
in Le Fanu's *House by the Churchyard,* and the holdup of Earwicker by the Cad. Orange, green, and rust are Ireland and,
probably, the dump, full of orangepeel. "Livvy," the last word,
goes with "riverrun," the first. Both mean Liffey, ivvy or Eve,
and Livy or Vico's favorite historian. ("Devlin" may include
Dublin's De Valera.) That my painful—yet partial and imperfect—analysis is more or less on the right track is proved by
Joyce's own partial and imperfect explanation of the first page in
a letter to Harriet Weaver (*Letters,* I, 247–48).

The matter of the first paragraph on p. 4 is heroic conflict,
whether of siege, "camibalistics," or boomerangs, followed by
peace, as rise follows fall. The conflicts include Ostrogoths
against Visigoths; oysters against fish and frogs (there by the
croaking chorus of Aristophanes); Irishmen (White Boys of
Howth and "Sod's brood." "Fear" is Gaelic *Fir,* men); Protestant against Catholic (*Ego te absolvo* indicates the Catholics
while "Bid me to love," a distortion of a song by Herrick, means
Protestant according to Mr. Bloom, *Ulysses,* 661); Jacob
against Esau again (hair and "false jiccup"). The sprawled "father of fornicationists" is fallen Adam or H.C.E. But the sky-
signs of Noah's rainbow and Times Square or Piccadilly promise
peace and renewal as does Isabel (Tristan's "Iseut") and her
soeurs ("sewers"). "Phall if you but will, rise you must" (4.16)
suggests free will, necessity, and the phallus, echoed by
"pharce," the farce of destiny and the Pharos of Alexandria.
"Phoenish," the key word, combines finish and phoenix.

The indelicate and very funny paragraph that begins on 4.18
concerns creation—the making of towers, love, and books. Like

Ibsen's Master Builder (*Bygmester* in Danish), Finnegan, the
bricklayer, built a tower—or at least a wall—before he fell from
it. He is not only the builder of the Woolworth Building, the
Eiffel Tower, and the Tower of Babel ("baubletop") but a primitive "maurer" (German mason) who lived before Genesis, Le-
viticus, Exodus and, indeed, the whole "pentschanjeuchy" Pentateuch. That Finnegan is stuttering-tottering H.C.E., a victim of
Punch-and-Judy conflict (4.25), is proved by his initials em-
bedded in proletarian "hod, cement and edifices" and in imperial "Haroun Childeric Eggeberth." Egg, child, and birth attend
or follow the begetting of children. Take up your partner means
dancing, but "tuck up your part inher," the dance of life, leads
to "the liquor wheretwin 'twas born." "Undress maisonry up-
standed" unites bricklaying with undressing at home and rising
to the occasion. The creator's partner, "addle liddle phifie
Annie," is A.L.P., as the initials show, and Lewis Carroll's Alice
Liddell. Sex and building vie as tools and buckets clitter up or
clotter down (5.3). Laurence O'Toole and Thomas Becket are
saints; but men of letters are builders too. "Sternely," "swiftly,"
and the tale of a "tub" (4.21–23) suggest Sterne and Swift,
who, like Jacob and Esau, Becket and O'Toole, are recurrent
twins. Helviticus committing "deuteronomy" is T. S. Eliot imitating *Ulysses* in Switzerland—"by the waters of Leman," as he
says in *The Waste Land*. "Balbulus" (4.30), Latin for stuttering, recalls *"Balbus was building a wall"* in *A Portrait of the
Artist,* by reference to which Joyce joins the creative company
of Ibsen, Sterne, Swift, Eliot, Lewis Carroll, and H. C. E. Finnegan.

Finnegan's coat of arms (Vico's heraldry) occupies the next
paragraph (5.5). Finnegan's? Known now as "Wassaily Boo-
slaeugh of Riesengeborg," Finnegan is a Russian-German giant
and a drinking man. But whatever his name, if Finn, having
taken a drop too much, falls from his ladder, he will be "Finnagain"—as "vine" will someday be vinegar. "Fined" (5.12), a
sinner's penalty, recalls his "tragoady thundersday this municipal
[original] sin business." The Near East (the Black Stone of
Mecca, Bedouins, and Arabic words) places him near or in

Eden. Adam-Finnegan's fall was caused by a "missfired brick" maybe, or maybe by "a collupsus of his back promises" (5.26–28), one of Joyce's happiest concentrations (cf. the "Cooloosus," 625.22, that also collupsed). That the tower Finnegan was building is "one thousand and one stories, all told" (5.29) suggests Babel, the Arabian Nights (heralded by Haroun, 4.32), and *Finnegans Wake* itself (heralded by "cubehouse," 5.14; for the incubating *Wake* is a cube or coach with "six insides," 359.24). If 10, 100, or 1000 represent completeness, 11, 101, or 1001 represent renewal—here the building of the modern city (5.30–6.7). Without the fall, indicated by "ivvy's holired abbles" (5.30, Eve, holly, ivy, and apple), there would be no cities.

Finn, the first builder and rebuilder, is Phil now because he is full of drink (6.8). Carrying his hod up the ladder, filled Finnegan falls and dies. If not the fall of man entirely, this is certainly the fall of a man. Dimb, Damb, Dumb, a suitable ablaut series, brings him to his Egyptian Mastabah tomb (6.10) and us, at last, to his wake.

At the wake of this "dacent gaylabouring" man (6.23)—a man like Joyce himself—the celebrants, conducting themselves "with the shoutmost shoviality," keen "Macool Macool" (Finn MacCool). "Duodismally" (6.16) and an abundance of words ending in -tion identify the twelve mourners: "plumbs and grumes and cheriffs and citherers and raiders and cinemen too." These are also the ingredients of "Miss Hooligan's Christmas Cake," one of several songs that enliven the mourning. As fragments show, the mourners also sing "Phil the Fluter's Ball" and "Brian O'Lynn." But "deepbrow fundigs and the dusty fidelios" (*de profundis* and *adeste, fideles,* 6.25) seem more agreeable to the occasion. There poor Finnegan lies "with a bockalips of finisky [Apocalypse, end, and whisky] fore his feet. And a barrowload of guenesis [Genesis, beginning, Guinness] hoer his head" (6.26–27). From last to first the funeral is a roaring success: "E'erawhere in this whorl [Vico] would ye hear such a din again?"

The "overgrown babeling" (6.31), a fallen tower and a big

baby, lies flat on his back like E supine. A sleeping giant, "he calmly extensolies" (H.C.E.) over the countryside from Howth ("Bailywick") to Chapelizod ("Shopalist") while oboes, ocarinas, and A.L.P. wake him. Her presence in the orchestra is established by sound, rhythm, and watery language: "the delldale dalppling night, the night of bluerybells, her flittaflute in tricky trochees" (7.2). With her are Stella, Vanessa, and Swift ("issavan essavans" and Peter, Jack, Martin from *A Tale of a Tub,* 7.4–5). This company, seated around the supine giant, proceeds sacramentally to eat him; for not only fallen Adam, H.C.E. is risen Christ or the Host (7.13–19). His icon, like Christ's, is the fish—the "Salmosalar" (Latin for salmon), canned and "smolten in our mist" (smolt is the second stage of the developing salmon as parr is the first). Down goes the holy meal, "schlook, schlice and goodridhirring." The grace before this meal (7.6–8) is so pleasing that I repeat it at table on feast days and other days as well: "For what we are, gifs à gross if we are, about to believe. So pool the begg and pass the kish for crawsake. Omen." Since Poolbeg is the lighthouse on the Pigeon House breakwater and Kish is the lightship farther out, Joyce's prayer implies leaving Dublin, Good riddance to it as to the eaten fish.

The supine giant is "brontoichthyan" now (7.20)—a thunder fish, by the edge of the "troutling stream." Bronto and Brunto, its twin banks, are thundering Vico and Bruno. *"Hic cubat edilis"* (Here lies H.C.E., an edible magistrate) with A.L.P., his little freewoman—"little Anny Ruiny" or "lovelittle Anna Rayiny, when unda her brella, mid piddle med puddle she ninnygoes nannygoes nancing by" (7.25–27)—like a piddling little goat. An abrupt switch of rhythm, sound, and tone recalls her sleeping partner.

Line 30 of page 7 marks the end of the dense and intricate overture, which, like many overtures, states the themes to be elaborated. So announced, the first movement of the suite begins after a brief introduction of its own leads to waterloose Waterloo.

At the Magazine in Phoenix Park, Earwicker's Eden, are two

girls and three soldiers (alluded to earlier, 7.4, as Stella, Vanessa, and Peter, Jack, Martin) who are the occasion of Earwicker's sin or its observers. These girls and soldiers, who reappear throughout the *Wake,* seem to be Earwicker's family, Anna, Isabel, Shem, Shaun, and Earwicker himself (271.5–6 encourages this hypothesis). The soldiers ("upjock and hockums," 7.35, or Up Guards, and at 'em), lurking in the "ombushes" at the "bagsides of the fort," are farting ("tarabom"), but the girls are making water. A pretty picture—like something by Renoir: "the charmful waterloose country and two quitewhite villagettes who hear show of themselves so gigglesomes minxt [*mingo* is Latin for piss] the follyages, the prettilees" (8.2–4). Earwicker may be peeping at them while the soldiers peep at him.

The Wellington Museum that we will visit now is a combination of the Magazine and the Wellington Monument in the Park. Kate, the old cleaning woman at Earwicker's pub, is "janitrix" (janitor and genetrix) and guide. Since the museum is a "Museyroom" (8.10), Kate seems the Mother of the Muses or Memory. "Tip," repeated nine times in the course of our tour of Waterloo, seems more than a pourboire for the guide and historian. (Cf. "tippers," 27.33.) A tip is a dump. So is a museum, so the debris of a battle, and so the *Wake* with all its litters.

"Mind your hats goan in" (8.9), the advice to "Penetrators" at the beginning and "Mind your boots goan out" (10.22) at the end make the episode seem the begetting and birth of a child and the nine tips the customary months of gestation. But literary creation is also proceeding, along with a game—played no doubt on the playing fields of Eton, where Waterloo was won, "(Bullsrag! Foul!) . . . (Bullseye! Game!)" 10.15,21. The main action, however, is military and familial. Pointing to the exhibits in the museum, Kate tells the story of Waterloo, here the conflict of Willingdone with Lipoleum (Napoleon distorted by female lip and flooring, Nat Halper says, to be walked on by Wellington boots). Willingdone, a man of will and doing, is H.C.E. Lipoleum, female and composite, is H.C.E.'s family, the two girls and the three soldiers ganging up on father—the one and the many. In short, Willingdone's Waterloo is family conflict. Puns on the names of battles, wars, and commanders (Goa, Peloponnesian, Thermopylae, Hastings, Agincourt, Boyne, Crimea, Salamanca, Bunker Hill, Byng, Cromwell, Grouchy, and Pickett) make family particulars general and confuse the times. Martial songs ("Tipperary" and "The Girl I Left Behind Me") accompany the action.

Lipoleum has a three-cornered hat and Willingdone has a "big wide harse," named Copenhagen like Wellington's own. The "three lipoleum boyne" (8.22) are "Touchole Fitz Tuomush. Dirty MacDyke. And Hairy O'Hurry" (8.26–27), Tom, Dick, and Harry combined with the female genitals. With these three soldiers are the two "jinnies" (8.31–34), girls who shelter the three lipoleums under their Crimea-Kremlin crinolines while making war "undisides" on Willingdone from "their handmade's book of stralegy." So attacked by the handmaids' handmades (or drawers), Willingdone gets "the band up" (*bander,* French slang for getting an erection). His "mormorial tallowscoop" with "Sexcaliber hrosspower" (8.35–36) is Wellington's Monument in the Park and his penis. ("Sexcaliber" is a dream condensation of sword, gun, and car.) Willingdone is now "Awful Grimmest Sunshat Cromwelly. Looted" or Arthur Guinness and Sons Company, Ltd. (9.1–2), and Belchum or Shaun, who tries to steal father's horse ("phillippy"), is a postman. On his shirtfront, to "irrigate" and "fontannoy" Willingdone, the Jinnies write a dispatch in a sort of German, suitable for men: *Lieber Arthur, Wir siegen. Wie geht's deiner kleinen Frau? Hoch Achtung.* Nap (9.5–6). Willingdone replies "tic for tac" in French no better than Nap's German, but suitable for women: *Chères Jinnies, Victorieux. Ça ne fait rien. Foutre.* Willingdone. The laughter that attends these insults ("Yaw, yaw, yaw. . . . Shee, shee, shee"), taking the form of yes, no, and all the personal pronouns, continues to the end, "Hney, hney, hney" (no, they, Marshal Ney, and a horse). And there are battle cries: "Arthiz too loose" (art, Arthur Wellesley, and the battle of Toulouse); "Brum! Cumbrum!" (Cambronne's *merde*); and "Underwetter"

(*Donnerwetter* and wet underwear, 9.26–27). "Poor the pay" (9.32) is soldiers' pay and *Pour le pays*. Aroused by the underwetter, Willingdone, brandishing his "marmorial tallowscoop," chases the Jinnies for his "royal divorsion" (Napoleon's royal divorce). "Gambariste della porca!" (9.35–36), apparently something to say after hitting one's thumb with a hammer, is— as one of my students discovered—Giambattista della Porta, who wrote a play about rival brothers.

Now the climax of hat and "harse" (10.1–22) and battle's end. Picking half of Lipoleum's hat from the blood and filth, Willingdone puts it on the backside of his big wide harse. The three soldiers (now "hiena hinnessy . . . lipsyg dooley . . . Shimar Shin") blow this half-a-hat off the tail of the harse and unhorse the Duke. "How Copenhagen ended" means the downfall of H.C.E.—Lipoleum wins this Waterloo—defeated by the family he thought he was defeating. A hat is a symbol of authority. Even half-a-hat on a harse is better than no hat at all. But Earwicker is left hatless and harseless too. Hinnessy, Dooley, and Shin (21 in Hebrew and the vaudeville team of Dooley and Hennessy) are equivalent to Shem, the laughing drinker and predecessor of Buckley, the young man who will shoot the old Russian General (353.16–21). The son must kill—or, at least, unhorse—the father before taking his place.

"What a warm time we were in there" (10.25) is what the foetus says on delivery and what we say on leaving the magazine-museum for the "keling" (cooling) air of peace outside; but here too is the debris of battle, "a verytableland of bleakbardfields" where "Lumproar" lies, "Skud ontorsed" (10.34–36). L'Empéreur confuses Willingdone with Lipoleum, but "Skud," less ambiguous if read backwards, means Duke's unhorsed or, read forwards, scut (tail) unhorsed from torso. Amid the corpses and other debris runs a little bird, a "gnarlybird" (10.32), getting the worm and picking up the pieces. References (10.26–28) to Deirdre ("Ussna"), Ophelia ("Downadown"), and Anna ("annaone") identify this bird as A.L.P. or LIV, an identification confirmed by numbers (10.29, 31): "quaintlymine" (twenty-nine or February of leap year) and fifty-four (LIV in Latin). The pair of pigeons and the three of crows, "kraaking of de baccle" (the two girls and the three soldiers) have left the scene (10.36–11.1). Anna, alone with her dead giant, says "byes will be byes" (11.8)—quarreling boys and past times; for she is a "peacefugle [*Vogel*], a parody's bird, a peri potmother" (11.9). Picking here and pecking there in the litter—a little hen now—she puts "clavicures and scampulars" and "all spoiled goods . . . into her nabsack" (11.9–27) or, as it is called later (20.7), her "muttheringpot." "Boaston . . . masses of shoesets . . . and foder allmicheal" makes it plain to rereaders that what the hen finds and puts in her bag or motheringpot for renewal is the letter from Boston, celebrated in Chapter V (111.5–23). From the litter comes the letter as from the dump (18.16–35) come letters. Literature, including the *Wake,* is essence of dump; and woman, the Muse's agent, if not the Muse, is collector of rubbish and its renewer. "That's cearc" (11.27. *Cearc* is Gaelic for hen). What Kate has shown, A.L.P. picks up, the one in her museum, the other in the dump. A.L.P. is making the best of "a pretty nice kettle of fruit" or the result of our fall in Eden—to be turned perhaps by Ichthos, the Redeemer, into a pretty nice kettle of fish. Not only Eve, she is Sarah ("sair") and her Isaac ("I saack") is also the "nabsack" of litter and letters. Rise, fall, and renewal—"Gricks may rise and Troysirs fall"—are the course of history, whether of Greeks and Trojans, bricks and cities or pricks and trousers (11.32–36).

While H.C.E. lies sleeping, A.L.P., practical and "mercenary," lights a fire and makes breakfast. Eggs "sunny side up" in the "mournhim" imply morning after mourning (12.6–16). That Swift is also there is shown by references to Queen Anne's bounty, first fruits ("quainance bandy" and "frutings for firstlings"), and "Wharton's Folly" (12.18–23). (Sir Thomas Wharton, Lord-Lieutenant of Ireland, built the Magazine in Phoenix Park, a folly for which Swift rebuked him.) As the sleeping giant lies with his head at "the macroborg of Holdhard" (Howth) and his feet at "the microbirg of Pied de Poudre" (the Magazine, 12.35–36), our "review of the two mounds" (another magazine,

12.20) includes Wharton's Folly and Swift's verses on it (13.1–3):

> Behold! a proof of *Irish* sense!
> Here *Irish* wit is seen!
> When nothing's left, that's worth defence,
> We build a magazine.

References to money, the real and the fake, punctuate Joyce's version.

"Dyoublong" and "Echoland" make H.C.E.'s Dublin seem a city of rejection and gossip. What is worse, it is a city of the dead, a "gravemure where used to be blurried the Ptollmens of the Incabus," where the fall from the Magazine wall and the wake (13.15) are appropriate.

History, the matter of the *Wake,* is recorded by four "herodotary" (hereditary and Herodotus) historians called "Mammon Lujius" or, later, Mamalujo (Matthew, Mark, Luke, and John, authors of the four gospels and, closer to home, authors of *Annals of the Four Masters,* a history of Ireland). These four old men—the "fear of um"—reappear throughout the *Wake* as judges and observers. Here (13.20–28) they have reduced the history of H.C.E.'s Eire to four things, *Unum, Duum, Triom,* and *Quodlibus,* which are associated with Jewish festivals throughout the year: Adar, Tamuz, Marchessvan, and Sukkoth. The four things of their reduction are: 1. A "bulbenboss" on an alderman or H.C.E., who is a little hunchbacked; 2. A.L.P.'s shoe; 3. An auburn maid to be deserted (Isabel in terms of Goldsmith's "Deserted Village"); 4. Shem and Shaun, equal twins, the pen of one no weightier than the post bag of the other. So all things proceed. It is plain from this that history is family history and all historical conflicts are conflicts within the family —as we have seen in Willingdone's Waterloo. As "innocens" plays "popeye antipop" with "anaclete" (Pope Innocent II and Anacletus or Julian, his rival), so all deeds and cycles of events come to pass (Passover) as "annals of themselves" (13.29–32).

Examples from 1132 A.D. to 566 A.D. follow. The big "hwide" (white in Danish) whale on which antlike men crawl in 1132 is

H.C.E. (cf. *Ulysses,* 45). 1132, a number that recurs throughout the *Wake,* combines 11 or rising with 32 or falling (32 feet
per second, as Mr. Bloom observed). There are thirty-two counties in Ireland. Add the digits and you get seven, and there are
seven in Earwicker's household. But little of importance happened in the year 1132. 566 (half of 1132) belongs to A.L.P.,
in whose basket or "kish" (cf. "nabsack") are shoes or children.
(Saul, son of Kish, enlarges the reference to Goody Twoshoes.)
"Hurdlesford" is Dublin, Ford of the Hurdles. After a period of
silence the course of history is reversed (reversal means renewal) by Anna's children. 566 A.D. is Isabel's year. She is
"brazenlockt" because she is "auburn" and because devotion to
herself is a girdle of chastity as good as any in the Cluny. The
ogre who steals her doll is papa, hence a pope, and hence bloody
wars in Baile atha Cliath or Dublin. 1132 A.D. is the year of the
twins, Caddy (cf. "kidscad," 3.11, cadet or Shem) and Primas-
Shaun, who, like St. Patrick, was an Irishman and came from
decent people. Caddy, a drunk, wrote words for Dublin. The
period of silence is explained now (14.16–17) as the Ginnungagap from Norse mythology, a period of Viconian chaos between cycles. A.D. means "antediluvious" in the first cycle and
"annadominant" in the second.

The record is unclear because in the confusion between
cycles, the "copyist" or recorder of history fled, frightened by
the worldwright's "bolt" (thunder) or by the galleys (*gallus* is
cock) of the invading Danes. "Bliddy duran" (cf. 111.5),
frightened by Danish cocks, is the hen who found the letter in
the dump (11.12). A moral aside (14.21–27): under the old
code a "scribicide" or writer-killer was let off while a "gyne-
cure" or woman-fancier was led on to the scaffold for "covertly"
(covet from the ninth commandment) meddling "with the
drawers of his neighbor's safe" (wife).

A period of peace, flowery, pastoral, and amatory—"how
paisibly eirenical"—follows the alarms of history (14.28–
15.11), the bouts, for example of Heber and Hereman, who, invading Ireland, conquered the Tuatha de Danann, as these had
conquered the Firbolgs and the Fomorians. (Any history of Ire-

land records these legendary conflicts.) But more important than
conflict are the flowers (women) that spring up during peace
and the jerrybuilding of cities by the "Joynts" (the twins, Jerry
and Kevin). Flowers, women, and rebuilders survive the confusions of history—as Edgar Quinet (suggested here and quoted,
281.4–13) observes—the confusion of tongues, for example,
after the fall of Babel (15.12–23), a confusion illustrated here
by fragments of Gaelic ("thigging thugs," Do you understand?)
and of Danish ("Elsekiss . . . piggy?" Do you love me, my dear
girl?). Let the "babbelers" confuse things as they must, boys
meet girls—"Norgels" (Danes) their "pollyfool" or Norman
fiancés and "duncledames" (dark Irish) their "hellish" (blond
Danish) fellows: "Who ails tongue coddeau. . . . ? (*Où est ton
cadeau, espèce d'imbécile?*). Whatever the confusion of
tongues, floras (girls) still say to their shy lovers: "Cull me ere I
wilt to thee! . . . Pluck me whilst I blush!" An abrupt change
of rhythm and tone (15.24) brings us back to Tim Timmycan,
once tamper of A.L.P., now lying flopping at his wake like "a
whale [cf. 13.34] in a whillbarrow" (not only wheelbarrow but
hill and barrow or tomb). "Flippety" may also mean the flapping of film at the end of a reel, as, full of hops, we hop like a
flea to the story of Mutt and Jute, another family conflict—
between the sons this time—yet in public history the battle between Irishmen and Danes on the field of Clontarf.

Mutt sees a queer, misshapen man "a parth a lone." This
strange creature, who is not unlike Joe Biggar (a member of
Parnell's party in Parliament), seems "mousterious" (Mousterian or paleolithic man). Indeed, he seems to be both "a dragon
man" (Blake's cave man in *The Marriage of Heaven and Hell*)
and a drinking man—as the confusion of months and drinks
indicates. Sucking marrow bones at the door of his cave, he is
evidently the "michindaddy," the Michael-Shaun element in
H.C.E. Mutt-Shem tries communication with this savage, first in
French (*Comment vous portez-vous, aujourd'hui, mon blond
monsieur?*), then in Danish, Scowegian, English, and Anglo-
Saxon. Nothing in this diverting interview works. By elimina-
tion, therefore, the man must be a Jute, "weak" whom it might

be instructive to exchange a few strong verbs about the battle of
Clontarf, which took place in 1014 on the Tolka ("tolkatiff")
where that bloody creek flows into Dublin Bay. Swapping hats, a
device that Samuel Beckett was to adopt, makes the pair a
vaudeville team—or comics like Mutt and Jeff. We occupy three
times: that of Mutt and Jeff, that of cave men, and that of Brian
Boru, who defeated the Danes on the Tolka.

Communication between Mutt and Jute, Irishman and invader, proves impossible, for one is "jeffmute" and the other
hardly "haudibble." The first of many recurrent conflicts between ear and eye or time and space or stick and stone (Shem
as ear-time-tree and Shaun as eye-space-stone), this conflict
comes, like all the rest, to nothing. In vain stuttering Jute asks
Mutt to become "more wiseable" (wiser and more visible);
"That side your voise are almost inedible [inaudible] to me";
for Jute is "surd" (deaf). The pointless exchange is so rich in
references that noting a few seems called for:

16.26   "Hasatency," a recurrent word, refers to Richard
           Pigott, whose forgery of a Parnell letter was exposed
           by his spelling of hesitancy, "Booru" is Brian Boru.

16.29   "One eyegonblack" is *Augenblick* (moment) and the
           patch over Joyce's eye. "Bisons is bisons" means let
           bygones be bygones, let two sons be two sons, and let
           American bison nickles be American bison nickles.
           Other references to money (guineas-Guinness and
           Wood's "sylvan" halfpennies, Swift's concern) show
           that the invader is trying to bribe the Irishman.

16.34   "Cedric Silkyshag" is Sitric, the Danish king of Dub-
           lin at the time of Clontarf. "Grilsy" (grilse is a stage
           in the development of the salmon) and "poached on
           that eggtentical spot" (fish and Humpty Dumpty)
           show that the subject of discussion has become H.C.E.

17.1–2   "The missers mooney" combines a Dublin pub with
           the twenty-eight girls of the month. "Minnikin passe"
           is *Le mannequin qui pisse,* a fountain in Brussels
           ("brookcells by a riverpool" or A.L.P.).

17.4   "He [H.C.E.] dumptied the wholeborrow of rubbages
        on to soil here." As the girls urinate, so Earwicker
        defecates and Clontarf becomes "Dungtarf" (16.22);
        but "rubbages" bring us back to the dump. The marshy
        field of Clontarf, filled in by dumping rubbages, is
        now Fairview Park. "Load Allmarshy!" "Wad for a
        norse": a Dane's nose and arse, holding one, wiping the
        other.

17.9   "Bull on a clompturf." Clontarf means Bull's Meadow.
        "Sutton" is the neck of Howth, north of Clontarf.
        "Woolseley side in . . . Brian d' of Linn": Brian
        Boru, the ballad of Brian O'Lynn, and Arthur Welles-
        ley or Wellington. "Baldoyle and rawhoney" (17.3):
        oil and honey and two districts north of Clontarf.

Annoyed by all this incomprehensible "rutterdamrotter,"
both "onheard of and umscene" (escaping ear and eye, like
Joyce's obscene works), Jute says: be damned to you, good-by.
But Mutt, obsessed with H.C.E., his dump, and all the past,
poetically pursues (17.17–36) the merging of races and all
those who have fallen on this beach since Clontarf, "flick as
flowflakes, litters from aloft . . . all tombed to the mound,
isges to isges, erde from erde" (ashes to ashes and *merde*). Attentive to the last word alone, Jute says, "Stench!" but Mutt
cannot abandon his cemetery-dump: here they lie, "alp on earwig . . . in this sound seemetery [ear and eye, A.L.P., H.C.E.,
and the *Wake*] which iz leebez luv" (Isolde-*Liebestod*).
" 'Zmorde!" Jute's composite French comment on Wagner, inspires Mutt's "Meldundleize" (*mild und leise* from *Tristan*) and
a line from "Desmond's Song" by Thomas Moore. Mutt's night
thoughts of mouldering and the sifting of dust (18.1–8) turn to
the Viconian process, the third stage of which is represented
here by the three castles of Dublin's coat of arms. As Vico says,
says Mutt, "the same roturns." His "whisht" (be quiet), misunderstood like everything else he says, provokes Jute's
"Whysht? . . . Howe? . . . Hwaad!" (18.8–15) The "vice-
king's graab" that Mutt has been concerned with is that of his

father, "the gyant Forficules [the earwig belongs to the genus of forficulidae] with Amni the fay." Jute is suitably "astoneaged" by all this learning and, like Vico's primitive, "thonthorstrok." His "Oye" (eye) is not attuned to Mutt's "Ore" (ear).

One sentence in Mutt's discourse serves as transition to what follows Clontarf: "he who runes may rede" the message of dust, grave, and dump (18.4–5) if he who can read the runes of earth runs "on all fours" or, at least, stoops. As the interlude that follows Waterloo brings the letter from the litter so the interlude that follows Clontarf brings letters from the dump, which, if you are "abcedminded," is an "allaphbed" (18.16–19) or "clay-book." Indeed, if you are "abcedminded" and can stoop enough, you can interpret *Finnegans Wake,* which, like the earth itself, is a lettered dump and a letter to someone composed of dumped letters. "Can you rede . . . its world?" (Compare the confusion of word and world in Martha's letter, *Ulysses,* 77.)

The examined dump discloses "a hatch, a celt, an earshare" (18.30. H.C.E. and primitive utensils); but letters are commoner than things in this "pay roll" (19.5, *parole*): "cued peteet peas," for example, and the other literate garbage. "What a mnice old mness it all mnakes! [mn for memory] A middenhide hoard of objects! Olives, beets, kimmells, dollies" (19.7–9, the Hebrew "allforabit"). The story of mankind, "Miscegenations on miscegenations," is told by "Many . . . Tieckle . . . Forsin"—*"Mene, tekel, upharsin,"* the writing on the wall at Belshazzar's feast (Daniel, 5:25), obscure enough to baffle the "Meades and Porsons" (Medes and Persians from Daniel, 5:28, and two eighteenth-century scholars, 18.20–22). The writing goes "furrowords, bagawords, like yoxen at the turnpaht" (18.32)—like the boustrophedontic cryptogram used by Mr. Bloom for Martha's address (*Ulysses,* 721). The "nameform that whets the wits" includes "Futhorc" (18.25, 34) or the runic alphabet that "he who runes may rede." Along with letters in this dump lie H.C.E. and A.L.P., face to face (18.36) like pied type—brought to this pass by the three soldiers ("upwap and dump em"). Indeed, "our durlbin [Dublin and dustbin?] is sworming in sneaks" (snakes and gossips) though St. Patrick is

said to have caught the "creeps of them" in his "garbagecans."
But the new world of "Racketeers and bottloggers" may offer
hope (19.12–19); and "ragnar rocks" (19.4, Norse *Götterdämmerung* or Ragnarok) promises a new cycle of world or
word.

This "meanderthalltale" (meandering, Neanderthal, tall tale)
is ours "to con as we can till allhorrors eve" (19.25). Conned, it
will yield the two girls, the three soldiers, H.C.E. and A.L.P.
("ahnsire" and "Damadam"), and "every sue, siss and sally of
us"—all "sons of the sod" (19.20–30) and "wrunes" of the
world: paper, type, and "misses in prints," left to "terracook in
the muttheringpot" until "Gutenmorg with his cromagnom charter" (Gutenberg, Cromagnon, Magna Carta) will bid us good
morning (19.31–20.18).

The door of death has not yet closed: "There's many a smile
[in the *Wake*] to Nondum" (20.17–19, Latin not yet). There
are still many stories to tell of the two girls and three soldiers in
the Park, and "of a pomme full grave and a fammy of levity
. . . or of what the mischievmiss made a man do" (20.20–
21.4). Adam, Eve, snake, and apple are involved; but more—or
less—than Eve, this "fammy of levity" is A.L.P. as the Prankquean. Rhythm, diction, initials, and a kind of prettiness con-
spire to shape her (21.1–4). So introduced, here is her story.

The story of the Prankquean begins, as Joyce says a fairy
story should begin, with "Once upon a time" or its equivalent,
and ends, as he says a fairy story should, with "They put on the
kettle and they all had tea" (*Letters*, I, 400). As in any well-
conducted fairy story, the witch comes and goes three times
(the third here is "the third charm," 22.21); and suitably there
are metamorphoses and a riddle. References connect this story
with the Bible—with Adam and Eve, a rib-robber (21.6–8) and
with Noah: forty days of rain, ark, and rainbow (21.22; 22.33;
23.1–2). Other references connect this story with Irish history
and myth, with the conflict of Catholic and Protestant, of Gael
and Gall, and with literature. As "grace o'malice" (21.20–21),
the Prankquean is sixteenth-century Grace O'Malley, who, denied admission to Howth Castle, kidnapped the young heir of

the St. Lawrence family and took him to her castle in the West.
In the myth of Dermot and Grania ("be dermot, 21.14; "red-
tom," 21.31; "grannewwail," 22.12), Grania, the young bride
of old Finn MacCool, could not resist the "love-spot" (21.27–
28) on the brow of young Dermot; so by her spells she kidnapped him. Old Finn, enraged by the infidelity of the pair, pursued them, in vain. The literary references include Laurence
Sterne ("shandy westerness," 21.21–22; "laurency night of star-
shootings," 22.12), Swift ("sulliver," 21.28; "histher," 22.2;
"lilipath," 22.8; "homerigh," 21.13), and Mark Twain (e.g.,
22.5). Since the Prankquean, like A.L.P., is a watery girl, associated with rain, rivers, and urine, Mark Twain means the
sounding of the river—of life or of art, if she is the Muse. Gael
and Gall ("dovesgall," 21.23; Strongbow, Cromwell, and William of Orange, 21.20, 22.14, 23.3), Catholic and Protestant
("luderman," 21.30, "baretholobruised," 21.35) complicate
the action, as does the conflict of ear and eye that we noticed in
the story of Mutt and Jute: "Stop deaf stop come back to my
earin stop" (21.23). "Handworded" (21.20) is German *Ant-
wort* and deaf-and-dumb talk.

These complications—and others—help make the simple
story obscure. Reduced to essentials, the story is this: H.C.E.,
now Jarl van Hoother or the Earl of Howth (a Dutchman because of William of Orange) is in his castle-inn-"lamphouse"
(the Bailey lighthouse on Howth) with his twin sons and his
daughter, the "dummy." (Isabel, a "dumbelle," is like the
"dummy" in "Clay.") Their felicity is interrupted by the arrival
of the "niece-of-his-in-law"—a niece instead of wife because of
dream-displacement perhaps—to confront him with a riddle:
"why do I am alook alike a poss of porterpease?" H.C.E. cannot
guess the question, let alone the answer, but we can try: A.L.P.
looks like the twins (who are as like as two peas in a pod)
because she is their mother, as "porter" (H.C.E., the publican,
who sells porter and maybe piesporter, a wine) is their father.
Baffled, he answers her "petty perusienne" French in Nassau
Dutch: "Shut!" (both shut up and shit). Offended in her turn,
the Prankquean kidnaps sad Tristopher (Shaun) and, aided by

the four masters, converts him to his opposite, Shem. (Not only Lutheran, "luderman" means joy, fun, play—from Latin *ludus*.) In vain H.C.E. wirelesses after her. She "swaradid" (answered in Danish): Nothing doing. Returning "to the bar of his bristolry," and asking her riddle again, the Prankquean sets a "jiminy" down and takes a "jiminy" up (*gemini*, twins in Latin). Tristopher has become Hilary, and Hilary, converted in his turn, will become Tristopher. (Hilary reversed is "Larryhill" as Tristopher reversed is "Toughertrees," 22.19, 24.) These interchanging twins owe their names and fates to Bruno's motto: *In tristitia hilaris, hilaritate tristis.*

The Prankquean's third visit threatens the dummy. Unable to endure the thought of this, incestuous H.C.E. emerges from his three castles (Dublin's coat of arms), dressed as usual in seven articles of clothing (22.34), including "ladbroke breeks," the snake-proof pants of Ragnar Ladbrok, a Danish king of Dublin. But H.C.E. has left the door open, and mother is now inside with daughter. Mother and daughter, ganging up—as composite "duppy"—on father, defeat him. He falls to the sound of thunder, and from what remains of him a city arises: "Thus the hearsomness . . . polis" (23.14) is the motto of Dublin, *Obedientia civium urbis felicitas.*

Earwicker's thundering fall, the second in this chapter, is connected, like the first, with defecation: "He ordurd" (23.5). His victorious family shuts the shutter of the pub, and drinks—including tea—are on the house; but "shot the shutter clup," anticipating the Russian General, also means: shot the shitter. Shooting him brings peace and illiterate "porthery" (pot, porter, pother, poetry) to the "floody flatuous [farting] world." Kersse the tailor, who makes a suit for the Norwegian captain, will reappear, like the Russian General, in Chapter XI. "One man in his armour" (23.8) is from Swift, but for his "shirts" Joyce substitutes girls' "under shurts" or drawers, as conspicuous here as at the battle of Waterloo. Here the Prankquean always arrives, to begin her "skirtmisshes," in a "brace of samers" or "another nice lace" or "a pair of changers" (21.19,32; 22.18, 21). Drawers bring us to the sexual aspect of this familiar story:

"laying cold hands on himself" (21.11), Earwicker appears to be masturbating. Making her "wit" (wet) against his door and pulling "a rosy one" or "a paly one" and lighting things up, she seems asking for sexual readmission. Denied this, "Annadominant" (14.17) contents herself with ruling what she cannot enjoy.

"Foenix culprit" (23.16), the right words for fallen and rising H.C.E., unite *felix culpa,* Adam's happy fall (from the Mass for Holy Saturday) with Earwicker's sin in Phoenix Park. From Nick's evil (*nihilo*) comes Michael's good—or the domestic adjustment of the Earwicker family, our general origin; for he and she are "our breed and washer givers" (23.30–36). But for his potent "halibutt" and her "pudor puff" neither you nor I nor, "to make plein avowels," the rest of the alphabet would exist. In this happy, evesdripping home—family seems equivalent to city—even ear and eye enjoy some adjustment (23.20–29). "Quarry silex . . . Undy gentian festyknees" seems to be corrupt Latin: Why are you silent as a stone? . . . Whence are you hurrying? But "Noanswa" (no answer) from Humphrey and Livia to these questions (cf. the opening lines of *Tom Sawyer*) proves communication less than perfect.

"Windfall" (apple, 23.34) shows that Larry O'Toole's Dublin, reversed and transported to the fertile Nile ("Nilbud," 24.1), is a kind of lost Eden, where Adam will earn his bread by the sweat of his brow until "the fiery bird disembers" (the Phoenix of May combined with Christ's December, 24.1–11). The rising Phoenix brings us back to the wake (24.14–15). "Did ye drink me doornail?" asks the corpse, "Did you think me dead?"

The rest of the chapter, simpler than what we have groped through, is an address to dead Finnegan, now "Finnimore," by a mourner at his wake. As "Guinnghis [Guinness] Khan" (24.35), Finnimore is both conqueror and keeper of a khan or pub. The milk and honey of "the madison man" (25.4), who combines medicine with Madison Avenue advertising, will sustain him while he rests like "a god on a pension." Rest easy, you decent man, says the mourner; your family is getting on without you:

Joe Behan and old Kate, Isabel, Jerry and Kevin, and even "your missus . . . the queenoveire" (Guinevere and queen of Ireland). "Repose you now! Finn no more!" (26–28) But "Finn no more" (28.34) promises "Finnagain" (5.10); for this is a wake. It becomes plain—or plainer—on the last page of this address to the dead (29) that Finnegan is H. C. Earwicker or "Humme the Cheapner, Esc," an "old offender . . . humile, commune and ensectuous" (like an incestuous earwig), who came to "Shop Illicit" (a shebeen in Chapelizod) by ship like a Danish invader. References to Egypt throughout this funeral oration (e.g., "Healiopolis," 24.18, "Totumcalmun," 26.18) suggest the tomb and hope of resurrection. "Edenborough," the last word, combines two times and the fall with the city. Building it from man's wreckage proves the fall a happy one.

3.9–10   One of the slighter motifs, "mishe mishe . . . tauftauf" recurs, bringing and acquiring meanings, in support of the twins and their girls: 12.22–23, 65.31, 80.7, 96.11–12, 102.28, 145.7–8, 211.14–15, 225.20–21, 240.24–25, 249.29, 277.11, 291.22–25, 446.18, 457.25, 459.3–4, 468.8, 485.8, 505.20, 601.25, 605.2, 606.36–607.1.

3.11   "Buttended." Isaac Butt, displaced by Parnell, takes the following places: 6.7, 23.32, 35.33–34, 85.15, 196.9, 254.13, 302.13, 421.4, 603.13.

3.13–14   "Rory . . . reggin" refer to Rory and Regan in Samuel Lover's novel Rory O'More. Contending opposites, Rory is hero and Shan (or Shaun) Regan, villain. (Sister Eileen Campion looked this up for me.) According to Joyce (Letters, I, 248) "rory" means the red and dewy (ros, roris) end of the rainbow. Joyce is right; for, as Paddy Henchy tells me, rory, an English version of Gaelic ruaidhri (pronounced ruri), is derived from ruadh, red. Rory anticipates Rory or Roderick O'Connor at the end of Chapter XI (380).

3.15–17   The first Viconian thunder is followed by nine more:

23.5–7, 44.20–21, 90.31–33, 113.9–11, 257.27–28,
314.8–9, 332.5–7, 414.19–20, 424.20–22.

6.8–27   *Finnegans Wake* owes its title and many phrases
(e.g., "the liquor wheretwin 'twas born," 4.34) to
"Finnegan's Wake," a ballad. (The title of the book
lacks an apostrophe perhaps because *Finnegans* is
plural as well as possessive.)

Tim Finnegan lived in Walker Street,

. . . .

And to rise in the world Tim carried a hod.
But Tim had a sort of tippling way;
With a love of liquor Tim was born,
And, to help him through his work each day,
Took a drop of the creature every morn.

One morning Tim was rather full,
His head felt heavy and it made him shake.
He fell from the ladder and broke his skull,
So they carried him home, his corpse to wake.

. . . . . , , ...

Micky Maloney raised his head,
When a gallon of whisky flew at him;
It missed him, and, hopping on the bed,
The liquor scattered over Tim.
"Och, he revives. See how he raises."
And Timothy, jumping from the bed,
Cried, while he lathered round like blazes,
"Bad luck to your sowls. D'ye think I'm dead?"

Whack. Hurroo. Now dance to your partners,
Welt the flure, your trotters shake;
Isn't it all the truth I've told ye,
Lots of fun at Finnegan's wake?

6.14–28   The songs in this paragraph and most of those that
appear throughout the *Wake* are identified in Mat-

thew Hodgart and Mabel Worthington, *Song in the Works of James Joyce,* 1959.

6.32   Literally, this E, lying flat on its back with its legs in the air, is fallen H.C.E., a giant extending across the countryside from Howth to Chapelizod. By a happy coincidence, this supine E is the Chinese ideogram for mountain—and H.C.E. is at least a hill. What is more, the ideogram for mountain is called "Shan." (See *Letters,* I, 250, 254, 257.) In this context "Shan" becomes Shaun, who will be the new and upright E. As a hieroglyph, the Chinese E suits Vico's divine age. Compare the hieroglyphic E, lying on its other side (299.F4), the sign of H.C.E. as a member of the "Doodles family" or the *Wake* itself. That E supine also looks like Sin and Shin (cf. "Shimar Shin," 10.18), the twenty-first and twenty-second letters of the Hebrew alphabet, improves the mixture; for Shem, who in Joyce's numerology is associated with twenty-one, is also an element of H.C.E.

7.5–6   Lady Morgan's "Dear dirty Dublin" becomes a motif: 60.33–35, 76.25–26, 105.18, 136.20–21, 180.15, 215.13–14, 305.7, 333.33, 370.9, 374.18, 570.3, 615.12.

8.9   For his Waterloo Joyce seems indebted to Freud's joke in *Wit and Its Relation to the Unconscious* about Wellington and his horse in a museum. See *Basic Writings,* Modern Library, p. 673.

8.29   "Mount Tipsey" and "Mons Injun," two of the three soldiers as mountains, seem to refer to Stephen-Joyce (*ipse* and tipsy) and Mulligan-Gogarty (St. John or Sinjin).

9.34–35   "Sophy Key-Po" combines *Sauve qui peut* with Li Po, the Chinese poet.

9.35   "Royal divorsion," the first of many references (e.g., 32.33) to *A Royal Divorce,* a play about Napoleon and his two girls, by W. G. Wills. The

authority on Joyce's allusions to literature is James
S. Atherton, *The Books at the Wake,* 1959.

12.26–32   Arbour Hill, Cork Hill, Summerhill, Misery Hill,
and Constitution Hill are streets in Dublin. Olaf,
Ivor, Sitric are Danish kings of Dublin.

13.33   Joyce liked playing with figures as well as with
words. 1132 (rise and fall) includes H.C.E. and his
sons. H is the eighth letter of the alphabet, C is the
third, and E is the fifth. Adding 8, 3, and 5 gives 16,
which, multiplied by 2 (the twins in him), gives 32.
Shaun's number is 11 (renewal) and Shem's is 21.
Add 21 and 11 and you get 32 or H.C.E. Elsewhere (in Chapter X) H.C.E.'s number is 10,
A.L.P.'s is 01. Put these together and you get 1001
or another of renewal's numbers. Consider A.L.P.
again: A is 1, L is 12, P is 16. Add these and you
get 29 or the leap-year girls.

13.36   "Baalfire." Cf. "balefires," 52.9, "bonfire," 501.27.
Baal is a Semitic god of fertility or fire. A balefire
(from Anglo-Saxon *bael,* fire) is a funeral or signal
fire, sometimes lighted on St. John's Eve.

15.13   "Thugs." A "thigging" thug may be someone, like
the Citizen in *Ulysses,* who pretends knowledge of
Gaelic. "Thawed" (15.15) is Gaelic *Tá,* to be.

15.30   "Parth a lone." Parthalon or Partholan was a
primitive invader of Ireland before the Firbolgs and
Fomorians.

17.14   Sturk. He and Ezekiel Irons (27.23) are characters
in Le Fanu's *House by the Churchyard,* a novel
about Chapelizod. (See *Letters,* I, 396.) The Salmon
House (25.14–15) is one of three pubs in this novel.
The others are the Phoenix (205.25) and the King's
House (32.26).

17.32   "Fiatfuit." Cf. "pfuit," 33.34, and "pfiat," 34.7.
Both *fiat* and *fuit* ("let there be . . . and there
was") occur in the Vulgate Genesis.

18.6   The three castles of Dublin's great seal recur: 22.34,

39.16, 101.23, 128.17, 230.35, 266.3, 414.4, 551.31, 594.9.

18.20–21 "Many. . . . Tieckle. . . . Forsin," Belshazzar's writing on the wall, is one of the lesser Biblical motifs: 118.19–20, 135.15–16, 146.13, 372.14–15, 373.3, 494.20, 598.14.

18.36 "Face to Face," the first F prone, the second F supine, anticipates "fux to fux" (177.36) and the situation of H.C.E. and A.L.P. in Chapter XVI.

19.33–35 "You gave me a boot. . . . I quizzed you a quid" seems to refer to Stephen-Joyce and Mulligan-Gogarty, *Ulysses,* 31, 49.

20.17 "Daleth," the fourth letter of the Hebrew alphabet, is equivalent to Greek delta, which, in connection with "mahomahouma" or Great Mother, implies that A.L.P., the delta, brings death as well as life.

23.8 "One man in his armour. . . ." Cf. *Ulysses,* 588: "Doctor Swift says one man in armour will beat ten men in their shirts."

23.14–15 Dublin's motto, *Obedientia civium urbis felicitas,* recurs: 76.9, 81.1, 139.29, 140.6–7, 266.1–2, 277.8, 347.35, 494.21–22, 540.25–26, 610.7–8.

25.31 "Liam failed." *Lia fail* is the Stone of Destiny on which Irish kings were crowned. Taken to Scotland, it was called the Stone of Scone. Now in Westminster Abbey, it serves at the coronation of English kings. "Liam" (William in Gaelic) may imply King William, who, though victor at the Boyne, failed. Here the stone appears with Le Fanu's "elmstree." Tree and stone are signs of Shem and Shaun.

27.10–11 "Encostive inkum" looks forward to solipsistic Shem in Chapter VII, 185.25.

27.28 "Lumbos," in connection with mist and sleep, seems an anagram of slumbo or slumber, distorted perhaps by Limbo. *Umbo,* a swelling or shield in Latin, seems irrelevant.

CHAPTER II · 30-47

THOUGH simpler than the first chapter, the second is like it in purpose. Both chapters are introductory. In the second Joyce names his hero, whose initials, H.C.E., appear in the first sentence of the book ("Howth Castle and Environs") and reappear through the rest of the first chapter to plague the reader alert enough to notice them. It is about time Joyce got around to giving the name the initials stand for—and about time to penetrate his hero's disguises, parallels, and pseudonyms: Finnegan, Willingdone, and Van Hoother. But Joyce is a teaser and suspense, if not too much of it, a value.

The first chapter abounds in fallers or guilty sinners. Now Joyce makes general sinning and falling particular. H. C. Earwicker is the sinner he has had in mind through all his mythical and historical parallels—H. C. Earwicker, the keeper of a pub in 1922, perhaps, in Chapelizod, Dublin, Ireland, Europe, the world, the universe, at all times. This particular-general man, the victim of gossip, suffers from the guilt that he displays during his encounter in the Park with the Cad.

The encounter of the young man with the old, said Joyce (*Letters*, I, 396), is the "basis" of his book. Elaborated here, this encounter was hinted at before: on the first page where the "kidscad" or young Parnell meets and replaces old Isaac Butt (3.11) and at the battle of Waterloo where young Shimar Shin blows the half-a-hat off the backside of old Willingdone's big wide harse (10.18–22). Later, in Chapter XI, the theme will come to climax in the shooting of the Russian General (353). Buckley, who kills the old general, owes his name of Gaelic *bouchal,* buck or young man, as the Cad, his predecessor, owes his name to French *cadet* or younger son. Indeed, the theme of this encounter is not only the young man challenging and replacing the old man but the son challenging and replacing the father and marrying the mother—a theme that had caught the notice of Sigmund Freud.

If Joyce's great theme is historical process and if this is centered in the family, here is the heart of the process: the son kills the father and, taking his place, will be killed by the son. The last chapter of the *Wake* concerns the rising son or father again, doomed by a later dawn. Waking up implies a wake. "The same," as Mutt tells Jute (18.5), "roturns." *'Zmorde* maybe, but what can we do about it?

As the theme of the Cad, elaborated in Chapter II, was stated or, at least, hinted in Chapter I, so were most of the themes elaborated now. The two girls and the three soldiers, for example, are still around. But, as we might expect from a chapter that is part of the general introduction, a few new themes are stated here, and a few remain for later statement. Essentially, however, the rest of the book is enlargement, rearrangement, and decoration of what we are given in Chapter I. Design is all—or almost all; for tone and feeling are important. Gaiety, the cheerful acceptance of horrors, continues from Chapter I through the whole elaborate design. "There's many a smile to Nondum" (20.19) before "allhorrors eve" (19.25).

No less formal than the first chapter, the second starts with a prelude: how Earwicker got his name, his alleged misdemeanor in the Park, and his defense. These preliminaries over, the action begins. Guilty Earwicker meets the Cad in the Park and, asked the time, unnecessarily defends himself. The puzzled Cad goes home, tells his wife, who tells her priest, who tells everybody else. Gossip about H.C.E. and his sin inspires a procession through the city and the composition of a ballad, which, exposing H.C.E., reviews most of the themes of the book. The odd thing about this simple story is that it is almost simple enough for the simplest reader. Chapter II is one of the first that Joyce

wrote. Maybe he did not have time, going over it, to complicate
it according to his habit.

Not from the Earwickers of Sussex nor from the Vikings, as
some say, Earwicker got his name from this: One evening while
a royal fox-hunt was in progress ("Hag Chivychas Eve," 30.14,
a strange union of evening with H.C.E. as A.L.P. in her triple
aspect of old woman, huntress, and temptress), the king and his
cocker spaniels, pausing on the turnpike at the "mobhouse" or
pub in Chapelizod, surprise the turnpike-keeper-publican catching earwigs in his garden after the manner of "cabbaging Cincin-
natus." Singing "John Peel" (a song that will recur), the king
names the gardener "earwigger" on the spot (31.28). This is the
best of the "andrewpaulmurphyc" (31.35) or anthropomorphic
accounts of the old humbug's naming. The prophets Nehemia
and Malachi, the bells of *Sechseläuten* ("seeks alicense") and
of the Angelus ("cumsceptres with centaurs stay") hail the
naming at the "khan" (pub, 32.1–4). (*Sechseläuten,* the Zurich
spring festival, and the Angelus, in corrupt Italian-French, are
new themes that will proceed throughout the book.) H.C.E.'s
initials appear unencumbered for the first time on p. 32 and his
full name for the first time on p. 33. That he is more than somebody or anybody is proved by his nickname, "Here Comes
Everybody" (32.18–19). The two girls are there at the christen-
ing and later, as Iris and Lili (30.1) and as those "nighttalkers,"
Skertsiraizde and Donyahzade, of the 1001 Arabian stories
(32.8). As Rosa and Lily, they played leading parts when the
matter was staged (32.11). The metaphor of the theater (all the
world's a "worldstage," 33.3) occupies the rest of the prelude
(32.10–33.13). Variously known as *The Bohemian Girl, The
Lily of Killarney* (Balfe), and *A Royal Divorce,* Earwicker's
"problem passion play" was given its 111th performance by
"Semperkelly's immergreen tourers" (32.29), who combine *always* in Latin and German with Irish green. This hilarious combination helps our growing idea of the "bossaloner" (32.36).
More than the boss, alone, of a saloon in his Borsalino hat, this
man is our "folksforefather" (33.4). The "King's treat house"

(32.26), where they put H.C.E.'s play on the boards, is at once
Le Fanu's pub, the King's House, and the King Street theater in
Dublin, named, appropriately in this context, the Gaiety.

A great man entirely, yet, according to some, he did something in the Park, as, according to others, Adam did something
in the Garden. What Adam did we know more or less; of what
Earwicker did we know less and less as we guess more and
more. His sin, like that of the "smugging" boys in *A Portrait of
the Artist,* remains indefinite. Maybe it is any sin of every man or
every sin of any man. The gossips, agreeing, accuse him of
"every enormity." Flora and Fauna, the two girls, say he annoyed the three Welsh Fusiliers in the Park (33.26–28). The
three fusiliers, those "shomers" (Hebrew watchers or peepers),
say he "behaved with ongentilmensky immodus" while watching
the two girls, who, in order to make water that "Saint Swithin's
summer," had pulled down their drawers (34.15–29). What
value, his defenders ask, has the evidence of peepers peeping at
a peeper at his peers? If the "guiltless" man did anything at
all—of this much we are sure—what he did had something to do
with, and rests on the dubious evidence of, the two girls and the
three soldiers. Arabic references and Hebrew words improve or
lessen our assurance.

They say that one morning H. C. Earwicker, dressed as usual
in seven ill-assorted articles of clothing, was walking through
Phoenix Park, the place of his "alleged misdemeanour," when
he met "a cad with a pipe." Greeting Earwicker in corrupt Gaelic ("Guinness thaw . . . ouzel fin?" How are you today, my
blond gentleman? Mutt's greeting to Jute), the Cad asks the
time of day—as if a doubting Seth Thomas Aquinas. Just then a
clock, striking twelve noon, answers this question. But the oriuolate's response (*oriuolo,* watch in Italian), surprising the luciferant (matches for a pipe and Stephen's Lucifer), is an uncalled-
for defense by the oriuolate of his character. Plainly the decent
man is "carrying his overgoat under his schulder [German,
guilt], sheepside out" (35.13). The puzzled Cad—Gaping Gill
now—thanking Earwicker, goes home to the pottage he shares
with Esau, and, thinking things over, spits.

Earwicker's uneasiness has several causes. First, the guilt that makes him stutter (e.g., 36.23–24). Second, fear, as if in New York, of mugging. Third, the nature of the Cad's question and his youth. When a young man asks an old man the time of day, the question implies that the old man is through—especially when the time is twelve, the end of one temporal cycle and the beginning of another. Fourth, politics. It is the Ides of April (35.3), a time that recalls not only Caesar's fatal Ides of March but "the fenian rising" (35.24) of Easter, 1916. Moreover, the Cad speaks sinister Gaelic. Earwicker's fear of a rebel is that of the established Englishman. Looking to the Wellington Monument and the Church of England for assurance, H.C.E. proclaims the respectability of his "hotel and creamery establishments" (36.18–29)—state, church, and commerce. Sinn Fein, the Boxer rebellion ("pingping K.O." or knockout, 35.23–24), and Cuchulain (35.32) define his fears. (Cuchulain's statue in the Post Office on O'Connell Street is a symbol of the Easter rising; and Cuchulain fought with his son.) Pigott's "Hesitency" (35.20) implies a young fraud attacking old Parnell. "Kidder" and "buttall" (35.33–34), recalling the first page of the *Wake,* imply young Parnell attacking old Isaac Butt. Buckley shooting the Russian General, another parallel but oddly displaced, occurs several pages later (42.11–12): "how the bouckaleens shout their roscan generally (seinn fion, seinn fion's araun)." The weight of these parallels is discouraging. Earwicker feels outnumbered five to one ("Me only, them five ones," 36.20–21) as Willingdone-Earwicker was at his Waterloo. ("Me only," five to one, and "sinnfinners," combining politics with masturbation, suggest loneliness and guilt.)

As Cadenus or Swift (36.35), the Cad brings literary parallels to bear. Earwicker, the Master Builder, is the established writer. The Cad, a "littlebilker" (37.35), challenges him. (As we have noticed, building and bilking are the same; for art as fiction is at once creation and fraud.) Earwicker's "Bhagafat gaiters" and "inverness" (35.10) and "the twattering of bards" in the Celtic twilight (37.17–18) associate the great man with old W. B. Yeats; and the Cad's "I have met with you, bird, too late" (37.13–14) is young Joyce's famous challenge to the older poet. But the Cad is also "ildiot" or T. S. Eliot, who "in his secondmouth language" repeated "as many of the bigtimer's [Joyce's] verbaten words" (verbatim and *verboten*, 37.14–16) as he could call to mind. (Joyce, as we have also noticed, always insisted that Eliot stole *The Waste Land* from *Ulysses*.) But Joyce, adept at relativity, is playing no favorites. As caddish young Joyce to respectable old Yeats, so caddish young Eliot to older Joyce. Anyway, the Cad, recalling as many of bigtimer-Earwicker's words as he can, goes home, spitting and leaving a trail of dandruff, to his supper. As "Mr. Shallwesigh or Mr. Shallwelaugh" (37.28), combining Tristopher and Hilary, the Cad is the composite son or the new father. Having replaced his old man, this risen son incestuously takes Earwicker's wife to wife.

That Mrs. Cad is that is made clear by this: née Bareniece, she is, like the Prankquean, H.C.E.'s niece-in-law. Maxwelton, confirmed by "annie lawrie promises" (38.21), establishes the niece as Anna and A.L.P., expert in "dumbestic husbandry" (38.11), or a letter-finding hen with chickens. Fascinated with the Cad's "spittoons" and his story of H.C.E., this hen whispers (Italian "pispigliando") her "gossiple" in the "epistolear" of her priest, who passes "a slightly varied version" on to Philly Thurnston. This priest, associated with Bruno of Nola, half Jesuit and half Paulist ("vincentian"), seems to embody the twins; and Thurnston, concerned with ethics and stone, seems Stanislaus-Shaun (38.18–36). Indeed, all the people who gossip about H.C.E. and his alleged sin through the rest of the chapter may be identified with one member or another of H.C.E.'s family. Before we proceed with their doubtful identification, one difficulty—and a very funny one—remains: the "ruah" (Hebrew spirit or wind) of the Bishop of Hippo (St. Augustine) and that of "Havvah-ban-Annah" (38.29–30), probably the Bible. "Ban," if a corruption of Hebrew *ben* (son), must mean daughter here. Eve, daughter of Anna, unites Havvah-Eve with the Virgin Mary; and Have a Banana, in this context, must imply forbidden fruit.

The twin priest passes the news to horse-loving Philly at Baldoyle, a race track near Dublin, where in the "doubles" of Peter and Paul (stone and tree or Shaun and Shem) the C.E.H. cup— a reversal of a sort for H.C.E.—was won by "two noses." At these races wee Winny Widget or A.L.P. is the tipster (39.1– 13). Her voice, like the voice of Solomon's "turfur," is heard in the land. At the track the gossip about Mr. Adams (H.C.E.) reaches Treacle Tom and Frisky Shorty, the twins again. Threecastle Tom, a Dubliner associated with meat ("Finnish pork" or Phoenix Park), seems Shaun, but, also associated with drink and pubs, seems Shem as well (39.14–36). (Shem drinks; Shaun eats.) In his flophouse Tom "alcoherently" passes on the gossip of the "evangelical bussybozzy" to Peter Cloran (stone-Shaun), O'Mara (a Buddhist devil and a singer—Shem), Mildew Lisa (Tristan's *mild und leise,* cf. 18.2, or Isabel), and Hosty, "an illstarred beachbusker . . . setting on a twoodstool on the verge of selfabyss" (40.5–23). Hosty, who figures most conspicuously through the rest of the rambling tale, is connected here by wood, beach, self-abuse, and solipsism with Shem, but he comes to be associated with H.C.E. As the Shem-side of H.C.E., Hosty is the Cad who has taken his place. Writer of the ballad of H.C.E., Hosty is a creator or father, at once the Master Builder and the "littlebilker." Exposing H.C.E., he exposes himself. Hosty's name shows his composite nature. As the Host (*hostie*) or Eucharist, Hosty is God. As *hostis* or enemy, he is the devil. As a host, he keeps a pub; and as a host he is a multitude. Never was Joyce's talent for concentration shown more happily.

Hosty and his companions cross "Ebblinn's chilled hamlet" (E.C.H., Eblana or Dublin, and "Molly Malone"); but Dublin, by virtue of the "metro" and "Simpson's on the Rocks," is also Paris and London or all cities (41.18,20; 43.7). As they cross the city, "the trio" is joined by "a decent sort of the hadbeen variety" (42.1–3) or H.C.E. What trio? They are a quartet before becoming a quintet and, later, a mob. But numbers and identities shift and merge in this dream sequence, "Where Riau Liviau riots and col de Houdo humps" (42.18). Trio, quartet or quintet, they are joined (43.7–18) by the two girls, Tarry the Tailor (H.C.E. as sailor-tailor), a fair girl (Isabel), a postboy (Shaun), and a plumodrole (Shem), and many others, including the four old men.

As they riot along, references to literature and music prepare us for their ballad, a union of words and song. Mangan and Davis, Shelley, Swinburne, Shaw, Yeats, Wilde, and Byron (41.4–10) adequately represent literature. Handel's "Messiagh of roaratorios" (41.28) and *Parsifal* (43.35) are the extremes of music. St. Cecilia, patron of music (41.33), presides over the tuning-up of Parnell's "inscrewments" (43.32)—all those fiddles and horns. At last we are ready for the ballad, "privately printed" (43.25) and publicly sung near the church of St. Anna.

The "rann" (verse) that Hosty made, his Shem-side out, about himself, is "the king of all ranns"—as the wren, sacrificed on St. Stephen's day, is the king of all birds (cf. *Ulysses,* 481). A tale of tree and stone, the rann buries poor Earwicker ("Here line the refrains of"), who, whatever his name, is everything and everybody. Some call him Vico or Michelet or Michael or Dublin. Others call him ear, bug or salmon. But the best thing to call him is Persse O'Reilly (44.7–17). As this chapter began with earwigs, so it ends: *Perce-oreille* is French for earwig. In this name, however, Joyce, never contented with one meaning, has also included Patrick Pearse and The O'Reilly of the Easter rising. Kersse the tailor (23.10) may also be there, along with Lady Gregory, née Persse, celebrator of Finn MacCool and Cuchulain. That *persse* is also Estonian for arse is fortunate because the ballad, like all literature, is defecation. (Joyce's other Estonian word, "sitta," 625.27, means shit.) The thunder (44.19–21) that signalizes Earwicker's third fall and renewal, includes "kak" (Latin *caco,* shit; Greek *kakos,* bad) and "pluddy . . . pkonpkot" (German *kot,* shit), which sounds like what it is. "It's cumming, it's brumming!" which introduces this thundering, recalls Cambronne, whose word is *merde*. Earwicker's thundering third fall is not unlike his second (23.4–7) at the end of the Prankquean's story.

Composed in "felibrine trancoped metre" (43.22), as good

a description as any of the cat-salty syncopation, Hosty's ballad approximates that return to the rhythms and diction of common speech that Eliot, Pound, and Yeats commended. As it bumps along, exposing H.C.E. entirely, it commends itself as one of Joyce's better poems—better than any in *Chamber Music* and better by far than any in *Pomes Penyeach*. In this bumping ballad, poor Earwicker, one with Humpty Dumpty, is a foreign invader—Oliver Cromwell, Black and Tan, or Dane—a sinner like Oscar Wilde, and a commercial, Protestant cheater—fit to be jailed in the criminal jail of Mountjoy. But what was his fall from the Magazine wall and what his sin in the Park? "He was joulting by Wellinton's monument . . . / When some bugger let down the backtrap of the omnibus / And he caught his death of fusiliers" (47.8–11). We knew that what he did had something to do with the three soldiers and the "collupsus of his back promises," but now we know little more. Sophocles, Shakespeare, false-teeth Dante, and anonymous Moses, however, imply creation after fall, and the last stanza, while denying resurrection, implies it; for if no king's horses or men can put Humpty together again, Abel, revived, may be able to raise Cain. If "The general lost her maldenloo" (46.36), his Waterloo is A.L.P.'s victory and his own.

31.7 "Silver doctors" are artificial fishing flies.

32.2–3 "Seeks alicence." *Sechseläuten* reappears: 58.24, 213.18–19, 268.2–3, 327.24, 339.22, 379.8, 492.14–15, 508.29, 528.19, 536.11.

33.23 "White caterpillar" is both the one in *Alice* and a name given to Oscar Wilde.

34.32 "Vollapluck" is Volapuk, an international language like Esperanto (cf. "voltapuke," 40.5). "Flesh nelly" is Fresh Nelly, a whore in *A Portrait* and *Ulysses,* 214, 217.

34.33 "Lilyth . . . allow." Not only Lilith and one of the two girls—Pauline the other—but "Lillibullero," a seventeenth-century song against the Irish Catholics, sung no doubt by William at the

Boyne. Becoming a refrain, "Lillibullero" recurs: 66.36, 83.34, 102.11, 206.4, 224.20–21, 450.29, 618.16–17.

35.2 The "hydrophobe sponge" is Stephen-Shem. Cf. "hydrophobe," *Ulysses,* 673. Stephen sponges on all his friends.

35.11 Samuel Beckett parodies the story of the Cad in *Watt* (Grove), pp. 45–46.

35.30 Fox Goodman, the mysterious bell-ringer, reappears throughout the *Wake,* e.g., 212.9, 328.26, 360.11, 403.20–22, 511.9, 621.35.

36.13 "Gygas." King Gyges of Lydia, provided with a ring of invisibility, was a peeping Tom. Plato mentions him.

36.17 E reversed, I am told, is a mathematical symbol for existence. Here it is also an example of reversal.

36.29 "Mrs. Michan" is St. Michan's Church, Dublin.

37.2 "Sweatagore," maybe in this context Yeats's Tagore, is certainly, Nat Halper tells me, Svyatogor, a giant in a Russian epic who met, and was replaced by Mikula, a sort of Cad. "Dublnotch" (37.3) is Russian good night and a postman's double knock.

37.19–22 This passage may reflect Lynch's experience in *Ulysses,* 224. "Pogh" or pogue is Gaelic kiss; and "ff . . . kk" seems one of those "verbaten words" (37.15), like "cowshots" (37.23).

37.25 *"Mawshe dho hole."* Gaelic: if you please.

37.33–35 "Senaffed . . . pibered . . . snevel." Swedish-German mustard, Danish pepper, and Danish snow (*sne*).

38.5 "Piessporter" is not only a German wine but an echo of the Prankquean's riddle. H.C.E. is Porter and the twins are peas.

39.33–40.2 "Hell fire, red biddy, bull dog, blue ruin and creeping jenny" are drinks and members of the family:

H.C.E., A.L.P. (the hen), Shaun, Shem, and
Isabel. "The Duck and Doggies" and the rest are
pubs.

44.12–13 "Arth . . . Barth, Coll," the Irish alphabet,
which, according to Joyce (*Letters*, I, 225–26)
—and Joyce is right—is "ailm, beith, coll, dair
. . . all made up of the names of trees"—elm,
birch, hazel, oak. Cf. "Dar Bey Coll" (433.16).

44.19 "It's cumming, it's brumming." *Le mot de*
Cambronne, alluded to on the first page of the
Wake ("konnbronn," 3.15, part of the first thunder) is a slight motif, part of the greater motif of
thundering defecation: 9.26–27, 98.3–4, 134.8,
151.31–32, 352.21–22, 421.13–14.

44.22 Arditi wrote "Il Bacio" (the kiss).

A note on Earwicker's name: In it Ear (or time) is combined
with wick (village or place, from Latin *vicus*, 3.2). Place is
space. A union of the twins (Shem, time; Shaun, space), Earwicker is time-space. Ear suggests Eire and wicker suggests
Ford of the Hurdles (made of wickerwork) or Dublin; hence
Earwicker could mean a dweller (wicker) in Dublin, Ireland.
In a pub time-place becomes "Time, please!"

CHAPTER III · 48-74

I F THE *Wake* is a dream, Chapter I seems oddly composed. Of dream materials perhaps, it is a conscious and rational, not an unconscious and irrational, structure. Chapter II is put together in the same way, except for Hosty's trip across the town, where something of a dream's deportment is captured. Chapter III, however, is dream entirely or almost entirely; for while the artist's hand is there, arranging, its arrangements approximate the disarrangements of dream. More than a careful ordering of sleepy matters, this chapter is their careful disordering. By inconsequence, uncertainty and repetition—the same things insistently over and over again—Joyce gives the effect of nightmare. This chapter our incubus, and we its succubi. Yet cheerfulness breaks through.

Joyce begins suitably with fog and cloud (48.1–5) and suitably ends with cloud and sleep: "Humph is in his doge [a dozing doge]. Words weigh no more to him than raindrips. . . . Rain. When we sleep. Drops. But wait until our sleeping. Drain. Sdops" (74.16–19). But words mean more than this to Joyce and to us, his readers; for through words alone we reach the wordlessness of the sleeping mind and enjoy it vicariously. Joyce had reason to call this work of unreason his "nightynovel" (54.21) and his "drema" (69.14). In a novel or drama characters have identity and constant names. Here names change, characters shift and "reamalgamerge" (49.36). So "intermutuomergent" (55.12) these people of the night that it is hard "to idendifine the individuone" (51.6). Earwicker's "cloudyphiz" remains "nebuless" (50.36; 51.1); and as for Hosty and the Cad, who, where, and when are they at all?

Hosty and the Cad are still around because this chapter repeats and confuses the already confusing matter of Chapter II. First, we hear something of what happened to Hosty after he composed that ballad. Then, a shifty cloud of witnesses and gossips tries in vain to pin shifting Earwicker down and to define his adventures in the Park, his encounter, if any, with the two girls and the three soldiers and his subsequent encounter with the Cad. The story of the Cad, displaced at last from Park to pub, recurs in several versions until it is hard for us to separate Earwicker from his supposed assailant. They may be the same person, if any, and so may Hosty and the Cad. As for the witnesses and gossips, they seem, like the crowd staggering across town from pub to pub in Chapter II, to be members of Earwicker's family. All that comes clear is that Earwicker sinned somewhere, somehow, and that everybody is talking about him.

That a mind is there directing this mess is made plain by the way in which matters from the first few lines of the chapter reappear and develop later on. The "Shanvocht" (Shan Van Vocht, Poor Old Woman or Ireland), Vercingetorix, and Caractacus or Caradoc (48.3,7) come back and by confusion of tongues illustrate miscegenation (54.3–19) and the difficulty of communicating. Husband and wife talk together but in languages foreign to each other. The "mixed sex cases" (48.2) reappear not only in these incompatible marriages but in "His husband" (49.2) and "her wife" (50.6). Lewis Carroll, suggested on the first page (48.4) by "treacle" and "liddled," reappears as old Tom Quad (Christ Church College, Oxford), who exposed H.C.E. as Humpty Dumpty (57.24–29) while watching in "clericalease" the sun "slithe dodgsomely into the nethermore" ("slithe" is from "Jabberwocky" and Dodgson is Carroll's real name as Liddell is Alice's). That there is a directing mind is also made plain by the themes that connect the apparently disordered matters. All, whatever their appearance, are variations on the themes of sin, conflict, fall, uncertainty, and incommunicability

—of "centuple celves" and the altered ego (49.33;51.2). On the first page and here and there for the next few pages (48.10–11; 49.29–30; 55.33–35) the "drema" seems about to take the form of a drama or "mime." This promise, not kept here, will be kept more or less in Chapter IX (219). Not only a prelude to this, the references to the play here recall the play in Chapter II (32–33). A play is a form of communication, the playwright hopes. In a chapter on incommunicability, a play would be out of place, and so are the other forms of communication that abound in this chapter: television, radio, telephone, dictaphone, and phonograph (52.18; 53.4; 59.15; 73.14). Whether directed to eye or ear, their messages, like the dead letter in the dump, never reach their destinations.

"Of the persins sin this Eyrawyggla saga (which thorough readable to int from and, is from tubb to buttom all falsetis- sues. . . .)" (48.16–18), the first in order of appearance in this chapter is Hosty, now "poor Osti-Fosti," a small poet with nice ear and tenor voice, like the author of *Chamber Music*. Of Hosty no one end is known—and who knows the ends of Joyce? Some say Hosty went as a wild goose to the Crimean War (with Buckley) or soldiered under Wolsey (Wellington). Others, thinking him Sordid Sam, say he died of drink, "pro- pelled from Behind into the great Beyond" (49.5–25). Anyway he disappeared. Before that he seems to have been the Cad with a pipe, "that same snob of the dunhill, fully several yearschaums riper, encountered by the General [H.C.E as the Russian Gen- eral and the Cad as Buckley] on that redletter morning or may- noon" (50.30–32). April has become May; morning or noon will become "evenchime" (51.32); for time around here is as fluid as the rest—and the Angelus, after all, rings out morning, noon, and evening. When asked by the three soldiers what hap- pened in the Park and what has happened to H.C.E., Hosty seems at a loss since he and H.C.E. have changed so much (51.11–19). Indeed, they seem to have changed into one an- other or, getting together, into one; for the two girls are his (whose?) only admirers. With both gun ("repeater") and watch ("repeater" and "timespiece"), the composite of Hosty, Joyce,

Cad, and H.C.E. is now "His Revenances," who, like Arthur and "Our Farfar," will return (52.7,16–17) maybe.

Changing sides and the intermerging of contraries are accounted for by calling on Nicholas of Cusa (49.33–36), who, merged here with his opposite, Michael Cusack, the Citizen of *Ulysses,* is himself an example of what he affirms. Another example (50.1) is the conflict and union of the Baxters and the Fleshmans or Shem as baker and Shaun as butcher. But the doctrine of Nicholas of Cusa anticipates that of Bruno of Nola, who appears here as Father Browne or Padre Bruno (50.18–23), the divided priest to whom Annie Maxwelton whispered in Chapter II (38.26–28). The "brothers' broil" (52.18), this one not between baker and butcher but between ear and eye, prepares us for the cloud of witnesses who need both if they are to get at H.C.E. This "bigboss," wise as Kang (Confucius), keeper of a tollgate, swearer by the Monument, now unites Napoleon's "elbaroom" with Wellington's "woolselywellesly" (52.23–31). United or not, he fell and the cause of his fall was woman: "(sukand see whybe!)" (52.35)—*suchen Sie Weib* or its identical opposite, *cherchez la femme* (64.28).

"Jauntyjogging," back to back, "on an Irish visavis" (53.7) or jaunting car, the two passengers learn about the Boomster's fall from the Jehu or driver, whose account occupies most of the next four pages. (Valentine Vousden, mentioned 50.15, composed a ballad called "The Irish Jaunting Car.") The gossiping Jehu appears to be Shem (563.7), exposing his father. Driving through the Park, past tree and stone (*"La arboro, lo petrusu"*) and the Wellington "monolith," at the "angelus hour," now midnight, the Jehu tells his passengers the story of Earwicker and the Cad. In this version (53.7–34) Earwicker, publican of the Eagle Cock Hostel, takes out a cigar to match the Cad's pipe and the Cad, wishing his Honour the "bannocks" (loaves) of Gort, Morya, Bri Head, and Puddyrick (God, Mary, Bridget, and Patrick), offers a box in the "pit of his St Tomach's" (stomach and Thomas Becket or Aquinas).

A martial interlude, bringing the three soldiers to mind ("Hup, boys, and hat him!"), establishes Earwicker as foreign invader,

King Billy of the Boyne or Cromwell (53.36–54.1). Another interlude on time, memory, succession, death, and sleep brings up mixed marriages—of Gaul or Briton with poor old Irishwoman (55.2–5). Mixture of races means mixture of tongues, illustrated in the following paragraph (54.7–19). Even in the "Casaconcordia" (home or pub), even between husband and wife words are as vain as when "ulemamen" talk to "sobranjewomen" (*Ulema* is a Moslem body of scholars; *Sobranje* is the national assembly of Bulgaria) or as when "storthingboys" talk to "dumagirls" (*Storthing* is the parliament of Norway; *Duma* is the parliament of Russia). Vain maybe, but not beyond all conjecture:

54.10–11   "Huru . . . frickans?" Swedish: how are you, young ladies?

54.11   "Hwoorledes . . . det?" Danish: how are you? "Losdoor . . . cue," English: last door on the left, ladies, thank you.

54.12–13   "Milleciento . . . scudi," Italian: 1132 scudi. "Tippoty . . . tippoty," Greek: nothing, lord, nothing. "Cha kai . . . sahib?" (India?)

54.13–14   "Despenseme . . . sabez," Spanish: Excuse me or grant me. "O thaw . . . gaily?" Gaelic: sorrow is upon me . . . Do you speak Gaelic?

54.15–16   "Lick . . . lang," pseudo-Chinese. "Epi . . . going," a mixture of tongues. "Lptit" seems Swift's "little language." "Ismeme . . ." may be Isabel's English.

54.17–19   "Os pipos . . . pocchino," a mixture, according to Elliott Dobbie, of Portuguese, Italian, and English. "Gruarso" seems to mean big arse. "We fee?" German. "Ung duro": one dollar? "Szabad": Hungarian? "Mercy": French. "Thak": Danish, thanks.

"Phew! What a warm time we were in there," as we said, leaving the museum. Whether this jumble of tongues is the Jehu's digression or Joyce's remains a problem. But it is plain that, continuing the story of Earwicker and Cad, the Jehu reviews Earwicker's defense of his respectability and adds something new, his invitation to "the adullescence who he was wising up" (the Cad) to follow his example (54.26–36). Earwicker's Miltonic "Great taskmaster" (36.27) has become his "Great Schoolmaster" (55.1).

Another digression: this one on fall and rise and the difficulty of establishing the facts of either (55.3–8). "The house of Atreox is fallen indeedust (Ilyam, Ilyum! . . .)": in the accusative case, first in a feminine declension, second in a masculine, Troy's decline and fall are not unlike accused Adam's. But fall means rise; for life is a wake. The fallen father—"the cropse of our seedfather," as Frazer said—is our nourishment and our sacrament (cf. 7.9–14).

Or our tree of life, "the gigantig's lifetree, our fireleaved loverlucky blomsterbohm, phoenix in our woodlessness, haughty, cacuminal, erubescent" (55.27–36), the Jehu continues, pointing it out in the Park to the couple "on their airish chaunting car," who, like Cyclopes ("round eyes") or Russians, behold the tree and its seasonal cycle with "intouristing" interest. Maybe the Jehu, "Dyas in his machina," learned about H.C.E. from Coppinger's cousin—Coppinger is H.C.E.—who, "in a pullwoman of our first transhibernian" (Irish-Russian) railroad, learned it from the three soldiers, those "factferreters" (55.12–22), or from "his biografiend" (55.6), Herbert Gorman perhaps. Confusing the issue with remarks on time and the "yawning (abyss)," the Ginnungagap, the Jehu returns to the Cad, the "gunwielder," and that "overgrown leadpencil," the Wellington Monument (56.3–14).

Goldsmith's traveller, Mr. Melancholy Slow, putting up at Earwicker's paradisal pub, "Inn the days of the Bygning," would find wine, women, and song, poteen and tea (56.20–30). But who is Earwicker ("Who was he to whom?") and where? At home? ("Kiwasti . . . kitnabudja," corrupt Finnish, means it is hard to make a house a home, 56.32–36.) The "hantitat" of this "ghouly ghost" is not here but rather with the "two peaches" and the three Chinese soldiers—and in Vico's tempo-

ral cycle: "plicyman, plansiman, plousiman, plab." Not even the
"forefarther folkers," the four old men, Blake's four Zoas and
the four quarters of Ireland, can tell us much. Nor can "Hee
haw," the donkey who follows them around. All we know is that
he fell and A.L.P. revived him, that we are just ants on his ant-
hill, "wee, wee" (57.3–15). ("Wee" means *oui,* and also in
connection with A.L.P., small and weewee or urine.)

Whatever he did, he is a pretty important man. Of his sin we
do not even possess the "unfacts." The "evidencegivers," who
appeal to our "notional gullery," are not to be relied on. "His
adjugers are semmingly freak threes but his judicandees plainly
minus twos" (the soldiers and the girls). Lewis Carroll's expo-
sure of Humpty Dumpty is no more reliable. All we have is gossip, "pillow talk and chithouse chat." Should he come to trial,
"Jedburgh justice" (hang first, try later) would be dispensed
(57.16–36). After all is said, "human, erring and condonable"
H.C.E. is "Greatwheel Dunlop" and we are his "bisaacles" (bicycles, Isaac and sons, testicles). He is Christ, Parnell, and Caesar. Christ's holly and Parnell's ivy are Caesar's triumph: "ulvy
came, envy saw, ivy conquered." Like Frazer's dying god, Earwicker is torn "limb from lamb" (58.2–7). Hence the wake.
The rest of the paragraph (58.8–18) repeats, almost word for
word, the wake in Chapter I (6.13–7.1–19). There are echoes,
too, of *Mannequin pisse* (17.2) and the Magazine wall, "Chin,
chin!"

So far the "evidencegivers by legpoll" (57.17) have pulled
our legs a little; but Hosty and the Jehu, working in a fog and
representing H.C.E. with his Shem-side out, have not convinced
us. Neither was around when what took place took place. Now
from the fog a cloud of witnesses, no more reliable but no less.
Here their sorry catalogue:

1. The three soldiers (58.23–33), now "Tap and pat and
tapatagain" (or appearance, reversal, and after union, reappearance) say that while they were walking down Montgomery
Street (not in Dublin) they saw Earwicker "souped" by Lilith
(evidently the wife of Martin Cunningham in *Ulysses*). As
Coldstream Guards they speak Norman French and a kind of

Danish Anglo-Saxon: "Wroth mod eldfar. . . ." Yet the bells
of *Sechseläuten* and the Angelus, promising renewal, precede
and follow their dubious evidence.

2. An English actress (58.33–59.14), a kind of "wastepacket
Sittons," interviewed in a London "pewty" parlor, sitting in her
theatrical bracegirdle at her mirror (surely she is Isabel who is
always at her mirror), says nothing in particular about H.C.E.
but in general the tart associates him with the rainbow, Arthur,
Cain, Adam, Christ, and building a tower of "wanderful noyth
untirely" (cf. 4.36), all of which we know about. She has one
great word however—one of Joyce's most radiant condensations: "goddinpotty," which, efficiently and hilariously uniting
Adam and Christ, fall and rise, means the garden party of Eden
and God in a potty or the Eucharist.

3. An "entychologist" (entomologist-etymologist-psycholo-
gist) says that Earwicker's pen name (Shem the Penman?) is a
properispomenon or word with accent on the penult. This scholar's obiter dicta seem Shaun's on Shem (59.15–16) or the comment by one half of H.C.E. on the other.

4. The dustman from St. Kevin's seven churches at Glendalough (59.16–24) is plainly Shaun, identified not only by Kevin
but by food—of an extraordinary kind. Eating "stenk and kit-
teney phie in a hashhoush," this dustman calls H.C.E. a temporal
(days, ages, avatar) brick, "buck it all" (bucket or chalice with
Buck Buckley).

5. The driver of a jaunting car (the Jehu again), while hosing
his horse in the manner of Leigh Hunt ("Jenny kissed me"),
calls Earwicker a "pink joint [roast beef] reformee" (changer),
who by the Brehon laws of ancient Ireland deserves a seat in
parliament (59.24–29).

6. Escoffier, as great a cook as Brillat-Savarin, sensibly favors
Humpty Dumpty: If you want a "homelette," you must break an
egg. French *foie* and German *Leber* attend him (59.29–32).

7. The "infamatios" of the perspiring tennis player in a pair
of flannels (Gogarty?) seems incompetent, immaterial, and irrelevant (59.33–35).

8. A concern with urine identifies the barmaid as A.L.P., who

defends H.C.E. against the Siddons creature (58.35) and all the "merrytricks" (Latin, whores) who tempt his "revulverher" (59.35–60.8).

9–12. A Board of Trade official, the Daughters Benkletter (Danish for drawers), Bryan O'Lynn, and a would-be martyr defend H.C.E. Those two bitches in the Park "ought to be leashed, canem." The martyr tells of Moody and Sankey or Sakyamuni (Buddha), playing mango tricks under a bo tree, and of Indra's thunder (60.8–21).

13. Ida Wombwell (cf. 529.1), the revivalist, is Isabel. What she says about "interfizzing with grenadines" and other "peersons" in the Park seems relevant. Concerned with fizz, she finds brutish father "brut" or rather sweet (60.22–26).

14–16. The antipodal bookmaker is concerned with reversal and revival. Captain Boycott is concerned with Yeats, his cape, and his meeting with Joyce: "We have meat two hourly" (cf. 37.13). And Dan Meiklejohn (Shaun) issues a papal bull to go with Yeats's cape (60.26–33).

17. Lady Morgan (60.33–61.1), who called her city "Dear dirty Dublin," takes and changes sides with a bully lord while those "dirty dubs," the three soldiers, undo their flies and the two drabs take down their "scenities" (obscene, scenic scanties).

18. Sylvia Silence, the girl detective (Isabel again), lisps for and against father (61.1–11). "Shew gweatness was his twadgedy," yet he should be tried by the law Oscar Wilde was tried by.

19. Jarley Jilke, a Jack looking for his Jill, thinks Earwicker, like Parnell, was sacked by Gladstone (61.11–13).

20. Walter Meagher, who will come back (e.g., 211.11), says something about the two girls, Questa and Puella, and their three drummers (61.13–27).

So they say. And what they say is "meer marchant taylor's fablings," worthy of sailor and tailor. So says an anonymous commentator. None of the outrages Earwicker is charged with can be proved to have taken place. Yet he fled Dublin, the seventh city, "his citadear of refuge," and, changing clothes with a "baggermalster," went, like Joyce, on a hejira to Trieste on the Adriatic, and married a "papishee" (A.L.P.–Nora). But even there he was subject to the gossip of "Errorland." The "perorhaps" that ends this eloquent defense and history of H.C.E.–Joyce combines deflation and doubt (61.28–62.25).

At this point the anonymous commentator begins a lecture on the encounter with the Cad—in a revised version involving new place, new time, and new identity. Commentator and lecturer are connected by a common "we" (62.23,26). Comment may be anonymous, but lecturing removes anonymity. This lecturer must be that man who lectures on and off throughout the night —in Chapter VI, for example, where he is named Jones (149.10). Jones (John's) is Shaun. It is likely, therefore, that the present lecture is Shaun's version of the Cad's story. Hence the displacement and the change; for the earlier versions are those of Hosty and the Jehu, both more or less Shem. Now the Cad, no longer a projection of Shem, is an "Abelbody in . . . butcherblue" (63.16). Shem is Cain and Shaun a butcher. Yet this butcherblueboy, a "pseudojocax" and a "Kane," pretending to be as jocax as Shem, drinks (63.7,30–31). The Cad, whatever the lecturer's bias, is still the composite son challenging the composite father, no longer in the Park but at the door of the pub. Since each of these "fenders" (63.11), offender and defender alike, is composite, we may conclude that Earwicker, outside and inside that door at once, is attacking and defending himself.

The lecturer on this confusing subject begins his paragraphs formally with "But resuming inquiries," "To proceed," "Now to the obverse" or "Fifthly," without having touched upon thirdly or fourthly; for this is a dream lecture, beyond logic. And like all lecturers, this one likes to digress. His versions of the encounter with the Cad begin (62.26) with a "Wednesbury" that neatly confuses time and place. On this day, on a street in this place, in "a dense particular" (like the fog or "London particular" in *Bleak House*) H.C.E., "humping" a parcel home has a Dickensian "barkiss revolver" shoved in his face by "an unknowable assailant," who says, like Buckley, "you're shot, major." (Assailant and victim have been rivals over one or two apple-tarts, Lotta Crabtree or Pomona Evlyn, maybe Lilith and Eve.) As "Whenn," the unknowable Cad is time or Shem, but as a voyager to Chapelizod from Brittany, he is Tristan or Shaun, though he does not come from Kevin's Glendalough (62.26–36). "Crawsopper" and "aunt" (Gracehoper and Ondt), Hobson's choice, and "twin alternatives" make the encounter seem, as it is, a battle of the twins, of Gael and Gall, of Cain and Abel (63.1–9). So they say, says the lecturer, but "No such fender." According to the drunken Cad's own statement in Gaelic (63.21–34), the Cad was trying to get into the pub after closing time with the "peaceablest intentions." Either by falling against the gate or by trying to open a bottle of stout against it he may have caused a disturbance. (References to Oscar Wilde—"cattlepillar" and "intentions"—add another side to the story.) Anyway, he made so much noise there that he woke up Joe Behan, the handyman of the pub, who clattered down with "homp, shtemp and jumphet" (like Noah's sons and the three soldiers). Never in the history of the Mullingar had Joe heard such a "battering babel," such a "belzey babble," as of "foreign musikants instrumongs"—a noise like that of *Finnegans Wake* itself. (Other versions of this disturbance in the pub and the origin of the *Wake* appear on pp. 382, 556–57.) Joe is followed down by "the young reine" (Isabel) and "the old liffopotamus" (A.L.P.), who, thinking of the butcher and baker's clothes she has been washing—like the two washerwomen in Chapter VIII —is "as mud as she cud be." She is "Rejaneyjailey" because, like the Blessed Virgin, she is *Regina Caeli,* and, since there is a jail of that name in Rome, she is H.C.E.'s jailer (63.35–64.21).

A digression (64.22–65.33) now provides a contrast between the real and the ideal—between the possibly real world of H.C.E. and the certainly "reel world" of the movies. Women—"Snow-white and Rosered"—cause the trouble (*"Cherchons la flamme!"*) and the fall from the Magazine wall ("Fammfamm! Fammfamm!"). Not only contrast, the movies (including *Blossom Time* and *Way Down East*) provide parallel. Take a typical movie about an old man and two young girls, a movie based on the actual affair of Daddy Browning and Peaches, in the 1920s, as reported with pictures in the *Daily Graphic*. The scenario (p.65), too plain for explanation, is among the most diverting passages of the *Wake*. "Finny" and "Ack, ack, ack" (cf. 15.26–27) mark the end of the reel and its flapping. Drawing a parallel, to hide his digression perhaps, the lecturer finds the two fenders —both, after all, connected with two girls—in Daddy Browning's boat in the "twiceaday" world of the movies. As "our mutual friends," the two fenders are associated once more with Dickens (65.35–66.4).

"Resuming inquiries" (66.10), far from doing this, introduces another digression, this one on the letter the hen scratched up in the dump. An echo of Chapter I (11.10–23), this digression is a promise of Chapter V (110.22–111.24). Written in "seven divers stages of ink"—all the colors of the rainbow—in "pothook and pancrook" and "siamixed twoatalk," the letter, like the "belzey babble" at the gate, is *Finnegans Wake* again. Signed by the "wisherwife" (A.L.P. as the washerwoman, 64.18–21), stamped with "gummibacks," carried by Shaun the postman and "semposed" by Shem, the letter is addressed to H.C.E. or "Hyde and Cheek, Edenberry, Dubblenn, WC," in three towns and two times at once. (Cf. "Edenborough," 29.35–36.) Cock's wife, Mrs. Hahn, poking her beak into the matter, has put the letter in her pillarbox pouch with other "litterish fragments." This implies renewal, but a meditation on death and "hashes" ends the digression on the letter (66.10–67.6).

Back now to the fender at the gate and the evidence of Tomkins–Tobkids (Joe?), special constable, who swears in court that he saw a "querrshnortt of a mand," carrying "mattonchepps and meatjutes," kicking at the gate. Meat makes the kicker Shaun, and so do the echoes of Mutt and Jute (16.1–12). Apprehended at the gate, the kicking meatman said to the confusion of the "peeler" (constable), "You are deepknee in error, sir, Madam Tomkins" (67.11–27). It comes out in court that the meatman's family is the oldest in the world except that of "nick, name"—of Shem, that is. (Shem is old Nick; and Shem, in Hebrew, means name.)

"Now to the obverse," a digression on women as temptresses
(67.28–69.28): first those two whores, Lupita Lorette and Lu-
perca Latouche, who "stripped teasily for binocular man," then
Delilah, Grania, Sheba, Mrs. Noah (in her "Arcoforty"), and
even Mary ("Angealousmei"). But most tempting of all is
A.L.P., "arrah of the lacessive poghue" (a play by Boucicault)
and "a sheebeen quean, a queen of pranks." As the prudent lecturer says, "There are certain intimacies in all ladies' lavastories
we just lease to imagination." Our publican knows the problem,
but "by the beer of his profit" he has no answer.

References to the first page of *A Portrait of the Artist*
(69.3–8) link this passage with the next: "wilde erthe bloth-
oms" and "once upon a wall and a hooghoog wall a was." Wilde
wrote *The Picture* of an aesthete, and the *Wake* concerns a
Magazine wall where Gyant Blyant (Danish, pencil) confronts
Peannlueamoore (pea, Ann, pen). There is not only a stone-
hinged or iron gate in this wall but a hole—maybe to let Adam
and Eve look from their "horde of orts" or dump into lost paradise. Swift's Stella and Vanessa and the twins (prime and
cadet, sheep and goat) are around to plague lost Adam (69.5–
20). The gate or hole in this wall, an "applegate," is "triplepat-
lockt" to keep lost Earwicker in or out after what he did, tempting divine providence, in Phoenix Park (69.21–29). Anyhow,
he is in his pub and the Cad at the gate outside. After this preparation, the lecturer's third version of their story.

Herr Betreffender (fender and the man in question), a German reporter, reporting the fall of Adam ("swobbing broguen
eeriesh myth brockendootsch") for a "Fastland payrodicule"
(*The Waste Land* as a parody of *Ulysses*), stated Germanically
that the knocker at the gate had bothered him. Betreffender
seems also H.C.E., whose "unsolicited visitor," Cad or Buckley,
blowing quaker's oats at him through the keyhole, tells the "hir-
suiter" (Esau–tailor) and "heeltapper" (cf. 381.9) in "mooxed
metaphors" that he would break his head unless given a drink
(69.30–70.36). A catalogue of all the "abusive names"—a
hundred and eleven of them—that the Cad called Earwicker follows reference to the two girls, three soldiers, and three battles:

Balaklava, Waterloo, and Clontarf (71.9–10). Plainly, there is
a battle at the hot gate. The catalogue, one of many in the
Wake, illustrates what Samuel Beckett, who used the technique
in *Watt,* calls "the comedy of exhaustive enumeration." The
"passive resistant," so besieged, made no "mocks for his
grapes" (Mookse and Gripes make this a conflict of twins, one
inside, one outside), but his pub has shrunk to a telephone
booth. 1132 leaves us uncertain of rise, fall, or outcome.
"Adyoe!" the inconclusive lecturer says at the conclusion of his
lecture (73.22). What more can he say? We know all that can
be known of Earwicker and his "unknowable assailant."

A meditation on rocks, clouds, children, and history leads to
a hopeful conclusion: We will wake after sleep; the heroes will
return; there will be an Easter rising, "some Finn, some Finn
avant!" Did you think me dead? Dramatic changes of rhythm,
sound, and tone on the last page (74) lead to a suitable diminu-
endo.

The place of Vico in the confusions of this chapter and its
predecessor is not immediately plain. There are references to his
system in both chapters, but placing them in it is a problem. It
may be —and, according to the plan, so it should—that the first
encounter of Earwicker and the Cad in Chapter II illustrates
Vico's heroic age, and their re-encounters through gossip in
Chapter III illustrate Vico's human age. Chapter IV, which
should illustrate his *ricorso,* is less problematical. This chapter,
though no less human than the third, ends with the river that
ends the book and begins it.

52.14–16   "Spegulo . . . fraulino" seems to be Esperanto.
53.29   "Lorenzo Tooley." Laurence O'Toole, Dublin's
            patron saint, first appears in Chapter I (5.3),
            associated with Thomas Becket, and reappears
            (24.1) before his present appearance. He usually
            stands for Dublin or with Becket, his twin: 59.7,
            77.2, 114.17–18, 138.26, 179.12, 228.25, 235.19,
            388.14–15, 405.24, 435.5, 510.18–19, 517.35,

519.5, 537.10, 557.7, 569.6, 601.28, 613.15, 616.34, 617.13.

55.18   "F.X. Preserved Coppinger." F.X. (Francis Xavier) and Preserved (a Protestant name) make Coppinger (one of H.C.E.'s identities) a mixture of Catholic and Protestant. Coppinger, like Porter, keeps bobbing up: 71.35, 211.20, 280.L2, 341.35, 524.8,18,27, 525.1, 575.6,24.

55.35   "Hypostasised." Hypostasis or underlying substance is formed by the merging of Nicholas of Cusa's contraries.

55.36–56.1   "Elrington bawl" is F. Elrington Ball, editor of Swift's *Correspondence*.

57.31   "Ceadurbar-atta-Cleath" combines Dublin, Baile atha Cliath, with a durbar or court in India.

58.1   "Thing Mod" is a Scandinavian court or assembly. Cf. "thing mud," 18.15.

58.13   "Chin, chin!" or "Fammfamm!" (64.28) or "tsin, tsin" or the like is a refrain for the fall from the Magazine wall.

58.18   "Eheu, for gassies!" is *"Eheu fugaces,"* Horace, II, 14. Cf. 57.22: "an exegious monument, aerily perennious," or *"monumentum aere perennius,"* Horace, III, 30.

59.4   "Mrs. F . . . A . . ." is Mrs. Fairfield Andrews or Rebecca West, who attacked Joyce in *Strange Necessity*. Fairfield is the maiden name of Mrs. Henry Andrews.

59.17   "Achburn, Soulpetre and Ashreborn" is death and regeneration in terms of Vico, fire, tree, and stone. "Soul" is *saule* or willow tree or Saul or Paul (Shem). "Petre" is Peter or stone (Shaun). The ash, a tree of life, is a kind of phoenix tree.

62.26–27   "Amenti" and "going forth by black" (day) are from the recurrent Egyptian Book of the Dead. The "sixth seal" is from the Apocalypse. Both imply death and renewal.

63.16   "One Life One Suit" may account for all the changes of clothing and the theme of the tailor. Cf. "Tawfulsdreck" (68.21) from Carlyle's *Sartor Resartus,* which, along with Swift's *Tale of a Tub,* supports Joyce's metaphor of clothing.

63.32   "Zozimus" or Zosimus is Michael Moran, a blind ballad-singer of Dublin in the early nineteenth century. Another Zozimus is one of Gibbon's principal authorities on Byzantium.

63.35   Joe Behan as Maurice equates him with Stanislaus Joyce, Maurice in *Stephen Hero.*

64.28   "Filons, filoosh!" recurs with variations. They say that from the trenches of World War I the Germans shouted *"Viel Uhr?"* to which the French, mistaking the question, replied *"Filou,"* pickpocket or fraud. Both question and answer suggest the Cad, a *filou,* asking the hour.

65.34   "Clap, trap and soddenment" are Vico's three ages represented by three customs: religion (thunder), marriage (trap), and burial (sodding), a "secular sequence" (66.6–7). Clap as a disease and claptrap offer further possibilities.

66.12   Vercingetorix (H.C.E.) appears here for the third time in this chapter. See 48.7, 54.3–4. He reappears 88.22.

71.8–10   On Joyce's three battles, Balaklava, Waterloo, Clontarf: Eckermann wrote *Conversations with Goethe,* but Inkerman, not only Shem the Penman, is a battle in the Crimean War, also suggested by Tennyson's Light Brigade, who at Balaklava charged "so on and sononward." "Lacies in loo water, flee celestials" combines the two watermaking girls, the three soldiers, and Waterloo. Clontarf is suggested by "clean turv," opposite to that of the General at Balaklava.

72.20   "Gripes" and "mocks" (72.27). Joyce liked to allude to a theme before establishing it. The con-

flict of the Mookse and the Gripes will not be
established until p. 152. Cf. "crawsopper" and
"aunt" (63.1,4), which anticipate the Ondt and
the Gracehoper, established p. 414. But the book,
demanding rereading, is circular.

74.7-8   "Add some" or *adsum,* here I am, is what Abraham said to God, Genesis, 22:1. "Mene credisti
mortuum?" is Finnegan's question at his wake,
"Did you think me dead?" Cf. 24.15, "Did ye
drink me doornail?"

CHAPTER IV · 75-103

D URING this fourth "traums halt" (81.16), as in the first three, the language of Joyce's traumway is "nat language at any sinse of the world" (83.12). "Nat" is English not and Danish night. Joyce's non-language of night, employing every sense of the word, is based, like that of Freud's dreamer (in *Traumdeutung*), on the sins of the world. Word and world are confused again.

Word and world imply order. The effect of their apparent dis- ordering here is dreamlike. This surface provides the feeling and texture of dream, but the underlying structure is orderly enough; for there is a shaper around. His shaping may not be logical— unless you take this word in its sense of verbal—but it is musical and poetic. Chapter IV consists of six movements or strophes— like those of a musical suite or of a long poem. Adding transi- tions or explanations would make the order of parts apparent there or here. Modern poets leave transitions out in the interest of intensity. Joyce left them out for that reason too—for the *Wake* is not unlike a poem in prose—and also for the effect of dream. Sudden juxtapositions of incompatibles and sudden shifts of rhythm and tone are what he needed for his designed effect.

The six parts of Chapter IV take this sequence: first, a brief introduction (75–76), second, a long meditation on death and burial (76–80), third, another story of the Cad (81–86), fourth, Earwicker's trial before four judges (86–96), fifth, a fox hunt and flight into exile (96–101), and last, a hymn to A.L.P. and the river (101–02).

Of these parts the last is most important—most important, that is, in the general scheme; for Vico's fourth age, more important to Joyce than to Vico, is the period of reflux after the cycle of three ages: the divine, the heroic, and the human. Death and burial call for revival; the horrors of night call for dawn and hope—hope perhaps of more of the same. Here in the sixth strophe A.L.P. will "wake" H.C.E. in both senses of the word. On the banks of her living river are washerwomen to wash and renew dirty clothes. The number 111 implies renewal, and A.L.P.'s "wee" (103.6) is a little like Mrs. Bloom's "Yes." Renewal, signalized in the *Wake* by reversal, abounds throughout this chapter. "Crowbar" becomes "Rabworc" (86.8, 13); sleeping and dawn become "the dorming of the mawn" (91.24); 1132 becomes 3211 (95.14); and as true as there's a tail on a cat becomes "as ture as there's an ital on atac" (89.35). Such "backwords" include initials: H.C.E., reversed, becomes E.C.H. These "tristurned initials" are "the cluekey to a worldroom beyond the roomwhorld" (100.28-29) or art after natural cycle and confusion. The hyacinth is the flower of this chapter (e.g., 86.15; 92.16); for Hyacinthus is one of Frazer's dying and reviving gods.

Introduction (75–76): As a lion unhappy in his zoo ("teargarten") remembers the lotuses ("nenuphars") of the Nile, so Earwicker, "besieged" by fender in pub, dreams of "those liliths undeveiled," the two girls who had "undone him." Still besieged? Dead rather; for he knows not the "watchful treachers at his wake." Maybe there is hope for the future in his three children, "Ysit? shamed and shone." But he has suffered the fate of Adam and the agony of Christ during the siege of that "wordwounder" (75.19. Cf. 71), the offending Cad. Insurance companies (75.28) are of no more help than Mountjoy jail (76.4–5) where such criminals as "Ham's cribcracking yeggs" (H.C.E. himself as fender, ham and eggs, Humpty Dumpty, and Noah's son) are put away. The introduction ends hopefully, however, with two assurances, one the calm judgment of the world and the other the city that rose from sin and fall: *Securus iudicat orbis terrarum* and Dublin's motto, *Obedientia civium urbis felicitas.*

Earwicker dead? Anyhow, they took the liberty of burying him—in a special watertight coffin in Lough Neagh perhaps or in Isaac Walton's river or, as reversed E.C.H., in the trueblue Danube, all of which, adding up to A.L.P.'s "sillying water of," promise dredging up (76.10–32). Many Dutch words, such as "maateskippey" (company), attend this aquatic burial. A leak in the dike? So "limniphobes" (Greek *limne,* pool) might conjecture.

Sinking the "misterbilder" of a "phallopharos" (at Alexandria) may be intended to foster Frazer's crops or help the tourist trade (76.34–35; 77.3), but sinking him in a coffin-submarine with conning tower and torpedoes (77.6–10) puts us all at sea, as uncertain of time (77.12–14) as of place; for the coffin of "Mgr Peurelachasse" (Wilde is buried in this cemetery) seems now to be the Tower of London and Dublin Castle (77.19–20). Such are the shifts of dream. And as for words: they lead us astray by "falsemeaning adamelegy." Our minds are diverted from Adam to Abraham by "Mac Pelah," his tomb (77.25–26). Nothing like this sepulchral meditation except Sir Thomas Browne's *Urn Burial,* which, strangely, escapes mention. Isaac Walton is here because fishing is more cheerful and wetter than "funebral pomp." (Eliot's "Burial of the Dead" may not be so irrelevant as it seems; for in the *Wake* Joyce always has Eliot in mind.)

As "hypnos chilia eonion," H.C.E. sleeps for a thousand ages as Vico's cycle of "explosion and reexplosion" proceeds from thunder to thunder. Meanwhile the three soldiers ("ramp, ramp, ramp, the boys are parching") and the Mookse and Gripes wage their civil wars ("the druiven [Dutch grapes] were muskating"); and the Pope fights the anti-Pope. While Earwicker is "hibernating," the two girls, "gigglibly temptatrix," are tempting others, and Swift is writing letters to Stella, his "pettest" (78.3–79.23).

"Tip" and Kate bring this "dreariodreama" back to the mu-

seum and the dump in the Park, the tomb's equivalent, filled
with "droppings of biddies, stinkend pusshies, moggies' duggies,
rotten witchawubbles, festering rubbages" (79.23–36). What
better "timeplace of the weald" for the burial of the dead or of a
letter? Dug up, each implies renewal: "So pass the pick for child
sake! O men!" Grace before Eucharist (80.13–19. Cf. 7.7–8).
The gods of India and Greece and all the Viconian thunderers
preside over dump, whether in Phoenix Park or Hyde Park, as
over tomb while the twenty-eight girls, "all the little pirlypettes"
(A.L.P.) and "Issy-la-Chapelle" (Isabel, the twenty-ninth)
conduct their "school for scamper" (80.20–36).

These girls are "pennyfares" on the Dublin tramline from
Lucan and Chapelizod to Ben Edar (Howth) with stops at
O'Connell Street and Phoenix Park, haunt of Skin-the-Goat's
Invincibles. "The viability of vicinals" (Dublin's motto again),
reinforced by references to "omnibus," pilgrims to Compostela
with scalloped hats, and St. Fiacre, constituting a vision of rapid
transit, is all the transition we have between the sections on
burial and the Cad. But since Joyce's tram is a "traum" and
Joyce is a traum-conductor here, this pseudo-transition, appropriate to dream, is all we can expect (80.34–81.17).

The Cad, who has haunted us through Chapters II and III, is
back again like an obsession of nightmare. But here the old story
reappears in new versions. Now an anarchistic "attackler"
(Kropotkin was an anarchist) engages the "Adversary" (H.C.E.
as Nick), whom he mistook in the rain for "Oglethorpe or some
other ginkus," old Parr (3.17) apparently. The attackler, abus-
ing H.C.E., a composite of Nick and Mick, threatens to exter-
minate the bloody bugger as soon as he has said "three patrec-
knocksters and a couplet of hellmuirries" (prayers combined
with the three soldiers and the two girls). The pair "apairently"
are also Buckley and the Russian General (son and father) or
the twins, equally rocked in Whitman's cradle by the hand of
Bruno (81.18–82.3). Whether son against father or son against
son, the pair, with a common interest in spirits, especially poteen, "pause for refleshmeant."

Identities are as uncertain as actions. In the next version of the story, the same man or maybe a different man, dropping his wooden gun and becoming friendly, asks H.C.E. for the loan of ten pounds. Stuttering Earwicker offers his "son" four shillings and sevenpence to buy Jameson's whisky and oysters at the Red Bank restaurant. The "starving gunman," pubs in mind, accepts the "danegeld" and, peace between "brothers" sealed by a spit in the fist, "tucked his friend's leave." This conflict, although like that of Mookse with Gripes, is not unlike the American Civil War. Union Earwicker, back in his pub, tells the story of "the confederate fender" to the astonished drinkers. This story of "self defience" combines self defense with internal conflict, one of Earwicker's sides against the other (82.4–84.27).

Now another version of the story: our "forebeer," having been almost "mistakenly ambushed" in the Park, goes, like Parnell's Butt, to sit on Butt Bridge to think things over. It must have been as clear to him as it is to us that "little headway, if any, was made in solving the wasnottobe crime cunundrum" (84.36–85.22). Who is who and who does what, if anything, to whom, remain puzzling questions.

Suddenly we are at Earwicker's trial at the Old Bailey in London for whatever he did in the Park in Dublin. As Festy King in the "dry dock" (raised from his watery grave), H.C.E. seems as composite as Hosty, a mixture of father and son. (*Festus,* joyful or merry in Latin, describes the Prankquean's Hilary or Shem. Cf. "Finnerty the Festive," 41.24.) P.C. Robort (police constable) testifies for the crown that King, alias Crowbar (C. Robort?), disguising his face with "clanetourf" (from Clane and Clontarf—not Balaklava), assumed the names of Tykingfest (Festy King) and Rabworc (Crowbar) at the Mudford fair with an unlicensed blind pig and a hyacinth, after having landed, two by two, from Noah's ark—after the deluge, into the mud (85.23–86.31).

Though comparatively rational, the constable's evidence suits the irrational trial that follows. Of a kind with Bloom's trial in the Circe episode of *Ulysses,* Earwicker's trial is from dream itself. Evidence makes no more sense than that of the trial in *Alice in Wonderland.* The charge is no more certain than that against Kafka's K. What is worse, the witness, the lawyer, and the prisoner at his bar, a shifty lot, unaccountably merge and, after merging, separate.

The eye-ear-nose-and-throat witness for the prosecution is a Shaun type, modeled on Dr. Oliver Gogarty (a specialist in nose, throat, and the rest) and Stanislaus Joyce, "a plain clothes priest." When grilled by the attorney for the defense (a Shem type), this witness testifies that he saw, heard, and smelt Hyacinth O'Donnell, B.A., "a mixer and word painter," threatening two old kings, Gush Mac Gale and Roaring O'Crian, Jr., "both changelings . . . of no address and in noncommunicables." Hyacinth O'Donnell is Festy King as reviver and liberator perhaps. As mixer and wordpainter he is a union of Shaun and Shem, who reappear in the royal "changelings." Shem-Shaun is fighting with Shaun-Shem again as allusions to the Mookse and the Gripes, the Ondt and the Gracehoper, Mutt and Jute make as plain as anything around here.

The "crossexanimation of the casehardened testis," at once legal and genital, introduces the "treepartied ambush," but whether of the Cad, the three soldiers, or pubic hair we never know although the witness relies on his senses for what happens in the "audible-visible-gnosible-edible world." Is he certain of "this king and blouseman [cf. 63.16] business?" As certain "as cad could be" (86.32–88.13). What is O'Donnell's name? Is it "Helmingham Erchenwyne . . . Yggdrasselmann?" (Take the eighteen initials of this enormous name and you get HERE COMES EVERYBODY, cf. 32.18. Take the initials of this reduction and you get H.C.E.) "A stoker [Bram or devil?] temptated by evesdripping aginst the driver who was a witness as well?" This loaded question, bringing up Shem the Jehu (cf. 53.8), leads to the twins by way of *The Comedy of Errors* and the Prankquean's riddle about "porterpease." "Peacisely" (88.20–89.4).

The exchange between attorney and witness, like that between Mutt and Jute in their comic strip or between a pair in vaudeville has been at cross-purposes. Communication has been as hard to establish as identity. But the "crossexanimation," getting

somewhere at last, brings up the three soldiers, the Ginnungagap, and the "two disappointed solicitresses" (90.3–16). Mark-
ing the end of a cycle, the Ginnungagap prepares us for the
thunder that marks both the fall and the beginning of a Viconian
cycle. Those two solicitresses, associated with "pox" and
"clap," caused Earwicker's fall. The fourth thunder, connected
with the third (44) by the reference to Persse O'Reilly, consists
of words for whore and dirt of all kinds (90.24–34).

At the request of a few jurors (are the twelve customers of
Earwicker's bar the jurors at this bar?), Festy King, now Pegger
Festy, defends himself in Gaelic, like a cad or "bouchal"—in
Gaelic interpreted by his interpreter. A few things emerge.
"Come on to Porterfeud" (91.15), Mutt's greeting (in French)
to Jute (16.4), defines this legal conflict as conflict within the
Porter family. Accused by one son and defended by the other,
Earwicker-Porter is their union and division. No wonder he is
shifty and no wonder he denies his innocence while protesting it.
Not having thrown the first stone at those two whores (91.31)
means that he is not without sin. His testimony, absurd even in
this context, ends amid general laughter (92.1–5), in which the
"testifighter," both Earwicker and the opposing witness, reluc-
tantly join.

The next two lines (92.6–7) are difficult. Bruno's Hilary and
Tristopher, Pegger, and the Wet Pinter seem to be included in
the following passage on Bruno's "equals of opposites . . . polarised for reunion by the symphysis of their antipathies" (92.7–
11)—included but not altogether accounted for. Pegger (Pegger
Festy, 91.1) is Earwicker, who got the "wind up" (was frightened) after his defeat by the Prankquean (23.14) and who, by
his testimony, wound up the case. But Pegger as Shaun is the
witness against Earwicker, and the Wet Pinter is the attorney
for the defense. (A West Pointer is a cadet or Cad from the new
world, and a Wet Pinter is a drunk—or Shem.) But Shaun, giving a "hilariohoot," has changed places with Hilary-Shem; and
Shem's "tristitone" shows that he has become Tristopher-Shaun.
The Prankquean must have had a hand in the changes of these
changelings. Earwicker, fallen apart, is now his changing sons.

As Shaun, he is given an ovation, and as Shem, that stinker, he goes off into exile. "Distinctly different were their duasdestinies."

Twenty-eight moon girls, "maidies of the bar," acclaiming Shaun the Post, ring their hero round, "stincking thyacinths through his curls," while that decorated witness, like Lady Chatterley's gamekeeper, loses the senses he has relied on. Twenty-ninth in the ring, Isabel, "a lovelooking leapgirl" (A.L.P.), approaches her "shayshaun" as Kitty O'Shea her Parnell (92.12–32). Shaun is the rising son, and the girls, as they are going to be again in Chapter IX, are heliotropic.

Distracted by disorder in the court, the "four justicers," Ulster, Munster, Pontius, and Pilate, lay their wigs together and arrive at a verdict of "Nolans Brumans"—the only possible verdict since Bruno's system has mixed things up. Leaving the court "scotfree" (the Scottish verdict of "not proven"), King, that "firewaterloover" (opposites joined in a Waterloo), receives the abuse of the twenty-eight "advocatesses," who, in love with Shaun the Post, cry "Shun the Punman!" Festy King, with his Shem-side out, has become the author of *Finnegans Wake,* where he "murdered all the English he knew." "The chassetitties belles," like the general public, condemn this "Parish Poser," who, like Joyce in Paris, a refugee from his parish, wrote all this "garbage abaht our Farvver"—about H.C.E. "You and your gift of your gaft . . . Hon! . . . Putor! Skam!" Seven words in seven languages confirm the shame of "Shames" Joyce (92.33–93.21), whose self-exposure is no less ignoble.

Finnegans Wake leads naturally to museum, dump, and letter. After the meditation on burial at the beginning of this chapter, Kate came appropriately before us with her museum-dump, another burial-place. Now, after the scene in the courtroom, she comes again with her "litter" (dump and letter), another confusion of evidence perhaps, but certainly the *Wake's* equivalent (93.22–27). In the first chapter passages on dump and letter or letters follow the battles of Waterloo and Clontarf. A pattern is beginning to emerge. Dump, litter, letter, letters, and *Wake* are depositories and vestiges of our living and dying—and part of

their rhythm. The motif of letter and litter attains its climax, but
not its end, in Chapter V, for which the passage before us is
suitable preparation. Old Kate, the "janitrix" of the "museyroom" (8.8–9) has the "kay" to all the past and all products of
the Muses, but it is A.L.P., the hen and Kate's younger self,
who, exploring the litter, will dig the letter up to renew life and
art. Not only guardian of the past, however, Kate must also have
a hand in the future; for her "kay" is both key and K, and K, the
eleventh letter, means renewal—as we learned from Mr.
Bloom's "K.11."

A dozen or more popular poems and songs, including the
ballad of "Finnegan's Wake" (93.27–94.3) make Kate's letter
and the *Wake* seem a union of words and music. But what is this
letter, and what is it about? "Of eyebrow pencilled, by lipstipple
penned," it seems the work of a woman; yet "Wind broke it
[H.C.E. breaking wind]. Wave bore it [A.L.P.]. Reed wrote of
it [Shem the Penman]. Syce ran with it [Shaun the Post]."
Plainly the family is responsible. That much is certain, but the
letter remains a riddle: "It was life but was it fair? It was free
but was it art?" (94.5–10. *Finnegans Wake* invites the same
questions.) Plainly the letter affects each member of the family
that is responsible for it. Maybe breaking into rhyme—a parody
of "Tea for Two," that domestic song—is the best way of getting at the matter, but the best is not good enough. What is it
then? It is everything from A to O—from Alpha to Omega—
like the *Wake* itself (94.10–22).

Preceding these terminal letters for the letter are four lines
(94.16–19) that exhibit with exemplary concentration Joyce's
use of interwoven motif. The three girls and the two soldiers,
here again, carry new—or, rather, old—loads. As "a pair of
sycopanties," the girls are drawers and fig leaves. Their
"amygdaleine" (almond) eyes suggest Mary Magdalene. As
"three meddlars," the soldiers combine meddling with apples, no
less appropriate to the fall than fig leaves. The faller is Humpty
Dumpty. But from his happy fall "acity arose . . . a sitting ar-
rows." "Finfin funfun," the motif for the Magazine wall, includes falling Finnegan and the fun at his wake. Renewal is

promised and old scandal uncovered by the refrain of the washerwomen: "Now tell me, tell me, tell me then!" This compendious arrangement of motifs is a summary of the *Wake*. The rest of the book is their rearrangement in other patterns of rhythm, meaning, and sound. Joyce disordered and ordered his limited materials endlessly.

After this pleasing interlude, we are back with the four judges, who, reviewing the case of H.C.E., find it "Well and druly dry. . . . Accourting to king's evelyns." There they sit in their chambers in the Marshalsea (court and prison in London)— "The four of them and thank court now there were no more of them"—with constable Lally Tomkins (67.11), drinking. They agree that, although acquitted, H.C.E. stinks—like the wind off the "manure works." So they go on, "the fourbottle men," the four "analists" (anal and *Annals of the Four Masters*), reviewing Earwicker's alleged misdemeanor in the Park with those Swiftian "saucicissters . . . meeting waters most improper (peepette!) . . . trickle trickle triss" (94.23–96.24. With "meeting waters" Tom Moore joins Stella and Vanessa). During these reminiscences, they break into song (96.1–3); for "all rogues lean to rhyme." Earwicker, a greater rogue, has fallen for those trickling girls, but without his fall there could be no *Wake;* for "the sibspeeches of all mankind have foliated . . . from the root of some funner's stotter" (96.30–31).

By a sudden metamorphosis, not surprising in a dream, Earwicker becomes a fox pursued by the hunt, "keen for the worry." Allusions to the beast epic of *Reynard the Fox* ("Mikkelraved," 97.17, is its title in Danish) make his story traditional, while hints of Mr. Fox (one of the names Parnell assumed when he hid himself—not, however, among maidens) and of James Joyce, hounded into exile, make his story immediate. Parnell is brought in by Pigott's "hesitency" and Joyce, an "underlinen overlord" (97.24–25), by many autobiographical details. A series of eight two-worded statements (e.g., "Wires hummed. . . . Jams jarred. . . . Mush spread. . . . Cracklings cricked") indicate the scandal that pursued the exiled "punsil shapner" (98.30). Gossips say he has "an infamous private ailment." Like Parnell, the exile is "envenomoloped in piggotry" (99.19). So envenomoloped, Earwicker-Parnell-Joyce follows Vico's cycle and an ablaut series: "A human pest cycling (pist!) and recycling (past!) . . . here he was (pust!) again" (99.4–6). "The latter! The latter!" (100.1–2) is Finnegan's ladder, the letter in its "envenomolope," and *Finnegans Wake,* written in exile and published in "transocean" or the magazine *transition.*

Our wandering dad is dead again, back in his undersea coffin (100.3–4). After some confusion of tongues (100.5–8), a new pope or papa is elected (199.15). The old pope has been a "prisoner of that sacred edifice," the submarine coffin. The reversal of initials, as we have noticed, promises his renewal (100.28–29). But what are we to do about "the canonicity of his existence [not reversed but scrambled, these initials are C.H.E.] as a tesseract" (100.34–35)? Webster tells us that a tessera is, among other things, a curvilinear rectangle, and a tesseract is an octahedroid. Joyce's symbol for the *Wake,* you will recall, is a square or cube. Make of this what you can. I make little or nothing—but, as Samuel Beckett says, nothing is better than nothing.

A transition of a sort—two sentences, one at the bottom of p. 100, the other at the top of p. 101—separates the hunt from the hymn to A.L.P. that brings this chapter to its close. "Quick" and "dumb," looking forward to Shaun's "deathbone" (193.29) and Shem's "lifewand" (195.5), suggest passage from death to renewal. Since *ulmus* is Latin for elm, "Ulma" must be its female variety or A.L.P. as tree. "Dispersal women" replacing "Assembly men" (97.28) change the hunters' sex. The men thought Reynard slow; the women wonder, "Was she fast?" Slow fox has become fast vixen. The chorus of washerwomen— "Do tell us all about . . . we want to hear allabout"—looks forward to 196.1–3. What they want to hear is news of H.C.E. and A.L.P., of his fall and her restoration.

Tell us about Earwicker and the girls (101.8–9), about Buckley and the Russian General. Cain and Cad make this encounter that of H.C.E. and the Cad in the Park. Who shot

whom? (101.15–22) But news of A.L.P. is more important; for
as Danish-Gaelic "murrmurr" (101.33) she is the Great Mother.
The "tell us" of the washerwomen suitably becomes "tellus"
(101.2) or the earth. Mrs. Bloom, the "Gea-Tellus" of *Ulysses*
and A.L.P. are not unalike—each in a way and in her way the
"bondwoman of the man of the house" (101.32).

It was A.L.P. who, like the Prankquean, "shuttered" (cf.
23.5) H.C.E. after his fall and "waked" him (102.1–2), who
"gave him keen and made him able." It is she, "finickin here
and funickin there," like a hen, who picked up his pieces and put
them in her "piecebag," the "nabsack" (11.19) of Earwicker's
Waterloo. Though she is Danish-Gaelic-English "Morandmor,"
the Great Mother again, she is "weeny" (102.18) or small,
given to trickling, and a yes-girl. It may be that H.C.E. fooled
around with the twenty-eight "haremscarems," those rainbow
girls, but she speaks up for him as Eve for Adam (102.25–30).

The all-but terminal verses, a parody of "At Trinity Church I
Met My Doom," celebrate this marriage in terms of fish, the ebb
and flow of the tide in the river (as far up as Island Bridge), a
long lease, a bottom, a fall, and babies. That her "wee," not
ultimate like Mrs. Bloom's "yes," is penultimate (followed by
"Woe") is less discouraging than it seems; for in our circle wee
brings woe and woe, wee.

The terminal lines are appropriately Biblical and Homeric.
"Nomad" could be Ulysses; but "Naaman," not only Homeric
"No Man," is also a son of Benjamin. Let no man laugh at jordan, the river of life or its commode. (Is Giordano here too, as
he is in the first sentence of the *Wake?*) Sheets, trees, and
stones predict the washerwomen of Chapter VIII. "Bibs" and
"babalong" suggest renewal by babies; but "the waters of babalong," from Psalm 137, suggest Eliot's *Waste Land* (line 182)
and this our exile.

The four chapters of the first cycle are centered in H.C.E. and
his fall. The four chapters of the coming cycle are centered in
A.L.P. and her children. She is dominant in the first and last of
these chapters. Shem, Shaun, and Isabel occupy the middle. But
H.C.E. is always around.

76.7–8   *Securus iudicat orbis terrarum,* sometimes attributed to St. Augustine, recurs: 96.33, 263.27–28, 306.R1, 513.1–2, 593.13–14.

79.25–26   "Arbour, bucketroom, caravan, ditch? [alphabetical] Coach, carriage, wheelbarrow, dungcart?" Such progressions of four elements, common in the *Wake,* stand for Vico's process. Cf. "Artha . . . moksa" (93.22), probably Sanskrit: *Kama* means sip or suck; *dharma* is legal, dutiful, virtuous; *moksha* is liberation or escape. *Artha* eluded me. Ever try using a Sanskrit dictionary?

79.27   "Pulls a lane picture." Context makes the lane Drury Lane, but Joyce also means Yeats's Hugh Lane, whose gift of pictures to Dublin went to the Tate. "Pulls" means pulling a fast one.

80.8–10   Park and dump are haunted by several of the characters of Le Fanu's *House by the Churchyard:* Dangerfield, Fireworker O'Flaherty, Nutter, Castlemallard, Archer, Sturk. Living at the edge of the Park, they are often in it.

80.27–28   "The House that Jack Built." Cf. 8.10–14; 72.9; 102.12–13. Nursery rhymes abound in the *Wake.*

89.27   *"Quare hircum?* No answer. *Unde gentium fe . . .* ?" An echo of 23.20: "Quarry silex . . . Noanswa! Undy gentian festyknees" (dog Latin for "Why are you as silent as a stone? From where among peoples are you hurrying?") Now it is changed to "Why are you a goat?"

91.13–14   "Markarthy" combines Tristan's King Mark with King Arthur. "Baalastartey" combines Baal, a Semitic god (here god

of fire; cf. "Baalfire," 13.36), with Astarte,
Phoenician goddess of love and moon. The
chapter is filled with gods and kings, e.g.,
the Hindu gods, 80.24.

93.8   "Fortytudor ages rawdownhams tanyou-
hide." The initials reveal Earwicker's indelicate answer to the bobbyguard.

95.8   "Dyinboosycough." References to Dion
Boucicault and his play *Arrah-na-Pogue*
generally appear in connection with A.L.P.
or Shaun. Shaun the Post (92.13) is a
character in this play.

96.13–14   "Peepette" in connection with "saucicissters" refers to *The Journal to Stella*.
"Peepette" is "ppt" (or poppet) in Swift's
"little language," modified by Joyce to
include peeping and peeing. Cf. "tapette
. . . pettest," 79.23. Like H.C.E. at this
point, Swift is an old man with two girls.

99.4–6   An ablaut series ("Pest . . . pist . . .
past") indicates the Viconian process perhaps. Cf. "Him . . . Hom . . . Hum.
. . . swimswamswum," 6.30–33; 7.1.

100.5–8   "Achdung! . . . ," a confusion of tongues
as at Babel, not meant perhaps to be
understood. Cf. 54.8–19. Such confusions
are also a comment on the difficulty of
communicating. The present instance, a
mixture of pig-Danish, pig-Gaelic, and
pig-English, seems to mean this: Attention!
The Viking king visits beautiful young
girls. Three somebodies adventure with
the giant foreigner in Phoenix Park. But
banana Anna bangs the ballyhoo out of
her buddy. (Bally is Gaelic for city.)

100.28–29, 34–35   H.C.E.'s initials are "tristurned" or reversed in the direction of Tristan-Shaun.

"En caecos harauspices," 100.18 (blind
augurer) is E.C.H. But "the canonicity of
his existence" makes him C.H.E., a
scrambled egg maybe.

103.6 "Wee." A.L.P.'s "wee" or *oui* is as extraordinary in Ireland as Mrs. Bloom's
"yes." There is no word for yes in Gaelic.
Irishmen, avoiding yes by tradition or
instinct, substitute "I am" or "I do" or the
like. Example: "Did you carry a gun in
the Easter rising?" I asked Mrs. Keating.
"I did," said Mrs. Keating. "Did you
shoot any Englishmen?" "I did," she said.

CHAPTER V · 104-25

THE great theme of the letter comes to climax in this chapter. In Chapter I the hen or *poule* finds the letter in the dump amid the litter of Waterloo (11). This litter, as full of letters as of other garbage, is an "allaphbed" (18–19). In Chapter IV the letter, ambiguously accosted (93–94), includes all between A and O. Now, in Chapter V, the hen digs the letter up again and for the first time we get a look at the text, such as it is, word for word, letter by letter. Our problem is what to make of what we have looked at.

Plainly more than life from Alpha to Omega, the letter represents all literature as well, especially *Finnegans Wake*. To confirm the idea of literature this chapter is crowded with references to works and writers from the Bible and Shakespeare to Walter Pater—Gay, Pope, and Sheridan, Ibsen, Eliot, and Pound. Literature is creation, and creation suits Vico's divine age. As Eve, Great Mother, river, Muse, and hen—the feminine creative principle—A.L.P. presides over a new genesis. From the debris of the fall comes renewal by letters. This chapter of renewal begins suitably with the river and suitably ends with Shem the Penman.

Structure is simple: First an invocation, next a litany of sorts, and then a long lecture or sermon on a text. A dream-lecture, this analysis, like all the materials of dream, conceals and reveals at once. Absurd maybe, it tells us a good deal about the *Wake*—more about this than about the letter—and a good deal about critical method and practice. Not only absurd—in the senses of beyond or contrary to reason—the lecture is funny,

like almost everything else at the wake. Nothing merrier than
that girl "deliberatively" somersaulting off her "bisexycle" to
show her "dinky pinks" (115.15–16).

The invocation (104.1), an echo of the first sentence of the
Wake and the end of Chapter IV, is less irreverent than it seems.
A parody of the Lord's Prayer, to be sure, it is the Lady's
Prayer. "Annah the Allmaziful," having replaced Allah the
Allmerciful, makes many of one or, like any creator, makes
power manifest. At once Eve and the river, A.L.P. deserves the
name of Plurabelle. The manifesto of this manifesting mother
goddess deserves the name of "mamafesta"—her letter to and
about the "Mosthighest" or H.C.E.; for as central Mrs. Bloom is
centered on Bloom, so central A.L.P. is centered on H.C.E. The
many titles of her "untitled mamafesta," crowding the litany,
concern H.C.E.

Her catalogue of his names is not unlike the catalogue of his
names in Chapter III (71–72) except that those are abusive and
these, although showing awareness of his sins, are not. The present catalogue of names for the sinner and for his wife's letter to
him falls into three parts separated by semicolons, each part distinguished by substance and tone. The first part seems Isabel's
view, the second Kate's, and the third Anna's—three views because A.L.P. is a triple goddess, young, old, and middling at
once. Isabel and Kate are two of her aspects, as Milly and Mary
Driscoll are aspects of Mrs. Bloom. A pity that Robert Graves,
celebrating his three-cornered White Goddess, did not know of
A.L.P., who, had she been created by someone else, would have
suited his taste entirely.

Since Joyce liked playing with numbers (1132, for example),
the number of items in this catalogue must be significant. How
pleasing if they added up to 101; but every time I try to make
their sum, I get a different figure. It is hard to fix the items; for
things are slipping around here and running into one another.
But it is easy to detect the literary allusions: to Shakespeare,
Swift (*The Drapier Letters,* 104.14), Mark Twain, and Gilbert
and Sullivan, a pair who wrote of Box and Cox, another pair
(105.5). It is easy to detect the popular songs and the motifs of

the *Wake:* Tristan, Buckley, the Mookse, the Ondt, and the rest. And it is easy to see that, whatever her devotion to H.C.E., Anna, in her part of the litany, is obsessed with his sin and fall. The stain of Adam's fall and the mess of Humpty Dumpty's calls for washing out near the tree and stone on the banks of the river (106.36–107.1). Yet Earwicker is a "Dear Man" despite the lies of all the conspirators about the three soldiers and that "Pair of Sloppy Sluts plainly Showing all the Unmentionability" (107.4–7). It was Anna, after all, who "waked him" (102.2).

After the litany the lecture, the third so far if we include Kate's lecture on Waterloo in the museum. In Chapter III (62–71) Shaun or someone like him gave a lecture on the "fender." The second lecture precedes the first litany (71–72) and the third follows the second litany—a reversal of sorts. The fourth lecture will be given in Chapter VI (149) by Professor Jones or Shaun again. Since all the lectures but Kate's are Shaun's, it seems evident that professors, scholars, and critics are of his tribe. The lecturer before us—both scholar and critic —is an American, intent on "normalcy" (Warren Harding's word, 112.13); for America is the new world and Shaun, as rising son, is its representative—as Shem the representative of the old. A "tombstone mason" (113.34), assisting at the burial of the old, Shaun lays the stone in Le Fanu's churchyard.

The lecturer's manner (like that of any academic old pro) varies from the formidably abstract to the breezily colloquial— from "proteiform graph" to "who . . . wrote the durn thing anyhow?" His approach to the text before him is commendably many-sided. Belonging to no school and doing what purists of any school deplore, he combines scholarship with criticism and any method of one with any method of the other, by turns, however. By turns he employs the methods of textual critics, contextual critics, biographers, paleographers, political and psychoanalytic critics. He examines the handwriting, the state of the paper, the punctuation (if any), each letter, sign, and word. In short, he is exhaustive; but what his exhausting analysis amounts to is an unintended criticism of criticism by an intending master of burlesque. The professor's "Extorreor Monolothe" (105.11–

12), apparently as objective as Wellington's monolith and the New Critics, is really a "steady monologuy of the interiors" (119.32–33), like all criticism, whatever its disciplines and pretensions. After this lecture on our academic ways, it is hard to see how any of us can still pursue them. Better to go home and write a letter.

The letter before him is a "proteiform graph" (both proto and Protean) or a "polyhedron of scripture" (a crystal or something like a Rosetta Stone inscribed by a sanhedrin or the Book of Kells). Questioning the authorship, this "hardily curiosing entomophilust," suspecting H.C.E., touches on insects (107.12–18) of a Swiftian variety. Unsure of this, "we must grope on"—as we must through the *Wake*. Closer inspection of the *"bordereau"* or account, seems to reveal "a multiplicity of personalities," coalescing, like Bruno's opposites, into "one stable somebody," maybe "a too pained whittlewit laden with the loot of learning" or two-paned (eyeglassed) Joyce's idea of Joyce, B.A. (107.8–108.7). But Earwicker, the "broadcaster," seems the likelier candidate (108.8–28).

Carlyle's "Naysayers" (108.29) lead us by way of *Sartor Resartus* to clothing and the letter's envelope. In spite of I. A. Richards and his school—"basically English" (116.26) makes it seem likely that Joyce had Richards in mind—meaning suffers as much from concentrating on the text to the "neglect of the enveloping facts . . . circumstantiating it" as, let us say, contemplating a feminine bottom to the neglect of drawers. No text or bottom is alone. No matter what the inventors of fallacies say, what encloses the thing is almost as important as the thing itself (109.1–36).

A meditation on "improbable possibles" leads to "Ahahn!" However impossible the events of the hen's story, "they are probably as like those which may have taken place as any others which never took person at all" (110.1–21). "Zot," as Hamlet said, "is the Quiztune" that we must solve.

"That original hen" (Eve as original sinner), scratching in the "dump" one April day in the "mistridden past" (mist is English fog and German manure), dug the letter up, but Kevin

(Shaun), one of her chicks claims credit for her find as by trick-
ery he claimed the credit due to Shem for finding the Ardagh
Chalice in another dump. At this point Kevin-Shaun is T. S. Eliot
stealing *The Waste Land* from *Ulysses,* Joyce's purple-patched
"massacre" (110.22–111.2). April, "future saintity," the chalice
(Joyce's gold cup and Eliot's grail), "strandlooper" (Prufrock),
"beachwalker" (Stephen), and "euchring" (Mme. Sosostris'
wicked pack of cards) establish identity and confirm the application of lines 108.33–36 on the suspicious absence of quotation marks. The "dual a duel" (111.2) is the conflict of twins,
Eliot-Shaun against Joyce-Shem, at whom "sticks and stanks"
are thrown by the "Jacobiters." But "transhipt from Boston"
(111.9), though suggesting Eliot's "Boston Evening Transcript,"
carries no suggestion of euchring or bilking. Generous Joyce
allowed something to the London publisher of the *Wake*—
ignorant of what is in it as he must have been—and the first
enthusiastic reviewer of *Ulysses,* who, from the gossip of Paris,
knew something of what it is about. Of these rivals neither
knew much about the other. The pleasing thing is that, whatever their misunderstandings and disagreements, they got along
so well together.

The letter, before us at last (111.5–24), begins and ends with
references to eighteenth-century literature: to John Gay ("to die
to day," 111.2–3, from *The Beggar's Opera*), to Alexander
Pope ("Belinda" from "The Rape of the Lock"), to Sheridan
("lydialike languishing" from *The Rivals*). "Relique" brings
Percy into this company. The hen scratched this literary docu-
ment up at twelve o'clock, the Cad's hour, end of one cycle and
beginning of another. Mailed from Boston, in the New World,
the letter is dated "last of the first," perhaps Omega and Alpha,
certainly January 31. "Dear whom it proceeded to mention"
leaves the addressee unnamed, but we know from the "mamafesta" that he is H.C.E. as we know the unnamed writer—or, at
least, dictator—to be A.L.P.

She mentions a wedding, a "funferall" (funeral and wake),
and the weather, so hot that it turned the milk in the cocoa (van
Houten's). "Hate . . . mild . . . general's elections" could

also refer to the Irish troubles and the establishment of a republic. Is the Russian general there too? People more certainly there
include Maggy (Isabel) and the "twoinns" (twins and two
pubs), Chriesty, and Father Michael. (Maggy in Boston and the
twins in Dublin?) The writer closes with four crosses for kisses
and Vico's sequence: "holy paul [religion] holey corner [mar-
riage] holipoli [the city of the human age] whollyisland [less
Ireland perhaps than Easter Island]." By way of postscript and
signature is a teastain, put there by the "masterbilker" or Shem,
who acted as scribe to the dictating Muse. Stephen Dedalus, as
we have noticed, is a forger and Shem a bilker since art is a violation of nature. Tea, as we know from *Ulysses,* is "family tea."
"Tea for Two" implies marriage. Boston had a tea party. "Pottery" associates the teapot here with the Prankquean's tea and
"illiterative porthery" (23.7–10).

However important this text, it is trivial, illiterate, and repetitious. However simple, it is obscure. Certainly about life, is it
art? If it stands for the *Wake,* it resembles it by simple difficulty
perhaps or by difficult simplicity. Anyway, detaining our lecturer, it teases him as the *Wake* teases us. For good reason the
lecturer calls A.L.P. "teasy dear." Writer of "some anomorous
letter, signed Toga Girilis" (112.29–30), she is a tea-girl who,
putting on a *toga virilis,* has taken man's place.

The literary style of Toga Girilis is that of Nora Joyce. Letters from her in the second volume of Joyce's *Letters* (e.g.,
400–04) and Joyce's comment on her "feminine" style (173)
make it plain that her letters are a model for A.L.P.'s letter and
Mrs. Bloom's monologue. Both letter and monologue, like
Nora's letters, flow in a redundant stream, unimpeded by punctuation or capitals. For Joyce such illiteracy became the heart of
literature—and life. Almost as strange as Nora's letters to Joyce
are his to Nora, selected from the collection at Cornell and
printed, one gathers, with suitable expurgation. (A good many
unprintable ones still rest in the library.) Nora's letters to Joyce,
with their news about Mrs. Bloom and A.L.P., may please us;
but Joyce's letters to Nora leave us puzzled. How, we ask, could
a man like that love a girl like that like that?

But back to our lecturer: long residence in the dump, he says, may be a cause of the letter's lacunae and imperfections. A photographic negative of a horse under similar circumstances might become no less distorted. Partly obliterating the negative, the ferment of the dump might cause "some features palpably nearer your pecker to be swollen up most grossly while the farther back we manage to wiggle the more we need the loan of a lens to see as much as the hen saw. Tip." (A "pecker" is what a hen has; and "tip," appearing now and again during the lecture, associates it with Kate's in the museum, 111.35–112.2.) If, on reading the letter—and the *Wake*—the lecturer continues, you feel "lost in the bush, boy" (D. H. Lawrence's *Boy in the Bush?* Pubic bush?), if, lost in the trees, you have only "the poultriest notions" of the forest, remember a new year is emerging from "the sack of auld hensyne" (112.3–8)—"Auld Lang Syne" and the hen's "nabsack" (11.19). "Lead, kindly fowl!" (112.9), suggesting Cardinal Newman, promises a new man for the new year and establishes his old woman as boss. A kind of Guinevere in January ("Janiveer"), she is "Misthress of Arths" (112.26–29). Not out to dazzle "adamologists" with "postmantuam glasseries from the lapins and the grigs," she is pastoral. ("Postmantuam" includes postman, Mantua, the birthplace of pastoral Vergil, Mantuan, another writer of pastorals, and Tuam, a pastoral town in Ireland.) In a somewhat murky passage pastoral Ann tells about milking cows, whose titties ("utharas" and "tutus"), whatever a milker might wish, are no farther forward than they are (113.1–9). Not even a cow in a tutu seems adequately responsible for the thunder clap, fifth of the series, that follows. But this thunder, appropriately pastoral with its shepherds' crooks, pastures, and "kinkinkankan" cowbells, is also appropriate to Anna's victory and to the larger context of Vico's divine age (113.9–11).

Announcing an end and a beginning, the thunder leads us back to the letter—to another version of what Anna wrote on the last of the first. Her French opening is balanced by the professor's Germanic "schwants" (tail) and "schwrites." All she wants, she writes, is, telling cock's truth about H.C.E., to see life

"foully" with all its "smut." Her present concern is his sin with
the two girls ("apple harlottes" and "peaches") and the three
soldiers or Earwicker as a composite figure: "there were three
men in him." As for those girls and their drawers, says A.L.P.,
reverting to French as a *poule* must: "Honeys wore camelia
paints." This time she signs her letter: "Add dapple inn" (a
union of Eve, pub, and Dublin). An old story, says the lecturer.
Think of Tristan and Isolde, of Gulliver, the man-mountain,
held by tentpegs and his "whatholoosed" on a Lilliputian fire, of
the Cad and his twin, of any conflict: Genoa against Venice,
man against Venus. In short, every element of the *Wake* tells
you "why Kate takes charge of the waxworks." Waxworks may
be static memorials of the past in Mme. Tussaud's museum, but
waxing, waning's opposite, is hopeful (113.11–22). Enough of
this negative horsing around. Let us draw nearer to the text,
defaced though it be by its experience underground. Have you
ears and cannot see? Have you eyes and cannot feel? (113.30)

If the professor is stone-Shaun-eye, his opposite must be tree-
Shem-ear or, here, just a Joycean beam in the eye, "poorjoist,
unctuous to polise nopebobbies." The two "cannot say aye to
aye." Having disposed of his rival, the professor looks at the
lines of the letter, some like longitude running north-south, others
like latitude, east-west. Longitude and latitude make the letter
"geodetic," like the measured world, yet by substance it remains
"domestic economical." Half the writing going "thithaways" and
half "hithaways," the hithering-thithering thing looks like Larry
O'Toole's "litters slittering up" and Thomas Becket's "latters
slettering down" (cf. 5.3–4), falling and rising like Shem, Ham,
Japhet, waking and sleeping like Hamlet ("tham Let"), Humphrey, and Humane Letters in the wasteland (113.34–114.20).

The terminal teastain, a "brown study" like *Dubliners* or a
"mademark" (maid and Latin *madeo,* to drip, flow) like *Chamber Music,* or just "a poor trait of the artless," helps to establish
"the identities in the writer complexus." Though written with a
blackthorn shillelagh (114.11–12), the letter is an arabesque.
No need to sign it, for every stain and stroke attests its authorship (114.29–115.8).

A kind of Ernest Jones now, the professor (called Jones, 149.10), trying the psychoanalytic approach to literature, becomes one of those "old Sykos who have done our unsmiling bit on 'alices, when they were yung and easily freudened" (115.21–23). "Sykos . . . on 'alices" implies the psychoanalysis of Lewis Carroll, an old man with little girls, that William Empson undertakes in his examination of *Alice*. "Oracular comepression" unites confession, sex, and the analyst's couch; and taken up "erogenously," a "gerontophil" unites T. S. Eliot, author of "Gerontion," with Buck Mulligan, to whom a nice old man is the supreme object of desire (*Ulysses*, 411). This analytic "drauma" centers on Father Michael in the text of the letter, who, under the "pudendascope," seems more or less than he is. So examined, the letter yields "as human a little story as paper could well carry" (115.11–36).

From Freud the professor passes to Marx, by whose approach Father Michael and Maggy seem actors in the "social revolution" and Anna's wedding cakes mean "party funds." (I once read in a Marxist magazine an article which, taking this passage seriously, concluded that Joyce's heart, in the right place, was red.) The social approach brings our lecturer to Irish politics: the volunteers, Howth guns, and "the froggy jew" (both Dreyfus and "The Foggy Dew," a song of the Easter rising). To Joyce Irish politics meant betrayal: "we tourned our coasts" as turncoats must (116.6–16).

Reinterpreted, the text of the letter yields Magazine wall, the pub, the two "sweet tarts" and other themes of the *Wake*, which, "however basically English," always uses appropriate language. If "wickerchurchwardens" (Earwicker and T. S. Eliot as churchwarden) should use the "languoaths, lesbiels, dentelles, gutterhowls and furtz" of the *Wake*, where would they be? And where the human race if, while making love, it made use of abstract jargon? *"Est modest in verbos"* or, to Latin it better, *Est modus in verbis* (116.16–35). Never modest in words, Joyce was always proper.

Love, appropriateness, and modesty lead to a lyrical digression on Vico, Bruno, and life's inevitable process. "So what are you going to do about it?" If youth ("juness") knew and if age could (116.36–117.12).

After this digression, for several pages, the letter and the *Wake* are plainly one, an "oldworld epistola of their weatherings and their marryings and their buryings and their natural selections"—as fresh as an "ould cup on tay" or a tale of a tub (117.12–32). Whatever doubts we may have "as to the whole sense of the lot" or as to the "interpretation of any phrase" or the meaning of any phrase, we cannot doubt its "genuine authorship and holusbolus authoritativeness." After all, somebody, whether "Coccolanius or Gallotaurus," wrote the whole cock-and-bull story, as somebody wrote the writing on the wall (Daniel 5). The trouble is that everything in this "chaosmos" is changing and shifting all the time, yet this maze of "changeably meaning . . . scriptsigns" is not "a misseffectual . . . riot of blots and blurs. . . . it only looks as like it as damn it" and we ought to be glad we have any writing at all (117.35–119.36). Professor on letter has yielded to Joyce on *Wake*.

The next pages (120–22) are an examination of the signs and letters of the text. Now a paleographer with his papyrus (121.2, 11), interpreting hieroglyphs (122.7), or an iconographer with the Book of Kells before him, the professor reviews the letters of the alphabet—after all the letter is composed of letters—and the strange hieroglyphs that Joyce used to keep track of his characters: an E on its side, a delta, a pothook, a T, or a caret (119.17–30; 124.9). Proceeding from "obeli" to "rubrics," through "whiplooplashes . . . ambiembellishing the initials" (as on the *Tunc* page of the Book of Kells), from arabesque to arabesque, the professor is not unlike "that ideal reader suffering from an ideal insomnia," who is condemned to nuzzle over the *Wake* "a full trillion times for ever and a night till his noddle sink or swim" (120.12–14). Hidden, still unexplained, in this "maze of confused drapery" are elements of the hen's letter: Father Michael, Maggy, the funferal, the date, and the crosskisses (*"basia"*) at the end. Among incidental beauties: "Jesuistically" (120.21) is Joyce at his best. At his best the professor is a good philologist: "to mpe mporn" (120.9) shows knowledge of modern Greek, in which mp serves as b. These words in mp are examples of what he calls "hapaxle, gomenon" (116.33) or hapax legomenon, a word used only once.

Passing from the *Wake,* the professor somehow modulates into *Ulysses* (123.3–10). But if the letter is all literature, especially the works of Joyce, why not? "Eighteenthly" reminds us of the number of chapters in *Ulysses,* and 732 is the number of pages in the first edition. "Penelopean," "leaping lasso," and "libido" bring Mrs. Bloom to mind. "Ulykkhean," the "Punic admiralty report" (Victor Bérard's book on a Phoenician Homer), Jason, the ancient mariner, and "periplic" Hanno, constituting a "dodecanesian baedeker," attend to the voyage of Ulysses-Bloom (123.16–32). Meanwhile, reverting to the area of "Tung-Toyd" (Jung-Freud improbably tongue-tied), the professor cites German studies of Sexophonology and the *"Semiunconscience,"* referring perhaps, in this context, to the Circe episode or the leaping lasso's libido (123.17–22).

The letter, now the "new book of Morses" (the Pentateuch in Morse code), is, as we have seen, without punctuation. How then can it be a "Tiberiast duplex"? Tiberian is a system of punctuating the Hebrew Bible. Yet holes in the manuscript should do for periods or commas—holes punched with a fork by a professor, like Holmes, at his breakfast table. (Through "Yard inquiries" Sherlock meets Oliver Wendell.) "Brotfressor Prenderguest," bread eater, is taker of the Host (123.30–124.19). As taker of the guest, he is H.C.E., publican (cf. "Prendregast . . . Innkipper," 144.6–7).

A medley of references to writers and to the themes of the *Wake* brings the chapter to its close. St. Jerome (translator of the Gospels), Solomon and his Song of Songs, Synge (there by diction and rhythm), Dermot and Grania, Shakespeare with his "little laughings and some less of cheeks," Walter Pater of "Bruisanose" College, and the three "Totty Askinses" (124.35–125.23). Most of these references lead by way of Noah and his sons to Shem the Penman. And "quizzing" (124.36) leads to the next chapter.

105.18–19   "I am Older northe Rogues among Whisht I Slips,"
from Walter Pater's essay on Leonardo da Vinci,
makes Kate-Anna, like *La Gioconda,* older than
the rocks she sits among.

107.2   "L.S.D.," not what you may think, is either pounds,
shillings, pence or *Laus Semper Deo.*

107.34   "As semper as oxhousehumper." As simple and
always as A.B.C. In the Hebrew alphabet aleph is
ox, beth is house, gimel is camel.

108.5–6   "Rightdown regular" is from *The Gondoliers*
(Finale, Act I) by Gilbert and Sullivan. Cf.
Patience (108.8). Both, like *Box and Cox* (105.5),
concern twins, actual in *The Gondoliers* and virtual
(Bunthorne and Grosvenor) in *Patience.*

110.17   "Harrystotalies." Aristotle joins Hegel (107.36),
Kant (109.1), and Aquinas ("tunnibelly," 113.36).
This chapter on literature needs "the light of
philophosy" (119.4–5).

111.1   "Puteters out of Now Sealand." Like America
(potatoes), New Zealand represents the new world
or renewal. Here New Zealand is a combination of
sea and land or Shaun, the new union of opposites.

116.2   "Esra, the cat" is Ezra Pound, Eliot's twin and,
like Eliot, Joyce's supporter. Pound liked cats;
hence the parody of "As I Was Going to St. Ives."
Here, inviting reversal, Esra is Arse, Joyce's idea
of most of his friends. Joyce was as difficult to get
along with as Ezra himself. See *Pound / Joyce,
the Letters of Ezra Pound to James Joyce,* edited
by Forrest Read, New York, New Directions, 1967.

117.1–9   "Thief us . . . liefest, mine": *Tief wie der Meer,
still wie die Nacht,* by Heine-Schubert. "Lightning
. . . birding . . . grave, everflowing": Vico's
system, repeated in "Feuragusaria iordenwater,"
the four elements or fire, air, earth, water (jordan,
like "commodius," 3.2, is both earthen pot and

Giordano). "Clap . . . marriage . . . wake . . . well" is Vico's system again.

118.16 "Baccbuccus." This combines Bacbuc, the oracle of the bottle in Rabelais (Book IV) with Bacchus and Hebrew *baqbuq,* flask, from which, if Pope's drinker, one "deeper thinks" (118.15). "And very potably so." Joyce may owe his tedious catalogues to Rabelais, whom, Joyce says (*Letters,* I, 255), he never read, "though nobody will believe this."

119.17–19 The signs used by Joyce in his manuscript notes to represent people and themes, first presented here, are listed in Note 4, 299 and explained in a letter (I, 213).

121.32–36 This learned footnote, which is introduced by reference to Hamlet's gravediggers and Shakespeare's "secondbest bed," seems to concern food: breakfast, lunch, dinner, and fullup (Vico's system again). Donne's deathbell becomes, in this context, a "muffinbell." To Joyce bread is the Eucharist and food the sign of Shaun, though Shem is a baker. Cf. "Brotfressor Prenderguest," 124.15.

122.23 The Book of Kells, on display in Trinity College, Dublin, is an illuminated manuscript of the four Gospels found in the monastery of St. Columba ("Columkiller," 122.26). The *"Tunk* page," on the crucifixion, is Matthew, 27:38 (122.28). An elaborate embellishment of a simple text, this page may be one of Joyce's models for the *Wake.*

CHAPTER VI · 126-68

SLEEPY TALK—"Who do you no tonigh, lazy and gentleman?"—begins the "quizzing" promised at the end of Chapter V (124.36). Jockit-Hilary-Shem Mic Ereweak, the same, no doubt, as Jimmy MacCawthelock or Jocko Nowlong (587.30, 36), quizzes Shaun, letter carrier for "Jhon Jhamieson and Song" or a double Dublin distillation of Earwicker and sons. The principal elements of the quiz are another catalogue and another lecture, both in accord with the sleepy opening.

Of the "twelve apostrophes" (turnings away, addresses, omissions, apostles or the twelve patrons of the pub) of this "nightly quisquiquock" (who's who) Shaun misunderstood three and answered four correctly. Which three, which four, and what about the other five? Beyond such questions, dream attends to its apostrophes. Some of these are long with short answers, some short with long answers; but the twelfth is a short answer to a short question. Numerical order provides an obvious structure. If the disorder of dream controls the parts, it is an "artful disorder" (126.9), perhaps the best brief description of the *Wake*. Apparently chaotic under an obvious order—the twelve questions here —it is a triumph of shape: a "shipshaped" thing "of buglooking words with a form like the easing moments of a graminivorous" (128.6–7). If this graminivorous is a horse, the *Wake* is horseshit or shaped like it. But as Hosty says (44.19–21), all literature, product of a fall, is *merde,* the more nearly globular the better. (Cf. the "three smoking globes" of *Ulysses,* 665.) Maybe the producer of globes is Pegasus himself.

The first and longest of the twelve questions takes almost thirteen pages (126–39). In the first draft, according to Hayman, this question occupied about a page; and in *transition* only three or four pages. Joyce's habit was to elaborate. All the matter from the first draft is here, lost among complications and arabesques. "Enough," as Blake said of this sort of thing, "is too much."

The form of the first question is the Rabelaisian catalogue used earlier in A.L.P.'s mamafesta (104–07) and the fender's abuse (71–72). Centered on H.C.E., these catalogues have consisted of opinions of him. Now, Shem's opinion is corroborated by Shaun's answer. The question, it may be, is centered on H.C.E., but the sons are central now. Yet only a catalogue could do justice to one so manysided as their father. "Larger than life" (132.28), he is everybody—and "you and I are in him" (130.34). A universal, he calls for particulars and analogies. He is faller, riser, and builder, hero, king, and giant, mountain, tree, and fish, politician and lover of "fraufrau's froufrous." The catalogue of his selves and qualities offers no great obstacle to readers so experienced as we must be by now, but a few emergent particulars call for notice.

As "maximost bridgesmaker" (126.10–11), he is a pope or supreme pontiff, a Roman emperor (*pontifex maximus*), and Adam, the tailor, who of fig leaves made the first breeches— Adam who "thought he weighed a new ton [Newton's apple] when there felled his first lapapple [A.L.P. as Eve]" (126.16–17). He is Jack's beanstalk and the tree of life (126.11–12), the hill of Howth with its "Rhoda Dundrums," and as "house as he was in heather" (135.31; 126.21). He waded "into a liffeyette when she was barely in her tricklies" (126.13–14). This Colossus, "our family furbear" (132.27,32), combines, according to Bruno, Shaun's "eatupus complex" with Shem's "drinkthedregs kink" (128.36; 129.1). He founded a house and built a city (136; 138–39), in which at "the softclad shellborn" (134.19), the hotel where Mr. Bloom bought Mrs. Dandrade's black drawers, he spends his hard cash. He is all the Norse gods, all the Danish kings (130.4–5; 132.17–18). He unites the four elements (127.5–6), and, according to Vico,

"moves in vicous cicles yet remews the same" (134.16–17).
Living, dying, and born again, he waits like Mr. Micawber
(131.16) for something to turn up. He is Phoenix and *"Bug of
the Deaf"* (134.36. The Egyptian Book of the Dead concerns
death and resurrection). He is the globe and its equator
(131.32,35). He is an Invincible in the Park and "a pigotted
nationalist" (132.33; 133.15). In short, as Shaun concludes, he
is Finn MacCool.

Weaving in and out through this catalogue are all the motifs
of the *Wake:* the Cad, the fender, Buckley, the two girls, the
three soldiers, the letter, the Host, the Prankquean, Cromwell,
William of Orange, King Mark and Mark Twain, and all the
rest. On every page the initials H.C.E. make Finn's identity
plain. And "babu" (133.28) connects the great man with Joyce,
whose children called him "Babbo" around the house.

In this confusion of "nuemaid motts [girls and words]," as
"truly prural and plusible" (138.8–9) as the *Wake,* there are
some signs of classification. Mountains appear together (129),
and politicians (132–33), but no more than more or less.
Mountains and politicians, slopping over, appear here and there
as well—as if to prove attempts at order vain. The first question,
for all the world like our world, remains—in spite of class,
genus, and species—a buzzing, blooming confusion. Less
Blooming here, of course, than Earwigging.

The second question (139) is a riddle with no certain answer,
for there is no certain question. It could mean: 1. Does your
mother know you're out? 2. Does your mother know you're
Mike or Michael? 3. Does your muttering suit your mike or microphone? Shaun's answer, made without pause in the rhythm
perhaps of Father Prout's "Bells of Shandon," concerns his father and mother. Shrewd enough to see that the important part
of the first question is H.C.E. as the builder of cities, Shaun hails
him here as "pontificator, [bridge-builder and mayor] and cir-
cumvallator." Mother is the dirty Liffey, flowing through the city
"for river and iver, and a night." (Her "pranklings" bring the
watery Prankquean to mind.) "Suchurban prospects" please
Shaun's optics.

Question three (139–40), another riddle, is about the pub. What is the motto on its hatchment or sign? Not "O'Faynix Coalprince" (*felix* and Phoenix culprit or devil), not "Ebblawn Downes" (Epsom Downs and Eblana or Dublin), not "The Dotch House" (the Scotch House is a pub near the Liffey), not what has been called *"L'Auberge du Père Adam"* (124.34). Not this or that, what is it? Not fooled by nots, Shaun comes out with a good answer: The pub's motto is the motto of Dublin.

If question four (140–41) is less confusing, the four answers to it are more; for now the answerers are the four old men, not Shaun alone. What Irish city, the question goes, what Irish city, having two syllables and six letters, begins with D and ends with n? Enlightened by Dublin's motto, we can guess; but those four men, intent on the four provinces they represent, Ulster, Munster, Leinster, and Connaught, give the capitals of their quarters. Only the man from Leinster is right—in a backward and accidental way. "Delfas," the answer of Ulster, is Belfast with its bolts, rivets, and shipyards. "Dorhqk," the answer of Munster, is Cork with its "good old chimes" of Shandon and its "soapstone of silvry speech" or the Blarney Stone. "Nublid," the answer of Leinster, is Dublin with its Georgian houses, Mansion House, Duke's Lawn, and the brewery at James's Gate. But best of all the "erroriboose of combarative embottled history" (E.C.E.H. or H.C.E. as a mixed-up drunk?) is Power's whisky—"(*more* power to you)." Dublin on the Oconee, mentioned on the first page, is a new version of the old place. "Dalway," the answer of Connaught, is Galway with its Spanish heritage and its salmon. The bells of Shandon, displaced or general, bring these answers to an end. Maybe the four old men are speaking through Shaun as Earwicker will speak through him to the four old men in Chapter XV.

Question five (141) is an advertisement for a handy man in the pub, someone to wash "smuttyflesks" (Danish, dirty bottles), empty "old mans" (dregs), and undertake other odd jobs. As the language of the ad implies, a Dane or a Dutchman is preferred. "Poor ole Joe" Behan, Kate's colleague (and Stephen Foster's slave?), answers the ad in Shaun's answer.

Kate, the subject of the sixth question (141), answers it her-self. Her "tip," transferred from the museum, is transformed in an ablaut series that includes all the vowels, tok, tik, tuk, tek, tak (the last, Danish thanks). Her tiktalk includes the dump ("me midden name") and defiance of her employer, who, ask-ing "whatinthe nameofsen lukeareyou rubbinthe sideofthe flureofthe lobbywith," gets the answer he or she has invited: *"Shite!* will you have a plateful?" The question that evokes her impatient answer distorts a song about domestic Dinah, sung in *Ulysses,* 443.

Question seven (142) concerns the twelve customers of the pub, their twelve occupations, and the twelve districts of Dublin from which they come. These twelve men, whom we first met "duodisimally" as mourners at Finnegan's wake (6), are "the year's round" now. Their sign is still words ending in -tion, of which twelve appear in this question. Under D'Oyly Carte's di-rection, they are a chorus from "deliberate but sullivans." Yet they are also the twelve apostles, including Jamesy Mor (the great) and Jakes Mac Carty (from *Ulysses*) or James the less. In his answer, calling them "the Morphios," Shaun combines Murphy, the commonest name in Ireland (as Beckett also knew), with Morpheus, god of sleep and shaper of dreams. W. B. Murphy, the lying ancient mariner in the Eumaeus episode of *Ulysses* (660), a sleepy chapter, is wrapped in the "arms of Murphy."

The eighth question (142), about the "maggies" or girls, re-minds us of Maggy in the hen's letter—or Isabel. The answer makes it plain that these maggies are the twenty-eight girls, who, with Isabel, the twenty-ninth, are a month of "elope year." Isa-bel as "Peck-at-my-Heart," one of the hen's chicks, picks her man in leap year and will peck him for years to come. As the three soldiers are aspects of H.C.E. and he their sum, so the twenty-eight girls of the month are aspects of A.L.P.-Isabel and her projections. These girls, like their concentrate, "hate think-ing . . . think feeling . . . feel tempting."

The ninth question (143), like much of the *Wake,* is about the *Wake,* that "panaroma" of "the course of his tory" (history and H.C.E.'s story), which "having recourses" to Vico's cyclical theory, explores the night until dawn. The conflict of opposites disturbs the watches of the night; but with appeasement comes the rainbow. Perhaps, the "earsighted" can smell this "pana-roma." Puzzled a little and partial to the eye, Shaun thinks the questioner has a "collideorscape" in mind. Shaun is less mis-taken than he seems; for, although directed to the ear, Joyce's "panaroma" has something in common with a kaleidoscope. Both, framed in a circle, offer endless rearrangements of a few elements, which, if "earsighted," you can enjoy.

The tenth question (143) brings Isabel back with all her twenty-eight classmates. Loving and home-making, their busi-ness in life, are suggested by the metaphor of hearth and fire (143.29–30). Recurrent flames in the long answer (143–48) remind us of the Prankquean, who, however watery, set fireland ablaze. This long answer takes the form of a dialogue between Shaun and Isabel, who, like any woman, does most of the talk-ing. That Shaun and Isabel, though brother and sister, are lovers is hardly surprising in a family so "ensectuous" (29.30). As for father, as ensectuous as his children, Isabel despises him now as much as she despises her mother, whose cosmetics she steals. To Isabel, H.C.E. is an "old somebooby" (146.6), a "rubberend . . . fleshmonger," who solicited "unlawful converse" with her in vain, through Mother Browne, a procuress (144.30–33). "Holy bug, how my highness [H.C.E.] would jump to make you flame your halve a bannan [cf. "Havvah-ban-Annah," 38.30]" —Isabel as half of Eve perhaps (145.34–36). Allusions to Tris-tan and Isolde, Dermot and Grania, Lancelot and Guinevere put H.C.E. in the place of King Mark, Finn MacCool, and King Arthur. Of the love the young lovers make the less said the bet-ter: "O mind you poo tickly. Sall I puhim in momou. Mum-mum. Funny spot to have a fingey" (144.34–35). Fruit and flowers provide the setting for such amours and popular tunes— like "Cuddle Up a Little Closer" (144.13)—the accompani-ment.

"I'm only any girl" (146.5–6) says Isabel; and her twenty-eight "classbirds," whose names are an alphabet plus two, are

just as any as she (147.7–15). Her chief interest outside loving
is clothing, especially her "underworld of nighties and naugh-
ties" and all her other "wonderwearlds" (147.27–28). Shaun,
admirably adapted to her needs, knows her "sighs in shockings"
(144.21).

Shaun's style, like hers, often parodies the "little language" of
Swift's *Journal to Stella;* for Shaun is Swift now as amatory
decanus or dean (cf. 413.22–29). More than a parallel to
Shaun, severalsided Swift serves elsewhere as parallel to H.C.E.
(an older man with two girls) and, as Cadenus, to Shem, the
writer and Cad. More than simple Jonathan, Swift is "Trinathan" (478.26), as triangular as A.L.P. or the triumvirate.
Here, in the tenth answer, not only Stella's curious lover, he is
arbiter of impolite conversation and epigrammatist, if these
verses (146.9–11) are his:

> How vain's that hope in cleric's heart
> Who still pursues th'adult'rous art,
> Cocksure that rusty gown of his
> Will make fair Sue forget his phiz!

Not even James Clifford can locate these verses, which, if not by
Swift or one of his contemporaries, are excellent parody.

Shaun changes now and again; but Isabel, wherever she appears, is a constant bonehead. (See her portraits: 65, 166, 268,
527, 556.) Yet this girl, our solace at present, is our hope for the
future. As an illiterate letter is Joyce's type of all literature, so
this bonehead is the center of living. Less contempt around here
perhaps than acceptance.

The eleventh answer (148–68) is the climax of this chapter.
The question, a rhythmic, rhymed parody of Campbell's "Exile
of Erin," is about Shem, a blind "fain shinner," partial to wine,
women, and song. If this ignominious devil begged you, Jones,
to save his immortal soul, would you? Jones (son of John) or
Shaun, the professor whose dream-lectures on fender and letter
we have listened to, is a "spatialist." His answer (after a brief
"No") to "this begging question" begs the question; for it is a
learned defense of space against time, eye against ear, stone

against tree. Stuttering like H.C.E., Jones allows that the "dime-dime urge is not with his cashcash charackstericksticks"—for time is money—but such temporalists as these have no merit: "Bitchson" (Bergson), "Winestain" (Einstein), *"recherché"* Proust with his "lost time," and "Miss Fortune," either Peggy Guggenheim or Gertrude Stein—all of them Jews (149.15–28).

Time and space are a matter of *qualis-talis* (such as) or *tantum-quantum* (as much as), not only Planck's "quantum theory" but a Jesuitical caution to Jesuits. It may be that *talis* and *qualis* mean the same thing, but the professor has mixed feelings about talismen: "Suchman" and that "swordswallower, who is on at the Craterium" (a vaudeville performer and T. S. Eliot, editor of the *Criterion* and swallower of Joyce's words). The "postvortex" school of Ezra Pound and Wyndham Lewis has investigated a case of "chronic spinosis." As yet—for Jones is lecturing in a dream—it is hard to separate his approval from his disapproval; but Joyce's disapproval, emerging from this academic confusion, is a disapproval of all anti-Semites (149.34–150.13). Anti-Semitic Jones attacks Lévy-Bruhl, an anthropologist who, having investigated time, myth, and dream, wrote *"Why am I not born like a Gentileman,"* published by Feigenbaumblatt, Judapest, in the year 5688 (A.D. 1928). Reference to "Jericho" (Jerry) and "Cavantry" (Kevin) makes this disagreement of Semite with anti-Semite a quarrel of twins. But anti-Semitism is only a distraction. "Spacious" Jones brings his eye back to his proper ball by way of television, a "nightlife instrument" that meets the eye with less than meets it (150.15–36). Pursuing his "romantic" temporalists—Spengler among them—Jones feels he need not "anthrapologise" for his championship of space. Meanwhile Lévy-Bruhl, his principal object, becomes Italian and Welsh, by dream metamorphosis and the demands of context, first a "neoitalian," then the "myrrdin aloer" (*merde alors*) of old Cambriannus, an Arthurian Cambronne. The proposed defense of *where* against *when* gets lost in this confusion, as even Jones becomes aware. To make his point plainer to the "muddlecrass pupils" in his classroom he abandons discourse for a "fabulist's parable," Aesop's story of the fox and the grapes. Jones disapproves of grapes and the tree they hang from; yet his "where I cling true'tis there I climb tree" makes him seem the grapes he foxily condemns. But opposites switch around in this dream where grapes grow on trees. Bruno Nowlan, one of his pupils, becomes Nolan Browne at fable's end (151.7–152.14). This conversion is not the conversion of his pupils from time to space and from ear to eye that Jones intended. Whatever his intention, his fable, proceeding according to Bruno, is actually about the conflict and union of all opposites—Irishman and foreign invader, Mutt and Jute, Earwicker and Cad.

"Eins within a space and a wearywide space it wast," echoing the first sentence of *A Portrait of the Artist,* makes time and space Einstein's space-time and a moocow of the fox. (Maybe the Mookse is also Alice's Mock Turtle.) But no sooner a moocow than a frog, the one who, in the nursery rhyme, would a-wooing go—like the Duc d'Alençon, whom Queen Elizabeth, the object of his wooing, called her frog. No sooner a frog, dining on "gammon and spittish," than a pope among the "borgeously letout gardens" and "horthoducts" of the Vatican. This pope is Adrian IV (Nicholas Breakspear), the only English pope, who by a bull, some say, gave Henry II the right to invade and occupy Ireland. From his whited Vatican, "chalkfull of masterplasters" the pope sets out like a whiter Candide "to see how badness was badness in the weirdest of all pensible ways." Girding on his father's sword, like Moore's minstrel boy, and his *"lancia spezzata"* (broken spear), Breakspear becomes a Norman invader of Ireland. (In *Ulysses,* 399–401, the drunks at the Holles Street hospital tell the story of the invasion of Ireland by Adrian IV and Henry II.) Arriving at the Liffey (time), the Norman-papal Mookse finds the Gripes hanging from a tree by the edge of the river (152.18–153.19), dried like a raisin. If the Gripes is up a tree, the Mookse, as Peter, is on a stone. His Rome or "Room" is *Raum* or space; but the Gripes has been having "the juice of his times." Like "Quartus the Fifth and Quintus the Sixth," Adrian has a "frisherman's blague" (wallet, ring, joke). The conflict of Whig and Tory and of Oscar Wilde

and the Philistines enlarges this meeting. ("Maudelenian" and
"intentions" are the clues to Wilde.) As "sly toad lowry" (tod
lowrie is a Scottish fox), the Gripes becomes the Mookse for a
moment (153.20–154.5). Disparaging asides by Jones, who ignores this transformation, condemn the Gripes throughout the
exemplary fable.

Like the Cad, meeting Earwicker in the Park, the Gripes asks
"How do you do it?" and "what is the time?" "Quote awhore?"
replies the Mookse, "Is this space . . . too dimensional for
you, temporiser?" The Mookse is no more outraged than the
professor, whose *"Culla vosellina,"* Spanish of a sort, sounds
suitably indecent (154.16–33). The "cannos" of the Gripes
adds to what is already complicated the submission of Henry IV
to Hildebrand or Gregory VII at Canossa. There is a lot going
on here.

Yeats, present at the first encounter with the Cad, is here
again. "Belowing things ab ove" (154.35; "as above so below"
of Hermes Trismegistus as well as bulls from egg), "russicrux-
ian" (155.28), Byzantium (155.5,9), and "we first met each
other newwhere so airly" (155.12), Joyce's remark to Yeats,
establish his presence. "Newwhere," Samuel Butler's *Erewhon*
(cf. "ere wohned," 152.18), is here because Butler is Yeats's
middle name. "Parysis . . . belongs to him who parises himself" (155.16–17) confirms the presence of Yeats's Joyce. The
paresis of his exile in Paris is Dublin's paralysis, which, celebrated in *Dubliners,* belongs to him as Ireland belongs to Stephen Dedalus. "Whose o'cloak you ware" (155.2) unites
Yeats's cloak with the Cad's question. At the end of this re-
encounter, the Gripes, as "Niklaus Alopsius" (155.31; *alopex* is
Latin, fox), becomes the papal Mookse again.

Setting about his "widerproof" (155.29) of a point still un-
made, the Mookse proves it widely by citing St. Malachy, the
"mummyscripts" (156.5) of the Book of the Dead, and "ipsofacts and sadcontras" (155.9–10). The conflict now includes
that of the Monophysites with the orthodox. Rival popes, the
Mookse is "belind" and the Gripes "botheared" (155.11–23).
The letter ("last of the first"), the Cad ("embouscher"), and

Macaulay's traveller from New Zealand, standing on the broken
arch of London Bridge, complicate the quarrel and predict its
end, an end also predicted by the "electress of Vale Hollow"
and the "Veiled Horror," the two women who will gather the
combatants up. Products of Bond Street support the Mookse
while an advertisement for a cure for bad breath exposes the
Gripes. This quarrel, beyond ipsofacts and sadcontras now, descends to abuse as papal "bullfolly" returns "volleyball"
(156.24–157.7).

   At this point Nuvoletta (Isabel), a little cloud, and her
twenty-eight "nubied" companions try to make peace, but "it
was all mild's vapour moist." Mookse and Gripes do not run to
the peacemaker with glad cries; for the first is too "farseeing" to
hear and the second too "auricular" about himself to notice. She
is as powerless as Tristan's Isolde at a papal conclave or as
"sweet madonine" at a theological cat-and-dog fight. "I see, she
sighed. There are menner" (157.8–158.5). The Mookse, she
sees, has eyes but cannot hear, the Gripes has ears but cannot
see. Moreover, as dewy night begins to fall—"Ah dew! . . .
Par la pluie!"—and as the Angelus sounds—"Vallee Maraia
. . . Grasyaplaina, dormimust echo!" (*Ave Maria, gratiae
plena, dominus tecum*)—Mookse and Gripes begin to disinte-
grate into Moo and Gri (158.6–24). The fall of night and dew,
one of the most moving passages of the *Wake,* proves that the
professor, changing in his turn, is less professor now than poet.

   The combatants, having changed to an apron and a handker-
chief on the hither or thither (cf. the "hitherandthithering waters
of. Night!" 216.4–5) bank of the river, are picked up by the two
washerwomen and put with other washing into the same basket.
Neither right nor wrong, despite the professor's insistence,
Mookse and Gripes are one—as we might have known before
had we known that Danish *mukke* means to gripe. The two
women (from Oscar Wilde and the Song of Solomon) will make
their dirty wash white again by the tree and stone on the banks
of the Liffey. Tree and stone, memorials or what is left of Gripes
and Mookse, and—"O! Yes!"—Nuvoletta survive the quarrel
(158.25–159.5). As after Waterloo, A.L.P. picks up the pieces

to renew them, so her daughter, after this verbal battle, drops into the river to renew the cycle of river, sea, cloud, and river again. Nothing more pleasing and nothing funnier than the fall of the "leaptear" into the river whose "muddied name was Missisliffi," still "lapping as though her heart was brook" (159.6–18). What are Mookse and Gripes—what, indeed, are all rivals but her *rivae* or banks?

Now that he has "successfully explained" the matter of time and space, exposing the wrongness of one and the rightness of the other, the professor gets lost in a jumble of things: the battle of Balaklava with its "charge of the night brigade," a forest with a variety of trees, the four old men from their four provinces— "allfore as foibleminded as . . . they are fablebodied"—and a little Esperanto (159.24–160.34). This disintegration of discourse, proving more perhaps than the professor's confusion, may show his anxiety. Perhaps the claim of pedagogical success was premature, perhaps his fable was "foibleminded." Perhaps he has not answered the question of the *"Bettlermensch"* (the begging exile of Erin), for whom "dime *is* cash." Logic tells the professor that you cannot have and not have a piece of cheese. Perhaps an example from cheesy history would make the point that the fable failed to make (161.3–14). Since Brutus and Cassius are as "sysentangled" as Mookse and Gripes, their history seems suitable.

Ernest Jones, Freud's disciple, has an account of Brutus, Cassius, and Anthony in *Hamlet and Oedipus* (Anchor, p. 139). These three, he says, are aspects of the son, who, according to Freud, must kill the father, Caesar in this case. "Regicide" (162.1) and "Caesar outnullused" (161.36, annihilated combined with Caesar Borgia's *"aut Caesar aut nullus"*) prove that our Jones and Freud's Jones see eye to eye. So reminded, we keep an eye on Buckley and the Cad, those father-killers.

Burrus (butter, Latin *butyrum*) and Caseous (Latin *caseus,* cheese and cash-time) are the elements in a mixer of food and politics. Burrus, the professor's favorite, is "full of natural greace" and "unbeaten as a risicide" (killer of king and laughter); but smelly Caseous is "not an ideal choose by any meals."

"The seemsame home and histry," expressing Joyce's conviction that home projects history, prepares us for a domestic-political salad, in which oil, vinegar, salt, pepper, lettuce, potatoes, parsley, and salmon represent Earwicker (salmon), Isabel and the twenty-eight girls, the four old men, the twelve men ("Murphybuds" or "Morphios") and A.L.P. As "shakespill and eggs" the twins are at it again—Shaun as Shakespill or Bacon claiming credit for what Shakespeare wrote. "Commons" and "benches" give the salad a parliamentary flavor. ("Schott," whose name recurs, is just one of the pupils in the classroom.) "Duddy shut the shopper op" recalls the tea at the end of the Prankquean's story (161.15–35). Of such is "the farce of dustiny," an opera whose composer thunders off a "pienofarte" as Caesar falls to the regicide. "Furst" (leader), "juke" (the Duke of Wellington, Duce, and joke), Yeats's Robert Gregory ("soldier-author-batman" he), and that man from Sandhurst (Caesar), author of "commontoryism," are fallers together; and on the *"champ de bouteilles,"* battlefield and pub, the "twinfreer types" (twin brothers), who killed the boss, remain. Persse O'Reilly and Finn MacCool lie dead. But the twins, like Cavalier and Roundhead, fight each other. Burrus has MacCool's "lac of wisdom" (the Salmon of Wisdom and lack of wisdom) while Caseous laughs with Yeats over the linnets. Burrus, who has replaced the old king, is Keats's new "king off duty and a jaw for ever," but he has a rival—god against god, Zoroastrian "arinam" (evil) against "ormuzd" (good). These rivals are like the *"Butyrum et mel"* (honey) of Isaiah, 7:15, or, like Haensli and Koebi, one is a *"Butterbrot"* and the other a *"Schtinkenkot"* or stinking shit (162.1–163.7).

"Cheesugh! you complain." But the struggle of "exiles or ambusheers" (the Cad) with the respectable citizen, of time with space—indeed, the conflict of all "antipathies" has been ordained by Nicholas of Cusa in his "learned ignorants" (*De docta ignorantia*) and by Bruno in his "heroicised furibouts" (*Eroici Furori*). ("Auberginiste" unites publican and eggplant or Humpty Dumpty himself.) The union of quarreling opposites that Nicholas and Bruno affirm, will be effected here by Sitric's "tyrondynamon" (Greek *tyron,* cheese), a kind of mixer or churn for making the new H.C.E. (163.10–32). The two male "pooles" (sons of A.L.P., the *poule*) will be "polarised" by the agency of Margareen or Nuvoletta, who by context has become margarine. In a way she is the tyrondynamon for mixing butter and cheese.

But the mixing is deferred while the professor digresses to "shamebred music" or *Chamber Music,* "the appetising entry [*entré*] of this subject on a fool chest of vialds [viands and viols] is plumply pudding the carp before doeuvre hors." This cheesy *hors-d'oeuvre* to Joyce's work is also a little buttery; for both Shem and Shaun had a hand in *Chamber Music.* And from "Tansy Sauce. Enough" (T.S.E.), the recipe for a garnish for drisheens, T. S. Eliot strangely emerges, perhaps as another author, when young, of "shoddy pieces." The extended metaphor of music and food ends musically with "true Bdur"—troubadour in B major or Burrus (164.15–165.7). Since Joyce liked *Chamber Music* more than the professor does, Joyce must be tolerating an academic critic who, like all critics of his work, is wrong.

Done with his literary aside, the wrongheaded professor returns to Burrus, Caseous, and Marge. Marge and her sister dress ALIKE; for Marge, as these initials show, is one with Anna, Isabel, and Kate Earwicker, who compose a *"Needlesswoman,"* needing nothing, while the twins need sewing together. The twins are now angles B and C of an "isocelating biangle," an isosceles, oscillating figure, new to geometry. To make a triangle —A.L.P. is a delta or triangle—of this imperfect figure, B and C need the help of Marge, A.L.P.'s representative, who, as "Rhomba, lady Trabezond," will impose a trapezoid on the biangle to form a "climactogram" up which B and C may ascend toward a still missing A. Her trapezoid is a kind of box with a roof that must be lifted by Sherlock Holmes, the domestic detective or roof-lifter, with his *"deductio ad domunum . . . movibile tectu."* Spatial Wyndham Lewis (the Slade school, for example, and other references on pp. 160, 167) and Australia, the new world of bush women, enlarge this dream-geometry (165.12–36).

Another digression interrupts the ascent of B and C to their union in A. Now, while taking a dim view of Marge, another Isabel, "ovidently" intent on Clara Bow's "it," the professor returns to *Chamber Music* and T. S. Eliot. Both young Joyce and young Eliot are "Master Pules," infants puking and mewling. Joyce, like the infant whom Marge holds over the gutter "to make waters worse," is the Joyce of "micturious" *Chamber Music;* while his "brieffrocked" rival is the Eliot of "Prufrock" (166.3–29). The professor's two digressions, excrescences that injure the progress of his theme, are a formal problem. Perhaps they agree with the confusion of dream or, in character, represent the professor's confusion; or perhaps Joyce, unable to resist a byway, spoiled his highway for its sake. Like the illuminator of the Book of Kells, Joyce could not resist an additional flourish, aesthetically right or wrong. Neither of the professor's two digressions was there in the more straightforward first draft.

Margareena, a "cleopatrician," introduces Antonius, "a wop," to complete the "Antonius-Burrus-Caseous grouptriad." A, the "Topsman" of this Tarpeian Rock, has enabled B and C to storm Olympus. Triangle ABC is now equivalent to triangle HCE, there by initials, and to triangle ALP. Usually female, the triangle, by a female's intervention, is male as well. After all, *talis* is *qualis, tantum* is *quantum,* and each thing joins its opposite. H.C.E., as "Hag Chivychas Eve" (30.14), is A.L.P. Her proper triangle will be constructed improperly by Shem in Chapter X. In the present triangle of father and sons, "eggs is to whey as whey is to zeed like . . . abe boob caddy" or father Humpty Abraham and the Cad (166.34–167.22).

A letter from Merus Genius (pure genius or Shaun's idea of Shaun) to Careous Caseous (decayed cheese or Shem) closes the lecture. Calling on the tables of the law, graven in stone, Merus Shaun claims to be a better writer than Shem, a changer like Protean Stephen. Shaun's "unchanging Word" means "the rite words by the rote order." Reverting to the rhythm of Question 11, Professor Shaun answers it at last. Were the begging exile his own brother, he would not help him.

Question 12 and its answer (168) serve as introduction to the next chapter on Shem the Penman. *"Sacer esto?"* is at once interrogative and imperative. Equally ambivalent, *sacer* is sacred and accursed. *"Semus sumus!"* both singular and plural, means I am Shem and we are the same.

133.29   "Brigstoll." Cf. "Mullingar," 138.19. The names of the pub are Bristol (from bridge) and Mullingar. The Mullingar and the Bridge Inn, across the bridge at Chapelizod, are still there. Note the "twoinns," 111.17. Maybe H.C.E.'s pub, like H.C.E. himself, is dual, half on one bank of the Liffey, half on the other. Mullingar: 64.9, 138.19–20, 286.L3, 321.33, 345.35, 370.27, 371.34, 380.5, 475.22, 558.35. ("Mead," in the last of these references, implies Meath, the county in which the town of Mullingar is situated.) Bristol: 21.34, 262.3, 353.35, 392.31, 405.27, 421.13, 443.29, 512.5, 537.25, 539.21, 545.20–21, 606.17, 624.33.

134.1   "Baulacleeva." Both Balaklava and Baile atha Cliath, Ford of the Hurdles or Dublin. Cf. "bally clay," 136.33 (*Bally* is Gaelic for city) and "Ebblannah," 138.23, the tide in Anna's Liffey and Eblana, a Latinized corruption of Dubh-Linn, dark pool or Dublin.

134.12–13   "The twentysecond of Mars . . . Virgintiquinque Germinal." According to Nathan Halper, one of the greatest authorities on the *Wake,* the night of Earwicker's dream is Saturday–Sunday, March 18– 19, 1922, night of the equinox or the union of opposites: "The Date of Earwicker's Dream," *Twelve and a Tilly,* London, Faber & Faber, 1966.

135.6–7   "Washes his fleet in annacrwatter . . . missed a

porter." Cf. Eliot's Mrs. Porter and her daughter washing their feet in soda water.

135.15 "Well of Artesia into a bird of Arabia." Phoenix Park owes its name to a corruption of the Gaelic word for well or spring.

136.1–2 "Mursque . . . sonagog." Cf. Mr. Bloom's progress in "The Lotus Eaters" from synagogue to church to mosque.

136.22–24 "Puffing from king's brugh . . . breach of all size." Doublin talk, according to James Gilvarry, for: 1. From Kingsbridge or the brewery to the Customs House, doffing his collapsible opera hat (*gibus*) to every considerable behind; 2. Like a tugboat on the Liffey, lowering its smokestack at every large bridge; 3. From Brugh, burial ground of kings, the progress of King Cormac's floating coffin down the Boyne in Ferguson's poem.

139.35 "O'Faynix Coalprince." The motif of *felix culpa,* associated with fall and rise, begins in Chapter I (23.16) with "O foenix culprit," reappears (105.18), and persists: 175.29, 202.34, 246.31, 263.29, 297.10, 311.26, 331.2–3, 332.31–32, 346.36, 363.20, 426.17, 433.30, 454.34, 506.9, 515.1, 536.8–9, 606.23, 618.1.

143.7–9 "Any camelot prince of dinmurk . . . eye of a noodle." 1. King Arthur of Camelot. 2. Hamlet of Denmark. 3. A camel passing through the eye of a needle. Cf. "a ghimel pass through the eye of an iota," 120.26–27.

143.13–14 Vico's cycle: "reverberration [thunder-religion] . . . reconjungation [marriage] . . . redissolusingness [burial]."

143.15–17 "None" to "gallicry" is the course of the night from evening to dawn: "none" is the ninth hour here; "comesilencers" is *conticinium* (cf. 244.31), the first part of the night when all becomes still;

"comeliewithers" is *concubium,* that part of the night in which first sleep occurs, and *concumbo* or lying together; "intempestuous Nox" is *intempesta nox,* the dead of night; "gallicry" (from *gallus,* cock) is dawn. See Lauds 1, hymn for Sister Eileen's Sunday:

Surgamus ergo strenue:
Gallus iacentes excitat,
Et somnolentos increpat,
Gallus negantes arguit.

145.29   "New Free Woman with novel inside" is the *Egoist,* which published *A Portrait of the Artist* and part of *Ulysses.* Before they named it the *Egoist,* this magazine was called the *New Freewoman.* Harriet Weaver was an editor.

145.32–33   "Brimstoker . . . Dracula's nightout." Bram Stoker, author of *Dracula,* lived on Ely Place, Dublin, near George Moore and Oliver Gogarty.

146.34–36   "Bigtree. . . . passdoor." These three lines are a complex of tree, stone, Alice's little door, and the Gracehoper ("cigolo") chirping to the "lug" (ear). Pigott's "hesitency" is mixed with Ondt-Shaun-Gladstone ("gravestone" and "Garnd ond mand"). Pigott and Gladstone belong with Parnell in the themes of father, son, betrayal, and "piggotry" (99.19). Pigott and his "hesitency" are a motif: 16.30, 26.35, 35.20, 43.32, 97.25–26, 119.18, 133.15, 149.16, 187.30, 282.F4, 296.F4, 305.4,9, 349.3, 350.13, 397.7, 421.19,23, 537.1, 599.14, 623.34.

148.24   "Charmermaid." This brings in Joyce, Nora, and "chambermade music" (184.4). Nora, to whom Joyce dedicated *Chamber Music,* was a chambermaid at Finn's Hotel on Nassau Street when Joyce met her. Finn's Hotel became Earwicker's pub.

149.3   "Dieuf and Domb Nostrums." 1. Deaf and dumb, like Mutt and Jute. 2. Dieu and Notre Dame. 3. Nostradamus, a sixteenth-century prophet.

151.18–19   "Deadbeat escupement." Pozzo in *Waiting for Godot* has a watch with "deadbeat escapement" (p. 31). Beckett's surds may owe something to "fortysixths," 149.12. A fortysixth or 6.66666 is a surd.

152.26   *"De Rure Albo"* and *"sus in cribro"* (155.4) or "sowsieved" (155.13) are from St. Malachy's prophecy to Adrian IV. See "Malachy the Augurer," 155.34.

152.36   Azylium, Aurignacian (153.21), Magdelenian (153.36), Mousterian (154.3), Robenhaus and Tardeynois (154.9) are primitive cultures. Cf. Mutt's "mousterious," 15.33. These references make the debate of Mookse and Gripes, like that of Mutt and Jute, one between cavemen.

154.22   *"Laudibiliter"* is the first word of the bull by which Adrian IV gave Henry II the right to invade and reform Ireland. At the time of the bull saints were around: Becket, O'Toole, and Malachy.

156.11–18   "But asawfulas . . . philioquus." A good example of dream language; but "philioquus" or *filioque* refers to the controversy between the churches of East and West over the Holy Ghost (*Letters,* III, 284–85).

158.12–13   Eyes-ears. This passage, like 113.29–30 and *Ulysses,* 148–50 (where, as Stephen tells his parable, Professor MacHugh keeps saying, "I see"), echoes Matthew 13:13 on parables: "Therefore speak I to them in parables; because they seeing see not; and hearing hear not."

159.4–5   "Elmtree . . . stone." "Polled [tree, Paul] with pietrous [stone, Peter], Sierre [stone, Peter] but saule [Saul or Paul and willow tree]." "O! Yes!"

are Joyce's two feminine words. The second is
Mrs. Bloom's last word, and the first is A.L.P.'s
omega and the first word of her chapter (VIII).

159.14   "Crylove" is Krylov, the Russian fabulist. The
Crimean War (159.27–32) is accompanied by
Cyril and Methodius, apostles to the Slavs, and
"Horoseshoew," Russian for good, a horseshow
in Dublin, and a horseshoe for the Light Brigade.

160.29–32   "Sgunoshooto . . . sinjoro," probably Esperanto.
"Malgranda" is small in Esperanto. "Fartas" must
be farts. "Mia nigra sinjoro" is my black gentleman.
Cf. Mutt's "blond monsieur," 16.5, and the Cad's
greeting to H.C.E.

CHAPTER VII · 169-95

SHEM the Penman, the exiled author of *Ulysses* and the *Wake,* is a problem. Joyce was always composing portraits of himself, but most of them, differing in kind from this portrait of Joyce-Shem, are distanced and controlled by irony or other device. So distanced, Stephen is nothing like Shem. Bloom and Earwicker, also self-projections, are objective and independent. The heavy—almost painful—jocularity with which Joyce handles Shem, no substitute for irony or comedy, fails to separate the embracing author from his embraced creation. In *A Portrait* Stephen calls this kind of art "lyric."

The best parallel to this chapter on Shem is Samuel Butler's *Way of All Flesh,* an embarrassing account of Butler-Overton hugging Ernest-Butler. Lacking distance from his object, the author lacks shaping power. Aware of his amatory predecessor, Joyce makes two references to him: "common to allflesh" (186.5) and "pleasures of a butler's life" (189.7–8). But awareness does not keep Joyce from Butler's aesthetic difficulty. Like *The Way of All Flesh,* the chapter on Shem is little more than the author's apology and his boast. The chapters on Shaun towards the end of the *Wake* are much more agreeable. No love distracts Joyce from that young man.

Franklin said, "A man in love with himself need fear no rival." But if a man in love with himself can find a rival, he should put him in a book. No fear of self-involvement there. It is not surprising that the involved chapter on Shem lacks shape and arabesque. Defensive jocularity is no substitute for wit, and sentiment no substitute for art. " 'The sentimentalist,' " says

Stephen Dedalus, quoting *The Ordeal of Richard Feverel,* " 'is he who would enjoy without incurring the immense debtorship for a thing done' " (*Ulysses,* 199). A thing done could be a work of art.

Shem was always writing "inartistic portraits of himself" (182.19). Not so his creator except in *Exiles, Giacomo Joyce,* and this chapter, which opens with a traditional character sketch or, better, with a caricature so unfavorable that, reacting to it, the reader may find it favorable. It may be that Joyce intended this caricature to be Shaun's idea of Shem, but Joyce, reporting it, breaks through with his own idea of Shaun's. Shaun embodies all disapproval of Joyce—and there was plenty. Disapproving of disapproval of Joyce, Joyce approves of Joyce. His feeling counteracts Shaun's tone.

The "lowness" of Shaun's Shem is exemplary. A scrounging apostate, he deserves excommunication on his way to Swift's madhouse. Though "all ears," he has a "deaf heart" (169.15–17). The sin of this "tragic jester" is the capital sin of pride. What seems worse to a butcher—see Shaun's advertisement (172.5–10)—Shem, the baker, detests meat, even the "Rosbif of Old Zealand" (170.25–171.4). Indeed, he prefers tinned salmon to the real thing, lax, parr, grilse or smolt, and to the real thing he prefers canned pineapple from Findlater's grocery. This "virgitarian" Esau sold his birthright for a "hash of lentils" that he liked better than the Prankquean's Irish "split little pea" (171.5–6). But worst of all, this drunk has an "artificial tongue" (169.15–16). Artifice or art, to Shaun's Philistine eye—and to Joyce's too—makes Shem a fraud, a fake, and a forger (172.21; 182.2; 185.25), like Jim the Penman, who forged checks. (*Ulysses* is Shem's "epical forged cheque," 181.16.) Ironically accepting this estimate of the artist, Shem, answering his riddle, calls himself a "Sham" (170.24–25). Because it is unnatural—let me remind you of what I said in my Introduction—all art, according to Joyce, agreeing and disagreeing with the popular estimate—all art is forgery or fake. Stephen Dedalus at the end of *A Portrait* is about to "forge" something in the "smithy" of his soul, after the fashion of

Daedalus, that "fabulous artificer" or smith. The literate little boy of "An Encounter," as if anticipating Stephen, calls his illiterate rival Murphy and himself Smith. And Earwicker's sacramental body, hammered out by Joyce, is "fraudstuff" (7.13). Naturally Shem-Joyce agrees that he is a fraud and a sham.

This forger's connection with H.C.E., his "Poppamore, Mr Humhum" (173.22–23), is plain. Not only does he stutter now and again, but he is at once the Cad (178.2) and Earwicker attacked by the Cad, the fender, and the three soldiers (179.2–8). Like Earwicker emerging from his trial, Shem stinks (181.9–12); and, as Earwicker is going to do (311.10–11), Shem puts "earwaker's pensile" in his "lauscher" or ear (173.9–10). But the introduction of ballad and catalogue makes the connection of interchangable father and son most apparent. The new *"Ballat of Perce-Oreille"* (175), recalling Hosty's original, makes Hosty and his victim, like Earwicker and the Cad, change places. Recurrent "Not yet" unites the new ballad with the first page of the *Wake,* and references to Adam, the Prankquean, Humpty Dumpty, the twelve men, the four men, Isabel, and the rest unite Shem not only with fallen Earwicker but with the rest of the book. The transition between ballad and catalogue (175.35), adding "Dina and old Joe" (141.27–29), establishes Shem in the household. So far the device of the catalogue has been associated with H.C.E. Using it for Shem (176.1–18) completes the identification and further confirms Shem's place in the pattern. A plexus of themes—"What's the Time," "Moggie's on the Wall, Twos and Threes"—the catalogue excellently shows how motifs work in the *Wake:* how, connecting the parts, they carry meanings from part to part and, as they carry, acquire.

Writers—like those who attend the letter—provide suitable environment for a penman. Goldsmith, Yeats, and Ibsen (170.14–18), appearing in the answer to Shem's riddle, are plain enough, but the intrusions of Swift, abounding in this chapter, take a little figuring out.

Deserting Goldsmith's village, Sweet Auburn or Dublin, Shem

sets out on his "gullible's travels" (173.3) from the house of
Mr. Vanhomrigh (174.25–31) where he has been seeing Vanessa to the dismay of all the Stellas (177.10). In Chapter VI
(143–48) Shaun sees a lot of Stella. H.C.E., plagued by two
girls, sees Stella and Vanessa. But each of the disunited twins,
both Swift, must be content with one of his girls or the other.
Appearing twice in Chapter VII as David and Jonathan, the
brothers become Jonathan Swift and his opposite, but which is
which is the question. From Swift's "asylum" Shem cables for
aid to "his Jonathan for a brother" (172.23–26). To add to the
confusion, Shaun's reply is signed David. A few pages later
Shem's "heavenlaid twin" and "privysuckatary" is Davy Browne-
Nolan (177.19–21). This makes Shem Jonathan; but since
Bruno of Nola is patron of opposites and their union, it is likely
that David and Jonathan, with one girl apiece, will become composite H.C.E. with two girls. Shem, Shaun, and H.C.E. are aspects of Swift; but in a chapter on the penman we would expect
Shem to be Swift the writer rather than Swift the lover of Vanessa.

Bruno adds Shakespeare to the mess. "Shakhisbeard" is
"either prexactly unlike his polar anthisishis or precisely the
seem" (177.30–32). But Scott, Dickens, and Thackeray, less
ambiguous, seem to represent literary convention, which, in a
fox hunt, hounds and "hivanhoes" foxy Shem for wiping "alley
english spooker, multaphoniaksically spuking, off the face of the
erse" (177.35–178.7)—the Irish arse.

Hounded by these and jostled by the football players of Ireland (Stephen Dedalus hated football at Clongowes), Shem flees
into exile, shaking, like Byron, the dust of home from his feet
(176.19–30). Not the only parallel for flight into exile, Byron is
joined by Oscar Wilde and Parnell (186.8, 13–14). England, no
refuge for Shem, attacks him, as it attacked Joyce, in the *Sport-
ing Times* or the *Pink 'Un* (185.9–13). So Shem holes up in his
"Inkbottle" house on the Continent, without heeding the advice
of the four conservative old masters (184.33–36). His inkbottle
retreat is near the "beerlitz" school (182.7), as Joyce's was,

and, like Joyce, Shem incontinently accepts a grant-in-aid from the islands he has fled from (182.35).

He occupies his exile by cooking and defecating, both creative acts. At first a specialist in eggs (184.13–32), he cooks what is left of Humpty Dumpty. (Escoffier has said, 59.30–32, *"Mon foie,* you wish to ave some homelette. . . . Your hegg he must break himself."*) Later, enlarging his menu, Shem undertakes a "new Irish stew" (190.2–9). His defecation, celebrated modestly in a mixture of Latin and English (185.14–26), provides ink. First *"in manum suum evacuavit,"* then *"minxit"* or "did a piss," and, mixing his products by hand and in hand, *"fecit"* (made or "faked") what he needed to cover "his own body" with writing (185.29–36). Drawn from "the bowels of his misery," this writing, like *Ulysses,* is "obscene matter not protected by copriright."

Writing from himself, on himself, and by himself, this ink-bottled exile seems solipsistic. Nothing of the kind; for, proceeding from himself (like Stephen's inscription in the geography book), Shem's writing on himself reflects from himself the whole of "cyclewheeling history" and what is "common to all-flesh." Far from autonomous, the work of this "squidself" is universal and human (186.1–7). Joyce's apology and his boast include *Ulysses* and the *Wake.*

Shem writes these and the others too. "May the Shaper have mercery [Swift, the drapier?] on him!" "Writing the mystery of himself," he proceeds through the "distortions, inversions of all this chambermade music" (184.4–10), chamber music composed in a chamber, about a chambermaid. Not only his first work, *Chamber Music* is the type of all the "inartistic portraits of himself" that followed it.

In *Ulysses,* a book about the author as a "greekenhearted yude" (171.1), Shem scribbles "nameless shamelessness about everybody ever he met" in "monolook interyerear" (182.14–21). *"Hanno,"* a voyager, stands for Ulysses or Bloom, who bought Mrs. Dandrade's black underthings at the Shelbourne. Shem's advertisement (181.27–33) for "abandoned female costumes," especially "culottes and onthergarmenteries" makes him one with Bloom and Joyce, both lovers of drawers. As "telemac" (176.36), Shem seems both Telemachus and, at a distance, Macintosh—and, indeed, everybody else in "his usylessly unreadable Blue Book of Eccles, *édition de ténèbres*" (179.26–28) or the blue-covered *édition de luxe* of Joyce's Book of Kells and Eccles Street that "bowdler and censor" had an eye on.

Shem's *Wake,* the subject of another catalogue (183.10–36), is equivalent to the dump, full of "alphybettyformed verbage," eggshells, "burst loveletters," puns, "quashed quotatoes," and "messes of mottage." *A Portrait of the Artist,* with its "tundish," is "astundished" Shem's "wetbed confession" (187.3; 188.1). The stories of *Dubliners,* getting more attention here, are listed one by one:

186.13–14	"Poisonivy . . . sexth day of Hogsober"—"Ivy Day in the Committee Room"
186.19	"Sistersen"—"The Sisters"
186.23	"Foul clay in little clots"—"Clay" and "A Little Cloud"
186.24	"Wrongcountered . . . eveling"—"An Encounter" and "Eveline"
186.31	"Bordelhouse . . . grazious"—"The Boarding House" and "Grace"
186.34–35	"After the grace"—"After the Race" and "Grace"
187.3	"Painful sake"—"A Painful Case"
187.7	"Countryports"—"Counterparts"
187.10	"The dead"—"The Dead"
187.11	"Arrahbejibbers"—"Araby"
187.12–13	"Two gallonts"—"Two Gallants"
187.13,15	"Murder. . . . mother"—"A Mother"

The troubles Shem had in getting these stories published—especially the troubles with Maunsel & Co. (185.1–5)—are those of Joyce.

A debate between Justius (Shaun) and Mercius (Shem)

concludes this shapeless chapter on shaping with Shaun's idea directly stated instead of "obliquelike" through another's apology. Now Brawn pursues his twin, Nayman of Noland (Ulysses), according to Bruno's laws, through all of Pigott's "hesitensies"—spelling and grammar alike—to an "empirative of my vendettative" (187.24–36). That what precedes Shaun's vendetta has been inspired by it is immediately apparent, but Shaun's attack is easier to take than Joyce's indirect and jocular defense. It becomes clear that Shaun is now Stanislaus Joyce or Immaculatus, the chum of angels, and "bosum foe" (191.13–30), blaming his brother for not having taken a job at Guinness' brewery or for not having become a priest (190.13–28). Following Vico's pattern of religion, marriage, and burial, Shaun blames the anarch, egoarch, heresiarch for all the sins of his youth and for refusal to serve. "Let us pry," says Shaun, whose *"cur, quicquid, ubi, quando"* (188.8–19) make him a confessor. "An Irish emigrant the wrong way out," sitting on Lady Dufferin's "stile" (190.36–191.4), Shaun's Shem is no better than a cosmopolitan "Europasianized Afferyank." Remember, Shaun says, what happened to "that hereticalist Marcon" (H.C.E. as Mark and archon), remember those two girls and "how bulkily he shat the Ructions gunnorrhal" (192.1–3, general with gonorrhea). Remember Hamlet's "Danmark . . . O Jonathan" (192.21–22), and remember the Mookse and the Gripes (193.5,8). Remember faith ("anchor"), hope ("host") and charity (193.25–27).

The answer of "Pain the Shamman" (192.23, a medicine man) to this attack, taking the form of a confession (193.31–32), is suitably brief because jocular Joyce has already implied all Shem could have said. Suddenly, speaking through her "lonly son," A.L.P. takes over: "sonnies had a scrap" (194.21–24). The voice of the river, concluding this chapter, introduces the next. But before turning to that, we must pause at Shaun's "deathbone" (193.29) and Shem's "lifewand" (195.5). The deathbone, an aboriginal device from Australia, kills living speech; but the lifewand, in the artist's hand, can evoke speech from elm and stone or those washerwomen by the

river. "Death banes and the quick quoke. But life wends and
the dombs spake!" (595.1–2). "Be still, O quick! Speak him
dumb! Hush ye fronds of Ulma!" (100.35–36)

Representing Vico's human age, this chapter proves great
Joyce to be as human as the rest of us. But the next chapter,
Vico's *ricorso* and Joyce at his most nearly divine, will bring
renewal.

170.24   "Sham." Other references to fraud, forgery, fake,
          bilking, and to smith, artifice, fiction: 13.3, 37.35,
          48.18, 111.21, 169.15, 296.7, 300.3–6, 305.2–5,
          342.8, 375.17, 418.3, 422.2, 423.6, 463.21,
          464.22, 473.3, 511.34, 532.15,29, 613.10.

171.4   "Hunself" is Danish for Irish herself or Nora.

176.25   "Maxims" (guns). Cf. "Kroukaparka," 178.33.
          These refer to the massacre by British troops of
          Dubliners leaving a football game at Croke Park,
          November 21, 1920.

176.36   "Telemac." The identity of Macintosh has puzzled
          readers of *Ulysses*. If Shem-Joyce is both Telem-
          achus and Macintosh, the puzzle may be solved.
          Maybe Macintosh is Joyce.

177.36   "Fux to fux." The "Face to Face" of H.C.E. and
          A.L.P. (18.36) transformed by context.

178.17–18 *"Pura e [et] pia bella."* A recurring tag from Vico
          on pure and pious war. See T. G. Bergin's transla-
          tion of *The New Science,* Book V, p. 358.

181.12   "Pozzo." A possible source for Beckett's Pozzo in
          Waiting for Godot. Pozzo means cesspool or privy.

186.19   "Sistersen." Constable Sistersen (Shaun) reappears
          as Sigurdsen (429), Sickerson (471), Seckersen
          (530), Seekersenn (586).

188.18   "God in the manger." Cf. the plays upon dog and
          God in *Ulysses,* e.g., in the black mass of the Circe
          episode (599–600).

188.27–30 "Underslung pipes." Possibly a reference to

Sterne's *Tristram Shandy:* "You've ruined spouts enough." Cf. "Yorek," 190.19.

189.33–36   "Raven cloud." Elijah's raven and little cloud and Noah's raven. The disasters that follow are the burning of the Four Courts and the Customs House in the Civil War of 1922 and of the College of Surgeons in 1916.

191.35–36   "Bourgeoismeister." H.C.E. as Ibsen's Master Builder and mayor combined with Joyce ("Baaboo") as builder and father. A "bourgeoismeister" is also the union of bourgeois Bloom with Stephen, the *Meistersinger.* Cf. "boorgomaister" (568.16–17).

193.29–30   *"Insomnia, somnia somniorum."* A good description of *Finnegans Wake* as dream and Vico's cycle, *per omnia saecula saeculorum.*

194.8–10   "Flowerpot on the pole." This refers back to p. 31 on the naming of Earwicker and forward to p. 622 —refers back and forward because, as Vico says, "all that has been done has yet to be done again."

CHAPTER VIII · 196-216

THE "riverrun" that begins the *Wake* and ends it comes to flood in Chapter VIII. Devoted to A.L.P., the river of life, this chapter is more agreeable than its immediate predecessor. Aesthetic distance brings us closeness now. Anna is the Liffey. Old maps of Dublin call its river Anna Liffey, and *liv,* appropriate to dear Danish Dublin, is the Danish word for life. Odd that a river so dirty as the Liffey can be the agent of cleaning the past up and renewing it, but this action, occurring a little to the west of O'Connell Street, at Chapelizod, is assisted by those two washerwomen on the banks, who, wringing out old clothes and the old year, ring in the new—the very women who, having tidied up the Mookse and the Gripes, put them with the other washing into a basket. Washing out the dirt in Earwicker's pants, these women, the one on one bank, the other on the other, find entertainment in gossiping about A.L.P. and H.C.E., the wet cleaner and her dirt.

"Tell me. Tell me," gossip's refrain, proceeds through the dialogue of the washerwomen, as verbal motifs proceed through the monologue of J. Alfred Prufrock. Indeed, Chapter VIII, put together like one of Eliot's longer poems, is a triumph of sequence, rhythm, and sound. Directed to the ear, as poems in verse or prose must be, this construction calls for reading aloud. The best way to prepare for your reading is to listen to Joyce's recording of the last few pages. Maybe Joyce is the *Wake*'s only reader and, though other readers dare other readings, the only reader's guide.

The dialogue, like the catalogue, is one of Joyce's recurrent devices. These women begin theirs with "O," which, as we have noticed, is one of Joyce's female words or signs—another of them Mrs. Bloom's "Yes," and still another the triangle or delta. "O! Yes!" (159.5) introduces Nuvoletta, the tear that drops into the Missisliffi. Now, displacing alpha at the beginning of things, the "O" is A.L.P.'s omega (94.22). The first three lines of her chapter compose, typographically, a delta, suitable for a river and calling to mind the triangle on a bottle of Bass. Bass's female triangle will figure in the geometry lesson (286.L3); and, in *Ulysses* (414, 416), Bloom is fascinated by this reminder of Molly.

Chapter VIII owes much of its fun and texture to appropriate punning. As, playing with words, Joyce made his battle of Waterloo a tissue of puns on the names of battles, so here his puns recall the names of rivers. There are hundreds of them. Joyce must have spent hours over a larger atlas than Stephen had at Clongowes Wood. So informed, Joyce uses not only the big rivers of the world—Nile, Rhine, Amazon, Euphrates—but little rivers as well: Wabash, Frome, Meander, and Isel—even the two rivers of Zurich, the Sihl (200.24) and the Limmat. "Yssel that the limmat?" (198.13). Earwicker gives Anna "the tigris eye" (202.33–34) and she knows "there's Zambosy waiting for me" (207.16)—and "so firth and so forth" (200.13). Dylan Thomas' Towy is there (215.11), along with such mythical streams as Acheron, Styx, and Teddy Roosevelt's Doubt (202.19). (I am disturbed by the absence of the Winooski and the Choptank.) Rivers—those that are there—meander between banks of Danish words; for, as Joyce insisted and we know, Dublin on the Liffey is a Danish city.

On their Irish banks, the women, washing Earwicker's dirty clothes and gossiping about his sins, are making "his private linen public" (196.16). Since Joyce, preferring words to things, often proceeded from words to things, "washing dirty linen in public," a conventional phrase, may have inspired this unconventional chapter. But verbal origin hides in verbal arabesque. Careless of things maybe and careful of words, Joyce has made from almost nothing a thing of words.

But back to Earwicker's washing with "the mouldaw stains.
And the dneepers of wet and the gangres of sin in it"
(196.17–18). Put under "loch and neagh" and brought to trial
—"King fiercas Humphrey" (all this in Chapter IV)—Earwicker, they say, was convicted of "illysus distilling"
(196.20–22). For these Dublin gossips, his greatest sin is the
illicit distilling of *Ulysses*. What Shem "faked" in the seventh
chapter, Earwicker distills in the eighth. "No man" is Homeric
Bloom, but "toms will till" (196.22–23) is peeping Tom Eliot
telling *Ulysses* over for the sake of his till in *The Waste Land*.
As for the reception of *Ulysses*, "Reeve Gootch was right and
Reeve Drughad was sinistrous" (197.1): the Left Bank in Paris
was right and the Right Bank in Dublin (*Droichead*, Gaelic for
bridge, means over the bridge here) was left or *sinister*. The two
Reeves are the *rivae* and the *rives* or banks of a river at once the
Liffey and the Seine, though one flows east and the other west.
Dexterous, what?—or, rather, ambidextrous, with "sinister dexterity" (384.26). Earwicker's "wee follyo" (197.18) is at once
Ulysses, a small folio, A.L.P., the foolish little weeweeing
woman who inspired it, and, since "wee" is *oui*, his yes-book,
ending with Mrs. Bloom's great word. As A.L.P.'s "gran Pheni-
cian rover" (197.31), Earwicker is Victor Bérard's Ulysses. The
"blooms of fisk" (199.15–16) that A.L.P. cooks for H.C.E. are
Bloom as Christ, whose icon is *ichthus*. Ibsen, "holding dooms-
day over hunselv" (199.4–8. *Hun* is Danish for her, and "peer"
is *Peer Gynt*), establishes H.C.E. as the self-and-wife-examining
Master Builder of *Ulysses*. "Was Parish worth thette mess"
(199.8–9), a play on Henry IV's comment, establishes *Ulysses*,
that mess, as the parody of a Mass (*Messe* is Mass in French).
"Parish" includes both Paris, where *Ulysses* was completed, and
parochial Dublin that the book is about. "He had been belching
for severn years" (199.10), the seven years Earwicker-Joyce
spent on his epic.

Having noticed the sin of *Ulysses*, these Irishwomen turn to
the marriage of its author and his wee Muse: "For mine ether
[eider] duck I thee drake" (197.13). "Don Dom Dombdomb"

(197.17–18) is their Wagnerian wedding march. Like that of Joyce and Nora, this was a wedding without ring (197.27), but happy enough for all that—except for a little trouble. H.C.E.'s possible birthplace reveals the discordant concord the pair enjoy: "Urgothland, Tvistown on the Kattekat? New Hunshire, Concord on the Merrimake?" (197.9–10) Their union unites the old world and the new, Goth and Hun, discord and concord. *Tvis,* Concord's opposite, is Danish for discord. References to music (200.4,8–9) make harmony dominant. Yet violation is its cause. "With his runagate bowmpriss" Earwicker "roade and borst her bar" (197.35). Like salmon-Solomon-Adam and Danish invader, he shot "swift up her sheba sheath. . . . In this wet of his prow" (198.3–7). Like a "ruhring" bull, he bellowed "Boyarka buah!" to her moo, "Boyana bueh!" (198.5).

At this point the women get involved with the word "proxenete" (198.17–19). Why can't you "call a spate a spate?" says one to the other. As a proxenete—procurer or pander—A.L.P., the temptress, throws "all the neiss [niece?] little whores in the world at him" (200.29–30), not only those two "boudeloire" maids (Baudelaire, boudoir, and mud of the Loire) in the Park (207.11–14) but Isabel and her twenty-eight friends (212.6–18). Yet A.L.P., attentive to her own chambering, "greased the groove of her keel," her "quincecunct," and "her little mary" with the "serpenthyme" oil these parts require for proper lubricity (206.32–36). And she cooked her husband "staynish beacons" (199.15–20) and eggs for breakfast, a time for those who are down to get up and begin again.

More than wife and temptress, A.L.P. is the great little mother of a "litter" (202.2), "the dearest little moma ever you saw" (207.34–35). Like the White Goddess—or like the triangle itself—she has three (or more) sides and capacities: "Some say she had three figures to fill and confined herself to a hundred eleven" (201.28–29). "Anna was, Livia is, Plurabelle's to be" (215.24). In a word, this singular being is as plural as her husband. He and she are like "petrock" and "laurals" (203.30–204.4) or Petrarch, that "bold priest," and his Laura, or stone and tree. If he is Patrick and Peter as well, she is also Boucicault's "Anna-na-Poghue," adept at kissing.

Her description, attempted by those gossips, amounts to the course of the river from its source in Wicklow to Dublin Bay (202–03; 207–08): "Casting her perils before our swains"— she is generous to a fault—"from Fonte-in-Monte to Tidingtown and from Tidingtown tilhavet [Danish, to sea]. . . . palling in and pietaring out and clyding by on her eastway" (202.8–12). Her clothing, from "nigger boggers" to "alpheubett buttons" (208.16,20) is the scenery through which she passes for "ffiffty odd Irish miles" (208.26). The four old men are around at the beginning and end of her journey; and the twelve men, sitting on the North Wall, are her last observers (209.1–9).

The "Continuarration" (205.14) of the two gossips is interrupted now and again by "tell me," their refrain, and by returns to the wash in hand, mostly drawers: "Denis Florence Mac-Carthy's combies" (a small poet, MacCarthy graced Mr. Bloom's library) and Mrs. Magrath's frilly, lace "hips' hurrahs." "Throw us your hudson soap . . . and don't forget the reckitts I lohaned you" (200.33–35; 204.26–205.15; 206.26–27; 212.22–27; 213.4–10). These recurrent interruptions of gossip, important parts of the poetic structure, keep the theme of washing before us.

A *poule* again—a pool in the river perhaps—A.L.P. finds another letter (201.1–20), which, though "trouved by a poule in the parco," differs considerably from the first. This one, according to context, concerns the banks of the river and Dublin Bay. Not the letter but the hen herself is important here; for that hen, pecking in the litter of Waterloo, has a "nabsack" to put the pieces in for renewal. Nabsack joins washing as renewal's agent. If we remember Chapter I, we know that the hen has a nabsack, but it is not mentioned here until several pages after the text of the letter, and then as a "sakbag" or "shammy mailsack" (206.9–10) and as "her mixed baggyrhatty" (209.10–13) with its reminder of Waterloo: "And where in thunder did she plunder? Fore the battle or efter the ball?" This bag, a womb for her many children and holder of presents for them, is the subject of the second part of this chapter. The hen and her bag serve as transition from the first, which, as we know, concerns marriage and the course of the river.

Standing "between two ages" (207.36), the poule makes a new age from fragments of an old: "Out of the paunschaup on to the pyre" (209.31), from the dump to the phoenix or, if you are a cynic, out of the frying pan into the fire. The hen's "culdee sacco of wabbash" (210.1) does not sound too hopeful, nor does the prospect of "potluck" for her children "for evil and ever" (210.5–6). Yet the number of her children, "a thousand and one," means renewal.

From the bag of children the hen brings presents for them, enough to require a catalogue (210–12): "for Saara Philpot a jordan vale teaorne"—three pots for her to fill—and "for Promoter Dunne; a niester egg with a twicedated shell" (210.30–36. Dunne is the author of a book on serial time and the two dates of Easter refer to an ecclesiastical controversy). But the best presents of the Muse are for literary men (211.1–6): "a collera morbous for Mann in the Cloack" (Thomas Mann and the mephitic *cloaca* of *Death in Venice*); "a starr and girton for Draper and Deane" (Swift as Shem's draper, Shaun's dean; starr as Shaun's Stella; girton—a garter and a college—as Shem's eggheaded Vanessa). "Will-of-the-Wisp" is Yeats and "Barny-the-Bark" Shaw (cf. "hushaby" and Shaw as Shakespeare, 211.35–36). "Sweeden their bitters" is Joyce's bitter comment on the Nobel Prize for Shaw, Yeats, and Mann, and none for Joyce. "Oliver" is Gogarty, "Seumas" is James Stephens, and "Sunny Twimjim" Joyce himself.

Elsie Oram, whoever she is, gets a slatepencil "to scratch her toby" and help with her "volgar fractions" (frictions? 211.12–13), but the rest of the presents on this page and the top of the next seem there to recall the first page of the *Wake* and the second chapter. Tauf-tauf, Dublin, Georgia, founded by Sawyer, and Armoricus Tristram Amoor Saint Lawrence are all from p. 3. "Caducus Angelus Rubiconstein" (a mercurial and Caesarean mixture of the Cad, his time of day [noon], Shaun

[stone], and their mother as Virgin and river, of tree and stone)
and Hosty's gang (212.1–3) are from Chapter II. Presents for
the twenty-nine girls follow. "Wardha bagful. . . . That's what
you may call a tale of a tub" (212.20–21) is one washerwoman's
comment on the other's catalogue.

No sooner the end of this than another, shorter catalogue of
books from Narcissus Marsh's library at Swift's St. Patrick's Cathedral (212.31–32). The two Esthers attend the Dean. Reviewing each "tattle-page," the gossips list *Die Windermere
Dichter* (Wordsworth and Wilde), Le Fanu's novel about Chapelizod, and, best of all: "Mill (J.) *On Woman* with *Ditto on
the Floss*" (212.36–213.4).

The conclusion and third part of the chapter begins (213.11)
where Joyce's famous recording begins. If the first two parts
with their motifs and sequences are a poem, the third part—and
that is why Joyce picked it for his record—is a greater poem, a
hymn to renewal, the fall of night, death, and the living river.
Hail Mary (214.19–20), other parts of the Angelus, and the
bells of *Sechseläuten* (213.18–19) celebrate revival; and
"Wring out the clothes! Wring in the dew!" (213.19–20) combines washing with Tennyson's new year, Vico's "seim anew"
(215.23). Washing continues through an ablaut series of Flip!
Flep! Flap! Flop!—the sound of wet clothes on the stone by the
Liffey. As night falls and the "Poolbeg flasher" on the breakwater lights up, "pharphar"—as far away as the Pharos—the
two washers see what they take to be the "great Finnleader himself" (or H.C.E. as Finn MacCool and Adam Findlater,
grocer); but the apparition is only the "ass them four old
codgers owns" (214.11, 33–36). (The ass's identity is a problem; but since the women confuse the ass with the Finnleader,
H.C.E. may be the ass.) The bats that flew from their belfry
over Gerty MacDowell fly over the two darkling women. Their
eyes, fooled by the ass, and now their ears, fail as they turn into
tree and stone. Tree, stone, night, and the river remain.

This metamorphosis echoes that at the end of the Mookse and
the Gripes. There the washerwomen, taking the rivals elsewhere,
leave tree, stone, and Nuvoletta in their place. Here the women,

themselves the rivals, become tree and stone. Since Shem is tree and Shaun stone, these women, in a sense, are Shem and Shaun, A.L.P.'s "swapsons" (206.11), gossiping about their mother, as they will gossip again in Chapter X.

The fall of night at the end of this chapter and of Part I of the *Wake* marks a change. The first part, although a night's dream, has concerned the day, for the most part. The next two parts will concern evening and night. Part IV brings the dawn.

A note on form: although the chapter is divided, like A.L.P., into three parts, the divisions are indistinct. The first part mingles with the second and the second with the third. The second part deals with the nabsack; but this receptacle, as we have noticed, is mentioned several pages before the beginning of the second part. Such intermingling agrees with dream and flow. Small motifs ("tell me" and washing) link the parts as larger motifs (hen, letter, Swift) link the chapter with the rest of the book.

That the three-part structure, as well as the verbal luxuriance, developed gradually is shown by six early versions of the text (manuscripts and proof sheets) in Fred H. Higginson's *Anna Livia Plurabelle, the Making of a Chapter,* 1960. The bag of the second part of the chapter is inconspicuous in the earliest versions, and the third part emerged only after a couple of tries. The hen is a late comer. "Tell me" is there from the start, but the motifs that connect the chapter with the rest of the book are as late as the hen. Words come first and last. Structure, far from being a preliminary imposition, grows from the words.

196.1   "O" (omega or zero), one of the principal motifs, makes its first important appearance, 94.22, as omega to H.C.E.'s alpha, recurs 158.23 and 159.5 in connection with rain and "Yes," before coming to climax here. But it continues, in the service of Joyce's "zeroine" and her daughter, throughout the rest of the *Wake:* 224.10, 251.31, 261.8,24, 270.25, 284.10–11, 286.2, 311.11–14, 327.27, 333.3, 383.4, 458.36, 478.27, 526.34, 527.21,

528.26, 555.5, 556.1, 570.20–31, 571.19–20,
585.5,26, 586.7,13, 593.3–4, 601.20, 617.3–5,
627.34.

200.12–13   *"High hellskirt . . . lilyhung pigger"* is Danish:
How I love those beautiful girls.

201.34   "Yakov Yea" is James J. and James Yes, in connection with Cain, Abel, Ibsen's Eyolf, and nay or
no.

203.12–14   "Neptune sculled . . . heroines two." Sculling,
rowing, two boat clubs (Neptune, Leander), Hero
and Leander, a bumping race at Oxford, the two
girls and the three soldiers, Tritonville Road, Dublin, are all involved.

204.1   "Parse secheressa." In the context of Petrarch this
must be Waller's Sacharissa combined with parching and drying out.

205.17   "Wakeschrift" is the *Wake* as a daily newspaper.

205.33   "Oddfellow's triple tiara busby" is H.C.E.'s hat
as the Pope's crown and Lipoleum's "threefoiled
hat" at Waterloo (10).

206.12–13   "Casey's Euclid." Cf. 286.9. This is the book on
which Shem will base his geometry lesson (about
mother) in Chapter X.

211.25   "Gouty Gough" is General Gough, whose statue in
Phoenix Park the Irish blew up as they blew up
Nelson's Pillar. (Cf. 334.18; 357.31.) Mr. Bloom
swore by Gough (*Ulysses,* 457) as Earwicker by
the Wellington Monument (36), already scheduled
perhaps for blowing up. Mr. Morkan's horse liked
King Billy's statue. They blew it up.

211.35   "Ida Ida." Possibly Gertrude Stein, who had as
little use for Joyce as he for her.

212.34–36   *"Senior ga dito. . . . ga facessà"* is a translation
into early Italian (of about the time of St. Francis
of Assisi) of Genesis 1:27, 2:22. Joseph Mazzeo
is my authority.

213.17   "My bach!" means brook in this context, but if

also a reference to J. S. Bach, "bach" is not inappropriate; for this composer devoted Cantata 206 (*Schleicht, spielende Wellen*) to the flow of four rivers: Vistula, Elbe, Pleisse, and Danube. However unlikely it is that Joyce knew Cantata 206, his catalogue of rivers includes the Vistula (199.27), the Pleisse (200.31), and the Elbe (208.01). His Danube, which escapes me here, appears before and after this chapter (76.32; 578.19–20).

214.18   "Ireland sober is Ireland stiff." Father Mathew (*Ulysses,* 95), Dublin's great crusader for temperance, said, "Ireland sober is Ireland free."

215.15–16   "Seven dams," according to *Letters,* I, 212–13, are the city being built at the mouth of the river. For Joyce's other comments on the chapter see *Letters,* I, 249, 259–61, 282; III, 164–65.

215.4   "Hitherandthithering." Cf. "thither" and "hither" (158.25,32) at the end of the Mookse and the Gripes and the "hither and thither" of the wading girl at the end of Chapter IV in *A Portrait of the Artist.*

215.26–27   "Latin me that . . . *Hircus Civis Eblanensis!"* —out of your unbelieving Sanskrit into our Gaelic. H.C.E. is the goat (*hircus*) of the city of Dublin (Eblana).

PART TWO

CHAPTER IX · 219-59

IF ALMOST every word of the first eight chapters of "the book of Doublends Jined" (two ends joined and Dublin's giant) carries three or four meanings, almost every word of this chapter carries "three score and ten toptypsical" meanings (20.15–16) or more. "Than this," we say, scratching our heads, "nothing is denser." Such density that Joyce must have had more of a later time on his hands. Indeed, he wrote Part II when, after hitting his stride "where the hand of man has never set foot" (203.15–16), he had finished Parts I and III. To explain all of Chapter IX—as one could if one could—would require a book and a big book too. I shall have to be contented, according to my space, time, and capacity, with bits and pieces.

The action is simple enough. As night falls, the children— Shem, Shaun, Isabel, and her twenty-eight friends—are playing in front of the pub. What they are playing is a guessing game on the order of the quiz Shem set for Shaun in Chapter VI but even closer to the riddle with which the Prankquean teased Jarl van Hoother (21). This time Shem is the victim. Three times Isabel poses her riddle and twice, unable to find the answer, Shem goes away in disgrace. Enjoying his discomfort, the girls dance in rings around Shaun; for the answer to their riddle is "heliotrope" (see *Letters*, I, 406) and unriddled Shaun, at sunset, is the rising son for those heliotropic Floras—flower girls and rainbow girls four times over in a leap year if we add Isabel to their number. They see Shaun only and he, good at eyeing, can see them, though maybe not through their game. Shem, good at hearing, cannot see or, since Isabel's question is asked in ges-

tures, hear. "Darwing" (252.28–30) presides over survival of
the fittest and "the assent of man." Round those girls go, around
their fitter, and, as is fitting, "roundagain before breakparts and
all dismissed." Not "breakparts" but supper threatens dismissal
now. A.L.P. is preparing it in her kitchen as H.C.E. in the pub is
serving drinks to his twelve unsteady customers and the four old
men. His summons to her supper brings all the teasing and dancing to an end. The twenty-eight girls go home, the animals in the
zoo in the Park go to sleep, and happy Shaun, unhappy Shem,
and Isabel, too knowing and dumb to be happy or unhappy, go
to supper, homework, and bed.

If the *Wake* is a narrative, this happy, sad little story is its
beginning, what happens in study, pub, and bedroom is its
middle, and waking up for breakfast its end. Hidden by extensions and arabesques, Joyce's simple narrative is not unlike, in
substance and character, one of the lesser stories of *Dubliners.*
However sad—and all stories about girls and boys and life are a
little sad—the beginning of his simple story about Dublin is as
gay as it is dense. Gaiety and density are odd companions but,
considering *Ulysses,* not without other example in the work of
Joyce. Gaiety is served here not only by action and tone but by
tripping rhythms, alliteration, rhyme. Singing games and dances
abound and, no less appropriate to terrible childhood, babytalk
and nursery rhymes (Bopeep, Mary's little lamb, Sing a Song of
Sixpence, and the rest). Lewis Carroll is there with A. A.
Milne's "Tigger" (246.32). The whole thing, with three comings
and goings like the Prankquean's, has the form of a fairy story.
Even the exiles of defeated Shem, though bringing the matter of
Chapter VII to mind—Joyce could never let himself alone—are
almost agreeable in this setting.

At the beginning of a new cycle, we are in Vico's divine age
again. The matter is also suitable to this. Childhood, if suffi-
ciently forgotten, seems the age of gold. But other things are
closer to the divine. The game the girls are playing, said Joyce,
is "Angels, Devils and Colours." (See *Letters,* I, 295, 300.
Shaun is an angel, Shem a devil, and the florid rainbow girls are
colors.) Christian holidays, sacraments, and rituals, the Bible,

and Jewish feasts crowd the chapter. And there are hints of
Moslemism, Buddhism, Zoroastrianism, Theosophy, and the
gods of Egypt. T. S. Eliot, with his "Shantih shantih shantih,"
represents Hinduism and holiness of an Anglican sort. Thunder,
which, Vico says, gave men the idea of gods, sounds for the
sixth time. Adam and Eve do again whatever they did in the
Garden.

Joyce accounts for density by three words and a reference:
"monthage" (223.8), "portemanteau" (240.36), "Calembaur-
nus" (240.21), and Wagner (229.34; 230.12–13). Montage, a
moving-picture technique developed by Joyce's friend Sergei
Eisenstein, is the juxtaposition or superimposition of things to
create a third thing. The verbal combinations that make this
chapter readable and unreadable can be thought of as montage
by superimposition. A "portmanteau word," defined by Lewis
Carroll's Humpty Dumpty, carries, like any portmanteau, several things at once. Since a *calembour* is a pun, "Saint Calem-
baurnus" must be the patron of punning. Double talk accounts
in part for a density improved by Wagnerian motifs.

This seems as good a place as any to see why motifs recur
where they do and what they do where they recur. Take the
motif of the Prankquean, who, after her first appearance in
Chapter I, has woven in and out through subsequent chapters.
This teaser, who, coming three times, asks an unanswerable
riddle, swaps brothers around, gangs up with Isabel, bothers father, and, after shutting the door, puts the kettle on and makes
tea, has obvious connections with this riddling chapter of the
twins, Isabel, tea for supper, three comings, and shutting the
door. Her presence in five places (223.24,33; 224.13–15;
229.24–26; 232.16–20; 250.29), serving to enlarge the situation, connects it with other situations and shows changing relations among the characters. Once A.L.P. alone, the Prankquean,
changing with context, is also Isabel now. (T. S. Eliot's technique of allusion, motif, and quotation serves a similar purpose.) Take tea, another recurring theme. Appearing several
times in this chapter (221.13; 229.25–26; 236.30–31;
242.14–15; 246.34–35; 255.4; 256.17), tea carries its usual

meanings of home, marriage ("Tea for Two"), urine, and peace
after conflict to support these matters here and, by recurrence,
to weave the book together. Home and marriage (whether of
H.C.E. and A.L.P. or of Isabel and her likely husband) are
plain enough, but A.L.P.'s urination is no more than hinted by
"po's taeorns" (236.30); and the teapot, taking from context
as much as it gives, takes on a new meaning: the two girls, back
again in the Park, now agitate H.C.E.'s "theopot" (242.14–
16). Tea, usually *thea* (229.26) or goddess, is now *theos* or
god. Earwicker's far from domestic teapot has a spout. The
domestic hen returns in support, not of the letter this time, but
of A.L.P., concerned with her chicks and her marriage to a cock
(e.g., 237.34; 256.2,6). Sinbad the Sailor, who appears now
and again, goes and returns here as a parallel to Shem (256.26–
27,33), sailing away to exile and back. As a "sin beau"
(233.5), Shem seems Sinbad's opposite, but the boy is mixed up
with Noah's rainbow here.

Take a page—almost any—for density's display and all the
wealth of allusion and motif. 245 will do. Part of the nocturne in
the zoo, this page is about animals going to sleep, the Rhinohorn
and the sleepy Hopopodorme—"Sobeast!"—while the children
play their last and drinks are lifted in the pub. As night falls,
lighthouses are lighting up ("arcglow's seafire siemens," 245.8)
for ships at sea, and "lights Brights . . ." (245.4. Cf. *Ulysses*,
447), nearer home, suggest feasts. Three Jewish feasts will serve
for familiar celebration: "Hanoukan's lamp" (245.5, *Hannukah*
and Aladdin), "simwhat toran" (245.10, *Simchat Torah*),
"Pouropourim" (245.36, *Purim* and pouring drinks). Out at sea
are Jonahs and whales; out in the Park the two girls and the
three soldiers are on the prowl, and the "ribber" (river, Eve)
runs its fishy "hoghly course" (245.12–16,19–20) through
"Finnyland," through the watches of the night. Before crossing
the bar, we are safe in the bar with H.C.E., near the washerwomen's "dithering dathering waltzers of. Stright" (245.22; cf.
216.4–5). So brought up, the Liffey suggests wrecks (e.g., the
Hesperus) and jimson weed on Jackson's Island in Mark Twain's
Missisliffi. While the bells (of the Angelus) ring in "Thundera-

tion," there is cure for Dean Swift's "mulligrubs" (*Polite Con-versation*) in the pub (245.23–28). The four apostles and the twelve men (-tion) are there, lifting their glasses which H.C.E., the "tuntapster," fills while Joe sees after the "rinsings" and Kate, the "homeswab," helps with A-one Bass (245.29–35). "Dapplebellied mugs and troublebedded rooms" bring Eden to Phoenix Park. "Chavvyout Chacer" recalls p. 31, where the turnpike-keeper-publican, serving the royal hunter, got his name. This public house by the churchyard with its neighboring "Brass Castle" (246.4–5) reminds us, if we have read Le Fanu's novel, of its three pubs, the Park, its houses—the Brass Castle is one of them—and all of Chapelizod. Dense and allusive maybe, but pleasing.

To begin at last with the beginning: the chapter begins in the "Feenichts Playhouse"—admission almost free—near Phoenix Park, a "childream's" theater offering "Somndoze massinees." The play in hand, in "four tubbloids" (like the *Wake*) is *The Mime of Mick, Nick and the Maggies* (Shaun, Shem, and the girls), a play we have seen advance notices of (48.10–11; 106.10). This play on which the curtain falls at chapter's end to Viconian applause—again, that is, and again—is less a frame or vehicle for the action than a metaphor for children at play. Their play is not unlike our best endeavors, for the sphere, great Shapesphere said, is a kind of stage and we the players on it. The cast of characters, including all the people of the *Wake,* includes us all. Glugg is Shem, Chuff is Shaun, Izod or Miss Butys Pott is herself, and the Floras or Maggies (142–43), her twenty-eight friends from St. Bride's, are what they always were and will be. (Mrs. Bloom is another Flora: "yes so we are flowers all a womans body yes," *Ulysses,* 782.) Father, Mother, their helpers, and the customers at the pub, though listed, are off stage until the end. Time: the present, past, and future. Elanio Vitale (or Bergson, 221.22) prompts what seems more of a movie than a play, and, as the following "argument" shows, is less of either, than of playing a game—or the game. (The play, as Hayman's first draft shows, was an afterthought, adopted per-haps to renew the motif of the theater.)

The tone and rhythm Joyce found suitable for girls (222.32–
36)—whether Gerty MacDowell or A.L.P.—reveal equal
amounts of acceptance and contempt. Standing "Aminxt
[*mingo*] that nombre of evelings" (little Eves in the evening)
and a rainbow "four themes over," Isabel poses her riddle by
"dipandump helpabit" and larger gestures (223.4,9–11). What
can the answer be? The "feinder" (Shem as devil, fender, and
finder) seeks in vain, "buzzling is brains" like an earwig in an
ear (223.25–26). Called upon, the four apostolic old men offer
no help (223.30–32). The maternal brook, solicited, "pranked
alone so johntily" (223.33) that she seems a Prankquean centered in Shaun. "Truly deplurabel" of Shem's "old fontmouther"
(224.10), "A dire, O dire!" No help from Alpha to Omega.
"His morrder had bourst a blabber."

By "gazework" Glugg-Shem tries to guess the colors of "the
youngly delightsome frilles-in-pleyurs" (224.22,26)—Proust's
Jeunes Filles en Fleurs? His eyes no help, his only "art" is the
exhibitionism he shares with his father. Shem's "pricoxity,"
however, elicits no more than "a little tittertit of hilarity." The
girls hold "their noises" while this Tristopher "make peace in his
preaches and play with esteem" (224.35–225.7). (Such artful
"pricoxity," more than sexual display, could represent the writing of *Chamber Music,* self-exposure of another sort. Making
"peace in his preaches" could also mean creating a work of art,
whose end, says Yeats, is peace.) Life, Shem concludes in
discouragement, is "breath and bother and whatarcurss. . . .
Then no breath no bother but worrawarrawurms" (225.12–14).

Regaining courage, he tries again; but his questions about
precious stones (225.22–28) are irrelevant and incompetent.
No nearer to heliotrope, "He has lost." The heliotrooping girls
turn to Chuff-Shaun: "Chuffchuff's inners even. All's rice with
their whorl!" (225.30–31) Shem has fled, and Isabel, a little
sad, consoles herself with thoughts of A.L.P. and Vico, both
eternal: "Mammy was, Mimmy is, Minuscoline's to be. . . .
The same renew" (226.14–17. Cf. 215.23–24). Consolation
indeed; for Minuscoline is Isabel. As the romping girls form a
RAYNBOW, "miss Endles of Eons efter Dies of Eirae"

(226.30–227.2, *Irae* and Eire) joins "the many wiles of Win-sure" in their dance of life. Boys may come and boys may go but this goes on foriver.

Poor Glugg, displaying "all the oathword science of his visible disgrace. . . . don't know whose hue." Isabel's jesting gestures are vain; for to him "no geste reveals the unconnouth" (227.22–27).

Shem's exile, parallel to that in Chapter VII, may delight some readers less than it delighted Joyce, whose hero, at once himself and another Stephen, takes heart from "the bruce, the coriolano and the ignacio" (228.10–11) or the silence of Bruce, the exile of Coriolanus, and the cunning of St. Ignatius Loyola. Obsessed by the Dublin he has left, Shem calls upon "Beate Laurentie O'Tuli" (228.25–26), Dublin's patron saint. Another "subustioned mullmud" (exiled Wilde as Sebastion Melmoth), Shem passes his time writing. Another Paul, he writes his "farced epistol to the hibruws" (228.33–34) or *Ulysses,* chapters of which (named 229.13–16) outraged the British "satiety of arthurs" (Society of Authors) and "the old sniggering pub-licking press and its nation of sheepcopers" (229.7–9). This "jeeremyhead sindbook" (Jerry's jeremiad or scapegoat book), more like the *Wake* now than *Ulysses,* bares to the world his father, his mother, and his home (229.17–36). But "Ipsey Se-cumbe," centered more on himself in exile now than on his home, sheds tears "such as engines weep" (*Paradise Lost,* I, 620; *Ulysses,* 184). "Was liffe worth leaving? Nej!" (230.20–25). Whatever the concern with self, his "ekonome world" (230.34–35) is home. "The first rattle of his juniverse" (prob-ably *Et tu, Healy?*) was about home, seen in terms of Gold-smith's "Deserted Village." "While itch ish a shome," the an-swer to his first riddle, is not unlike "When he is a . . . Sham" (170), a later riddle of a riddler now helpless before Isabel's riddle (231.1–8). "Pugases," the winged horse of his youth, car-ried the young poet from chambering music to heights occupied by Denis Florence McCarthy and other minor bards (231.13–22), whose verses are like "gnawthing unheardth!" The irony with which Joyce treats his beloved early work may seem no more convincing than the heavy jocularity with which, in Chapter VII, he treats his beloved Shem. But taking sides, Joyce took both of them at once.

Echoes of the Prankquean's goings and comings (232.15–20) accompany the exile's return. Echoes of the *Journal to Stella* mean little more here than Swift's return to Ireland and his "little language," which "decoded," serves to introduce the wireless of a returning sailor (232.9–36). Anyway, back from France, where they say "can for dog" and England, where they say "now for know," the "seagoer," home from the sea, tries Isabel's riddle for the second time: "Hark to his wily geeses goosling by" (233.11–14). We may expect a third try because Joyce, another guessing wild goose, returned twice from exile to solve Ireland's riddle before giving up and going away to solve it in his books.

Shem's second try at heliotrope, a symphony in yellow, ends with "nunsibellies" because, if we believe one of his letters, Joyce thought nuns' bellies yellow—as, for all he knew, they may be (233.25). Another failure, another flight.

References to the Mookse and the Gripes (234.2,10) suggest the success of "mookst kevinly" Candidatus and the failure of the "debuzzled" Gripes. References to *Don Quixote* (234.3,-4,6,23) and to Lewis Carroll and his hookah-smoking caterpillar (234.15,31–32) may debuzzle us a little though it is clear that Shaun is Carroll here and Shem, the "tristiest cabaleer," has been "donkey shot at." Shaun must be "Sin Showpanza" and Isabel "dulsy nayer," who knows all about "the farbung and . . . the scent and . . . the holiodropes" (235.5).

The orison of the girls arises "misquewhite" as dusk falls from the "turquewashed" sky. "Allahlah lahlah lah!" and "Xanthos!" remind us of the divine age (235.6–9) while a vision of the suburb—much like Bloom's ideal—discloses Chuff's bourgeois world (235.13–32)—and T. S. Eliot's too: "come on, ye wealthy gentrymen wibfrufrocksfull [Prufrock] of fun" (236.12–14). The sugary fairy tale of Lady Marmela (Isabel) and Prince Le Monade (Shaun) is a suburban view of reality— every day a holiday: a Candlemas, a Christmas with its holly, ivy, and mistletoe, or a Saint Tibbs' day that never comes at all (235.32–236.18). "Tintin tintin" at the beginning of this happy dream and "Thin thin! Thin thin!" at the end are ominous: we too can fall from the Magazine wall.

A parody of Edgar Quinet (236.19–32), the second of four in the *Wake* (the others: 14.35–15.11, 281.4–15, 615.2–5), brings us back to flowers, persisting in spite of politics and war, and to the Floras, "troping" around their sun—the "dumbelles" (237.2–9). To Shaun, their sun, they say: "Outcaste thou art not. . . . Untouchable is not the scarecrown is on you." "Stainusless" Shaun, having been Eliot, is now Joyce's brother Stanislaus (237.11–25). Expert beyond experience, and knowing the Book of the Dead without reading it, these girls know that Shaun, not Shem, is their hope. Egyptian divinities attend him—in reverse, since reversal means renewal. In "Amanti," the underworld, there are these goddesses: Elleb Inam (Belle Mani), Titep Notep (Petit Peton), Enel-Rah (Harlena) and Aruc-Ituc (Cuticura).

Nothing much happens in the interlude of several pages that follows "And they said to him" (237.10). What the girls say to Shaun (238–39) is mostly about "drawpairs" or drawers. "Next to our shrinking selves," as the advertisements say, "we love sensitivas best" (238.1,9)—as next to himself Joyce loved drawers best. (He kept a miniature pair of drawers in his pocket to wave at parties. Bloom too. Mrs. Bloom, who thought Bloom invented bloomers, promised him "the pair off my doll to carry about in his waistcoat pocket . . . hes mad on the subject of drawers," *Ulysses,* 746.) Their words are something like the words of the Angelus: "Behose our handmades for the lured!" (239.10. Cf. "handmade's," 8.32) But interrupting such intimacies, they tell Shaun about the bees and the flowers (238.31–35), the "iris riflers." "Honey swarns where mellisponds" (*Honi soit, mel* or honey, and Hero and Leander). After bees, flowers, and drawers, little is left to talk about but marriage, a German "Hightime" (239.16–27), celebrated with fragments of the Angelus, while "ringing hands" in Vico's (or Yeats's) gyre.

Rejected by these "bright elects," baffled, like a reader of the

Wake, by "punns and reedles" (239.28–36), "poor Glugger was dazed and late in his crave" (240.3–4). But like Finnegan, he rises. People say this fallen riser, like H.C.E., has "shape of hegoat where he just was sheep of herrgott" (240.34–35). A "greyed vike cuddlepuller" with "smugpipe" (241.9,14), he is not only Oscar Wilde and a creature from Lewis Carroll but a union of Earwicker and the Cad with a pipe. Indeed, from here to the bottom of p. 243, Shem, the son, becomes Earwicker, the father, and rules his "howthold." The presence of Finn Mac-Cool and Persse O'Reilly makes their union plain. After "trial by julias," the double pontifex becomes a "pointifox" to be hunted down (242.14,35).

Now back to children at play (244.3–12): Not much time is left; for the lamplighter is making his rounds. It's "time for bairns ta hame. Chickchilds, comeho to roo." The supper that awaits them is a cheerful family affair, a Seder or Feast of Tabernacles, while out in the dark, after curfew, "the wildworewolf's abroad" (244.5–12). But in the zoo in Phoenix Park our "funnaminal world" beds down, and furry sides are "rugs." The "Nocturne" (244.13–246.2) calls, as *Paradise Lost* calls, for reading aloud, in a small tiled room preferably.

From the door of his pub "Housefather calls enthreateningly" (246.6). The twenty-eight girls scamper off, "vamp, vamp, vamp," to their homes in Bray or Sorrento along the Vico Road, far from Chapelizod (246.22–26). But as they go, Shem is back, like a colt on a track, a brook running to the sea, "a time-killer" to his "spacemaker" or a hiker from elm to stone—back to Isabel for a third try at her riddle (246.36–247.7). "Secs" and "yougend" are his drives.

This time his futile guess (247.14), in a composite of Greek and English, seems, in English, to be about tea for supper. Isabel's answering "Teapotty" (cf. 54.12) combines Mother Grogan's tea and water potty with Greek *tipote,* nothing. Nothing doing, she says. Shem weeps again. His weak eye has reduced the "Prettimaid tints" of the rainbow girls to black and white (247.31–36). His ear is blind to colors. But all is not lost: "Turn again, wistfultone, lode mere of Doubtlynn" (248.7).

Giving him another chance, she hints at heliotrope, "the flower that stars the day," and more obscurely, "Achill's low, my middle I ope" (248.11–13), which, if you substitute Achilles' heel for his "low," is almost heliotrope. Clearly the incestuous girl hates to give Shem up. Shaun is her tutor, but Shem can be another. Both can replace "old Deanns" (248.26. H.C.E. as Ann's Swift) in her favor. It may be that "my lord of Glendalough" (Kevin or Shaun) now commands the "approaches to my intimast innermost," but Shem can share "their pink of panties" (248.30–36). If Shem could "see with its backsight," he could guess "the winning word" (249.2–4). Her "Luck!" is both good luck and look. What he must look at—besides the pink of her panties—is "the house of breathings" or her body. "There lies her word, you reder" (249.6,13).

The girls we had thought gone are still here or back again, "Twentynines of bloomers, geging een [one and eye] man," dancing in their ring (249.21–36). In vain "Misha Misha" Shem pretends to be "Toffey Tough" Shaun (cf. 3.9–10). Shaun himself is there, tousing the girls, "buytings of their maidens and spitting their heads." Their real tutor—the professor again—he says: "So now be hushy, little pukers!" (250.1–15). Now is "the time for being now, now, now"; for "Lack breath" can "leap no more." So "their prunktqueen kilt her kirtles up" and her heliotropic "troup came heeling" (250.14–33).

Though "thrust from the light" by a "young sourceress" (a river at its source as well as a little Prankquean), Shem, she thinks again, would "be good tutor two." She would be "waxen" in his hands as he turned "the most dantellising peaches in the lingerous longerous book of the dark. Look at this passage about Galilleotto [Galileo and Dante's Galeotto] . . . Turn now to this patch upon Smacchiavelluti." "Monitorology" has been the same since "Headmaster Adam became Eva Harte's toucher"—a matter of head and heart. "I is a femaline person. O, of provocative gender. U unisingular case." Given her I.O.U., each of Bruno's dueling opposites has something to commend him. We have listened to this "mocking birde" (of the New World) since "songdom was gemurrmal" (251.6–36).

Meanwhile her "crown pretenders," the twins, fight for her favor like lion and unicorn; and, like Cain and Abel, "each was wrought with his other." But of these combatants one, bound to win by Darwin's "natural rejection," represents and assists the "assent of man" (252.14–36), his yes the echo of hers. Shem, on the other hand, "does not know how his grandson's grandson's . . . grandson will stammer up" like another stammering H.C.E.

Shem has failed "as tiercely as the deuce," but the careless girls of this "village childergarten" play on with "screams" and "ejaculations of aurinos" in their "tug of love" with Shaun (253.19–32) until H.C.E., like the "god of all machineries," comes out to end their play. Whether "splitten up or recompounded," this "Ipse dadden" is himself alone; and when most himself is the "product of the extremes." Whether washed ashore by the three waves of Ireland (Rury, Toth, and Cleena), whether the Brut of Layamon or somebody else from Clio's library, here he is, and, in concert with A.L.P., determines the course of history; "for ancients link with presents [A.L.P.] as the human chain extends [H.C.E.], have done, do and will again." A.L.P. is his necessary partner, turning her "minnelisp extorreor to his moanolothe inturned," as "the water of the livvying goes the way of all fish"—a Sarah to her Isaac (253.33–254.17). This Viconian interlude, that covers all from birth to burial—writing, phonetics, and groceries too—is one of Joyce's recurrent celebrations of "cycloannalism" (254.18–36). Old "summonorother" summons the children because "the hour of his closing"—life as well as pub—is at hand. To lend authority to his call to supper Mr. John Baptister Vikar, producer of the play, brings on the scene the tailor's daughter who, in Chapter XI, will marry the sailor. A "cutletsized" girl? A.L.P.'s measurements, given here, prove her to be less wee than we have come to think (255.5–36).

So dismissed, those girls at last go home; so summoned, Shaun, Isabel, and Shem come to supper, radio, homework, and bed. Isabel, "that little cloud, a nibulissa," is contented in her sky, but "Singabed" Shem, making chamber music and coming home like Sinbad from his voyages, sulks (256.1–36). Can Vanessa be unhappy? Her Stella's vesperine laugh, proving happiness, may excite old "Daddy Deacon" (H.C.E. as Swift), the twins, and even those twelve customers in the pub (257.1–26). The sixth thunder (257.27–28) means closing the door (cf. "shot the shutter clup," 23.5): "Lukkedoer" (shut the door in Danish), "unandurras" (*dún an doras,* in Gaelic), "fermoyporte" (in French). "Kapakkapuk," the hen's cackle that also follows the fifth thunder (113.12–13), implies that, closing the door, A.L.P. has got her chickens home. The thunder that once gave Vico's men the idea of gods gives children now an idea of father and mother.

The curtain falls on the play to applause in German ("Byfall") and English. "Byfall. Upploud" imply fall and rise, and, by three bursts of applause, Vico's system. "The gawds" or the departed girls are gods of the gallery. "Orbiter" is H.C.E. as Vico or God. "Where the huer," combining the Cad's question about the time of day with the hewer of all things, ends a series: when, who, where—time, space, and color (257.31–36). Ragnarok and *Götterdämmerung* suggest the end and beginning of a cycle (258.1–2). "Loud, hear us!" is the prayer of Viconian man to the thunderer, their "phonemanon." (The *Wake* is our phonemanon.) Babel and its reversal, "Lebab," may explain the confusion of all things here: a mixture of Finnegan at his wake ("didits dinkun's dud?") with Shem's "Immi ammi Semmi" (cf. 168.14) and of Buckley with the Cad (258.2–26).

A prayer for the children fittingly ends this divine age. Thank "Gov" (God, Jove, Governor) for shutting the door. May "Garda Didymus and Garda Domas" keep them and open their minds to light from the Book of the Dead. (Didymus, Greek for twin, is Thomas, the apostle, and a *garda* is an Irish policeman.) May they grow like trees until "under stone for ever." "Grant sleep in hours time, O Loud!" Fragments of the ten commandments and the liturgy ("with laughters low" means "incline our hearts to keep his law") introduce the five vowels or the word. "Mummum," silence after laughter and speech, could also mean champagne with bubbles rising.

The movement of this chapter—or at least of its second half —slows down beneath a load of decoration and repetition, which Joyce, expanding the first draft, was unable to resist. Playing around, he almost loses himself and the reader. Maybe, however, the feeling of getting lost among repetitions and arabesques or of being impeded by them is what he was after. The *Wake,* after all, is dream, and in a dream we sometimes find ourselves trying to run through a sort of glue that arabesques, here, could be meant to give the feel of. Yet his possible intention cannot lessen our probable response. A parallel and a likely source could be the chapter's proper excuse. The *Tunc* page of the Book of Kells displays less text than decoration, and we must agree that this page is a work of art. Maybe Joyce is the last illuminator—if I have read his "tunc's dimissage" (298.7) right.

221.34–36   "Silktrick twomesh" is Sitric, a Danish king of Dublin, Silken Thomas, a pretender (see *Ulysses,* 45), and a silk stocking. "Grabstone beg" is a little gravestone and a Gladstone bag. "General Orders Mailed" (G.O.M.) is Gladstone as Grand Old Man and a Russian department store.

223.3   The "willy wooly woolf" is both Satan and Virginia Woolf, who rejected *Ulysses* when Joyce offered it for publication to the Hogarth Press.

223.9–11   Like Isabel, Stephen uses expressive gestures, *Ulysses,* 432–33.

223.11   "Holytroopers." Heliotrope, Isabel's color (*Letters,* I, 406), that of her twenty-eight sun-turning friends, and of "Heliotropolis," the Dublin of Tim Healy and a city in Egypt, is a motif that, starting 89.19, finds its climax in this chapter, and persists: 235.5, 236.35–36, 237. 1–2, 248.11–13, 265.L1, 273.24–25, 303.F1,

461.9, 470.7, 509.22, 533.2, 561.20–21, 594.
8, 603.28, 610.36, 626.17–18.

223.33 "The skand for schooling." H.C.E. is a Skand,
and the twenty-eight girls go to school. One of
many references to Sheridan, e.g., 80.34, 111.
23, 184.24, 256.12.

224.30–31 Cinderella's slipper is "chiny": glass, shiny, and
as tiny as a slipper in China.

227.29–35 A mixture of Scotland (Calvin?) with the seven
sacraments: confirmation, holy communion,
penance, extreme unction, marriage, baptism,
and holy orders.

231.1–8 Some think this poem, with its echoes of Goldsmith, a parody of Joyce's first poem, *Et tu,
Healy?* Others think Hynes's poem in "Ivy Day
in the Committee Room" a more faithful parody. No copy of the poem itself survives.

231.12–15 Besides Denis Florence McCarthy, the minor
poets with whom Joyce compares himself are
John Boyle O'Reilly, Thomas D'Arcy McGee,
and Kevin Izod O'Doherty. Mr. Deasy's school
was in McCarthy's house at Dalkey. That
Bloom owns a copy of McCarthy's poems is
another connection between Deasy and Bloom,
both flowering father-figures.

235.9–12 "Xanthos! Xanthos! Xanthos!" and other
versions of *Sanctus, Sanctus, Sanctus,* recur
throughout the *Wake* to suggest holy Shaun and
T. S. Eliot (the "Shantih" man), who, in this
passage, performs bourgeois "desk jobduty" in
a bank. Cf. Prufrock, 236.13. Other appearances of *Sanctus, Sanctus, Sanctus,* (the trishagion): 305.23–24, 377.1, 408.33–34, 454.
33, 528.9–10, 593.1, 605.14.

239.10,22–26 Fragments of the Angelus: "The Angel of the
Lord declared unto Mary. And she conceived of

the Holy Ghost (*Et concepit de Spiritu Sancto*).
Hail, Mary. . . . Behold the handmaid of the
Lord. Be it done unto me according to thy
word. Hail, Mary. . . . And the word was made
flesh. And dwelt among us. Hail, Mary. . . ."
Commonly associated in the *Wake* with *Sechseläuten,* the Angelus is a motif: 32.2–4, 35.33,
51.32, 53.17–20, 58.32–33, 63.26–27, 68.18,
211.16, 213.19, 267.16, 268.3, 278.11–12,
296.16, 327.24–25, 336.17, 379.8, 392.31,
517.5, 528.19–20,25, 561.26–28, 604.10–11.

242.11–32 On this page are many books of the Bible, from
"ecrazyaztecs" and "praverbs" to the Apocrypha
and Revelation. The Koran ends this list.

244.21,34–36 We are in the zoo. "Isegrim" is the wolf from
Reynard the Fox. "Panther monster" is *Pater
noster* and Christ as the black panther of the
Bestiary and as Bloom, the black "pard" of
Ulysses. "Eliphas Magistrodontos" is the tusked
elephant and Eliphas Lévi, the magus, in whom
Joyce, once interested in Theosophy, was interested. Theosophy adds a little, if not much, to
the divine age.

250.16–18,34 The parody of *Macbeth* is one of the many references to Shakespeare and his plays that crowd
the *Wake* and the library scene in *Ulysses.*
Those to *Hamlet* are most frequent.

250.36–251.1 The parody of Stephen Foster's "Campdown
Races" belongs with the motif of the race:
rivalry on a circular track. Cf. 246.36 where
Shem is a chestnut colt on the track.

251.22 The "tutor" serves as introduction to the next
chapter. Neither twin is tutor to Isabel, who
needs no teaching, but in Chapter X Shem tries
to teach Shaun.

252.7–13 The three cemeteries of Dublin: Glasnevin,
Prospect, and Mount Jerome. "Grassy ass ago"

means I lay my ass in the grass and *gratias ago,* thank God. Mowy or Mobhi or Berchan, a saint of the sixth century, founded a monastery on the Tolka at Glasnevin.

253.16   "Noodynaady" seems Blake's Nobodaddy (*Ulysses,* 205).

254.20   "Hocus Crocus Esquilocus" is H.C.E., Esq., proprietor of a "local" or pub, and *Hoc est enim corpus meum* or the Eucharist, a hokus-pokus or Mr. Bloom's "Hokypoky . . . Pious fraud," *Ulysses,* 81–82. The crocus also promises rebirth. H.C.E., the Eucharist or "fraud-stuff," is sacramentally devoured by all his people (7.9–19).

255.18–20   References to writers: Aulus Gellius, *Noctes Atticae,* Macrobius on dreams, Vitruvius on architecture, Cassiodorus, whose history of the Goths preserved manuscripts as the others, by quotation, preserved lost writers. All amount to *Finnegans Wake.* The Book of Lucan (Lecan) is an Irish manuscript preserved at Trinity College, Dublin. The "Coombe" is a street near St. Patrick's Cathedral.

256.11–15   The "ramsblares" of Jewish horns include Burke, Gay ("cease your fumings"), Seymour Bushe, an oratorical lawyer celebrated in *Ulysses* (139: "Kendal Bushe or I mean Seymour Bushe"), Sheridan, Goldsmith, Wilde, Shaw, Swift, and Sterne—all users of the "holy language."

256.20   "Grandmère des Grammaires." Cf. 268.17, "gramma's grammar," from which, having learned all, Isabel needs to learn nothing more. Another introduction to the next chapter.

256.29–32   A matter of initials: G.P.O. is the General Post Office. D.U.T.C. is the Dublin United Tram Company. N.C.R. and S.C.R. are North

Circular Road and South Circular Road, Dublin.

257.5 "Geamatron" or Earth Mother. Cf. "geomater," 297.1 and "Gea-Tellus" or Mrs. Bloom, *Ulysses*, 737.

CHAPTER X · 260-308

IF CHAPTER IX is denser than what preceded it, Chapter X should be densest; but Chapter XI is even denser. A more elaborate comparison of adjectives is called for. Lacking it, we must content ourselves with calling Chapters IX, X, and XI the densest part of the *Wake*. After these, as dawn approaches, things are no more than dense again. Here, in Chapter X, in deepest sleep, we are sure, as the first sentence tells us, that "As we there are where are we are we there." Our uncertainty about where and there is improved by the absence of syntactical divisions, which, if added, after a little unscrambling and punctuating, might yield this: We are there. Where are we? Are we there? A sound statement and good questions.

After these, what puzzles us is the form of the chapter: a text with marginal comments and footnotes. (See *Letters,* I, 406.) But a moment's reflection shows its suitability. Since children doing their homework is the theme, why not mimetic form? Mimesis no more than parody, however; for the form is a parody of all scholarship—as Professor Jones's lecture on time and space is a parody of all lectures. Jones gets nowhere. Getting there too, the three commentators on the text before them are all commentators on all texts, especially *Finnegans Wake,* and, since this book is a world, shaped by a great, punning "Shapesphere" (295.4), all commentators on the world in the world.

The three commentators on its tenth chapter, of which they compose the text to be commented on, are Shem, Shaun, and Isabel. Their ostensible concern is with grammar, history, and mathematics. Their real concern is with their parents. Through history they arrive at H.C.E. and through geometry at A.L.P., who, working at home, created these little homeworkers.

Shaun's comments, abstract, professorial, and profounder than their occasion, occupy the right-hand margin at first. At first, Shem's comments, gay and irreverent, occupy the left. But in the middle of the chapter, after a passage without marginal comments, the twins change sides. Changing with them, italics become capitals and capitals, italics. We should be used to the shifting of this shifty pair. Remember how the Prankquean changed Tristopher to Hilary and, according to the rule of Bruno, Hilary to Tristopher. Twins may come and go, but Isabel, the little brook, goes on for ever. There she is with her footnotes, at the bottom, where she belongs, constant. She may be a "dumbelle," but her footnotes are the most instructive part of the chapter—and the funniest.

When this chapter was published separately as a little book in 1937, Joyce called it *Storiella as She is Syung* (267.7–8), a title that, bringing Isabel from the bottom to the top, illustrates perhaps the domestic career of woman. "Syung" means young, sung, and sewing (*sy* is Danish for sew). There she sits, as her brothers argue, sewing or knitting, as her terrible predecessors at the guillotine sat and knat. The brothers, talking and striving, try to get somewhere. Silent, she is already there without trying. Her footnotes, the voice of silence, are at once more frivolous than Shem's marginalia and profounder than Shaun's. Like E. M. Forster's Mrs. Moore, Isabel knows. Shaun says: "CONSTITUTION OF THE CONSTITUTIONABLE AS CONSTITUTIONAL" (261.R1). Shem, referring to H.C.E., ribs, and dump, says, *"Dig him in the rubsh"* (261.L2). Isabel, passing peripheries by and going to the heart of things, asks: "Is love worse living?" (269.F1); for, as she says, she is following "the law of the jungerl" (268.F3)—of the jungle, of the young girl, and of Jung's Anima or female archetype.

The studies of these children are framed suitably by the mediaeval trivium and quadrivium (grammar, rhetoric, logic, arithmetic, geometry, astronomy, music). "We've had our day at triv

and quad" (306.12–13), says Shem at the end; and, at the beginning (260.9–15), a list of seven scholars in seven areas suggests triv and quad. These seven scholars are also streets,
squares, and gateways that lead the enquiring traveller to the
pub and its creative occupants. How, says the traveller, echoing
the Prankquean, "do we hook our hike to find that pint of porter
place?" The answer, seemingly irrelevant to "UNDE ET UBI," is
"Am shot, says the bigguard" (260.5–7); but Buckley's victim is
the publican. It is through the streets and squares of triv and
quad that the three children get to H.C.E., the pub, and environs. The traveller, approaching E.C.H. and A.L.P., must cross
the bridge, come to the Castleknock gate of the Park, and,
knocking, join the wake of the fallen Persse O'Reilly
(262.1–19). Less wake, perhaps, than an ordinary evening in
the pub (262.25–29). As "the babbers [children] ply the pen"
upstairs, "the bibbers" drink downstairs, while "the papplicom,
the pubblicam he's turning tin for ten" or making what money
he can before closing time.

The scene is Chapelizod, Isolde's chapel, with its "Lefanuian"
elm and stone (264.12–14; 265.4), a town not unlike Goldsmith's "Distorted mirage, aloofliest of the plain" (265.28–29).
Here is the "phoenix," one of Le Fanu's pubs (265.8), here the
"creepered tower" of Le Fanu's church and his King's House
(264.30–32); here the famous strawberry beds on the banks of
"the winnerful wonders off, the winnerful wonnerful wanders"
of the washerwomen's Liffey (265.15–16). "Riverside . . .
sunnybank . . . buona the vista" (264.23–24) are villas in
Chapelizod. This place, a part of Greater Dublin, is the pub's
setting, where we soar from "the murk of the mythelated"
twelve customers to the "childlight in the studiorium upsturts"
(266.1–19). "The tasks above are as the flasks below, saith
the emerald canticle of Hermes" (263.21–22). Hermes Trismegistus, celebrated as Thoth in *A Portrait of the Artist* and
Ulysses, is the philosopher or god of correspondences and a
clue to Joyce's method. Though correspondence between above
and below is no more at this point than that between upstairs

in the study and downstairs in the pub, the *Emerald Tablet* is at home with other references to the occult, mostly kabalistic, at the beginning of this chapter.

As "Ainsoph" (261.23), Earwicker is God in the Kabala, a maker who, mating with made (261.8), descends to it through ten emanations or *sephiroth* (cf. "zephiroth," 29.13). Earwicker's number is ten, the number of completeness, that, recurring at the end of the tenth chapter (308.5–14), brings the *sephiroth* back to mind. If his number is 10, that of the made or maid he mates with, a "noughty . . . zeroine" (261.24, zero-*eine*), is 01. Combined, they make 1001, the number of renewal. Nothing kabalistic about this numerical play or about the alchemical matters of mercury and sulphur (261.25–26) that follow or about Earwicker's "hairy face" (260.L1), although the *Zohar,* a kabalistic text, has much to say about God's beard and the stars in it. Joyce may have looked into McGregor Mathers' English version of the *Zohar* or the version in French; but what he certainly intended was Stephen's father who, on the first page of *A Portrait,* has a "hairy face." No kabalist, Joyce was using his smattering of kabalism, as he used his smatterings of all else, for the sake of analogy. Like the God of kabalists and alchemists, H.C.E. is father and creator; and this is all those need to know who ask: "Whose is he? . . . And what the decans [ten, Dickens, and Dean Swift] is there about him anyway, the decemt man?" (261.28–262.1)

Other analogies—Hermetic correspondences if you like—broaden him. He is a "montan wetting his moll," the "Brook of Life" (260.17; 264.6). As "Cronwall" (261.L3), he is Cromwell and King Mark of Cornwall. He is "Whiteman" (263.9) or fair-haired Finn MacCool, "Ignotus Loquor" (263.3), a publican, the voice of sleep, and builder of the Seven Wonders of the World (261.9–13). If his name is the "Groupname for grapejuice," as Isabel says (261.F3), he is the Eucharist. As "original sun" (263.27–30), he is at once Adam and God. In short, "more mob than man" (261.21–22)—"not a feature alike and the face the same" (263.16)—H.C.E. is an "archetypt" (263.30) like, in respect of this, his Jungian daughter, Isabel.

This "flickerflapper" (266.31), a Nova among twenty-eight Nereids, "speaking nots for yestures" (267.9,23–24), is another gesturing yes-girl, fittingly announced by *Sechseläuten,* the spring festival of Zurich, and the Angelus as renewal's agent. Like her twenty-eight companions of the itching It, she knows the business she "was bred to breed by" (268.2–6). No longer abroad, this girl is a homeworker now.

While her brothers quarrel, like Ondt and Gracehoper, over Browne and Nolan's "divisional tables" (268.7–17), she meditates "gramma's grammar" (cf. 256.20). No need for the sitting knitter to study Lindley and Murray's grammar (see *Letters,* I, 278) with the twins (269.29); for "all is her inbourne" (268.16) and, instructed by grandma, she knows her "genderous towards his reflexives" and all about conjugation: "Jeg suis, vos wore a gentleman, thou arr, I am a quean." The unnecessary homework of this "hortatrixy" proceeds through three hilarious pages (268–70). Perhaps while she is detained by gramma's grammar, the twins are studying Lindley and Murray's or perhaps they are still preoccupied with their divisional tables while Isabel is freewheeling "on youthlit's bike" with her feet on the "algebrars" (270.23–24). Lewis Carroll is there (270.20–22) less for the sake of mathematics than for the looking glass that Isabel shares with Alice: "O Evol, kool in the salg and ees" (262.F2). A looking glass, reversing what is before it, may imply renewal.

Done with grammar of two schools and with two kinds of mathematics, the children turn to history (270–71), over which Clio and the four old historians from their four provinces preside (270.30–271.3,L2). History, as mixed and dubious as grammar, is ancient and modern, local and universal at once. "Hireling's puny wars" (270.30) unite Ireland with Carthage; the affairs of "Sire Jeallyous Seizer" unite Earwicker with Rome. His "druidesses" are the two girls in the Park and his triumvirate is the three soldiers: "Oxthievious [Shem as Cad or *filou*], Lapidous [Shaun as stone] and Malthouse Anthemy [the publican himself]" (271.3–6. Cf. Antonius who, with Burrus and Caseous, forms another triumvirate, 167). Centering on

H.C.E. and A.L.P., history from Adam and Eve to democracy ("Impovernment of the booble by the bauble for the bubble," 273.6–7) proceeds according to Vico's "whorled without aimed" (272.4–5), from B.C. to A.D. (So goes the music in the margin, 272.L2). The "passing of order [Arthur] and order's coming" (277.18–20) are attended to by A.L.P., the Viconian river: "And Sein annews" (cf. 215.23). "Pappapassos, Mammamanet . . . and whowitswhy" (272.5–6). "Please stop" (272.12) and "Tip" (273.21), motifs from the first chapter, prove history a museum and a dump.

The two "scribbledehobbles . . . are head bent and hard upon" (275.7–24) these familiar studies while their sister, thinking history a hen's letter (278.7–24), devotes her longest footnote to a letter of her own (279.F1): "This isabella," she says, "knows the ruelles of the rut." Her concern with the letter continues until the third appearance of Edgar Quinet (281.4–13. Cf. 15.1–11; 236.19–32), speaking in his own words at last, on flowers remaining, cities passing.

Careless of letters, flowers and the little cloud, the twins, now Brutus and Cassius, resume their quarrel (281.14–27). Killers of Caesar, hence father-killers—"Sire Jeallyous Seizer" has already appeared—Brutus and Cassius remind us of Burrus and Caseous who, on their "isocelating biangle" (161–67), seek completion in a triangular triumvirate by Antonius or Anthemy (271). The "totients quotients" of their rivalry, reminding us of Professor Jones's *talis-qualis* (149–50), also concern time and space—"Sieger" (clock or time) and "Ruhm" (*Raum* or space) this time. No better example than this paragraph of how the *Wake* hangs together. "Either or," that ends the paragraph, introduces a new but parallel idea of the conflict between son and son, father and son. Since "Enten eller" is Danish for either-or, Joyce reminds us of Kierkegaard on father and son without, perhaps, having had him in mind.

A.M.D.G., the Jesuit motto with which students commonly begin their themes (282.6), begins the lesson in mathematics, of which, during the exercise in grammar, we have already had anticipations. Counting on fingers, measuring and weighing, suggest the area of "nucleuds and alegobrew" with its signs of infinity and its surds (282–85). Like history, mathematics illustrates "the family umbroglia," the "zeroic couplet" of A.L.P. and H.C.E., and even the two girls and the three soldiers (284.4,-10–16,22–23); for two, three, division, and multiplication come under the heads of mathematics and family alike. The bicycle or tricycle that Isabel rode with her feet on the "algebrars" (270.23–24) is here again to carry ones, twos, and threes along (284.22–27) to the troubles they have invited.

At last, by way of bridge (286.11–18)—a game that unites, divides, has four players of four Viconian suits and a dummy (cf. the Prankquean's "dummy," 22.1), together with a family of kings, queens, and knaves—we cross over to Casey's Euclid, which has been mentioned before (206.12–13) as one of A.L.P.'s books of reference (cf. crossing the bridge, 262.3–4). The geometry lesson given by Shem or Dolph to Kev or Shaun is the heart of this chapter. Shaun as Jones is usually the teacher and Shem the learner. Shifting now, Shem takes the place of didactic Shaun. (A few pages later they swap margins.) Expert in "mythametical tripods," like the oracle at Delphi, Dolph demonstrates the first problem of Euclid's first book: to construct an equilateral triangle—not an "isocelating biangle"—on a given line. "Ann aquilittoral dryankle" or "trillitter" (three children) makes this triangle A.L.P. "Probe loom" could refer to Bloom and his weaving Penelope (286.19–24). "Know . . . Oc . . . oui" introduce Mrs. Bloom's "yes"; and "mud" makes mudder A.L.P.'s triangle her delta (286.25–31). Her triangle, as we learn a few pages later (294.3, "in Fig., the forest"), is pubic, calling for Eve's fig leaf. Raising this fig leaf, Shem is exposing and peeping at his mother—her "whole," like Eve's, in "applepine erdor" (order and error). The naughty boy, unboxing his compasses, finds "a locus for an alp [to] get a howlth on her bayrings as a prisme O." Plainly the discovery of her Omega involves local geography: muddy, prismic delta, Howth, and Dublin Bay or the "coastmap." "I cain" do it, says one of Eve's sons to the other, "but are you able? Amicably nod" (287.7–17). Dean Swift and Berkeley together (287.18–19),

Dolph-Shem is also Balbus, another constructor, who, in *A Portrait,* is building a wall.

The passage in Latin that begins an interlude without banks or margins connects the river of life and her banks with Vico's historical flow and Bruno's interacting machinery. I owe the following translation to Gilbert Highet, on whom—since his Latin is even better than mine—I called for help:

Come, you people of the past (or you dead), without delay, and while in a little page in the manner of Livy an explanation is given rather gracefully in the Roman language of the dead, about the beings who are still to be born, sitting in joy (*letitiae* should be *letitia*) over pots of flesh, or rather looking at the site of Paris (*lutetiae,* a play on words that may justify *letitiae*) from which under favourable omens such great races of humanity are to arise, let us turn over in our minds the most ancient wisdom of both (*amborium* should be *amborum*) the priests Jordan and Jambaptista: that the whole universe flows safely like a river, that the same things which were poked (*fututa* is obscene) from the heap of rubbish will again be inside the riverbed, that anything recognizes itself through some contrary, and finally (*demun* should be *demum*) that the whole river is enfolded in the rival banks along its sides.

In uncovering A.L.P., then, Shem is disclosing the world and its laws of time and space. As he says (296.30–297.1): "I'll make you to see figuratleavely the whome of your eternal geomater." Geometry or measuring the earth can measure the Earth Mother, whether A.L.P. or Mrs. Bloom, the "Gea-Tellus" (Earth-Earth) of *Ulysses* (737).

The interlude that defers this geometrical exercise (287–92) concerns Shem, Shaun, H.C.E., A.L.P., Isabel, and Joyce—in short, the whole family and its creator, enlarged by memories of Dermot, Grania, and Finn MacCool, Tristan, Isolde, and Mark, and a variety of invaders from Patrick and Strongbow, the Norman, to Swift, who, like Patrick and Tristan, came twice from abroad to Wickerworks or Dublin, the Ford of the Hurdles.

In the beginning, Shem, teaching school like Stephen in *Ulys-*

ses and Joyce in Trieste, is taking the place of professorial Shaun (287.30–288.1) "for a dillon a dollar" like any ten o'clock scholar. But metamorphosis of dream allows no constancy here. Suddenly Shem, dealing in "tropadores and double-cressing twofold thruths," becomes the author of the *Wake,* "a reel [movie] of funnish ficts apout the shee [A.L.P.]." No sooner author than invader. Becoming H.C.E., Shem is all invaders coming to Ireland's shores in Sir Thomas Lipton's "strongbowed" yacht. As "Mr. Dane," Shem-Earwicker is a Danish invader and Dean Swift leaving Sir William Temple for Dublin (288.1–28). Persse O'Reilly, Finn MacCool, and Patrick bring us to King Mark, Tristan, and Isolde—or father, daughter, and rival son. Mark, his "craft ebbing," is no match for Tristan-Shaun and his Isolde, both first and second, as Finn is no match for Dermot and his Grania. Isabel devotes a footnote at this point (291.F7) to "Just one big booty's pot." (The part of Izod in the *Mime,* 220.7, was taken by Miss Butys Pott.) Now, disposing of father and his amatory troubles, dream shifts from Mark to Joyce and his troubles with the critics, especially Wyndham Lewis, who, in *Time and Western Man* (*"Spice and Westend Woman"*) had said of the *Wake:* you must "draw the line somewhere" (292.1–31). A peep into "the cerebralised saucepan of the eer [ear, air, Eire] illwinded goodfornobody" (Joyce) would reveal the making of the *Wake,* "a jetsam litterage . . . of times lost or strayed" and of "novo takin place of what stale words." "No mouth," says Joyce, echoing Parnell while defending himself against critics, "has the might to set a mearbound to the march of a landsmaul."

With "Coss? Cossist" (*Was ist* and cosine) the lesson in geometry resumes—as if the demonstrator were saying, "Lead us seek" (266.27) or "Let us pry" (188.8). "Somnione sciupiones" and "murphy" (Morpheus), telling us that prying will occupy a "Dreamcountry," arouse expectation of Lewis Carroll, who, indeed, will soon appear to assist the mathematics of dream. Not only Eve, a faller and riser, and "liv" (Danish, life), A.L.P. is also "ann linch," a brand of tea (293.1–33,F1). Apply-

ing his "passer" (Danish, compass) to "Modder ilond," Shem
evolves her delta from two Viconian cycles with the aid of
"loose carollaries" (294.2–15). The construction of mother
compels thoughts of father, who, after those two girls and his
volcanic "magmasine fall," needs reconstruction. H.C.E. is
doomed to Swift's "galehus" (Danish, madhouse): but "thunder and turf" (Buckley and the Russian General), he is not
through yet. Gaudyanna, like Shaw's Anna, will make him repeat himself, like Shaw's Tanner or the sailor's tailor
(294.15–31). Like "Tate and Comyng" (Tutankhamen)—so
the Book of the Dead assures us—he will rise tomorrow.
"Straorbinaire!"

"A daintical pair of accomplasses" (identical twins with compasses and accomplices like the two lasses), they apply their
"twain of doubling bicirculars" (peeping eyes and compass-
circles) to "tew tricklesome poinds" (of mother and the two
girls). Shem's "Gyre O, gyre" suggests Yeats and Lewis Carroll's "Jabberwocky." "Shapesphere" and the book of a thousand-and-one nights, claiming places in this literary company,
promise revival through the word (295.3–31).

Mother's "doubleviewed seeds" (sons, peeping, and W.C. to
go with "Pee") provoke more thoughts of parents and their fall:
"Hoddum and Heave, our monsterbilker" (Tim Finnegan and
his hod as Adam and Ibsen) and his "bawd of parodies," who
will become "awful angelous" as Mary, the second Eve. Before
this rise, Earwicker's fall was "the muddest thick that was ever
heard dump." Not only his defecation, this fall is also that of
Lewis Carroll's Humpty Dumpty (296.1–31).

Lifting "the maidsapron" of A.L.P. (the lower triangle of the
construction), Shem exposes her "triagonal delta," her "midden wedge," or "safety vulve." Under the "serpumstances" (of
Eve's fall), Shem thinks of Solomon setting his seal (composed of two triangles) on the witch Sheba, his "hexengown,"
and of Noah's sons peeping at father. All this from a "trickki-
kant" (Danish, triangle) which, we must agree, is the most significant "since fillies calpered" (*felix culpa*, 297.1–30). Shem's
"Quicks herit fossyending. Quef!" (Q.E.F.) is justifiably trium-

phant (298.4–5). He is more than the "elementator joyclid" (302.12) Shaun thinks him.

But the descending and ascending twins, one always greater than the other—these "circumflicksrent searclhers," whatever their "gyribouts," are unable to reproduce themselves. They owe their production and reproduction to "Frivulteeny Sexuagesima," from whose "redtangles" they have just removed "the calicolum of her undescribables" (drawers) to "see her it" (298.1–33).

Shaun's response to Shem's Q.E.F. or Q.E.D. is "mooxed." Becoming Stanislaus Joyce, Shaun advises the demonstrator to get a job in Guinness' brewery, the only place for a boy so lacking in faith, hope, and charity (299.1–300.8). Becoming James Joyce, a sorrowful exile in "trieste, ah trieste," Shem ignores his brother's "Sink deep or touch not the Cartesian spring" of egocentricity. Echoes of the hen's letter bring the quarreling twins to the matter of writing. Shaun could write as well as Shem— even *The Day of the Rabblement* or *Pomes Penyeach*—if he put his mind to it (302.1–30). Shem, who created "all the charictures in the drame" (the *Wake* with its caricatures rather than characters), agreeably tells Shaun how to emulate him. Take Steele, Burke, Sterne, Swift, Wilde, Shaw, and Yeats as models. "Tip!" makes Shem seem Kate in another museum, where Dan O'Connell and Parnell are among the exhibits. This is too much for Shaun, who, like Private Carr in *Ulysses,* and like Cain, "wreathed with his pother," knocks Shem down. A good thing too, Isabel implies in her footnote: Mr. Tellibly Divilcult, who was unable to guess heliotrope, deserves what he got (302.31–303.F1). What can Shem expect "after all his . . . writings of paraboles of famellicurbs and meddlied muddlingisms"? The "countinghands" of a referee, signifying a knockout, conduct Tristan's love-death music (304.1–3). Rising from the floor, Cartesian Shem says, "cog it out, here goes a sum" (304.31), and, taking heart from the bilking and forgery of art, forgives his "bloater's kipper." Shem hails his "popular endphthisis," now T. S. Eliot, with a suitable "slanty scanty shanty!" (305.1–24). Though Eliot-Shaun received the "Noblett's surprize" and Joyce-Shem did not, noble Shem says, "let us be sin-gulfied"—something that the laws of Bruno would attend to anyway (306.4–6).

They have had their day at "triv and quad" and, apparently, have written their themes, the titles of which appear in a cata-logue. Shem's margin is silent, but Shaun's, academic as usual, provides parallels from the illustrious past (306–07). The ten *sephiroth* of the beginning descend to another manifestation at the end. A "Nightletter" from the children to their obsessive parents concerns birth, death, and renewal ("youlldied . . . new yonks"). Isabel's hieroglyphics thumb a nose at the old ones and their crossbones.

260.9–15   The seven representatives of the trivium and quadrivium are Livy (history); Mezzofanti (a cardinal and linguist); Lavater (phisiognomy and theology. A "Lavatery Square" is a urinal like the "square" in *A Portrait*); Tycho Brahe (astron-omy); Berkeley (philosophy); Gainsborough (painting); Guido d'Arezzo (music). All follow "New Livius Lane" (cf. "vicus," 3.2) or Vico's historical process.

261.9–13   The seven wonders of the world are examples of creation: "cones" (Pyramids), "mured" (Hanging Gardens), "pensils" (Pharos), "olymp" (Phideas' statue of Zeus), "diana" (Temple of Diana), "culosses" (Colossus), "mosoleum" (at Hali-carnassus). There are many references in the *Wake* to the Colossus and the Pharos.

262.15–19   "Requiestress" is *requiescat*. "And let luck's . . . ease" is *Et lux perpetua luceat ei* from the Mass for the Dead. "Lucy" is patron of eyesight. "Sow byg eat" combines "So be it" with feasting at a wake.

263.13–15   "Hispano . . . Helleniky" combines Spain-China-Black Sea with Spain-Ireland-Scotland and Spain-Wales-Greece (or everywhere) with H.C.E.,

C.E.H., and E.C.H. (or everybody). Why Spain
thrice? And what does the variety of the initials
mean? Cf. "hce che ech," 284.1. E.C.H. is a reversal of H.C.E., but what about C.H.E. or C.E.H.?

265.4 "Elm Lefanunian above mansioned" (264.12–14)
proves Joyce's elm and stone those that Le Fanu
establishes in the first chapter of *The House by the
Churchyard*. The stone is a tombstone and Shaun
is a "tombstone mason" (113.34. Cf. 293.23–25).

272.18–21 "Taletub" introduces Swift with his Houyhnhnms
and a Viconian sequence of horses: "Whoan, tug,
trace, stirrup."

280.32 Horace again: "fount Bandusian" and "lalage,"
229.10. See 57.22; 58.18.

286.3 "P.t.l.o.a.t.o." See 286.18: "Plates to lick one and
turn over."

287.19 "Balbose." After his first appearance (4.30),
Balbus recurs: 37.16, 467.16, 518.34, 552.19.

290.5 "O Shee . . . 4.32 M.P." O'Shea is Parnell's
Kitty. Parnell was an M.P. 432 is the year St.
Patrick landed in Ireland.

291.5–6 "Inseuladed as Crampton's peartree." Isabel is as
isolated as the bust of Sir Philip Crampton in
Dublin. The bust is gone now along with Nelson's
Pillar and Bloom's house. The Pigeon House was
being demolished in 1967. Dublin blows up or
tears down reminders of Joyce or, as in the case of
the beach where Stephen walked and Gerty sat,
fills them in to build factories. The Wellington
Monument, the National Library, and the Magazine next. Lucky that Joyce had so little to do
with the Hotel Shelbourne or, for the matter of
that, with my other favorite hotel, the Savoy in
London, though he mentions the Savoy operas
often enough.

292.26–27 "No mouth has the might to set a mearbound to
the march of a landsmaul" parodies Parnell's

speech at Cork: "No man has a right to fix the boundary of the march of a nation." (*Landsmaal* is the common speech of Norway; "Mear" or *Meer* is German, sea.) Cf. "If you soil may . . . guett me prives" (614.16), a free version of Parnell's "If you throw me to [my enemies] . . . see to it that you secure value for the sacrifice." See St. John Ervine, *Parnell,* London, 1925, pp. 219, 295. Joyce recommended Ervine's book (*Letters,* I, 241) as guide to the matter of Parnell in the *Wake,* e.g., Pigott's "hesitency," Parnell's fire escape, Kitty O'Shea, Joe Biggar, Isaac Butt.

293.4–5   These lines, echoing a passage in *A Vision,* are among several references to Yeats, mostly in connection with gyres, on this page and the next two pages, e.g., "lazily . . . lapis" (293.11), "Ellis" (one of Yeats's collaborators, 294.8), Ossian (294.13), "Byzantium" (294.27), "dreaming back" (295.10–11), "instructor" (295.22), "Gyre" (295.23–24).

293.9–11   "Murphy." Cf. Murphy-Morpheus, *Ulysses,* 639, 660, and "Murphybuds" (*FW,* 161.29), beds and potatoes. Joyce liked Beckett's *Murphy.*

293.22   "Vieus Von DVbLIn." Add the capitals with a liberal imagination and you get 566, the number of woman (pp. 13–14), half of 1132. Cf. "liv" (293.29) or 54, another of A.L.P.'s numbers.

293.L2   "Sprung Verse." A possible reference to Hopkins. "Pantifox" (bridge-builder, 293.F2) may be Robert Bridges, who preserved Hopkins' poems. "Dappled" (294.1), though one of Yeats's words, is Hopkins' favorite word.

295.32   "Dunloop." Dunlop tires, standing for cycles, appear frequently in the *Wake,* e.g., 44.12; 58.4.

295.F1   The Jukes and Kallikacks (twins) appear several times, e.g., 33.24; 137.11–12.

296.1–2   "Lemmas quatsch," one of many references to

"Lebens Quatsch," a waiter's interpretation of Joyce's request in Zurich for lemon squash. *Lebens Quatsch* (*Quatsch* is German, nonsense), said Joyce, is what life is. Cf. "woman squelch," 392.36.

296.F1 "Parsee ffrench" is Percy French, who wrote "Are you there, Michael, are you there?" (296.13–14) and "Phil, the Fluter" (297.18–19).

297.20 "Hurdlebury Fenn." Huck Finn confused with Ford of the Hurdles (Dublin) and a muddy swamp or delta. Despite his many references to Mark Twain, Joyce never read him. In a letter (III, 401– 02) he asks a friend to read *Huckleberry Finn* for him and note words or passages that might be of interest: "I have never read it. . . . I shall try to use whatever bears upon what I am doing." Joyce made excellent use of all he did not know— Thomas Aquinas, for example.

297.24 "Triagonal delta." Thematic occurrences of triangle and delta (aside from those in this chapter): 20.17 ("Daleth"), 119.19–22, 165.13–23, 167.1–8, 196.1–3, 221.13, 229.23–24, 492.9, 594.4, 600.6, 608.23, 614.25, 626.31.

299.F4 "The Doodles family." These hieroglyphs were used by Joyce in his manuscript notes to indicate characters and themes. The E on its side is H.C.E. The delta is A.L.P. The reclining T is Tristan. The X is Mamalujo. The square is the title of the book. The caret or inverted V is Shaun. The imperfect E is Shem. These and other hieroglyphs are ex- plained in a letter of March 24, 1924 to Harriet Weaver (*Letters,* I, 213. Cf. I, 216, 242; III, 145, 147).

303.L1 The four centers of serpentine fire seem to refer ironically to D. H. Lawrence at his most occult, e.g., *Psychoanalysis and the Unconscious* and *Fantasia of the Unconscious,* those queer mixtures of Theosophy and Yoga.

305.27–29   Here Joyce mixes up two Moores, George, author of *Ave* and *Vale,* and Thomas, who celebrated "the meeting of the waters" in the Vale of Avoca. Moore's meeting waters and his statue over the urinal near Trinity College pleased Bloom (*Ulysses,* 162). Cf. "meeting waters" (the two girls urinating), 96.14; "Ovoca," 203.15. Here, "maiding waters" are those of the two girls at it again in "the charmful waterloose country . . . minxt the follyages," 8.2–4.

308.R1   "BEEFTAY'S FIZZIN OVER." Cf. 421.9; *Ulysses,* 568. God knows why Joyce was obsessed with this.

CHAPTER XI · 309-82

CHAPTER XI is divided into four parts, in the first of which are the sailor and the tailor. These quarrelers are followed, in the second part, by Buckley and the Russian General. After Earwicker's apology and boast in the third part, comes closing time ("time jings pleas," 310.25–26) in the fourth. All the drunken patrons of Earwicker's bar go home and Earwicker, drunker than they, falls. To celebrate Vico's human age the choice of a pub is fitting: "plubs will be plebs" (312.33). The plebs in the plub are the twelve men, who judge "the pilsener had the baar" (313.14–15), the four old men, and the three soldiers; but the pilsener on trial at the bar, serving drinks, drinking, and making change, dominates the scene. The stories about the Norwegian Captain and the Russian General are about Earwicker, whose marriage is the substance of the first and whose replacement by his son, of the second.

As if poems, these two narratives and the conclusion are interrupted, united, and distinguished by appropriate refrains. "Take off that white hat" and "John Peel" with his coat so grey suit the story of tailor and sailor; the royal wren, sacrificed on St. Stephen's day, and "The Charge of the Light Brigade" suit the story of the Russian General at Balaklava. "Waters parted from the sea," though less obvious than these, seems good enough for closing time. The motifs that link and enlarge the parts of the *Wake* are working here, as appropriately in their contexts as the refrains. Coming and going, the Prankquean supports the comings and goings of the sailor, whose voyages also receive support from the motifs of Noah, Sinbad, and W. S. Gilbert's *Pinafore*. Pidgin English, a language of business, reappears during the business of the suit of clothes. The Cad, back from displacing his father, lends precedent and courage to Buckley, killing his. Echoes of Mookse and Gripes, Box and Cox, and anticipations of Ondt and Gracehoper accompany the conflicts in these stories, both of which come down to earth through the obsessive themes of urination and defecation, the first in the first story, the second in the second. Never was Joyce's use of motif as parallel, link, and enlargement better displayed; and never, as these recurrent analogies suggest, has it been clearer that under each particular of the *Wake,* and whatever the peculiarity of each surface, the same old things go on, over and over—as in life itself.

Earwicker's apology in the third part and closing time in the fourth are clear enough—as simple as anything around here; but the stories in the first two parts are the obscurest part of the *Wake.* Joyce himself (*Letters,* III, 422) called his story of the tailor a "wordspiderweb." Nothing more intricate or more forbidding to assurance and comfortable reading. The reader—if I may change metaphor in midweb—finds himself, in the tale of the sailor, all at sea or, when landed now and again, unable to see the wood for the trees or even the trees in the wood. The causes of confusion are plain. Now in the period of deepest sleep, we dream of drunks, whose exchanges, even in periods of lighter sleep, might tax our sobriety. The problem is who among those drunks in the dream is telling the story of the sailor and who the story of the Russian General. Deferring the latter, let us try the former.

A good guess is that Earwicker at the bar is telling his patrons the story of sailor and tailor. To distract or forestall the "Guinnesses" (309.1), gossiping about what is "no concern" of theirs, Earwicker tells them the truth about his inner conflict and his marriage. It is clear that sailor and tailor embody two of his capacities, that of rover, caught at last, and that of creator. As tailor, he is the father of A.L.P. (cf. "my cold mad feary father," 628.2) and, as a sailor lost on land—not unlike Dylan Thomas' sailor in the "Long-legged Bait"—her husband. That

this "host of a bottlefilled" with his "canterberry bellseyes" is
the "teller" (310.26–30) seems likely; but "teller" could mean
counting money at his till, and, although "canterberry" suggests
tales, blue Canterbury bells could mean the color of his eyes. A
"talerman" suffering from "rheumaniscences" (319.8,17) could
be Earwicker giving his reminiscences or Earwicker as rheu-
matic tailor. A little later, however, the customers are the "tailors" (324.14) who "thricetold the taler" (317.27). "Taler"
(Danish, speaker) could also be the tale of a tailor thricetold by
the Guinnesses. "Pukkelsen, tilltold" (316.1) is hunchbacked
Earwicker (*pukkel* is Danish, hump) telling the story or counting money at his till or both together. If the customers, by way
of gossip, are telling the story of Earwicker's life—our second
guess—they must be co-operative tellers, a sort of "concertium"
(310.14), like those drunks who contribute bits to the story of
the papal bull in *Ulysses* (399–401). As a two-way radio
(309–10), the customers, tuned to H.C.E., receive gossip about
him and broadcast it to the "auricular forfickle" (or an earwig's
ear) of the "Vakingfar sleeper" (310.10). Maybe, after all,
they are broadcasting the story; but earlier (108.21–24) Earwicker's ear is the trademark of a "broadcaster . . . (Hear!
Calls! Everywhere!)." What is broadcast now may be "the balk
of the deaf" (309.3) and Earwicker, a little deaf, may cup his
ear in vain (321.22), but he is cupping his ear for orders for
drinks. In this confusion of broadcaster and receiver, of teller
and told, of taler and tailor all we know for sure is that someone
is telling a story in a pub about a publican. But, taking one thing
with another, we may conclude, without assurance, that Earwicker, the tailor, is the likelier teller. It may be that in this
"foggy doze. . . . among incomputables about an uncomeout-
able" we feel, while agreeing to this, that "threestory sorratelling
was much too many" (367.15,24,31–32). The three sorrows of
twostory telling are more than enough for me.

While the "tolvtubular high fidelity" radio of the Ibsen-Swift
"Ligue of Yahooth" is broadcasting gossip about H.C.E. to his
ear (the anatomy of which is given in detail, 310.11–21), our
"hoary frother" is serving drinks—"slaunty" (310.33–311.4).

The story of Kersse, the tailor, and the Norwegian Captain—whoever is telling it—begins amid a confusion of befores and afters with "once there was" (311.5–9), a good way to begin a story. Bloom thinks of a Norwegian captain in *Ulysses* (61), and in "An Encounter" the little boy is fascinated by a Norwegian sailor. Adding a tailor to the sailor, the Prankquean's story predicts their encounter (23.10–11): "How kirssy the tiler made a sweet unclose to the Narwhealian captol." Since "pughs and keaoghs" (349.3), unless minded, are easily confused, it is likely that Kersse is Persse O'Reilly, who, as Scandinavian invader, is also a sailor. Sailor and tailor are twins of a sort, like Mookse and Gripes. As twins without, so twins within, where all twins are divided and united. If Earwicker is telling this story of the twins within him, he must be picking at the wax in his ear with a pencil (311.10–11) the better to hear himself.

Hardly has the tailor "buttonhaled" the sailor than Kate, intruding, tells the "lord of the barrels" that she has not lost the key of "Efas-Taem" or, by Egyptian reversal, the meat-safe. Reversal and female O promise a renewal that the Book of the Dead (309.3) has already hinted. Her interruption is the first of many that plague narrator and reader alike: calls for drink, pauses to make change, visits to the urinal, and gossip about the host, that Norman "strongbowth" and "leadder," who, having fallen from his ladder, deserves "awake." To wake him decently the three soldiers call for Bass and O'Connell's Dublin ale (311.15–20).

The present distractions over, the story begins again. Where, the sailor asks the "ship's husband" (a shipping agent), can I have a suit made? Though echoing the Prankquean's riddle and Isabel's enigmatic footnote (301.F1), his question receives an answer: at the shop of Kersse, successor to Ashe and Whitehead. In this shop, the sailor bargains suitably in pidgin English for a suit for "his lady her master" (whoever that is) with trousers cut like Cardinal Manning's cassock. The bargain sealed by a spit in the fist, the sailor takes his "fringe sleeve"—"A barter, a parter." "Stolp, tief," shouts the unpaid tailor, now one with the ship's husband and the Prankquean's Van Hoother, "come

bag to Moy Eireann!" Like the Prankquean herself, the depart-
ing sailor answers, "All lykkehud!" and off he goes on a voyage
for Noah's forty days and forty nights. "Holey bucket, dinned he
raign!" (311.21–312.12. Cf. 21.18–27).

The story pauses for comments to the "earpicker" by the
drinkers on "the rigout for her wife's lairdship" that the tailor
has been stuck with. After reviewing the story of that "queen of
Prancess," the Earl of Howth's "niece," the twelve men stray to
religious, civil, and legal matters: Occasional Conformity, the
Pilgrimage of Grace, and the Petition of Right (all to be found
in Webster's dictionary). A list of the twelve customers assures
us of "all quorum." It is about time "to have another"—another
"agitator" (O'Connell) and another "bassabosuned" Bass
(312.13–313.6). Kersse-Earwicker, agreeing to serve drinks to
the twelve on his jury and, maybe, to continue the story, pauses
at his till to make change and count his Irish coins, while his
jury "pushed their whisper in his hairing" (313.7–30).

Their gossip, reminding him of his "misshapes," his fall, the
sins and flood of Genesis, Babel, and the divorce of "kiddy"
O'Shea (with Parnell as "correspondent"), leads to the seventh
thunder (313.32–314.18), which includes "humtadump" and,
hopefully, "turnup." The three soldiers, noting his fall, remember Humpty Dumpty's from the Magazine wall and Finnegan's
departure from this "mortar scene" by way of a ladder. "Arbo-
riginally" brings Adam into Earwicker's company. The scandalous radio with "extravent intervulve coupling" broadcasts
news of the whole family, from aunt and uncle to those "sohns
of a blitzh." Suddenly a movie projector, this machine, pleasing
eye as well as ear, also brings a family picture with "flash substi-
ttles" to a silver screen. But what about his "dopter. . . . The
lappel of his size?" those gossips "addled" (314.19–315.7).

At this point "Burniface" (a blushing Boniface or publican)
leaves the bar to "let flow." After the "deluge" (at once Noah's
and the Prankquean's), the "skibber breezed in . . . drip-
ping," with "his stickup in his hand to show them none ill feeling." Once the tailor, this exhibitionist is now the sailor, returning from his voyage to "bierhiven," or a Dane landing near the

Tolka at Clontarf. The phone number of his Danish beerhaven is "clown toff, tye hug fliorten" or Clontarf 1014, the date of the battle (315.9–36). The "good mothers gossip" welcome "Brewinbaroon" (now Brian Boru), who, they feared, had gone "down to the button of his seat" with McGinty—down to "Divy and Jorum's locquor." When he gets canned, Earwicker says, a "pusspull" of tomato juice is a good pick-me-up. "What's the good word?" (what will you have to drink?), asks the "shop's housebound" as he spreads on the bar a repast of fishballs and other dainties (316.8–317.21). "Say wehrn!" If Adam was the first "breachesmaker," say the drinkers, Kersse was the second. Their talk, turning to Grace O'Malley's Howth and from that to A.L.P., begins and ends with the singing of "John Peel" (cf. 31.28–29). Between songs they allude to Tristan, Guinevere, marriage, Omar, Annapolis (Ann's school for sailors), Eden, and Earwicker's rainbow of the seven sins (317.22–319.2). Allusions to Shakespeare, Congreve (*The Double Dealer*), Berkeley (tar water for tars), and Rimbaud ("tromb" and "gulpstroom") precede Earwicker's second departure for relief (319.20–35).

"Hops!" says he as he leaves for the "oasthouse" (a fitting outhouse for a beerhaven) to "empty dempty him down to the ground" (319.23,36) . . . "And, soaking scupper, didn't he drain (320.30–31). Before, after, or during this departure the story resumes. Back in port, the sailor, quarreling with "stitchimesnider," objects at his second fitting to the cut of what is supposed to be the latest "civille row faction." (Plainly this row about Savile Row is a civil war.) So off to sea he goes again, pursued by the shouts of the tailor (320.1–31). "As the baffling yarn sailed in circles" (320.35), it is more and more difficult to separate Earwicker in pub or can from sailor, tailor, Prankquean, and Van Hoother or pub from ship or shop—and will be "Till Irinwakes from Slumber Deep" (321.17–18).

Aware that the drinkers have "liquorally no more powers [whisky] to their elbow," the publican comes back from "outback's" to "Wazwollenzee Haven [*haben*] to give them their beerings" and to count the money in his till "with an arc of his covethand." Whether it is called Le Fanu's "Phoenix" or the "mulligar," the pub is the scene of Finnegan's wake (321.1–36), where songs ("Take off that white hat" and "John Peel") accompany the publican's revival and the resumption of his story. The "bespoking" tailor calls the sailor a "welsher," and he accuses the tailor of having "misfutthered" that "shook of cloakses." During this exchange, talk at the bar strays from the races at Baldoyle and the Curragh to Vico's "recoursing" race from "spark to phoenish." The "dielectrick" (electric dialectic?) strays again through "mhos" (ohms) to the blowing up of British monuments: Nelson's Pillar, King Billy's statue, and Cromwell's "millestones." It was Dan O'Connell who "ham muncipated" these drunks from foreign oppressors and their memorials. Three new patrons, who have been "malttreating" themselves, join the crowd (322.1–36).

The "bugganeering wanderducken," a union of Earwigger and the Flying Dutchman, leaves the pub again to pump ship (see *Ulysses,* 335): "One can smell off his wetsments how he is coming from a beach of promisck." The "salestrimmer" (at once sailor and tailor), coming back like a Danish ghost walking ("spoeking, gen and gang"), is hailed by his guests: "their joke was coming home to them" (323.1–36)—their "encient, the murrainer, and wallruse. . . . ye seal that lubs you lassers" from H.M.S. *Pinafore.* "Heave, coves, emptybloddy!. . . . sod the tailors" (324.8–14).

At this point in the proceedings—if you can call them this—a radio takes over, not the metaphorical twelve-tubed machine but seemingly an actual radio that broadcasts a variety of news (324.18–325.10): First an announcement of missing persons (call Clontarf 1014), then a weather forecast (a "suite of clouds" and a "sotton retch of low pleasure"), then the news ("Giant crash in Aden," followed by Vico's religion, marriage, burial, and divine providence), then advertisements (for Arthur Guinness and Sons Company, Ltd. and Ann Lynch's tea), and, last, bedtime music from the "fourposter harp quartetto" of the four old men. The days of the week in Finnish (325.10–12) mark the broadcast's finish. Jesuitical A.M.D.G. ("for the greeter glossary of code") begins the broadcast and Jesuitical L.S.D. (*Laus semper Deo*) precedes its end. But coming before the advertisements, L.S.D. also implies pounds, shillings, and pence.

After the broadcast, the story, obscured by overlays, draws slowly to an end (325–32). What happens—for those able to brush the overlays aside or to penetrate them—seems this: the tailor, tired of quarreling, proposes peace through union of the contenders. Let the "nowedding captain" (325.27) marry "Nanny Ni Sheeres" (328.14), the tailor's daughter. By this arrangement the "faulter-in-law" (325.15) will become son-in-law to a father-in-law, "jonjemsums both, in sailsmanship"; for "the two breasts of Banba [Ireland] are her soilers and her toilers" (325.15–26). Such agreement of squabbling twins—a *Détente Cordiale*—deserves the blessing of the four apostles and their ass and the approval of "tome, thick and heavy" (325.31–34).

Before "A Trinity judge will crux [his] boom" (326.4. Cf. 102–03), however, the sailor must submit to baptism and other sacraments of "our roomyo connellic relation" (326.6–15). "Tina-bat-Talur" (tiny, Sinbad, bat), the tailor's Catholic daughter, seems a combination of A.L.P. and Isabel, "the lippeyear's wonder." Rivers, girls, flowers, and a mirror surround her "trickle bed." The bells of *Sechseläuten* and the Angleus and the litany of the Blessed Virgin ("house of ivary, dower of gould") help set an "Eriweddying on fire." As Swift's *Journal to Stella* ("peepat my prize") makes the wedding private, so newspapers, the "airish timers" and the "racy turf," make it public (327.3–36). Lord Nelson and Lady Hamilton will attend the wedding at "Sing Mattins in the Fields" of "our fiery quean," a Prankquean from Spenser, who wrote an "Epithalamion" for a similar occasion "with Elizabeliza blessing the bedpain" (328.21–36). Nevertheless, on this "hooneymoon" of Noah's raven and dove, the groom, a "blondblubber" now, feels "Cawcaught. Coocaged." He fears a "rain of Tarar" (329.11–35). And Father Mathew, the advocate of temperance, looks "taytotally" at all the drunks at the wedding (330.5–6).

Norway's national anthem about "this land with a thousand homes" (330.7–8) introduces the domestic life of those "phaymix cupplerts," united till "deaf do his part" (331.2–5). "He goat a berth." And she, happy that "her faiths is altared," "cot a manege" (got a bed, man, menage, 330.28; 331.3). She says: "I'll tittle your barents [?] if you stick that pigpin upinto meh!" (331.12–13). Children, arriving in due course, are the twins and "An apple" or Isabel (330.30–31).

"Snip snap snoody" go the fatal sisters, like three tailors. Now at our "historyend," Earwicker "put off the ketyl and they made three." When they put on the kettle and have tea at the end of the Prankquean's story (23), Vico's second thunder rumbles; for woman's domestic triumph is man's fall. Now the teakettle of A.L.P.'s triumph precedes the eighth thunder (332.1–9), which, starting with "Pappa" and "parr," includes "fall," and ends with "daddydoodled." But "Fine again" is hopeful. "The act of goth" (thunder) interrupts for a moment "the tolk of Doolin" (gossip) in the pub, the "landshop" to which his "loudship was converted" (332.10,23–24). A father now, the proprietor can expect trouble from the Cad (332.32–34). As the Cad's faint presence is a premonition of Buckley, so "Check or slowback" and a scattering of Polish and Russian words are a premonition of a Slavic general checked at the bottom of his career.

But before the Russian General appears, there is "Enterruption. . . . Dvershen." Kate comes in again, this time with a message from A.L.P., announcing bedtime. "Pierce me, hunky, I'm full of meunders" (333.22–23), says H.C.E.'s "hot and tot lass." However "whishtful to licture her caudal," our "fader huncher" (*Vater unser*) prays—suitably in a context of insects: "lead us not into reformication" (333.26–35). Kate's embassy recalls her tour of the Wellington "mewseyfume" (333.16–18; 334.6–16), in which, under the auspices of Browne and Nolan now, Earwicker is at once Napoleon and Wellington on "his speak quite hoarse. Dip." "Dip" replaces Kate's original "Tip" because Earwicker-Gladstone (hoping for Home Rule) thinks it "time for my tubble." Yet business detains him at the bar, on

the "mizzatint wall" of which are two pictures, one of the charge
of the Light Brigade (looking forward to the Crimean War—
"crimm crimms"), the other (recalling the tailor) of John Peel
going out with his hounds in the morning (334.24–34). Kate
leaves while the "pub's pobbel done a stare" at her and the picture of the Light Brigade, which puts them in mind of "Bully-
clubber burgherly" and "the rush in general." So they call "on
the one" (H.C.E.) for another Hibernian nights entertainment,
another "tale of a tublin" (335.13–28).

That they have Earwicker's sin in mind is proved by allusions
to Wellington, Grace O'Malley, and the two girls in the Park,
"where obelisk rises when odalisks fall" (335.30–33). It is long
since Earwicker has made the sign of the cross, gone to Mass
("enterellbo all taller Danis") or paused at the Angelus (the
"wold made fresh"). Thoughts of Adam's apple and "the welt
of his plow" delay the story (336.1–29). And while the "tale
tarries" there are thoughts of Earwicker's trial (337.2–3), of
the affair in the Park with the two girls and the three soldiers,
and of the evidence of Sylvia Silence (337.15–31. Cf. 61.1–
11). This review of Earwicker's guilt prepares us for the punish-
ment he deserves. Buckley had reason to shoot the Russian
General. Shooting him in the Crimea is less crime than retribu-
tion for crimes; and a general, more than a particular man, is all
sinners, all fathers—as Buckley or *bouchal* (Gaelic, young
man) is every son, who, as the story of the Cad makes plain,
must kill the father and take his place. Now it is time for the
story.

"We want Bud," shout the drinkers, "the man that shunned
the rucks on Gereland"—we want Taf ("Tancred Artaxerxes
Flavin") and the story we have heard a thousand times. Let
"Milster Malster" take the chair (337.32–338.3). Taking the
chair does not necessarily mean telling the story. If H.C.E., the
chairman, is telling the story of his own destruction, the form he
chooses is odd. Why should his story, echoing Mutt and Jute,
take the form of a dialogue between Butt and Taff, his sons? It
may be that Joyce, recasting Earwicker's more or less straightforward narrative, put it into dramatic form; but it is no less likely

that Butt and Taff are a vaudeville team—with Taff as stooge—
on television. Calling for Butt and Taff, the customers may be
asking Earwicker to turn the set on. As chairman, he may be
part of the audience. But as author of the *Wake,* Earwicker
commands any form. The broadcasts on TV (341–42, 345–
46, 349–50, 353) may be interruptions of the story rather than
its source. Why, if its source, should these interludes be enclosed
in square brackets? On the whole, I feel, at this time and without
conviction, that Earwicker himself is telling another on himself.

Since Butt and Taff are the twins, talking again about father,
we can expect parallels: the Mookse and the Gripes, for example, and the Ondt and the Gracehoper. We get what we expect. Since they are also talking about war, we can expect—and
we get—other parallels: Waterloo, Clontarf, and the Boyne. As
for the Crimean War, there are appropriate references to the
battles of Sevastopol, Balaklava, Inkerman, and Malakhov, to
Generals Raglan and Totleben, and to the Turks. Russian words
abound. And Tennyson's "Charge of the Light Brigade" provides a refrain.

Taff (Shaun) and Butt (Shem), friars or brothers, talk of the
"boss," that "intrepidation of our dreams which we foregot at
wiking . . . and the bleakfrost chilled our ravery." Killing "old
Dolldy Icon," the Russian bear, the Czar or "little farther," is
the dream, straight from Freud's unconscious, of every "little
soon" (338–39). Butt does the important talking. Taff, as
stooge, makes comments: "Say mangraphique, may say nay por
daguerre!" *La guerre,* in Taff's French, becomes Daguerre because a photographer suits a conflict which, like most between
the twins, is one between ear and eye—a conflict to be settled
here perhaps by "verbivocovisual" TV, which often offends eye
and ear alike. (What matter that there was no TV at the time of
Earwicker's dream or Joyce's writing?)

Freud's dream-work—censorship with all its displacements
and condensations—may account in part for the extreme obscurity of Butt's Oedipal story, which, if separated from the work of
dream and Joyce's compulsive arabesques, is this: Butt, an Irish
private in the British army, catches the Russian General with his

pants down, defecating and stinking—the "so so sewn of a fitchid" (340.2. A fitchew is a polecat. See "polecad," 341.1). There the General is, "expousing his old . . . tailtottom by manurevring in open ordure" (344.16–17). But Butt is unable to take immediate advantage of this opportunity. The "frighteousness" (343.34–35) of the great man—despite his lowly occupation—accounts for Butt's "hissindensity" (350.13; 349.3), a "hesitency" like that of Pigott, trying to kill Parnell, Ireland's father. "I adn't the arts to" (345.2–3), says Butt, who finds himself in the position of Noah's peeping sons (344.36) or of Milton's Adam, in the act of "manifest 'tis obedience" (343.36) to God the father. It is not until, defecation over, the General wipes himself with a "sad of tearfs" (346.22) that Butt finds the courage to shoot the terrible old man.

The Cad's interview with Earwicker provides precedent and parallel. *Cadet* and *bouchal* are plainly the same young man. Each kills father, the first by asking the time, the second by pulling a trigger. Echoes of Chapter II abound. Hosty's wren (44.16) reappears at the present sacrifice: "the Riss, the Ross, the sur of all Russers" (340.35) and, later, mixed with Eve and the Prankquean, "The rib, the rib, the quean of oldbyrdes" (348.33–34). The Cad's Fox Goodman (35.30), the bellmaster who rang the bell for noon, is around, somewhat displaced (328.26); and it is precisely at the Cad's hour, "tolfoklokken" (353.15), that Butt shoots the General. Yeats, who figures in the Cad's story, is also here: "I met with whom it was too late" (345.13). His Celtic Twilight, responsive to the context of defecation, becomes his *"cultic twalette"* (344.12). Like the Cad, Butt has a pipe (341.17). That Taff also "smugs to bagot" (345.15,25) prepares us for the eventual union of the two sons, who, once they are together, are Buckley.

Other parallels enlarge the story: Sinn Fein and the Easter rising (346.28), the "Boxerising" (347.29), the Soviet rising against the Czar, "with the sickle . . . [and] hummer" (341.10). A parody of Synge's *Playboy* (344.12–16) reminds us of another son killing his father or trying to. Inevitably in this context old Cambronne is back with his *mot* (352.21–22), and

Wellington with his big, wide harse (352.12–13), confused at
the moment with the Ondt and the Gracehoper—as the Boxer
rising is confused with Gilbert's *Box and Cox;* for the conflict,
not only between father and son, is also between son and son,
for whom, when united at last, the shooting of the "roshashana-
ral" (340.27) marks a new year—as twelve o'clock, a new day.

Of the television programs in their italics and square brackets,
the first (341–42), broadcast by Bett and Tipp, "our swapstick
quackchancers" (the exchanging twins as slapstick comedians),
and sponsored by "The Irish Race and World," is about the race
track, a Viconian round that involves all the people of the
Wake, from Mick, Nick, and the Maggies to the two girls showing a clean pair of heels to "Immensipater" or H.C.E. himself.
Taff is aware of this "sports report" from the London Regional
(342.34), but whether, as Tipp, he is in it, is problematical.
The second program to be "teilweisioned" (345–46), including
the drinkers in the Mullingar, the shooting of the Russian General, and the new year, makes the connection between broadcast
and pub even more problematical. We wonder again if the story
of Taff, Butt, and the General is on television—a program which
these reports are interrupting—or whether television programs
interrupt Earwicker's story. Such uncertainty could be the work
of dream. The third program (349–50), "following a fade of
transformed Tuff and . . . Batt," shows General Earwicker
confessing his sins to all "his tellavicious nieces" while his sons,
their "bitts bugtwug their teffs," seem horses of the "light barri-
cade." Maybe it was wrong to feel that Earwicker is telling the
story or maybe Earwicker is telling it on television by the aid of
tape, which Joyce, having invented television, could easily have
invented too.

To identify all the allusions that clot the dialogue of Butt and
Taff would require more space than at my disposal, and to explain all the difficulties of this *"eeridreme"* (342.30), more time
and brain. But I have space enough and time to notice a little of
the action: Annoyed by impiety, Taff hits Butt, as in the school-
room (303.23) Kev hits Dolph (344.7–8). The blow forgiven
by magnanimous Butt, the twins take communion (345.26–33).

Tell me, says Taff, like a good stooge, just how Buckley shot the
Russian General—and don't leave out the sod of turf (346.20–
22). Before getting to that, Butt pauses to drink a toast in "ab-
sents wehrmuth" (348.13, a combination of absinthe, ver-
mouth, German sweet melancholy and military courage) to the
old bugger whom, at story's end, he will shoot.

"I shuttm. . . . Hump to dump!" (352.14–15) says Butt,
that fitting representative of a nation of "shorpshoopers"
(352.26). I shot the "connundurumchuff" with "backsights to
his bared." "Bullyclaver of ye" (352.23), says Taff. You shot
the "mangoat . . . in souber civiles?" "Yastsar!" says Butt,
"In . . . sobre saviles!" (353.2–9. Savile Row connects the
General with the tailor.) Butt overcame his hesitancy when he
saw the General wiping himself with a sod of turf, an insult to
the old sod—to Ireland itself—that could not be endured; so,
like the sparrow, he shot Cock Robin (353.15–21).

The italics in square brackets that follow this climax may be
another broadcast, but, if so, it differs in kind and function from
its predecessors. Not an interlude, it concerns the cataclysmic
effects of shooting father: the *"abnihilisation of the etym,"* the
"moletons skaping with mulicules." Atomic fission (that Joyce
invented along with television) joins the destruction of the word
(*etym*) that creates *ab nihil*. *"Coventry," "Pinkadindy"* (London), and *"Hullulullu"* predict the bombing of those cities—
cities that H.C.E., the builder of cities, built. (As Joyce, who
with some reason thought himself a prophet, predicted these disasters, so, a few pages later, he predicts—or so I fancy—my
class in *Finnegans Wake:* "the same old tincoverdull bauble-
class," 359.12.) *"Plumpkins fairlygosmother,"* introducing Cinderella, indicates twelve o'clock, the end of a cycle and the beginning of another, a Donnybrook *"dawnybreak in Aira"*
(353.22–33).

After the cataclysm, the "birstol boys" (Borstal and Bristol,
the pub) return—antagonists no longer, but *"now one and the
same person"* or Buckley himself. Taking the *"pledge of fianna-
ship,"* they join the company of "Faun MacGhoul," killed by
"Goll's gillie." In short, these "samuraised twimbs" after their

"murdhering idies" of March have become the "rising germinal." They will constitute the new father "till butagain budly" gets out his gun again (353.34–354.36). Such is "the toil of his tubb." Another interlude in italics and square brackets (355.1– 7) announces the end and the beginning of a cycle, *"ideally reconstituted,"* according to Vico.

The harrowing of hell, the fall of Finnegan from his scaffold, and the "enjined Egyptians" promise revival after death. "Khummer-Phett," which sounds like something from the Book of the Dead, is only Danish *kumme* (toilet) and French *pet* (fart), straight from the *"cultic twalette"* (355.16–32). The story we have heard is true of "each and ilkermann of us," says the teller, drawing his moral. Since the "gentlemen" he is addressing are the "guiltshouters" in the pub, this passage (356.1– 10) makes H.C.E. either the teller or the moralist of another's story. An echo of Shem's riddle (170.4–5,23–24), making H.C.E. "asame," may assure us of his continuing identity but does little to settle our doubts about the teller (356.12–14).

Earwicker has been reading, he continues, a suppressed book, distinguished by "wordcraft" (*Ulysses?*) and "expurgative plates" by Aubrey Beardsley, who delighted in arabesques (the *Wake?*): "Ars we say . . . *Kunstful.*" Arse and *Kunst* remind him of those two girls: "one which I have pushed my finker in for the movement. . . . another which I have fombly fongered freequuntly" (356.16–357.26). Public confession of what the pub has suspected all along precedes a profession of innocence. "Cad's truth," says he, "I am, I am big altoogooder" (358.9– 16).

"He beached the bark of his tale" (358.17) with the whole family aboard. Is this, we ask, an assurance at last that H.C.E. has told the story of Butt and Taff or is his "tale" no more than a tale about him or the confession and profession we have just heard? As for what they say the boys or girls did to him, he may have done it himself to himself. A catalogue indicates other possibilities (358.27–359.20).

A radio program takes over at this point. You have been listening, the announcer tells the hams, to the "fiveaxled produc-

tion" of *The Coach With The Six Insides.*" (If this production
has been broadcast, we ask, how can Earwicker have "beached
the bark of his tale"?) Since Joyce thought the *Wake* a square
(299.F4) or a cube ("cubehouse," 5.14), it is likely that this
coach—a kind of cube, and cubes have six sides—is the *Wake* itself. A cubical coach with six insides can also mean with six
passengers inside. But there are only five in Earwicker's family
—the five axles on which the *Wake* moves. Who is the sixth
inside? Kate or Joe? Six are listed (335.7–9): "Holispolis
[H.C.E.] . . . with mabby and sammy and sonny and sissy
and mop's varlet de shambles." The last of these seems a composite of Kate and Joe. Maybe, however, the sixth passenger is
Joyce; but he should be the producer instead of John Whiston,
whoever he is (359.22–29). John and stone suggest Shaun,
who, though the unlikeliest producer in the world, carried the
letter in his mailbag before producing it.

Having made this announcement with appropriate songs
(359.27–29), the radio "hookup" diffuses a program of music
(359.31–360.16), which, mixing singers, songs, instruments,
and composers, is among the most pleasing parts of the *Wake.*
Jenny Lind (the Swedish Nightingale), Rossini, Bellini, Merca-
dante, Meyerbeer, and Pergolesi are there, along with Bach,
Mozart, Haydn, Gluck, John Field, Beethoven, Arthur Sullivan,
and Fox Goodman, the Cad's bellmaster. Every "sound of a
pitch" in the book is there from mother and father to Isabel, the
twins, Swift, and the "Hitherzither" washerwomen. These make
an agreeable composition in which rhythm and sound are in
more than customary accord with sense. (Willard Roosevelt, unable to resist this concert, has set it to music—a double fugue.)
An interlude of birds, flowers, insects, fruit, and trees commends
fertility (360.23–361.35).

Back to the pub now, where the twelve customers condemn
the guilty publican again (361.36–363.16). Recalling the affair
of sailor and tailor (363.17–19), Earwicker begins his apology
and boast: "Guilty but fellows culpows!" All he was doing in
the Park was listening to the "thud of surf" as those two girls
made water "through minxmingled hair" (263.25–26). He is

incapable of "unlifting upfallen girls"—whatever the prudish misunderstandings of "angelsexonism" (363.32–36). Yet girls and snoopers alike "bare whiteness against me" (364.1–2).

The rest of his monologue (to 367.4), which is not unlike Bloom's in the Circe episode, offers few difficulties. Earwicker's rambling—sometimes stuttering—defense covers most themes of the book: the hen and the letter, the Mookse and the Gripes, the trial, Buckley, Swift, the washerwomen, the Floras, those two "lilliths oft I feldt" (366.25), and Isabel, "my deepseep daughter" who rose "out of medsdreams unclouthed when I was pillowing in my brime" (366.13–15. "Brime" includes the crime of incest, prime, bride, and, in the context of stream, sea, and billow, Aphrodite's brine). "Increaminated" (366.17), no doubt, he is nevertheless important, a kind of shitting Russian Caesar ("thit thides or marse makes a good dayle to be shattat," (366.29–30) or "Jukoleon" (367.20), who combines Deucalion, Napoleon, and the "Juke" of Wellington.

At the end of his speech—even during it—the pub takes over with song and gossip. Those drunks sing "Down went McGinty to the bottom of the sea" (366.32–33) and "Casey Jones" (368.27–29), a substitute in this context for Davy Jones. They recite a quatrain from Omar (368.24–26), who has come to mind earlier in the evening (318.17; 319.34). The four critical old men "underrupt" from their "fourdimmansions" the "foggy doze" of pub and publican (367.24–27). Six of those twelve "noodles" resume their gossip, this time about Earwig and the royal hunter (369.6–22. Cf. 30.16–31.3) and A.L.P.'s letter (369.23–370.14). The uncomfortable host has "one on the house" (369.3) and by no means the first one.

Closing time at last. Joe Sockerson, the Danish bouncer, after "rancing there smutsy floskons," prepares to "Shatten up ship" (370.30–371.5). "Tids, genmen, plays," says the host of this "hostillery" as he serves the "Porterfillyers and spirituous suncksters" their "last dropes of summour" before Joe locks the door. Another last drink, another last song before "the Mullinguard minstrelsers" leave for home (371.1–36). Their parting refrains are "Water parted from the sea" (371.7; 372.26;

373.10) and Hosty's ballad about H.C.E. (371.9,21–22;
372.32; 373.9). Shutting up shop recalls—as Bow bells recalled
Dick Whittington—the end of the Prankquean's story: "While
the dumb he shoots the shopper rope. And they all pour forth"
(372.5–6. Cf. 23.5–7). The four senile senators, still singing, go
off in four directions (372.34–373.8) over the "walters of,
hoompsydoompsy walters of" A.L.P., the washerwomen, and
the next chapter, so introduced. "Horkus chiefest ebblynuncies"
(373.12) is at last alone.

A sketch of his character might help us pin the shifty man
down—a man who "shook be ashaped of hempshelves, hiding
that shepe in his goat." This sheepshaped goat or goatshaped
sheep gave "our kindom from an orse" (horse, arse, bear). All
he did was hunting the "pairk" (the pair in the Park) and "begetting a wife which [like the Prankquean] begame his niece."
He conceals himself under many identities but is always Persse
O'Reilly. Now alone in the pub, like Finnegan in his coffin
(24.6–7), he is taking his leisure like a god on a pension
(373.13–36).

Like the reader of "Dadgerson's dodges" (Lewis Carroll's
Alice) or the "trancedone boyscript" (the letter and Eliot's
early poem), the reader of Earwicker's character must look
closely with ears open. "The auditor [of the *Wake*] learns." We
recommend "Epistlemadethemology for deep dorfy doubtlings"
(374.1–18). Finn MacCool's sin, fall, wake, and trial prove that
"You'll have loss of fame from Wimmegame's fake. . . . It
will wecker your earse" (375.16–19). This resumé of Earwicker and the *Wake*—in which, as everywhere else in the book,
everything in the book comes up again—is not unlike Kate's
tour of the museum. "Tik" and "Jik" (376.5,13) replace her
"Tip." Vico's sequence of religion, marriage, burial, and renewal (377) enlarges the scene and expands the time. "Our
myterbilder his fullen aslip" but the cock of "gallus day" will
wake him (377.21,26). The risen host is the Host; so "pass the
grace for Gard sake" (377.30–31. Cf. 7.7–8). Eucharist or
Word, this "traumconductor" knows that words assure his resurrection; for "In the buginning is the woid" (378.29). A "non-

irishblooder that becomes a Greenislender overnight" (378.11)
deserves a letter (though "We don't know the sendor to
whome," 379.2–3), but not that "pairsadrawsing" in the Park
and those three soldiers. Let the bells of *Sechseläuten* and the
Angelus ring out his renewal: "BENK BANK BONK" (379.4–
8,30). So informed about the hero, we return to the pub to see
how he takes advantage of his solitude.

What did he do? And who was he at all at the time? To answer the second question first: Earwicker, alone in his "house of
the hundred bottles with the radio beamer tower," is Roderick
or Rory O'Connor, the "last pre-electric king of Ireland." This
king, who has appeared earlier as "rory" (3.13) and "rudrik"
(369.18), was an incompetent, who, having the force to expel
the invading Normans, lacked the enterprise. His predecessor in
the dynasty of Tara, "King Arth Mockmorrow"—"(God guard
his . . . comicsongbook soul!)"—seems a combination of Cormac MacArt and Dermot MacMurrough, whose wife brought
the Normans in. Like Rory among Strongbow, MacMurrough,
and Laurence O'Toole, Earwicker is alone and incompetent.

To answer the first question second: alone in his pub, Earwicker, drunk already, "went heeltapping" or drinking the
dregs of all the glasses left on the bar. His action emerges here
and there from the sweep of one long sentence—or something
more or less than a sentence—that is like Mrs. Bloom's monologue except for the commas. Redundant and intricate, this gush
from a pub has an Irish intonation and rhythm—not that of
Synge's Wicklow or Galway, but of Joyce's Dublin. This more-
or-less-than-sentence is one of the merriest parts of the "comicsongbook" *Wake*.

"With the wonderful midnight thirst was on him" and with
"Hauburnea's liveliest vinnage on the brain," the heeltapper begins "allocutioning in bellcantos" and speaking in "diversed
tonguesed," for which references to Goldsmith, Smollett, Congreve, Scott, Hood, and Gay establish a literary context. What
was Earwicker going and doing at all? Like Joyce, sopping up
the dregs of old literature to make new "bellcantos" in "diversed
tonguesed," Earwicker is writing *Finnegans Wake*. Like every-

thing else in it, this has happened before: once, when alone in his pub, Earwicker feared the fender pounding on the door (64.1–21) and again (70.13–36). In the first of these previews, the "battering babel" and "belzey babble" downstairs, awaking the whole family, brings them down to see what the matter is. In the second, the fender shouts abuse in "mooxed metaphores" at the "heeltapper" in the pub. It may be that the caddish fender at the door, not heeltapping Earwicker, is composing the "belzey babble" of the *Wake* on these occasions, but reversal is common around here, and the parallel holds. On the present occasion, Earwicker's *Wake* is the hen's letter (382.10–14), a "Newestlatter . . . seen, sold and delivered and all's set for restart after the silence."

What did he do before restarting? After drinking the various leavings—of Guinness, Jameson, "Coccola," and O'Connell's Dublin ale—and, so inspired, writing the *Wake,* "he came acrash a crupper" with so great a noise that "cathering candled" or Kate with a candle comes downstairs to see what the matter is (382.17–19). She finds Earwicker "sort of a sate on accomondation and the very boxst in all his composs. . . . just slumped to throne"—at once the throne of poor old Rory and the commode or toilet of the pub. (In a later parallel to this scene, 556.31–557.12, Kate comes down to find Earwicker "in his honeymoon trim" [naked] with his "clookey in his fisstball.")

"Slumped to throne" though he be, a voyage promises change for the better. The good ship *"Nansy Hans"* is about to sail away to nightlands with "Larry" on the forecastle and "Faugh MacHugh O'Bawler" at the wheel. Feagh MacHugh O'Byrne is a character in "Follow Me Up to Carlow" (382.30), a ballad by P. J. McCall. (See *Letters,* III, 428–29.) But Faugh MacHugh O'Bawler is also Ford Madox Ford, who published an early version of the next chapter in his *transatlantic review.* (See *Letters,* I, 405.) "Larry's on the focse," preparing us for Tristan and Isolde in the next chapter, must be D. H. Lawrence, a specialist in "focse." "As who has come returns" looks forward to Vico's *ricorso* after this all-too-human human age, in which communicating, no longer a matter of gestures, hieroglyphs, or misses in prints, has been entrusted to radio and television.

309.19   "Bellini-Tosti." Bellini composed *La sonnambula,* which seems appropriate to dream. Tosti was a teacher of singing in London.

313.22–28   The pigs, hares, chickens, and the hounds and horses (321.26–27) are images on Irish coinage from the halfpenny to the half crown. Yeats had a hand in their designing.

314.17   "Sortor's risorted" is one of several references to Carlyle's book, e.g., "shutter reshottus" (352.25), "Tawfulsdreck" (68.21), "Naysayers" (108.29). These references, along with some to *A Tale of a Tub,* support the theme of clothing: "One Life One Suit" (63.16).

322.1,5   "Take off that white hat" is a music-hall song or gag mentioned by Bloom (*Ulysses,* 167). Cf. 322.-5,8; 342.11–12,22–23; 607.3; 623.9. White hat or white head includes Whitehead, the name of the tailor, and blond Finn MacCool. Other references to hats (signs of identity?): "toll hut" and "nate-cup" (334.7,10), "topheavy hat" (335.35). Cf. "Whitehed. . . . Whitehowth" (535.22,26).

330.24   "Finn's Hotel" on Nassau Street, Dublin, the place where Nora worked as chambermaid before her elopement, unites Joyce with H.C.E., the caught captain.

334.33   The two pictures on the wall are Christmas calendars from Adam Findlater, the Dublin grocer. Cf. "Foundlitter," 420.35; 558.10; 619.3–4. Findlater's name, including Adam, suggests Finnegan, ladder, and leader. ("Finnleader," 214.11.) Findlater is "our grocerest churcher" (619.3–4) because he built a church known in Dublin as "Findlater's fire escape": "Kerk Findlater's" (533.23).

335.16–17   In his manuscript Joyce calls this passage a "Maori warcry."

349.25   *"The Martyrology of Gorman"* must be Herbert Gorman's biography of Joyce, the martyr.

350.11–17   This passage on Oscar Wilde, the Big White Caterpillar, with his *"sunflawered beautonhole"*—*"the whyfe of his bothem was the very lad's thing to elter his mehind"*—makes it plain that buggery must be included among Earwicker's "deboutcheries." Cf. "drumbume of a narse" (340.23–24), *"pedarrests"* (349.34), "back excits" (368.17–18), "Burgearse" (371.22). The last of these is from Hosty's ballad (46.21). Cf. "breach" (136.-24). "Osion buck" and "fairioes" (326.18) combine Wilde with Mann's Aschenbach (also referred to, 211.1).

359.24   *"The Coach With The Six Insides."* Six insides could also be the six main relationships within the family: of father with mother, son, daughter; of mother with father, son, and daughter. But what about son and daughter and son and son? Maybe, as son and son are the same person, so mother and daughter. But this mixes the count up again. Joyce liked to puzzle us.

361.1–3   The mathematics of nothing anticipates Samuel Beckett. Consider *"Slippery Sam"* (341.36) and "eye of a gull" (377.4–5), which recurs in Beckett's *Malone Dies.*

371.7–8   "Water parted from the sea," which recurs (371.-19–20,31–32; 373.10–11), is an old song, mentioned by Charles Lamb in "A Chapter on Ears" (*Elia*). Hodgart and Worthington ascribe the song to Dr. Arne.

376.11–12   "Delphin. . . . Grusham. . . . Real Hymernians" are three Dublin hotels, the Dolphin, the Gresham, and the Royal Hibernian, all under the management of innkeeper "Umpthump."

377.5   Like "oasthouse" (319.23), "greenhouse" is a urinal. See *Ulysses,* 153, 252.

380.22 Maybe Joyce thought Dermot MacMurrough's first name was Art. See "Art MacMurragh," *Ulysses* (296).

382.26 "Throne" is a W.C. in *Ulysses* (537).

382.27 *"Nancy Hans."* Is this ship named after Nancy Hanks, Lincoln's mother? As "Emancipator" (342.19), Earwicker could be Lincoln as well as O'Connell. But "Nancy Hands" (244.20) is A.L.P.

CHAPTER XII · 383-99

WHAT we are concerned with now is more the four old men than what they are concerned with. These four have Tristan, Iseult, and Mark in mind. But as Conrad's Marlow, talking about Kurtz, is more important than Kurtz, so the four, talking about Tristan and Iseult (or Isolde if you prefer to be Germanic about it), are more important than those lovers. Four commentaries on them are before us. Taken together, the commentators are "Mamalujo" (397.11. See *Letters,* I, 204, 241; III, 81, 82) or, taken apart, Matthew, Mark, Luke, and John, who devote their "gastspiels" (393.35) to the secular "matther of Erryn" (389.6)—Irish sinning, a matter that these representatives of Ireland's four provinces (389.5) are qualified to handle. More than Irish writers of secular gospels, the four, all at sea, are the "foremasters" and the "four maaster waves" (384.6; 385.35) or, writing their reminiscences ashore, are "fourmasters" (394.17) of another kind, authors of *Annals of the Four Masters,* devoted now to one aspect of Irish history. Since the annals of these "fourbottle men, the analists" (95.27) are in a sense the bones of history and a little of its flesh, these four records of an elopement parody the four ages of Vico's "evelopment in spirits of time" (394.10). Like Vico's ages, the four historians and their histories are always "repeating themselves" (394.6). The four ages are there—implicitly—but "add them" (396.4) and you get *ricorso.* Commonly associated with this, the four men, whether as judges or observers, make three of their four principal entrances in fourth chapters: here in the twelfth, earlier in the fourth (94–96), and later in the sixteenth.

Through this "regnumrockery roundup" (Ragnarok) or this *ricorso*—King Arthur's "Runtable's Reincorporated"—the new world of the next chapter "presses" (387.36; 388.34). To signify the end of things and a fresh beginning Joyce used the device of reversal—a kind of off-stage peripety. Peeping John and the three "synopticals" (394.5–6) reverse their gospel order. John, the last, comes first, and Matthew, the first, last, with Mark and Luke between them. Reversal of names—as if the Prankquean's prank—abounds. "Kram of Llawnroc," his "Wehpen," and "Tuesy" (388.2–4) take the places in this exchange of Mark of Cornwall, his nephew Tristan, and Iseult. Those ancient Egyptians "Nush" and "Mesh" (385.5–6) are Shaun and Shem. Sexes reversed, the four old men become "four dear old heladies" (386.14–15). To signify renewal, as in almost all fourth chapters, Joyce uses the image of water—not the river this time but the sea and the perils or successes of voyaging. There are drownings, wrecks, and landings—that, for example, of Mrs. Sheman's Pilgrims (397.31). But now the effective agent of renewal is love. When "Amoricas Champius"— Tristan at once from Brittany and the New World—"with one aragan throust, druve the massive of virilvigtoury fishpst . . . rightjingbangshot into the goal of her gullet"—at this "joysis crisis she renulited their disunited" (395.32–396.2). Not Lady Iseult's lover—and this is one way Joyce differs from Lawrence —but Lady Iseult herself brings new light and life to the dead, divided world of the peeping four. Another Nuvoletta or Margareen, a younger A.L.P., this water-girl works Vico's process as she always has and will.

The story of Tristan, Iseult, and King Mark emerges here and there from the incompetent and immaterial testimony of the four witnesses. But if we did not know that old King Mark sent young Tristan from Cornwall to Chapelizod to fetch Izod from her chapel, we could make little of these accounts of their voyage back. Looking through the windows of the first-class cabin, and listening (395), the "deepseepeepers" (389.26) saw and heard more than they tell us and what they tell us is less than we know, though there are references to the nurse (392.9), the potion (397.18), and Wagner's love-death music, "mild aunt Liza" (388.4). This story, however displaced by irrelevant muttering, is central nevertheless in being of local interest (Chapelizod) and in illustrating again the great theme of father and son. As Buckley and the Cad disposed of father, so Tristan disposes of Mark. Taking father's place, the young man—more enterprising than Conrad's Marlow—goes to bed with father's Intended. "Where the old conk cruised now croons the yunk" (388.1). If we relate the story to the pub at Iseult's Chapelizod—as we must—Earwicker-Mark's incestuous designs on Isabel are disappointed by Tristan-Shaun's incestuous triumph, which will be celebrated in the next three chapters.

This pathetic story of father, son, and daughter seems displaced and peripheral in the present chapter because, a commentary on commentaries, it is centered on the nature of history, whether annal or gospel—on every "stole stale mis betold" (396.23). Not what is there but what historians make of it is central here. "All puddled and mythified" (393.32–33), history or gospel is a dream of "narcolepts on the lakes of Coma" (395.8). Peep as they will, the recorders, not all there or there at all, must go on repeating themselves, and what we get is a jumble of repetitions like the *Wake* itself, which, in a sense, the four old historians are writing. Their sleepy digressions and overlays are of a kind that, having read this far, we must be getting used to. No surprise, therefore, that "the matther of Erryn" gets lost in errant manner. No surprise that senile men, not only drunk and fast asleep but obsessed with "bygone times" (386.7)—tradition claims their individual talents—and missing most of what they have before them, talk about what comes to mind. "Or so they say" (392.1) is a comment on all history and what we take for gospel.

This chapter of repetitions is simple in structure. An introductory poem precedes an introduction as a conclusion precedes a concluding poem. Between these extremes come the four gospels. The themes of the *Wake* chosen to link and enlarge these parts are functional. Noah, the Prankquean, Buckley, and the Cad provide obvious parallels. The recurrent Book of the Dead promises revival. Yeats's *A Vision* reminds us of cycles and his *Ossian* of voyaging. Le Fanu's *House by the Churchyard* establishes place as Vico's system, time. Not only these common themes, motifs or references but others peculiar to the four old men thread their gospels, the introduction, and the conclusion.

Repeated "up" suggests renewal. "Auld lang syne," the favorite song of the four, celebrates the end and the beginning of a year. Colleges and auctions, by which they are obsessed, imply collection and dispersal. The Protestant sects take care of reformation. 1132, if reversed, attends to fall and rise. King Arthur, possessor of a round table, is an old king displaced by a young lover as Wellington with his half-a-hat is an old general unhorsed by a cadet. But some of the themes are less apparent. Martin Cunningham (from *Dubliners* and *Ulysses*) may be there to suggest trouble with a wife. Constable Lally, who testified against the fender and attended the four judges after Earwicker's trial (67, 94), seems a kind of Shaun. "So pool the begg and pass the kish for crawsake" (7.7–8) reappears with variations to suggest perhaps the Eucharistic eating of the dead father. Divorce, much on the minds of the four, seems not altogether inappropriate to the affair of Mark and Iseult. Dion Boucicault, with his *Arrah-na-Pogue* and *Colleen Bawn,* supports all the cuddling and kissing. But I do not know what to make of recurrent "sycamores" nor do I give a fig. Several of these themes—Boucicault and Cunningham, for example—were stated (94–96) at the meeting of Earwicker's four judges in their chambers. These themes, becoming topics in the present chapter, distract the old men from their ostensible object. Almost all we get is their muttering about divorce, the Eucharist, colleges, auctions, bootybuttons, and, when they break into song, "Auld lang syne." So "the four of them and thank court now there were no more of them" (94.31–32) or, as they sing and pray now, so "the four of us and no more of us and so now pass the fish for Christ sake" (384.14–15).

As for style: most of the story, such as it is, is told in the Dublin talk of the Rory O'Connor episode; but the amorous passages receive the treatment in rhythm, diction, and tone that

Joyce thought appropriate to Gerty MacDowell, Peaches Browning, and Isabel. An abstract intrusion—from the human age perhaps—lends variety to the manners of Dublin and Peaches. One of the first parts to be written and the first to be published (an early version in the *transatlantic review*, April, 1924. See *Letters*, I, 204), this chapter lacks the density that has detained us. But the *Wake* at its lightest is no less diverting than the *Wake* at its densest. Thick or thin, the *Wake* is the funniest book in the world—a book at once the most resigned and the most cheerful.

The "quarks" for Mark are seagull talk, at which Joyce was good. Talking gulls defend Mr. Bloom: "Kaw kave kankury kake" (*Ulysses*, 453). Here gulls and other birds attack Mr. Mark, who, they say in the introductory verses, will be replaced by Tristan, "the spry young spark," whose bedding of Iseult is what the gulls are looking at and "shrillgleescreaming" about. These gulls are either the four old men with feathers on—a glee is a song for three or more voices—or else the gulls are shipmates on the "rockbysuckerassousyoceanal" (384.3–4) sea. (This Homeric adjective, recalling *poluphloisboio* in the Iliad, is worth the analysis that I leave to others.) Birds and men, listening in and crying out "when they smacked the big kuss of Trustan with Usolde," are under the auspices of "Mr Deaubaleau . . . Kaempersally" (383.21–22), who, reversing "immergreen" Mr. "Semperkelly" (32.29), combines French water, a German champion sallying forth, and a green sally or willow tree— maybe Joyce himself. "Mistlethrushes" (384.3) among the birds, introducing the theme of Frazer's mistletoe (e.g., 385.2, 392.24, 393.30–31), agree with all the kissing and reviving. The capercailzie (383.17) is a bird that, once all but extinct, was reintroduced.

There they are, the four of them, saying grace before Eucharist and thanking God there are no more of them. There they are, listening and peeping, as Tristan cuddles and kisses his "colleen bawn"—Tristan that "sexfutter," who, however "handson," is doing what is "palpably wrong and bulbubly improper" (384.6–34). Long ago in Egypt when Shem cut the reed to write the letter that Shaun carried, and long ago when in college, reading the fables of Jean de Florian, the four had had some experience in "communic suctions and vellicar frictions with mixum members." What they did not learn from these exercises they learned from twin "Totius Quotius" (cf. *tantum quantum,* 149.35) and Brian Boru-Ladbrok-H.C.E., the "mad dane" with his snakeproof breeches. Memories of such a past improve present observations (in "Luvillicit" or out on Byron's ocean) of a "seatuition" that calls for the style of Peaches and Gerty. Isolde is not unlike the tailor's daughter catching her "tar" (385.1–36). Her "woman squash" (recalling *Lebensquatsch* or life's nonsense) makes the envious four rogues lean to rhyme in iambic "duckasaloppics" (386.4–11), "all their mouths making water" the while. So introduced, their gospels begin, not in first person, however, but recorded in third person by some person, maybe Joyce, who overhears these peepers and commands Dublin talk.

Johnny MacDougall's evidence, straying among auctions, colleges, races at the Curragh, the Dublin horseshow, Dame Street, College Green, and "barrancos" and volcanoes in the New World, comes at last to Wellington-H.C.E.'s "half a tall hat," a sign perhaps of authority divided or impaired, like the "half a tall hat" the four men share. As Lally, Martin Cunningham, and Pharoah—all drowned—H.C.E. seems finished. But "Mind mand gunfree" (*My Man Godfrey,* a movie, and a general free from Buckley's gun) will revive (386.12–387.36). The evidence seems irrelevant so far, but before the end John gets down to the matter before him with a brief reference to Mark, Tristan, Iseult, and *"mild und leise"* (388.2–4). These matters, a little confused by reversal, are further confused by thoughts of Parnell "fairescapading in his natsirt" from Kitty's room and of "luftcat revol," not only Tristan in reverse as tactful lover but the Cad with a revolver. Napoleon with his two girls, Josephine and Marie Louise (388.7–8), completes the confusion. Obsessed with Earwicker and Dublin, John has been unable to tell us much about Tristan and Iseult. But that John has kept renewal in mind is shown not only by the reference to King Arthur

(387.36) but by that to Yeats (386.20–21): "Darkumound numbur wan," the dark moon of phase number one in *A Vision,* promises a new cycle.

The testimony of Marcus Lyons repeats that of John with variations. Drowning is now the fate of those on the Armada from "Hedalgoland" (388.11–20). Cunningham becomes "Cominghome," and the Cad with a revolver becomes Buckley with his gun (388.33–34). Now John's water is the "raining water" of "Nupiter Privius" (390.22–23), patron of those two girls in the bushes. Confusing H.C.E. with Shaun (or King Mark with Tristan) and A.L.P. with Isabel or Iseult, Mark devotes most of his attention to "Porterscout" and his Spanish "Dona," our "first marents," all at sea. As Lipoleum-Wellington, on his "whuite hourse of Hunover," and Brian Boru, "rising Clunkthurf over Cabinhogan," H.C.E. has "half a grey traditional hat" (388.15–22). As old "galahat, with his peer of quinnyfears," he repeats himself with the two girls "in his old futile manner, cape, towel and drawbreeches" (389.23, 35). But A.L.P., "the Fatima Woman" (Catholic Mary) and "unitarian lady" (Protestant unifier), also repeating herself, takes charge, and the college suitably becomes a "gynecollege." *Pater familias,* having been displaced by "Fatimiliafamilias" (389.9–19), Vico's round, "difinely developed in time," moves on from past to future at present. Vico's process demands Bruno's contraries, "Battleshore and Deaddleconchs," who appear "in their half a Roman hat" (390.16–17). The "Artsichekes Road" (390.9) must be Dedalus-Shem's road of art for art's sake, egocentricity, and heartache.

From such orderly confusions, Tristan emerges twice: once "poghuing her scandalous" (388.23), and again, "kiddling and cuddling" (389.22).

Although Lucas Tarpey repeats his predecessors with variations, he alone fails to notice the affair of Tristan and Iseult. Luke's eyes, like those of John and Mark, are on H.C.E. and A.L.P. Earwicker goes on trial before "Dowager Justice Squalchman" (A.L.P.), who seems related less to "woman squash" than to "woman squelch" (392.36). This "materfamilias," like Bella Cohen, asks H.C.E.-Bloom to button her boot (391.9–10, 34). But having eaten a bad fish (Jesus) and a "bad crab" (Adam), "poorboir Matt [H.C.E.] in his saltwater hat," that "queenly man," is taken to Mater Misericordiae hospital. Dying in this "housepays for the daying," he is waked in the pub and buried (392.4–33). "Now pass the loaf for Christ sake," say those at the wake, "And so. And all" (393.2–3).

In the testimony of Matt Gregory, H.C.E. is Martin Cunningham, Sitric Silkenbeard, and a bearded "Bargomuster"; but A.L.P., with her "mudhen republican name" and her bootybuttons, is always the same (393.5–24). Repeating predecessors becomes Vico's repetitive process: "cycling, and dooing a doonloop" until you are "tyred" (394.14–16). A passage in abstract language (394.30–36), suitable to Luke's human age, seems out of place in this *ricorso*. But suiting it, Matt gives the best account of "eysolt of binnoculises" (394.30). Not only using his binoculars, he tells what he saw in the "honeymoon" cabin of those lovers, and what he saw (395) might cheer Lawrence's gamekeeper up, as Matt's gaiety—or Joyce's—would have saddened Lawrence. Would have? Did. "My God," he said on looking into the *Wake,* "what . . . deliberate, journalistic dirty-mindedness."

The Book of the Dead—"the chaptel of the opering of the month of Nema Knatut" (Tutankhamen)—and the Eucharist affirm the renewal promised by that "vivid girl, deaf with love" (395.23–29)—that "strapping modern old ancient Irish prisscess" with "nothing under her hat but . . . solid ivory," red hair, and a fine pair of "bedroom eyes" (396.7–11). Where Matt's excellent report ends and the conclusion begins is uncertain. Let us guess that it ends with "Plop" (396.33), a very good word to end with.

A commentary on the "mummurrlubejubes. . . .(up one up four)" is penultimate. Old Luke's "kingly leer" (398.23) may have accompanied his silence about Tristan. Now "at the end of it all" all four historians of the "death and . . . love embrace" (398.10) are dead and "happily buried." Their "tellmastory repeating yourself" (397.7–8) is not unlike the *Senchus Mor,* a

mediaeval "codex book of old year's eve 1132, M.M.L.J. old
style" (397.30–31; 398.23). (This codex is the principal collection of the Brehon Law, which promised order in Ireland from
the time of Patrick to the sixteenth century.) But the *Annals of
the Four Masters* are a better analogy. As the authors of this
"mousework," the four old men are Michael Ó Clery, Cucogry
or Peregrine Ó Clery, Cucogry or Peregrine Duigenan, and
Fearfeasa Ó Mulconry ("O'Mulcnory. . . . Peregrine and Michael and Farfassa and Peregrine," 397.36; 398.15). Cf. 14.28.

A "caschal pandle" (397.26–27), reversed, lights their Irish
Easter rising; Lazarus comes forth (398.26) to the tune of
"Auld lang syne"; and "Miss Yiss," who, like the Prankquean,
"ran, when wit won free" (398.17–20), utters Mrs. Bloom's
great "yes." Miss Yiss or Iseult is renewal's agent, but Tristan,
with a part in her, has had a part in it. "Heroest champion of
Eren," Tristan is the new H.C.E. His "braceoelanders" are
H.C.E.'s two girls and the two Iseults. "Gowan, Gawin and
Gonne" unite an auction, an Arthurian champion, and Yeats's
girl Maud (398.5–6). Yeats is another "heroest champion of
Eren."

"Iseult la belle" and "Tristan, sad hero," the Prankquean's
Tristopher, deserve the music of drum, reed, bagpipe, fife, trumpet, and the word of five vowels that celebrates their achieve-
ment (398.29–30). More than one of the brasses of this concert, "Brazenaze" is another college, which, since it is Walter
Pater's, may imply a new father. "Lambeg," recalling Protestants—Joyce is tying loose ends together at the end—may imply
a new archbishop at Lambeth.

Tristan's song to Iseult, with her *"silverymonnblue mantle
round her"* in her boat *"of daughter of pearl,"* recalls the song of
A.L.P.'s river at the end of Chapter IV. Why should the new
"Brinabride. . . . bide with Sig Sloomysides," Mark-H.C.E.,
when Tristan-Shaun, her "nursetender," will give her money
every day of the week? Why indeed? says she, rising up on Saturday, *"whatever your name is, you're the mose likable lad
that's come my ways yet."*

At song's end, Mamalujo and "Haw," their ass, make a farewell appearance, but there is new light on the river and the way of "john, johnajeams" (Hamlet's "John-a-dreams") is clear. The next three chapters concern Shaun and his dream. Its interpretation is the concern of the four old men, who, in the fourth chapter of Part III, provide another *ricorso*, a less encouraging one than this.

383.1   A "quark" is also German for cottage cheese. Recently a physicist chose Joyce's "quark" as the name for a new particle of matter (*New York Times,* April 26, 1966).

384.17   "Augusburgh," the first reference to Protestants in this chapter, is the Lutheran Peace of Augsburg, 1555. Anglican Hugh Latimer, martyred in 1555 (388.32), is accompanied by sectarians: Anabaptists (388.14), Plymouth Brethren (389.1), Unitarians (389.11), Methodists (391.11), Presbyterians (391.-29), and Quakers (395.12). Anglican Lambeth (398.29) closes the Protestant circle.

384.26   Joyce's witty "sinister dexterity" was anticipated by witty Herman Melville in *Billy Budd.*

386.26   "James H. Tickell" (alluded to 387.6, 388.-27, and associated with law (J.P.), cricket, and Trinity College) must be Joyce's invention. Patrick Henchy, Director of the National Library, Dublin, has been unable to track him down. There was a George Tickell, J.P. Thomas and John Tickell were both connected with Dublin.

389.6–7   The matter of Erin consists of four Kills. But the kills of state are no worse than the kills (*kil* is Gaelic, church) of church.

389.13   "1169" is the date of Strongbow's landing in Ireland. "1768 Y.W.C.A" that appears after 1169 (391.2), though apparently connected with an association of Protestant women (founded 1855), is really connected with Lucas (390.34): the death of Charles Lucas, M.P. was erroneously reported in the *Freeman's Journal* in 1768. (Patrick Henchy is my authority.) The "buy in disgrace" is Dermot MacMurrough, who, in 1169, invited the English to Ireland.

389.28; 392.18   "Mnepos" combines Cornelius Nepos, the historian, with grandson, in Latin, and memory, in Greek.

391.8   The "hing" (asafetida) is the fetid ass who follows the four old men—inconspicuously in this chapter: "Dubbledorp, the donker" (383.23), "their familiar" (389.33), and "Haw" (399.32). Almost as elusive as Macintosh, the ass may be Dublin (383.23), Ireland, Earwicker, or Joyce, the historian of these historians.

394.26   "Aithne" is a legendary Irish heroine, one of Cuchulain's two girls in Yeats's *The Only Jealousy of Emer.*

398.15–16   "Navigants et peregrinantibus" (voyaging Peregrines) echo *Benedictio Peregrinorum* and *Benedictio Navis,* prayers for travelers, and the Introit of *Missa pro peregrinatoribus* or *peregrinantibus.*

PART THREE

CHAPTER XIII · 403-28

"SHAUN" is the title Joyce picked for Part III—or so he said in a letter—and a very good title too; for three of the four chapters of the third part are Shaun's. (See *Letters*, III, 93, 131, 140.) The "beamish" boy with his postman's lamp, following the Cad, Buckley, and Tristan, is now the immediate son. Indeed, having disposed of old H.C.E., Shaun is becoming the new H.C.E. It may be that, although ringed by Floras and Maggies, he still lacks experience of two girls in the Park. Preferring food to drink, he seems disqualified for keeping a pub or, at least, for slumping grandly to its throne. Maybe, after delivering the letter, he will open a butcher shop. But already he stutters a little, and, like H.C.E., he finds it hard "to isolate i from my multiple Mes" (410.12). The i of this comedian as the letter i is smaller than father's, his eye less than father's ear.

If the four parts of the *Wake* are Vico's four ages, this part is the human age. Shaun is as human as those drunks in the pub. But within the third part, as within the second, four Viconian ages—wheels within a wheel—proceed. The present chapter, a divine age within a human age, is affected by its position. The Son becomes the son. Shaun is Jesus the postman, as Bloom is Jesus the canvasser for advertisements. Shaun's "jehovial oye-glances" beam from "a picture primitive" (405.3, 20), but, however "tarabred" (411.22), Shaun belongs to the New World, where "a starspangled zephyr" (a western wind) harps "crinklydoodle" (404.27–28). Carrying a tea-partied letter from Boston, this divine postman, following the example of Elijah-Bloom, enjoys a kind of ascension at the end of the chapter.

But before getting to that—and we have Joyce's assurance for this—Shaun follows the Way of the Cross. (*Letters*, I, 214, 216.) No more than hinted in this chapter, his *Via Crucis* will be a little more evident in the next. Now, Jesus-Shaun takes up his "heaviest crux" while "we," his devotees, hail him as "salve a tour" (409.17–18, 31), a *Salvator* about to tour his fourteen stations, of which taking the cross up is the second. It is not without pertinence that "we," acclaiming him as he proclaims himself, ask fourteen questions, one for each station of his cross. "The most purely human being that ever was called man, loving all up and down the whole creation" (431.11–12) is incarnate God. Shaun, missing by a hair the divine humanity of his great example, loves all but Shem.

This local incarnation, more than Jesus the postman, is Jesus the Guinness barrel. Shaun is either this barrel, floating down the Liffey while we applaud from the banks or else—and this is more likely—he is "in the barrel" (419.19) and his voice comes out of the "bunghole." Here's "hooprings," we say (428.12–13). After his sermon from the bung, "over he careened . . . by the mightyfine weight of his barrel . . . and rolled buoyantly backwards" down the river, "*via* Rattigan's corner out of farther earshot" (426.30–35). He has "disappaled and vanesshed . . . from circular circulatio. Ah, mean!" (427.7–10) We piously attend his second coming.

This Swiftian tale of a "vanesshed" tub, under the "stellas," is not unlike that of secular Diogenes, who emerged from his tub with a lamp to seek an honest man. "Smoiling . . . up his lampsleeve," our barreled "diogneses is anonest man's" (411.25–29). For his admirers, this *non est* cannot impair honesty's is.

In the divine age a man from the human age must be a little childish. It is fitting therefore that nursery rhymes, fairy tales, fables, and parables accompany Shaun's sermon. Anderson and Grimm (413.15; 414.17) sponsor "Little Red Ridinghood" (411.24). "Mooseyeare Goonness," not only Mr. Guinness, patron of barrels, is also Mother Goose or French "Mery Loye" (414.11–12; 428.7), patron of "Little Miss Muffet" and

"Simple Simon" (408.20; 413.19–20). Such things put children to sleep, sometimes. As fast asleep as the four old men, Shaun addresses a sleeping congregation. His "dreambookpage" (428.16) of this Viconian dream-book is a "dreamskhwindel" (Danish, dream-spiral, 426.27).

Not even Vico's thunders, of which there are two in this chapter, wake him. The eight thunders we have heard so far, associated with H.C.E., have echoed or announced his fall and, sometimes, rise. Now the last two of the ten thunders, announcing fall, rise, and the beginning of a cycle, are Shaun's. What better evidence that son is taking father's place? The ninth thunder (414.18–20) is the protracted cough of a lecturer clearing his throat perhaps before his climax. Introductory "casus," both the case of the Ondt and his fall, predicts fall after rise. Divine entirely, the ultimate thunder (424.20–22) predicts rise after fall. This Norse thunder proceeds from Midgard to Loki's Ragnarok and beginning again. "Thor's for you!" "The hundredlettered name again," we say of this last thunder, "the last word of perfect language," a word that Shaun, however penultimate, could "come near" (424.23-26). Come near? Hundredlettered? We are wrong on both counts. Shaun is already near or beyond, and his last word, no longer of a hundred letters, like H.C.E.'s, has a hundred-and-one letters. The ten thunders then, their letters added up, compose a word of 1001 letters. 1001 is renewal's number. The Arabian Nights, the Tower of Babel, and the *Wake* (5.28–29) have 1001 stories, "all told." Penultimate, ultimate or postultimate, the word is the creator's tool. The word of in the beginning was Joyce's end.

Mostly a lecture by Shaun, this chapter echoes answer 11 of Chapter VI, in which Shaun, as Professor Jones, lectures his pupils on time and space, ear and eye, bad Shem and good Shaun. Unable there to convince by discourse, he resorts to fable, the Mookse and the Gripes. Here, unable to make the same points, he resorts to another fable or, since he is more or less Jesus now, parable, the Ondt and the Gracehoper. The results, as usual, are the same. Exposing his "other," Shaun-Jones exposes himself. Brother conflict, accounting for the reappearance of Bruno (412.36), proves Shaun an imperfect H.C.E. Not until he unites again with Shem at the end of Chapter XIV will he be the great man entirely—for a while. As yet in the state of becoming, still plagued with a rival, Shaun requires and gets a host of parallels for his condition. The chapter is crowded with Shauns: Frank O'Connor with his *Guest of a Nation* (409.6; 414.8; 426.20), Oliver Gogarty (410.13–14), Wyndham Lewis, champion of space against temporal Joyce (415.29; 418.29), T. S. Eliot (408.33–34), John McCormack, Joyce's successful rival in song (418.3–4), and, above these, Stanislaus Joyce, who finally takes charge of Shaun's delivery. Like these parallels, the motifs that reappear are carefully chosen. Swift is here to support "cadenus" and "Mr. O'Shem the Draper" (413.27; 421.25) and, in his other capacity of dean and lover, to support Shaun (413.22–29). The letter is here because of the postman, who carries what he cannot understand or deliver. Aladdin is here again to suggest the Arabian Nights and to carry another lamp ("New worlds for all!" 412.2), and the washerwomen are back to wring in the new (404.1–2). As these, so all.

At the beginning of this chapter, the clock is striking twelve, its strokes "the heartbeats of sleep" (403.1–5). Twelve is the "zero hour" that Fox Goodman tolled for Earwicker and the Cad (403.20–22. Cf. 35.30–33) and the hour at which, by happy coincidence, Buckley shot the old general. No rainbow now. Only a "white fogbow" of sleep, from which the Jute-like "fixtures" of H.C.E. appear, especially his nose, and, after this, the features of A.L.P. This parental apparition (403.6–17), ending in a blackout, introduces another dream-vision, recounted in first person by the "poor ass" of the four "concordant wiseheads" (405.4–7). "Methought as I was dropping asleep," says the ass, as if John Bunyan reporting a vision, that I saw in the murk by the washerwomen's "affluvial flowand-flow" the glow of Shaun's lamp, then Shaun himself, dressed, like H.C.E., in seven articles of clothing: "What a pairfact crease" in those trousers, "how amsolookly kersse!" This well-tailored "primitive" has been having a good feed in H.C.E.'s "porterhouse." No less obsessed with food than Bloom among the Lestrygonians, Shaun, that "card," has been eating by "spadefuls" what he cut with his "knives of hearts," as if a Jew at the "faste of the tablenapkins" (403.18–405.36). The Australian glutton "grubbed his tuck all right." Growing "butterand butter," he washed down Boland's bread and oysters with parental "old phoenix portar" and Anne Lynch's tea: "Houseanna. Tea is the Highest! [*Hosanna in excelsis* from the Mass] For auld lang Ayternitay" (406.1–407.9).

"Mesaw mestreamed," the visionary ass goes on, that "I heard" the music of Shaun's voice—like Palestrina sung by Mario, who, in *Ulysses* (117), is said to look like Jesus, or like something broadcast on the radio from Swift's birdy "morepork" (407.11–22). Seven gestures of Shaun's directing hand, bringing this "overture" to an end, half prepare us for a "general address rehearsal" of his fourteen movements (407.10, 23–33).

Tired of carrying the letter "on his majesty's service" over the "sod of Erin" and along what the ass has called "the winding ways of random ever" (405.8–9), Shaun feels it is time for a change—an ascension perhaps, "unwordy" though he be for the honor. He is also tired of Shem, "that other of mine." Of this "musichall pair," who "shared the twin chamber and . . . winked on the one wench [Nora]," Shem, like the Cad's Yeats, "bit his mirth too early or met his birth too late," but Stanislaus-Shaun, had he been more canny at the time, could have done better than Shem, who is always "imitating me" anyway. Anyway, "what Sim sobs todie I'll reeve tomorry." Away with him to the "dustbins"; for I am the "heart" of the matter. A toast to their mother transforms Irish *slaunti* to Eliot-Shaun's "Shaunti and shaunti and shaunti again" (408.1–409.7). This brotherly discourse, interrupted by our first question, prepares us for the parable of the Ondt and the Gracehoper.

Who was it, we ask, "who out of symphony gave you the permit?" This permission to leave the mailman's round on the sod for higher regions may represent the first Station of the Cross: "Jesus is Condemned to Death." Shaun's response corroborates this guess. "Goodbye now," says Shaun, echoing Buck

Mulligan's ballad of "Joking Jesus" (*Ulysses,* 19). Taking up his "crux," he proceeds to the second Station: "Jesus Carries His Cross." All goes according to Saint "Colleenkiller's [Columcille's] prophecies": after six days of the week, comes the Sabbath. So "Tilvido! Adie!" or, as Mulligan's Jesus says, "Goodbye, now goodbye" (409.8–30).

Were you ordered to undertake this tour? we ask our "salve a tour." It was "put upon me from on high," says Shaun, and "condemned on me" (the first Station again) by the hierarchy in their "Eusebian Concordant Homilies" (E.C.H. as Eusebius, an Arian bishop). Besides, I was "about fed up be going circulating" down here in the "meddle of this expending umniverse" (409.31–410.19). After you have left us, we ask—this is our third question—who will carry the mail? Shaun's answer, however evasive, contains a reference to "Barbe" (bearded father), who accounts for a strange "hairydittary" (410.2, 20–27. Cf. 260.L1).

Fourth question: "where mostly are you able to work?" "Here!" says Shaun, where "there's no sabbath for nomads," as he is always telling those "pedestriasts . . . Top, Sid and Hucky" (Mark Twain's trio and the three soldiers). His "vacation in life," down here in this "nightmaze," was walking for "the relics of my time." The Lord's Prayer was his comfort, from "His hungry will be done!" to our "daggily broth." In short, "I believe. Greedo!" (410.28–411.21).

The fifth question, less question than remark, is about painting the town the "wearing green" of little red "ridinghued." "Dogmestic" Shaun (at once dogmatic, domestic, and a dog about to become a god) responds by confession and denial: "You never made a more freudful mistake." The lamp of this Jungian "extravert" promises, like Aladdin's, new lamps for old (411.22–412.6).

The sixth question put to the "mielodorous . . . songbird," who somehow, while singing, blows his own horn, is so obscure that his sudden and heated response is surprising. (The "furniture would or verdure" of the question could be the tree or cross.) Defending himself against such "intinuations," Shaun calls on his old friend "Miss Enders, poachmistress and gay receiver" of the parcel post office—probably A.L.P. (412.7–28). "Mrs Sanders" and her sister, "Mrs. Shunders," may be Earwicker's two girls as they certainly are Dean Swift's two Esthers, like as two legs and two Easter eggs. Shaun's letter to H.C.E. (413.3–26), "my last will intesticle," attempts the little language ("ptpt . . . M.D.") of the *Journal to Stella*. Like Stephen Dedalus, Shaun remains obsessed with the parents he thinks he has escaped from and will have to escape from before, merging with his opposite—as Stephen with Bloom—he can become his father or another like him. It is Shaun who is making the "freudful mistake."

Pouncing, in our seventh question, on "Biggerstiff" Swift and his "Two venusstas," we demand the whole truth now and nothing but the truth. "Hooraymost!" (*Oremus*), says Shaun, alluding in H.C.E.'s stutter to the "rawcawcaw romantical" story of Jarl van Hoother and the Prankquean. My meaning, he continues, is as plain as a letter sent in care of one of Mr. Guinness' barrels—a letter you will "now parably receive" (413.27–414.13).

Shaun's letter, parable or "feeble" fable—not from Aesop but from La Fontaine (Book I, Fable 1)—is meant, like Professor Jones's fable of the Mookse and the Gripes, to illustrate what discourse has proved inadequate for. Like the Mookse, the Ondt (Danish, evil), representing space, is the hero in a quarrel with his opposite or time. Since this quarrel is one between insects—sons of an earwig—puns in several languages yield insects or their parts. Example: the Grasshopper has a "smetterling [smattering and German, butterfly] of entymology [etymology and entomology]." Puns on Russian affairs and the names of philosophers are no less evident. "So vi et" (414.14) introduces socialist, party, Beria, Moscow, and the like, to suggest perhaps a society of ants. Philosophers—Aristotle, Mencius, Confucius, Spinoza, Grotius, Leibnitz, Kant, Hegel, Schopenhauer—are there perhaps because they deal with time, space, ethics or process—or, maybe, to establish the Ondt's bourgeois philosophy of life. Freud, unnamed but there with his "Libido" and "imago,"

and Vico, there with his rounds, round out this thoughtful company. References to Egypt, not in the service of revival now,
seem there to imply the Ondt's world of death and burial.

The Gracehoper (Shem) wastes the time he stands for in having a good time—a victim of Hilary's "joyicity." Associated
with music and dance—or keeping time—he scrapes his "findle-
stilts" in "overtures" to his four girls, "Floh and Luse and
Bienie and Vespatilla" (flea, louse, bee, and wasp), whom he
urges "to commence insects with him, their mouthparts to his
orefice and his gambills to there airy processes, even if only in
chaste" (414.22–34). When away from his house, called "four-
millierly [French, ant] Tingsomingenting [Danish, a thing like
no thing]," he passes his "schoppinhour" in buying them
"housery." At home sometimes with grandfather Zeus
(H.C.E.), the Gracehoper likes to strike up "funereels" (dances
and movies at a funeral, 414.35). At this festive funeral, plainly
a wake or "dance McCaper," old father Saturn is ringed by his
sons as old father Chronos, crumbling in his coffin, by his
(415.9–10, 19, 21–22). A.L.P., the two girls (now "Dehlia and
Peonia"), Shem and Shaun, kicking time, join the "wheel of the
whorl" around the "wormcasket" of the "oldbuoyant" old boy
(415.1–8, 23–24). Such festivities get the Gracehoper nowhere.

The Ondt, disapproving of this "Inzanzarity" (Italian, mos-
quito), will not come to the "party" because the Gracehoper is
not on his "social list": "Nixnixundnix," in answer to the yes of
that "sommerfool" (Danish, butterfly), like a Russian vote in
the United Nations, is the Ondt's everlasting No (415.25–31).
Thoth and the scarabs of Egypt support his refusal, while
"windhame" Lewis makes spaces for his "raumybult and abel-
boobied" follower (415.25, 28–29; 416.3). Go to the ant, thou
"sloghard" (415.32) is less of an invitation than it seems.

A life of doubts, loves, debts, and "bilking" (or creating
works of art) leaves the Gracehoper worn out, broke, and ac-
tively contrite: "I am heartily hungry" (416.8.–20). Hunger
drives him, as it drove Joyce, to make "mundballs of the ephemerids," mouth-and-world shapes of the ephemeral—in *Ulysses*
and *Finnegans Wake,* for example—or eating short-lived in-

sects. "Artsaccord" (415.18) bringing neither cash nor food, the improvident Gracehoper, a traveling wreck on the way to "ragnowrock," makes three Viconian rounds (416.21–36). Unlike the three journeys of the Prankquean, that "boss of both appease" (417.7), these rounds are vain. Meeting the Ondt, the miserable Gracehoper, still hoping for grace, is consumed with envy; for there the Ondt sits, smoking a "spatial brunt of Hosana cigals," surrounded by the four "houris," Floh, Luse, Bieni, and Vespatilla, who, pleased by his "comfortumble phullupsuppy" (philosophy and supper), have left the failure, to his "chronic's despair," for his successful rival—like those heliotropic girls in Chapter IX. "Artalone . . . with his parisites" (the exiled artist in Paris among his followers) wasted time "writing off his phoney," but Papal Count John McCormack—once Joyce's rival in song—makes money: *"Ad majorem l.s.d. . . .* So be it" (417.8–418.8). Professor Jones's fable of the Mookse proved nothing, whatever its intention; but Shaun's parable of the Ondt and the "spindhrift" convinces us that making spaces and money is better than wasting time, prudence better than art, and bourgeois better than artist.

Terminal verses by the Gracehoper forgive the Ondt for his "mocks for my gropes." What more can we expect of Bruno's world, where *"These twain are the twins that tick* Homo Vulgaris?"* The volumes and spaces of the Ondt may be immense and his *"genus . . . worldwide,"* but how much nicer if, having *"song sense"* or literary sensibility, he could *"beat time."*

Question nine: After complimenting the "foibler" on his "explosition" and his "volupkabulary," we come, by way of "fokloire" to literature in general. Can you read, we ask, "the strangewrote anagylptics of those shemletters"—of the letter inspired by A.L.P., written by Shem, and directed to H.C.E.?

Whether it is written in Greek, Turkish or "Oscan wild," says the "letter potent" carrier of the letter, he can read such "furloined notepaper" (Poe and A.L.P.) and would too, were it "a nice production." But like "theodicy" (*Ulysses*), it is "a pinch of scribble. . . . Puffedly offal tosh," and full of "filth." In this abominable letter, as in *Finnegans Wake,* there is "nothing beyond clerical horrors" (419.12–36) and scandals about A.L.P. and H.C.E.—how he met a cad with a pipe, two girls "on the makewater," and three fellows in the bushes. Shaun defends the parents so exposed: May their "livetree" flourish and be their "ecotaph" a stone (420.1–16). If "all the mound reared" at the publication of the letter, Shaun seems singular in his disapproval; but "reared" and "mound" are ambiguous, and Shaun's disapproval, far from singular, is that of Stanislaus and all the bourgeois journalists and censors.

An interlude on the letter (420.17–421.14) proves that, more than unreadable and discouraging, it is undeliverable. The addresses to which Shaun carried the letter in vain are not only those of H.C.E. (or everybody) but—some of them at least—of James Joyce, who, while in Dublin, lived at 13 Fitzgibbon Street, 12 North Richmond Street, 8 Royal Terrace, and 7 St. Peter's Terrace, Cabra. Delivery seems impossible: addressee unknown, name illegible, opened by mistake, no such person. A medley of references improves the confusion: Finn's Hotel (where Nora worked), Adam Findlater (now Foundlitter from context), Sir Arthur (Guinness or Wellesley), and Isaac Butt. "Step out to Hall out of that, Ereweaker, with your Bloody Big Bristol." "Bung. Stop. Bung. Stop. Cumm Bumm" combines Van Hoother's telegram to the Prankquean, Cambronne with his *mot,* and Shaun's barrel.

Tenth question: Has not your voice from the barrel used "tun" times as many words of "used up slanguage" as your "cerebrated" brother—a kind of Pigott—used with such "hesitancy" in his forgeries?

Shaun's answer makes Shem the Pigott one with H.C.E. ("HeCitEncy") and Swift, author of the *Drapier Letters.* If called upon for a "dieoguinnsis" (Diogenes-Guinness) in the "irelitz" of Berlitz, Shaun continues, that "pixillated doodler" ("pixillated" is from *Mr. Deeds,* a movie) of "illegible clergimanths" is just about through. His mother or Muse is not responsible for the *Wake.* Let the drunken "Homo" be sent to "some drapyery institution," like Swift's madhouse, for "wordsharping." Can the leopard change his spots? Am I my brother's keeper? (421.15–422.18)

Eleventh question: Putting his prince's pride in your pauper's purse (like Mark Twain), can you make your point clearer with another "esiop's foible"?

Shem's work, says Shaun, avoiding fable, is "partly my own," isn't it? What is not mine in it is borrowed—and this is as plain as Nelson on his Trafalgar pillar—from the two girls, the three soldiers, and "Ananymus" or A.L.P., Anima and Muse, who made his "litterery bed." Shem, that forger of farces, is as bad as "jameymock farceson," the forger of *Ossian*. That "ambitrickster" is as bad as Dean Swift. During an exile like that of "Childe Horrid," Shem claimed the invention of an "idioglossary," but I gave him that too. The "beogrefright" he began *in medias res* was stollen from me: "Swop beef!" He would rape the pad off Pope's lock. No wonder "Berkeley showed the reason genrously." No wonder Shem, that "middayevil" devil, left the Society of Jesus for "the society of jewses" and, though warned against it, entered the "ricecourse of marrimoney." He is as bad as Chekhov's seagull. His wild goose is cooked. The four X's with which Shaun concludes make his account of Shem seem another letter (422.19–424.13).

Twelfth question: Why? For his "root language," says Shaun. The tenth thunder that interrupts his answer illustrates this language (424.14–22).

Thirteenth question: Could you approximate this language? Every word of Shem's work, says Shaun, like every word of Eliot's "Sweeney," is a "copy. . . . the last word in stolentelling." "The lowquacity of him!" He was "rising my lather" as he stole the "tale" of my shirt (424.23–425.3). The voice is the voice of Stanislaus.

Shaun is always answering questions. In Chapter VI, the "briefdragger" answers twelve questions put by Shem—twelve because of the "twelve apostrophes" or apostles of H.C.E. Now Shaun answers fourteen questions put by "us"—fourteen because of the crucial context. In Chapter XV, he responds to the inquisition of the four old men. The identity of his inquisitors is plain in VI and XV; not so in XIII. Who, we ask, are "we"? We could be the twelve men who, in Chapter VIII, are sitting on the bank of the river. Or "we" could be as general as Yeats's "they," our common enemy. Anyway, "our" questions, shrewder than their tone leads the holy victim to suspect, expose what we desire.

Fourteenth question: As bright and "well letterread" as "Shamous Shamonous, Limited" (John Jameson), you could use your own "worse" if you took the time and trouble. That is "show," says Shaun, the blood of his mother beginning to transfuse. I could write the "blurry wards" (cf. 14.5, 12) of "Siamanish" better than most if I put my mind to it. My *Ulysses*— "my trifolium librotto, the authordux Book of Lief. . . . Acomedy of letters"—would be as good or better than Shem's. Cutting "my throat with my tongue," I would "introvent" the thing and "a hundred and eleven other things," all of which are "tame, deep and harried in my mine's I." After all, "annyma" is my Anima, Muse, and mother too. But all that is too much trouble (425.4–426.4).

Thoughts of mother bring a tear and a smile to Shaun's eye and lips, respectively. The inquisition over, the barrel takes off down the river. If this departure is a kind of ascension, it is more or less horizontal and no better than penultimate; for there is another departure at the end of the next chapter after other stations of Shaun's cross. Maybe now he is just taking off down the river to St. Bride's school, where all the Stellas and Vanessas (427.7, 10) await him. Now, as he passes hence and his lamp goes out, we, the "twelve o'clock scholars" at his wake, praise the goodness of our "Spickspookspokesman." Be coming back to us, we pray, back to "Biddyhouse." Since the four elders join our prayer, we are not they, though as "twelve o'clock scholars" we may be the twelve men (427.34; 428.3–4). "Turn your coat" and come "rolling home" as "Jonnyjoys," a successful Joyce, back from exile. Success would make Joyce—as it made John McCormack—a Shaun.

405.16   "Beamish" makes Shaun the hero of Lewis Carroll's
         "Jabberwocky." An archaic word for shining brightly,
         "beamish" was made current by Carroll.

411.18   "Hek domov muy" is the Czech national anthem,
         "Kde domov muj" (Where is my home?), distorted
         by the intrusion of H.C.E., who reappears as "Hek"
         (420.18).

415.17   "The Great Sommboddy within the Omniboss" must
         be the sleeper, dreamer, H.C.E., and God.

418.29   *"Accident Man"* is Occident Man, an allusion to
         Time and Western Man by Wyndham Lewis, a spatial-
         ist. Lewis also appears in Jones's fable of the Mookse.

421.13   "Bung" in the context of a Guinness barrel recalls the
         Guinness brothers, "Bungiveagh and Bungardilaun"
         (*Ulysses,* 299).

424.3–7 "Demonican skyterrier" alludes to the Dominicans,
         who by a mediaeval pun, *domini canes,* became dogs
         of God. See "bulldog of Aquin" and "san Tommaso
         Mastino" (mastiff) in *Ulysses* (208, 637). The
         "Hooley Fermers" may be the Jesuits, whose principal
         establishment in the British Isles is at Farm Street,
         London. "Cecilia's treat" and "Galen" refer to Joyce's
         early desire to take up medicine or music. A medical
         school, taken over by University College, is on Cecilia
         Street, Dublin; Galen is an authority on medicine; and
         St. Cecilia presides over music.

CHAPTER XIV · 429-73

SHAUN'S barrel halts on its crucial way at Saint Bridget's "nightschool" (cf. 220.3) where the twenty-nine pupils (Isabel and her attendant Floras), sitting on the bank, splash in the water of the Liffey with their "eight and fifty pedalettes" (430.1–10). Saint Bridget or Bride, whose feast is February 1, is a good patron for these "once-upon-a-four year" girls, whose feast is February 29. From his "pulpitbarrel" (472.4) Shaun— now Jaun (all-but Juan) on account of those girls—delivers a sermon to the paddling congregation, which, as heliotropic as it was in Chapter IX, gladly receives the good word of the Son.

His sermon or "dream monologue" (474.4), suitably didactic, is a model of the art Stephen Dedalus condemned as "kinetic" in his aesthetic discourse with Lynch. Shaun's "kinantics" (441.28) or kinetic antics with his kin—Isabel, after all, is his sister—are among the most diverting of the most diverting book. "Never park your brief stays in the men's convenience," says preaching Shaun. "And look before you leak, dears" (433.24–25,34). Not only preaching what seems to be a paschal sermon, Jaun is also celebrating a Mass from "introit" and "offertory" (432.5,17) to *Ite Missa est.* "Eat a missal lest" (456.18) includes communion—with himself, as those girls, exclaiming "O salutary" (*O salutaris hostia,* 454.18), are aware. As they might expect, the "lithurgy" of Shaun, the stone on Peter's rock, does not lack "me saries" (432.22,32) or *miserere.* So "Sussumcordials all round" (453.26, *Sursum corda* or Up, hearts! is from the Mass). All this—for the Mass is high—to organ accompaniment. Seated at his "console," Jaun pulls all

the stops of the "voixehumanar" (441.25–26). No problem
here, but problems from Chapter XIII, the fourteen stations and
a possible ascension, remain to plague us.

Shaun's ascension there—if any—was horizontal, but so was
Bloom's at the end of the Cyclops episode (*Ulysses,* 345). Ascending metaphorically "at an angle of forty-five degrees over
Donohoe's in Little Green Street," Elijah-Jesus Bloom, after his
crucifixion by the Citizen, actually ascends the street in a jaunting car. No time elapses between his crucifixion and ascension.
But if Shaun, at the end of Chapter XIII, is following Bloom's
great example, why is he back on his *Via Crucis* in Chapter
XIV? A second coming? Surely the second coming is beyond the
fourteen stations of the last of the first. On the whole, we must
agree that Shaun's departure in Chapter XIII, however like
Bloom's ascension, is just a departure for more stations, greater
applause.

The *Via Crucis* is hinted in Chapter XIII by fourteen questions and by reference to at least two of the fourteen stations.
Now, while preaching to the girls, celebrating Mass, and playing
his organ, Jaun is going through the fourteen stations again—
not, however, in their customary order. To some he returns, at
some he lingers, at others pauses briefly. In identifying these stations, immediate context is less important than the general context of a chapter which, numbered fourteen, seems qualified by
number for the fourteen stations:

Station 1   (Jesus is condemned to death), hinted in
                Chapter XIII, is hinted again by "privy-
                sealed orders" (448.29).

Station 2   (Jesus carries the cross), also hinted in
                Chapter XIII, is now attended to by "gross
                proceeds," "load on ye" (431.27–28), and
                "the Lord's stake" (433.14).

Stations 3, 7, 9   (Jesus falls with the cross). These three
                falls, "footslips" of "staggering humanity"
                (442.15; 451.20), are associated with
                Adam's fall: 433.28–31. The "fellow that

fell foul" (465.20–21) is old Adam, falling for that "snailcharmer," and Jesus, the new Adam, who "felt the fall" (469.13). Cf. "falls down to his knees" (434.33).

Station 4   (Jesus meets his mother): Becoming her mother, Isabel is a "virginwhite . . . manonna" (433.3–4). My "mutther . . . a Runningwater" (469.14) is not only A.L.P. but the Virgin weeping and giving birth at the expense of amniotic fluid.

Station 5   (Simon of Cyrene helps Jesus carry the cross): "You're sitting on me style, maybe" (445.33) is not only Lady Dufferin's "I'm sitting on the stile, Mary" but St. Simeon Stylites, who, sitting on his pillar (or style), serves to recall Simon. (Sister Eileen Campion Kennedy helped me over this stile and over that running water too.)

Station 6   (Veronica wipes the face of Jesus). The piece of cloth Isabel tears from her drawers is Shaun's "veronique" (458.1–14).

Station 8   (The Daughters of Jerusalem weep over Jesus). This "miry lot of maggalenes" is "sweeping" and emitting "lost soupirs" (453.-8–12,19). Cf. "weeping" (462.7).

Station 10   (Jesus is stripped of his garments) is hinted by "undraped divine" (435.14–15), "undress," "overdressed if underclothed," "strip off that nullity suit" (441.2–5,30), and "gentleman without a duster" (432.24). Cf. "Mulligan is stripped of his garments" (*Ulysses,* 16).

Station 11   (Jesus is nailed to the cross): "forstake me knot" (441.6). Shaun's "hat with a reinforced crown" (430.17–18) must be the crown of thorns. His "cup of scald" (456.1), more than tea, must be vinegar and gall.

Stations 12–14 (Jesus dies on the cross and, taken down, is buried): "Marie Maudlin . . . weeper" (434.16). The litany of the girls (470.5–23), says Joyce in a letter (I, 263), attends to the death of Jesus and taking His body down. Shaun's burial ("Gravesend," 434.34) is his departure from view in a barrel. "How wrong will he look till he rises?" (434.33–34).

So much for "the Shaun way" (442.22) on that "good friday" (433.12).

It may be that, according to the stations, Jaun is dead and the litany of the girls is a "mourning for the passing of the last post" (470.26), but how are we to take his "take off" (469.22) and what about the "retourneys postexilic" (472.34) of this "Joss-el-Jovan" (472.15) or God-God-God? And what about the phoenix on the last page of this chapter? Is Jaun's death an ascension to be followed by a second coming or part of a week end in springtime: dying on Good Friday, dead on Holy Saturday, rising on Easter Sunday? Whatever the case—ascension and second coming or death and resurrection—we shall look into it again. Meanwhile, let "Doremon's" (433.4) be our caution and our guide; for this good possessive-subjunctive combines Roman words for sleeping and praying. However sleepy and possessed, "let us pry."

The ass is our "preambler" (429.4). Usually ambling after the four historians, the ass, preambling here as in Chapter XIII, provides the preamble to Shaun's amble with the cross. "God's son," a little brighter after these "barrelhours," seems about to "fill space and burst in systems" (429.3–13). This barreled pedestrian, suitably careful of his shoes, comes to rest against blond Constable Sigurdsen, who, drunk and asleep upright on the bank of the river, is like a "log" awaiting top and bottom sawyers (429.18–24; 430.12–13. Cf. 3.7). Commonly associated with Joe, the Danish handyman, and with Shaun himself (186.19–20; 471.30; 530.21–22; 586.28), this blond, sleeping

like a log, seems H.C.E. now, although a line or so in Danish
(430.15–16) keeps Joe in mind. Ignoring his snores, the twenty-
nine Floras, "on their best beehiviour," rush "sowarmly" to
Shaun, as "buzzy" as flowers can bee. "O nice" for the florid,
ladykilling "young chapplie of sixtine" and his florid swarm
(430.12–33), to which he addresses a few "prelimbs" (on hams
and hems) to his "general delivery." But this "martyr to the
dischurch" of his duty soon fixes his "eroscope" on Izzy, who,
"splabashing and . . . blabushing" like her twenty-eight companions, is his particular pet. Like Zeus, their father, both Phoebus and Pollux, the twins, are incestuous, but Phoebus, the sun-
son, more than Pollux, who mixes "Castor's oil" with "Parrish's
syrup," whether in parochial Dublin or Paris (431.5–432.1).

That Father Mike, the parish priest of A.L.P.'s letter, is
H.C.E., is proved by his initials, his conference "teat-a-teat with
two viragos intactas," and his "buckling time" as a Russian general. That he is also God the father is proved by his words "from
above" (432.6–19). So inspired, Jaun rises like a "preaching
freer" to exhort his "massoeurses," who, during his brief absence, should obey "as many as probable" of the ten commandments. Giving such advice is the "mokst" he can do for "his
grapce" (grace and Eucharist) in the diocese of "Gay O'Toole
and Gloamy Gwenn du Lake" (Hilary and Tristopher mixed
with O'Toole, Guenevere's Launcelot, and Kevin of Glendalough, 432.23–424.6). Preliminaries over, Shaun proceeds with
his advice, but his remarks on faith, hope, and charity are complicated by asides on drawers (434.2–3,21–23) and *Hamlet
and Oedipus* by Ernest Jones, an authority on incest (434.4–5,
19,27).

Thackeray's *Vanity Fair,* Dickens' *Our Mutual Friend, David
Copperfield,* and *Old Curiosity Shop* (confused here with the
"cupiosity shape" of a corset) introduce Shaun's warning
against literature. Beware, the vice-crusader says, of "Autist
Algy" (Shem, the Swinburnian egoist), alias "Mr Smuth" (Smut
and Shem as fabulous Smith), who, in his "low bearded voice"
may invite you to the "playguehouse" to see the *"Smirching of
Venus"* or, commending painters, persuade you to be "an artist's

moral" (434.25–435.9). I shall keep an eye on you, Jaun continues; for "Secret satieties and onanymous letters make the great unwatched as bad as their [artistic] betters" (435.31–32). Music is as bad, musicians worse. Some "Melosiosus MacShine" (Shem) may inch up to you, "disarranging your modesties and fumbling with his forte paws in your bodice"—a "whorable" affair that might get into the newspapers (437.32–438.18). Consider the girl who "ran off after the trumpadour that mangled Moore's melodies" (Nora and Joyce, author of *Chamber Music*) and turned the "tubshead of the stardaft journalwriter" (Joyce-Shem as Swift, 439.8–10).

Burning bad books, Jaun commends the good: "pious fiction . . . licensed and censered" by the best bishops, the "best sells on the market," lives of the saints, "instructual primers," and "Mary Liddlelambe's flitsy tales" (*Alice,* Mary had a little lamb, and Lamb's *Tales from Shakespeare*). Cinderella and Little Bopeep are no less improving (439.34–440.27; 435.25); and "Funnymore" Cooper is tolerable because a cooper makes beerbarrels (439.12).

Whatever his concern with dangerous and improving art, Shaun always returns to sex and food, the centers of his circlings. He advises "love through the usual channels, cisternbrothelly" or with some other "respectable relative of an apposite sex" (436.14–22). Such "prurities" are as good as food: "I never open momouth but I pack mefood in it" (437.19–20). And so "adlibidinum" (441.9); but his mood is commonly imperative.

Suppose, he says, switching to the conditional, you should meet some dog of a "saxopeeler," let us say "Attaboy Knowling" (Bruno), my twin, who takes after his parents, now seeking a divorce in New York. If I were "Blonderboss" (H.C.E. as God), I would dispose of this outsider and "insister"—this "joyboy" (Hilary), who should be brought to trial before twelve good men. A drunk like his father, Shem is also a "general omnibus character" (441.31–444.2). "I hereby admonish you": Incest, to be avoided with H.C.E. or Shem, is all right with me. When I return from my journey, "I'll be all over you myselx

horizontally" and "teach you bed minners." As Shem has been
confused with H.C.E., so Isabel is confused now with A.L.P.
Together, they are the two girls in the Park (444.6–445.1). "I
am, I do and I suffer" (445.18), says Jaun, confusing himself
with Christ and Caesar—a double confusion, beyond Bloom.
"Christ or Pilate?" asks Father Vaughan (*Ulysses,* 82).
"Christ," says Mr. Bloom, "but don't keep us all night over it."

On his return, Jaun, like H.C.E., the builder of cities, will
"circumcivicise" Dublin and improve its piety. Burning "only
what's Irish"—turf and books, for example—he will attend to
"Meliorism in massquantities." He will lay boulevards, establish
sweepstakes, and make a park of the dump at Fairview or Clontarf—and do all this as well as Buckley-Persse O'Reilly, that
constable, "now snoring," could do (446.35–448.33).

Swift in his turn, with Izzy his "stellar attraction" (449.3–4)
—"O, the vanity of Vanissy!"—Jaun Swift tells her about birds,
fish, music, and champagne. However rambling and incoherent,
his discourse to Stella presents few difficulties to the moderately
hardened reader (449.31–451.25). (Maybe that is why pages
449 and 450 have been explained in such detail by Joyce's inter-
preters.) Shaun would live with his sister "in the lap of lechery,"
he continues, but for one thing: fear of old "shoepisser pluvi-
ous," the godlike father whom we thought had shot
(451.28–452.2)—"perish the Dane."

Reading the letters of Denis Florence M'Carthy the other day
and inspired by such respectable reading, Jaun thought he would
like to remain at "Hothelizod," but historical necessity compels
departure on a "glorious mission . . . to meet a king." Without example in the annals of Livy or the Pharaoh's Book of the
Dead, this mission is celebrated in the work of Vico, whose cycles and "recoursers" reconcile the missionary to his "dutyful
cask." Joining the king up there, Jaun knows, means replacement by a young successor down here—some "newlywet fellow
that's bound to follow" on the Vico Road. Knowing this, Jaun is
beginning to get "sunsick"; for he is not "half Norawain [Nor-
wegian, Ibsen's Nora, and, like Giorgio, son of Nora Joyce] for
nothing." His "fine ice" (*finis*) is not so far off as he could wish;

but let there be no weeping or sighing at "my poor primmafore's wake. . . . It's my gala bene fit." The "tunc" page of the Book of Kells proves that he has the crucifixion in mind (452.8–453.20). But "Once upon a drunk and a fairly good drunk it was" makes the subsequent wake, like the first page of *A Portrait,* a beginning. So, "Parting's fun. . . . Goodbye, swisstart, goodbye" (454.1–4).

"Jaunathaun"—closer to Swift than simple Jaun—turns "swifter" and "rather sternish" to the girls to see "what's loose" as they hail him with prayers, glorias, and "doxologers" or hymns of praise. A final word, says he, about heaven his destination—Sanctus! Sanctus! Sanctus! To be "felixed" you must be "parked" up there in heaven, where the former sinner enjoys his "latterday paint" and the "whole flock's at home." There is no "apuckalips" up there, "nor no nothing." For what is beyond Macbeth's burrow and barrow, postmortem is the word. "Bouncer Naster" (*Pater Noster* as Death) is in charge. To his keeping we come "touch and go, from atoms and ifs" to become "odd's without ends." Down here all is uncertain, but up there all is "dead certain." Up there you will be nothing whatever for ever and ever. Time's last joke is putting all space in "a Notshall" (454.8–455.29).

More like Beckett perhaps than Shaun at his best; but thoughts of food, bringing him down to earth, cheer him up. "Boiled protestants" (potatoes), "Huguenot ligooms" (French beans), "naboc and erics" (partly masticated), and "a cup of scald" you could trot a mouse on (tea), reminding him of the Eucharist, remind him more of the postman's round, postage due from the Jukes and Kallikaks of Ireland, and a new coat to turn. Though the "grame reaper" will come for him someday, he will return as "His Diligence Majesty" (a divine H.C.E.) while "sinnerettes in silkettes" (drawers) line the route of his triumph (456.1–457.24).

Isabel, at this point, interrupts the monologue of her brother and "male corrispondee," who, corresponding with her, corresponds to her in respect of intellect. Indeed, her gift of a bit of her drawers, more than a "veronique" on Shaun's way, is a kind of valentine or letter, to be answered from heaven by "pigeon's pneu." Her sister Maggy (from the hen's letter) is A.L.P. herself, Isabel's mirror-image or "linkingclass girl." With this "Sosy" sister (cf. 3.12) she will meet her latest lad, one of the three soldiers, in the Park: "Ope, Jack, and atem!" The "wellingtons" of her "second mate" identify the soldier in question and Jaun's replacement as H.C.E. While Jaun is away, she will miss his "lupstucks," but will try to console herself in love's game of tennis with one who is "immutating" everybody. Like Mrs. Bloom, Isabel has more than one lover. The names of these "boysforus"—Leanders to her Hero—will be inscribed by this *Jungfrau* in her "Jungfraud's Messongebook," to be handy for her Freudian dreams and Jungian lies. Trees and waters associate the girl with A.L.P., as her style associates her with Gerty MacDowell. Shaun, once her "professor," is now her "dean," for whom, "turned a star" (Stella) on his return, she will "duberry my two fesces [faces and *fesses*] under Pouts [Pond's] Vanisha Creme." Meanwhile, buying herself a raincoat at Elvery's Elephant House, she will try to please her Russian general, the "chambermate" for whom "with other lipth I nakest open my thight." The baby talk of her peroration may approximate the replies of Stella to her baby-talking Swift. One cannot blame Jaun for adding to her terminal "ah" an ambiguous "MEN" (457.25–461.33).

Shaunathaun Swift replies to this stellar effusion with "chalished drink" in hand to toast the "living waters" of Isabel-A.L.P. and all the "Esterelles" around her. Mixing champagne, the two girls, and bubbies, he tosses his Eucharist off to "her peepair of hideseeks . . . nippling her bubblets." But Shaunathaun is also Jonathan to Shem's David. That dancer and "froubadour," could he stop "doubling" and "tippling," would be just the boy to leave behind with Isabel; for Shem, always imitating Shaun, says Shaun, is "the shadow of a post." Jaun's commendation of Shem, less surprising than it seems, may mean that if his sister insists on incest, incest with a brother—"like boyrun [Byron] to sibster" (465.17)—is better on the whole than in-

cest with father. So "gullaby," says Gulliver Shaun, about to set
out on his travels. A parting commendation of his "darling
proxy" has this proviso: let there be "nothing between you but a
plain deal table" for no more than a Protestant communion.
Happily Dave-Shem is cycling back to Ireland "just in time as if
he fell out of space" from his "old continence . . . after his
French evolution," like Patrick on the "4.32." This "home
cured emigrant," another H.C.E., is Jaun's "altar's ego." It may
be that, a "poisoner of his word," Shem has "novel ideas," but
these can be overlooked; for, once as opposite as Christ and
Caesar, the twins are now as nearly compatible as Shaun's
Caesar-Christ. After "slanderising himself," Shem is "johnny-
thin," says Shaunathaun. If Jaun turned his coat, Shem turned
his shirt—a tale of a shirt that makes Swift, like H.C.E., a great
composite (461.33–463.29).

However close the union of opposites, Stanislaus-Shaun, obsessed with differences, continues to be "terribly nice" about
Shem-James, who, although "the closest of chems," is Shaun's
"intellectual debtor" and "crib." It may be that Shem-James
"with his blackguarded eye" is the living spit of "Shemuel Tulli-
ver" (H.C.E. as Lemuel-Gulliver Swift), yet Shem is as "sym-
patrico" as any son of Patrick when not "absintheminded" in
Paris. Maybe Shem is a "phoney"—a Yankee doodler wearing
the green—yet Shaun magnanimously takes the hand of this
"dapper dandy" (napper tandy) in a "Claddagh clasp"
(464.2–24). (Claddagh rings of Galway display clasped
hands.) Maybe Shem, retreating like Jack Horner, refused
"three female bribes" (church, country, and mother: the three
loves at the end of *Chamber Music*), yet this triple goddess has
"plenty of woom . . . for the bothsforus." Anyway, "no martyr" how humble, "there's no plagues like rome," both church
and country (465.4–35). If that "illstarred punster" wears a
"schamlooking leaf" in his buttonhole, "our national umbloom"
proves him no more Irish than Mr. Bloom (467.10–11). In the
domestic triumvirate, Shem is "a full octavium" below Shaun;
but both approve of "cesarella," who, like Margareen, created

the triumvirate; for her "flesh-without-word" has the last word
(467.8; 468.4–6). Whatever their differences, Nick and Mick
now compose a "nikrokosmikon" (468.21).

It is time now, says Jaun, "to be up and ambling. . . .
Here's me take off." His departure, far from being the ascension "take off" implies, is putting out to sea, where "Dinky
Doll" (A.L.P.), who will put out to the paternal sea in the last
chapter, rides, like Venus, in her shell. The maternal sea of
death and life will be Jaun's "bride" (468.23–469.20). "Fik
yew!" his parting ejaculation, suitably combines fruit tree, tree
of death, and his opinion of the twenty-nine girls he leaves behind him (469.27). Cf. 9.13.

Those girls, unable to interpret this ambiguity or else distracted by "You watch my smoke," his four last words on the
cross, are "kneedeep in tears" over the death of their "sunflower." They express their grief in a "Maronite liturgy"—we
have Joyce's assurance for this (*Letters*, I, 263–64)—of twenty-
nine words (470.6–21). According to these, the Maronites of
Lebanon ("Leafboughnoon") seem to have been devoted to
trees: not only the cedar, but the cypress of Mount Sion, the
palm, the plane, and the rose of Jericho—the cross, after all, is a
tree—and to the game of tennis besides. But "Oasis . . . Oisis
. . . mirage" complicate Lebanon with Egypt, Isis, and
Osiris. Osiris, one of Frazer's dying and rising gods, was torn to
pieces by Set, his brother; but Isis, the sister and wife of Osiris,
gathered his pieces up and restored them to life. Horus (see "the
chamber of horrus," 455.6), the son of Isis and Osiris and a sun
god, avenged his father by killing Set. It is easy to see why the
girls evoke a legend which prefigures that of the Earwicker family: the killing of father, the renewal of his pieces by mother, the
rivalry of brothers, incest, and the confusion of son with sun.
Jaun, our "sunflower" (Jesus-Wilde), dying on Good Friday,
lying in the dark of the sepulcher on Holy Saturday, will rise on
Easter Sunday. Before his resurrection, let the barrel be his
tomb.

With a "hermetic prod" (470.2–3. Hermes, the magician, is
Egyptian Thoth) Jaun pushes his barrel off—all sealed and

stamped for the "last post" (470.26–29). Blowing "his own trumpet" and with a parting "glance of Irish frisky"—*"hasta-luego,"* so long—he floats down the Liffey while the twenty-nine "pacifettes" utter twenty-nine words for peace in twenty-nine languages (470.36–471.5). Good-by to Izzy, whom, though "dizzier" than the other Stellas and Vanessas, Jaun loves the best. Adjusting the trim of his "corporeity" (*corpus*-barrel), with his "bungaloid" hat "bucketing after," he is off on his "easting" towards Easter and the Irish Sea, far from "that region's general," Sickerson, that son of a Danish bear, and the girls waving handkerchiefs. In the barrel maybe, the "bouchal" who shot the Russian General is also running along a road like a last postman. Whatever his mode of departure—it is Holy Saturday now—the "export stout fellow" is soon "lost to sight" (471.6–36).

We of "Shamrogueshire," keening him with Tom Moore's "wail of evoker," praise a boy who, as "wideheaded" as Finn MacCool, deserves the best of wakes. As many-sided as Yeats's Robert Gregory or his Fisherman, Jaun is our "Songster, angler, choreographer." The four cantons of Ireland unite in glorifying our "pattern sent." Every wake means a waking. Here in "this grand continuum" of the *Wake,* ruled by Vico's "fate" and Joyce's "accidence," we await Jaun's "retourneys postexilic" and the new day (472.1–34).

As an exile, Shaun is Shem. Returning in triumph to Irish applause, Shem will be Shaun. When Johnny "comes marching ahome," after his civil war, he is Haun or Shem and Shaun, who will enjoy their Easter rising together. All this on p. 473, the last and most important page of the chapter.

While the phoenix, burning and aspiring on his "spyre," attends to resurrection after death, the "devil era" of De Valera (473.8,20–21), bringing resurrection beyond the limits of "sphoenix spark," makes it the Easter rising of 1916 and the founding of the republic. The "Bennu bird," from the Book of the Dead, is the phoenix or the *be new* bird; and *ben* is Hebrew son. *"Va faotre!"* not only an echo of Shaun's "Fik yew" (*foutre* in French) is Breton *Va faotre,* my son. When the cock of the

morning crows "the east awake," Haun, the "lightbreakfastbringer," is at once Stephen's Lucifer, the light-bringer of the
devil era, and Mr. Bloom, bringer of Molly's light breakfast on a
tray.

This union of opposites—"Janyouare" (John-Shaun) with
"Fibyouare" (Shem-Joyce as February faker) or "Walker" with
"Waltzer"—is the author of Joyce's works, which require co-op-
eration of Stephen with Bloom or of Shem with Shaun. The
book that minds us "of the withering of our ways"—paralysis—
is *Dubliners*. The docile boy who runs round the track with
"high bouncing gait"—Stephen in training under Mike Flynn
—reminds us of *A Portrait of the Artist*. "Breakfastbringer"
brings *Ulysses* in. Surely, "Work your progress," what "will be
contested . . . for centuries to come," and "awake" are the
Wake itself.

What Shem needs is being Shaun a little. Only a partnership
—a conspiracy of Hic and Ille—can do the creative job. The
trouble with the Shem chapter of the *Wake* is too little Shaun.
The little that is wrong with Shaun's second chapter is too much
Shem. *A Portrait, Ulysses,* and most of the *Wake* are in accurate
balance.

430.35–36   These virgins, like St. Bride, are suitably from
            February; for February is the month of the
            twenty-nine leap-year girls. The feast of Agatha,
            Virgin Martyr, is February 5; the feast of Our
            Lady of Lourdes, seen by Bernadette, is Feb-
            ruary 11; the feast of Juliana, Virgin Martyr,
            is February 16; the feast of Eulalia, Virgin
            Martyr, is February 12. (Although not men-
            tioned, the feast of Joyce, the martyr, is Feb-
            ruary 2.) Agatha's lamb and Juliana's rabbit
            predict Easter; but Bernadette's amorous dove
            requires an Annunciation.

431.12–13   Here, the wren, king of all birds, martyred on
            St. Stephen's day (see *Ulysses,* 481), is mixed
            with architecture; for Shaun, the martyr, is a

builder of cities. Inigo Jones and Christopher
Wren are architects; Samson is an architect in
reverse. "The whole creation" from dogs, birds,
and fish to infusoria—the descent of dog to
origin of species—is a kind of architecture.

432.35–36 Hobson's choice (cf. 63.2–3), if we believe
Milton's poem on the University Carrier, is no
choice at all, but Hobson as "hopesome" means
here's hoping. As for "the sinkts in the colan-
der": both saints in the calendar and colanders
in the sink are holy.

433.16,20–22 The "Dar Bey Coll Cafeteria." Three or more
trees (the Indian dar or Irish oak, the bay or
Irish birch, and the hazel, *coll* in Gaelic) are
confused with the Derby and the D.B.C. (Dublin Bakery Company) cafeteria, near Trinity
Coll. (*Ulysses,* 248). "Bun . . . bisbuiting
His Esaus and Cos . . . box. . . . tin's
nearly empty" suggest a tin of Jacob's biscuits,
the ciborium of the Cyclops episode (*Ulysses,*
342–43). Cf. "Jacobs Vobiscuits" (*Ulysses,*
473). The substitution of Esau for Jacob, im-
plying brothers in conflict, allows the appearance, through initials, of H.E.C.

434.4–5,19,27 Ernest Jones's *Hamlet and Oedipus* is brought
to mind by "errors of outrager's virtue" from
Hamlet (434.4–5), "swell foot" or Oedipus
(434.19), and "Jonas" (434.27). Professor
Jones's history of Burrus and Caseous (161–
62) seems to owe something to Ernest Jones's
account of Brutus and Cassius in *Hamlet and
Oedipus.* Not only one of Shaun's authorities,
Ernest Jones seems one of his surrogates.

435.13–14 "Ramrod, the meaty hunter" is one of the
beauties of the *Wake.* This confusion of
Nimrod, the mighty hunter, with a penis seems
echoed by Dylan Thomas' "old ram rod." But

at Cavanaugh's bar one day, Thomas told me he had never noticed Joyce's Ramrod although, said Thomas, he prized the *Wake* above all other books. He liked words.

440.34–36 A pretty mixture of above and below: the "treasure . . . where extremes [legs and other opposites] meet" is at the crotch and in heaven. "Merry Hal and do whatever his Mary well likes" combines Hail Mary, Henry VIII, the Lord's prayer, H.C.E. and A.L.P.

443.20–25 The "man in brown about town" seems to be Macintosh as Joyce: "about fiftysix or so . . . five foot eight . . . with a toothbrush moustache."

447.9 "The sludge of King Harrington's" (cf. "Harington's invention," 266.12) is the watercloset invented by Sir John Harington and celebrated in his *Metamorphosis of Ajax,* 1596. Jaun's city requires adequate plumbing, like Professor MacHugh's England and Rome (*Ulysses,* 131).

448.34–452.7 This passage is analyzed at length to some depth by Stuart Gilbert in "Prolegomena to *Work in Progress," Our Exagmination,* Paris, Shakespeare and Company, 1929. The sentence that begins with "I could sit on safe side" (449.26) is analyzed in depth at some length by David Hayman, "From *Finnegans Wake:* a Sentence in Progress," *PMLA,* LXXIII (March, 1958), 136–54.

450.5 "Swansway," repeated 465.35, is more than a possible reference to Proust and one of two directions. The swan is Leda's Swan or God. His way, taken by Jaun, is the way of the cross.

454.35–36 "The seanad and pobbel queue's remainder" and the "SPQueaRking" (455.28, *Senatus*

Populusque Romanus) stand, in this context, for the Holy City. "Seekit headup," echoing the Ondt's "Seekit Hatup" (Sekhet Hotep, 415.34–35), is a cup of scald from Egypt. Perhaps seeking heaven is like seeking immortality in an Egyptian tomb.

460.27 "Boysforus" (Bosporus and boys for us) and "bothsforus" (465.9) call for "hero and lander" (466.14). In the first case, the Bosporus is the Hellespont and the boys are Leanders to Isabel's Hero. In the second case, one of the twins, like a Dane at Clontarf, is a hero and lander.

466.18 "Mr. Jinglejoys." Wyndham Lewis, in *Time and Western Man* (New York, 1928, Chapter XVI, p. 105), compares Joyce's style with Mr. Jingle's.

466.21 "Sedulous to singe" mixes R. L. Stevenson's "I played the sedulous ape" (*singe*) with J. M. Synge, sedulously aped by Shem. (Once I played the sedulous Gibbon.)

467.16 "Tower of Balbus" (cf. "balbulous," 4.30). In *A Portrait*, Balbus is building a wall. In the *Wake*, he builds towers, especially Babel. Since the fall of this rising tower involves confusion of tongues, the Tower of Balbus is the *Wake* and Finnegan-Joyce its Balbus or Master Builder.

469.33–34 "Leap . . . fall" recalls Stephen as "Lapwing Icarus" (*Ulysses*, 210). The lapwing owes its name to Anglo-Saxon *leap* (rise) and *winc* (fall). Lapwing Finnegan.

471.23–25 The "hankerwaves" after the "paketshape" (packet ship and postman) allude perhaps to Mallarmé's "l'adieu suprême des mouchoirs" ("Brise Marine").

471.35 "Haun." Helmut Bonheim (*A Lexicon of the German in Finnegans Wake*) finds Haun a *Hahn* or cock. Context ("cock" of the morning, 473.22) justifies this finding.

CHAPTER XV · 474-554

His "cruxway" over, our "messio" (478.15–17) is lying "dormant" on a mound. His "dream monologue" in the hearing of the leap-year girls has become a "drama parapolylogic" (474.1–5, a paraplegic staging of many-worded asides) before an audience of four old men. Sleepy Shaun, having been Jaun and Haun a while, is "metandmorefussed" now (513.31) to Yawn. His Easter rising at the end of Chapter XIV was only predicted. Easter itself must wait until Chapter XVII. If Yawn's present dormancy represents Holy Saturday, Chapter XVI could represent the Harrowing of Hell.

The four old men, who have served as Earwicker's judges, customers in his pub, and the annalists of Tristan, are "psychomorers" now (476.14–15). Shaun is always answering quizzes, and it is "question time" again (476.32). The inquisition of the inquisitive four takes the forms of a fishing, a hunting, a séance, a trial in court, an analysis in depth, and the sounding of an ocean—what Gerard Hopkins called the "ocean of a motionable mind" and Andrew Marvell, "that ocean" of the mind "where each kind / Does straight its own resemblance find." Yawn's mound is a couch for the convenience of his analysts, whose object is his "soul's groupography" (476.33). Who he is and what is in him are in question.

Who he is remains a problem, but what is in him becomes almost clear as, uncovering layer below layer, the four probers find him, like his father, the host of a multitude. Each layer of Yawn's unconscious contains a member of the family. Isabel, Anna, and Kate emerge to speak through Yawn, their *persona:*

"I have something inside of me talking to myself" (522.26).
Deepest of all in Yawn and the most difficult of all to bring to
light is H.C.E. "You may identify yourself with the him in you"
(496.25–26), say the four, trying to combine the old Earwicker
with the new. Since Yawn, exposed from top to bottom, contains
all the people of the *Wake,* he amounts to the *Wake* with its
"tales within tales" (522.5). The "cubical crib" (476.32) on
which he lies is also the *Wake;* for this book is an incubating
cube with "six insides." What the four men are after, then, is not
only H.C.E., the *Wake's* personal concentrate, but the *Wake* itself. Like a college of critics or critics in a college, examining the
levels of a text, they are trying to discover what they are in.
Their success in this endeavor is no less than that of any four
critics in any college or, for that matter, any four colleges. What
more can we expect of "psychomorers," however senior?

What they are after, on "the twelfth day" of Christmas or
January 6, is an epiphany or showing forth. As Earwicker's
trousers fall, someone says, "How culious an epiphany!"
(508.5–11) It is not surprising that these epiphany-seekers—or
at least the synoptic three of those cards—are the "three kings"
(474.18), who shuffled to the manger on January 6 to see a
baby. What he shows forth shows us a good deal about H.C.E.
that we may have been unsure of or reluctant to agree to.

The inquest, for example, establishes Earwicker's place
among the three soldiers, the *"Three in one, one and three."*
Two of this trinity are Shem and Shaun; and the third person is
"the shame that sunders em." This *"tertium quid"* or Holy
Ghost is plainly H.C.E. (526.11–14). "Arise, sir ghostus!"
(532.4)

The inquest accosts, but fails to solve, the problem of Earwicker's name. Sir Holy Ghostus, having arisen from Yawn,
speaks of the "necknamesh" the king gave him (31–32), a nickname "which is second fiddler to nomen" (546.3–4). If Earwicker is his nickname—like the "nickelname" Adam imposed
on "every toad, duck and herring" (506.1–2)—what is Earwicker's true *nomen?* It could be Persse O'Reilly, as Hosty insisted (44.14); but *perce-oreille* is only an earwig of another

color. Earwicker's name could be Porter if we trust the Prankquean's riddle about "porterpease" (21.18–19. Cf. 560.22–31;
570.15–20); it could be Coppinger (524.18), Oglethorpe
(81.21), or even Finnegan. Since Earwicker is everybody,
he requires a new name for every "Time, place!" (546.23–24),
which, more than "daybowbreak" and closing time in the pub, is
every time and place in Vico's continuum. Earwicker's pub may
be the Mullingar, the Bristol or even the Phoenix. His favorite
son and successor may be Kevin, Shaun, Chuff, Taff, Tristan,
Yawn or What's His Name. What the "hek!" To name is to fix,
define or identify; and nothing in the *Wake* is certain enough for
naming. Whatever his name, Earwicker is general, the Russian
General in particular. "Who are you?" the four old men ask
Yawn, "Is it yourself?" "I'm not meself at all" (487.18), says
Earwicker-Yawn. Let us settle, then, for H. C. Earwicker, as
good a name as any and one, since its initials crowd the book,
that keeps our hero in mind. Let the four old men worry about
identity. Earwicker's card of identity, forged by a card, is the
Wake that we have to be content with.

For the matter of that, who are the four old men on their
"octopods" (484.2) and who their quadrupedal ass? These
questions find readier answers. That the four are the Four Masters again is indicated by "peregrines" (484.29), "O'mulan-
chonry" (482.12), and "Michael Clery" (520.3), which, in
case you have forgotten, are names of the Masters. Having
served Tristan in this capacity, they now serve Yawn, who is
still Tristan on occasion. As "mamalujo" (476.32), the four are
Matthew Gregory, Marcus Lyons, Lucas Tarpey, and John (or
Shaun) MacDougal (475–76). "Jonny na Hossaleen" (little
horse, 476.27–28) or "Johnny my donkeyschott" (Don Quixote, 482.14) is followed as usual by "Esellus" (*Esel,* 478.8),
the ass, who abides our questions. The four apostles, also "quar-
termasters" (477.13), stand for the four quarters or provinces
of Ireland: Matthew, from the North, is Ulster; Mark, from the
South, is Munster; Luke, from the East, is Leinster; and John,
from the West, is Connaught. The four are Vico's ages too:
Matthew, the divine age; leonine Mark, the heroic age; Luke of

Dublin, the human age; and John, the *ricorso*. John's West is connected with renewal in "The Dead"; and here, sharing Shaun's name, John suits a son who, after sleep, will wake, rise, and shine. The ass, attending this renewer, may be Joyce, the "interpreter" (478.8).

Back now to that sleeper who will wake when the four around him, at a wake of a sort, wake him enough. Himself entirely, Yawn, as we have seen, is not himself at all. So qualified, he is at home in the human age of this chapter. The age of "gossipocracy" (476.4)—its language often suitably abstract—is the time of cities. H.C.E., Master Builder and the Balbus of Babel, is their builder. H.C.E.-Finnegan, hodcarrier and bricklayer, fell from his ladder while a wall was under construction. Now awake and emerging from sleeping Yawn, he carries his hod up the ladder again to build New York, London, Paris, and Dublin. The Master Builder's celebration of building is the climax of this chapter.

Since this chapter represents Vico's human age, the abundance of reversals—Bruno, for example, as "Nobru" and Nola as "Anol" (490.26–27)—is curious; for since the device of reversal appears most often in fourth chapters, we have come to connect it with renewal. To be sure, the building of cities is commonly their renewal; and reversal suits the switching of identities—Yawn as Isabel, for example—and the conflict of twins. Maybe reversal here is a promise of renewal in the next chapter, which reverses that promise.

Curious too the inordinate length of the present chapter, rivalled in respect of this by Chapter XI alone. Both XI and XV concern the human age. This age, Joyce's particular province, is the one in which he was most and least at home. Perhaps the abstraction of humanity—his virtue in the *Wake*—detained him. It takes time and space to pin the unpinnable down. Old H.C.E. of Chapter XI and Yawn in process of becoming H.C.E. in Chapter XV are important enough to justify all those "enduring long terms" (519.20), which, if of the better sort, we gaze on so fondly today; but other chapters seem no less important. If, as a summary of the *Wake* and its people, this chapter—like the

Circe episode, a summary of *Ulysses*—demands length, other chapters are equally demanding. Maybe Joyce, always adding, leaving nothing out, and distracted by the joys of complication, forgot that more than enough is too much. But too much of Joyce is too little for Joyceans. Even if not one of those yet, courage! Chapter XI is one of the most difficult, and Chapter XV, except for a few "traumaturgid" (496.24) pages, one of the easier ones. If the chapter were shorter, we should miss a lot of fun.

An obstacle, preventing our descent to easiness, confronts us at the start. This "sevenply sweat of night blues" consists of seven formidable words, from "Feefee" to "ooridiminy," and an ascending scale of exclamation points (475.1–2). Although the first three of the seven words suggest a fearful giant, the sequence is puzzling. Of no common tongue, the words may be Swahili or Eskimo for all I know, or, like the *"nebrakada femininum"* of *Ulysses* (242), the nonsense of a spell or incantation. Associated with celestial phenomena (meteor, nebula, rainbow) and with parts of the body (navel, ribs, entrails) these words, uniting above and below, are Hermetic enough to please a magician—and seven is a magic number (475.12–17). When added, the exclamation points, rising from one to seven, total twenty-eight, the number of a month, and, reappearing with changes (492.4–7), the imperfect "gammat" of words and exclamation points becomes the days of the week. Plainly, we have to do with time in month, week, and music. But the thing, like Yawn himself, remains a riddle. Coming upon Yawn in this setting, the four men, like Oedipus coming upon the Sphinx, wonder what "class of a crossroads puzzler he would likely be" (475.3–4). A likely answer to this riddle, as to that, is Man.

The man the old men come upon—no walker on two legs now—is a baby, flat on his back, his four legs in the air, "dormant" yet wailing with "earpiercing dulcitude" as if you had stuck a pin in his bum. The "three kings" came to see a big baby. Our four kings—or, considering the incantation, Magi—find a very big one indeed: a giant, "ells upon ells of him" on his "mountainy molehill" of a mound (474.11–475.12) "amongst

. . . the flowers of narcosis." Gigantic Earwicker, the supine E, lay "dormant"—"like an overgrown babeling"—between "two mounds" (6.31–32; 12.19–20,35–36). Yawn is only half the babeling his father was.

Nevertheless, the four circuit judges think Yawn worth a "starchamber quiry"; for, if he is Man, he is "everybug his bodiment," in which "they would see themselves" (475.18–21). In short, the proper study of mankind is man in the *Wake*. The study of this man by these men in the *Wake* is a little perplexing at times because their questions and his answers are indicated, in the manner of France, by simple dashes that leave speakers unidentified. Identifying the speakers, though not altogether beyond our ingenuity, requires a lot of it.

The first attempt on Yawn, that "slipping beauty" with the "blurbeous lips" of a whale, is a kind of fishing (477.20–30). "—Y?" or Why? asks the first questioner. Taking this literally, Yawn ambiguously and inaccurately answers, "—Before You!" (477.31–32) Jute's "Yutah!" comes to mind. Here, as in the conference of Mutt and Jute, communication will be difficult. Identity and communication, as strangers say—Camus and Beckett among them—are problems around here now.

Yawn's mound is a "prehistoric barrow" or "orangery," the dump from which the hen scratched the letter up (110.27–29). Roman letters and runes carved on trees also recall Mutt's "allaphbed" (18.16–36). Lying in the litter of the *Wake*, Yawn answers a questioner's "Whure yu" (where or who are you) with a complication of clover (shamrock), Swift, Patrick, and H.C.E. "Trinathan" Swift of St. Patrick's is as triple as Yawn's "fatherick," and no less devoted to "Typette" (Swift's Stella and Isabel in a context of letters. 477.36–478.30. Cf. "peatrick," 3.10). Bad French fails to distract the questioners of "Pat Whateveryournameis."

Their fishing turns by way of "padredges" (Patrick, father, birds), foxes, and wolves to hunting (478.34–479.21), and then, by the inconsequence of dream, to boating. The "dungcairn" on which Yawn is sprawled, says one of his inquisitors, was once a boat perhaps: the burial boat of the Book of the

Dead, the ship of a Danish invader or of voyaging Hanno, or the boat that sailed for "Weissduwasland" (Goethe's *"Kennst du das Land"*) and never returned. Since "Knowest thout the kind?" (Yawn, *das Kind*) is the question, one of the questioners says, "Spake ab laut!" "Warum night!" says Germanic Yawn (479.19–36). But his French distortion of Goethe, "Conning two lay payees" (480.1, Earwicker's two girls), is an attempt to change the subject—an attempt that fails; for Earwicker in Yawn is what the men are trying to get at. Earwicker, says Yawn, is Danish "Spadebeard," a perfidious foreigner ("welsher"), who did no more than give suck at his "breast-paps"—an epicene wolf of the sea who, like the wolf of Romulus and Remus, was no more than foster parent. Or else, "Ecce Hagios Chrisman"-Earwicker is Jesus Christ. "Oh, Jeyses, fluid!" (an English cleaning preparation), says one of the impatient men: Who is the real "Bill of old Bailey?" (the cape and lighthouse of Howth and the court in London). Still hunting sea wolves and moving in the "beast circuls," the men think Yawn has got himself into a "wrynecky fix" (Goethe's *Reinecke Fuchs*). Mooksey Yawn feels less fixed than foxed by the "whole totem pack" of Johann Wolfgang von Goethe (480.4–36).

Yawn's "tristich" on H.C.E. (481.1–11) confuses the great man with Vico, as one of the four men observes. But, he adds, coming down from "the asphalt to the concrete," let us rather consider Father Abraham and "Gun, the farther" as the builder of cities (481.12–30). That, says Yawn, is the very "man I go in fear of . . . he could be all your and my das" (Midas), and the Trinity of "Petries [*pater*] and violet ice [*filius*] . . . and spiriduous sanction." Yawn and Lewis Carroll's Tom Tower (at Christ Church, Oxford) used to refer to him as "Dodgfather, Dodgson and Coo [pigeon]." Ignoring Carroll-Dodgson and the Trinity, an inquisitor reverts to golden Midas and his ass's ears: What's his name? "Me das has or oreils," Yawn admits. But ears suggest "Piercy. . . . Pursyriley" and "Vulva," his wife. Diverted by A.L.P., the four men discuss the letter found by the hen in the dump and its more literate equivalent, the *Wake*, "our

book of kills" in "counterpoint words" which, though never
"coded" (one sign for each meaning), can be "decorded" if ear
and heart can catch what Joyce's eye grieved for: "The gist is
the gist of Shaun but the hand is the hand of Sameas." Kevin's
"counterfeit" claims to finding the letter and Pigott's "hesitancy" confirm Shaun's role as Jacob to Shem's Esau and Cain
to his brother's Abel: "Been ike his kindgardien?" (481.31–
483.26).

Shaun, not Shem—that "fakesimilar," is father's boy. It was
for "patristic motives," says Yawn, that, circumcising his hairs
and reciting "meas minimas culpads," he donned the "habit" of
a monk. (His austerity anticipates that of St. Kevin in Chapter
XVII, 604–06.) "I," Yawn continues, or "the person whomin I
now am," always attentive to the commands of "Spheropneu-
maticus," faithfully said the "night office" with the "other cata-
chumens." Yet the four "laycreated cardinals," unfair to one
who saved and taught them, have held his "lapsus langways"
against him. "My . . . decanal caste is a cut above you peregrines [Annalists]. . . . I'm of the ochlocracy" (the ruling
mob, 483.27–484.36). Indeed, like those of the Prince of
Wales, Yawn's crest is three feathers and his motto is "Itch
dean." As Prince of Wales, Yawn is heir apparent of "Yod" or
"Bog," the royal (and divine) father (485.2–6). As orator, he
is not unlike Lucky in *Waiting for Godot.*

Little wonder, then, that Luke—identifiable here—exclaiming, "Gags be plebsed!" asks: "Are we speachin d'anglas land-
age or are you sprakin sea Djoytsch?" (485.10–13) This excellent question is ours when we read the *Wake,* where quarreling
opposites—land and sea, French and German, English and
"Djoytsch"—confuse us a little, however certain we may be that
the result is *echt* "Djoytsch." Anyway, Luke continues, what we
really want, "Master Monk," is news of your "old fellow . . .
through the ages," that "twicer," born in a stable (Jesus), that
sinner (Adam) who fell from the Magazine wall and went to
prison: "Tsing tsing!" (485.8–28) Inspired by the Chinese air
of this, Yawn's reply, in pidgin English, concerns "Jackinaboss"
(485.33)—Jack, the boss, who built the house that Jack built,

popping up from the box of the *Wake,* or, like the three soldiers, popping from the bushes: "Upjack!" and at 'em (487.4).
"Hell's Confucium!" says philosophical Luke, discouraged by
the "chinchin chat" of a "postal cleric" with "a chink in his
conscience." Enough about your "lambdad." Are you St. Patrick—432 and all that? Yawn's reply in a "tristich" concerns
432 and Tristan, another invader of Ireland. Patrick's 432 and
Tristan or "History as her is harped" by the Irish, reminding
Luke of Vico's four ages, suggest the need of stronger measures
(485.35–486.13), the substitution of magic for "psychosinol-
ogy" (China, analysis, and sin). Taking up a "T square"—the
Wake is a square as well as a cube; tea is domestic; and T, a
member of the "Doodles family" (299.F4), is the "tripartite"
sign of Tristan—Luke places his Masonic device against Yawn's
temple, lips, and breast to see what "irmages" of "oneir"
(dream) will be evoked. Responding with eye, feeling, and ear,
Yawn comes up with a "triptych vision" of H.C.E. and A.L.P.,
Tristan and Isolde, Swift with Stella and Vanessa (486.14–35).

Did it ever occur to you, asks an inquisitor, that Shem, your
"complementary character," might be substituted for you? A
monk's "Hood maketh not frere. The voice [in the *Wake*] is the
voice of jokeup." Reversals—Trickpat, Roma-Amor, Lapac-
Capal, Upjack-jokeup—attend this return to the rivalry and
interchange of brothers (487.1–25). "God save the monk!"
says Yawn, reminded by these "crossqueets" of his messianic
past. Good "Freeday's child," dead, like Jesus, between "loving
and thieving," will return (487.26–34) and, an unrecognizable
dark horse, will win the race.

By way of Bruno—"alionola equal and opposite brunoipso"
—the conversation returns to Shem and Shaun. A "skipgod,"
expelled from Ireland "for looking at churches from behind"—
as Mr. Bloom looked at statues—Shem, says Shaun, was always
cabling home for financial aid from "switersland" (Zurich) or
wherever his colonial expansion took him. May God "half muxy
on his whole!" says the griping Mookse. Yet, like "castor and
porridge" (Pollux and Esau), the two are brothers, and Shem,
"my shemblable! My freer!" (as Baudelaire and T. S. Eliot re-

marked), deserves something, preferably a place in the "antipathies of austrasia" (Trieste and the Australia to which Jim the Penman was transported). This speech or "letter selfpenned to one's other," says an inquisitor, is quite "a study." Yes, says Yawn, "this nonday diary, this allnights newseryreel" of his is equivalent to the *Wake*, for which he claims credit, or to the letter he claims he found. Any rooster, says a skeptical master, "can peck up bostoons" (the letter from Boston and T. S. Eliot, 488.3–490.1). Returning to Bruno and the quarrel of twins, the conversation centers on "Baggot" (Shaun, carrying his bag on Baggot Street), and "Gottgab" (Shem), that "mispatriate" with God-given gab who is really a "doblinganger." After all, says one of the men, when opposites are united, "Tugbag is Baggut's" (490.1–491.13), but enough of this. Have you heard of "Van Homper" (H.C.E.) or of *"Ebell Teresa Kane"* (A.L.P., the mother of Cain and Abel)? Yawn responds with verses on King Mark and Earwicker's sin in the Park—Swift's Brobdingnag on the bum with "lillypets" (the two Lilliputian girls) or, adds one of the four men, "Mr. Hairwigger" with "twinned little curls," and the Russian General, taking down his trousers to take the temperature of the grass one turdsday (491.16–36). Talk of Earwicker's sin reminds a questioner of A.L.P., who, in "deltic dwilights," like Yeats in a rivery, sang to her "henpecked" husband through the bars of his jail (492.8–12).

Speaking suddenly through Yawn's mouth, A.L.P. rises to defend her husband, the "Djanaral," against all detractors. Her references to India are more puzzling than those to *Sechseläuten,* to the Angelus, and to bringing a specimen of urine to the "family drugger" to see "was my watergood." "I hindustand," she says, that my "dodear . . . mainhirr"—a menhir is an upstanding monolith—was jailed and arointed with "tummy moor's maladies . . . below the belch" by the "sexular clergy," but he always did his duty by me: "He hidded up my hemifaces . . . he locked plum into my mirrymouth . . . and . . . showed me his propendiculous loadpoker." Disconcerted perhaps by this connubial revelation, an interrogator asks: "Which was said by whem to whom?" But, in spite of Yawn's evasions, this interro-

gator soon recognizes A.L.P., renewal's agent, Isis to H.C.E.'s
Osiris, bringer of "Nu-Men, triumphant" (*lumen* and numinous
new men): "Be thy mouth given unto thee!" ("Let our cry come
unto thee," *Salve Regina,* 492.13–493.33). Yawn, too, recognizes the voice from his mouth as that of his mother, the domestic rainbow. After muttering awhile about volcanoes, serpents,
planets, stars, the points of the compass, the writing on the wall,
and the city, the four men hail "heva heva," center of them all
(493.34–494.26): "Holy snakes . . . Eva's got barley under
her fluencies."

So evoked, A.L.P. resumes the defense of her husband: "I
will confess to his sins and blush me further." What if they accused him in "annoyimgmost letters and skirriless ballets?" He
adored her as his triple goddess, "Granny-stream-Auborne"
(Kate, A.L.P., Isabel), and "I cool him my Finnyking." It may
be that he put "pennis in the sluts maschine" of those two
"legintimate lady performers of display unquestionable," but
"O'Neill saw Queen Molly's pants" (*Honi soit qui mal y pense*).
This oral letter to her husband (494.27–495.33) ends with
"R. . . . S.V.P."

You may wish, "Frui Mria," to convince us "by degrees"
(Hail Mary, full of grace) that you are patroness of letters and,
as poor old woman, Ireland's Muse, but you are mistaken, says
one of the four men: "Lordy Daw [H.C.E.] and Lady Don
[river]!" Whatever you say in defense of "that old humbugger,"
he was properly "conspued" (*conspuer,* Lenehan's favorite
word in *Ulysses*). Yawn, resuming in his proper voice, confirms
this opinion: Persse O'Reilly was "flappergangsted" in the Park,
and peeping Toms at home saw all that passed—as we shall too
in the next chapter—between "Ma's da. Da's ma"—or, if you
prefer a palindrome—"Madas. Sadam" (495.34–496.21).

Changing the subject from father and the watershedding girls
of the family, the questioners turn to the H.C.E. within Yawn
and identical with him, the "dadaddy" who was in domestic tea
before "he went on the bier" (in his pub and at his wake). Let
us, they say, discuss Finnegan's wake and *Finnegans Wake*
(496.22–497.3).

Yawn obliges with an elaborate account, echoing Chapter I, of the wake: first, the arrival of mourners at "the licensed boosiness primises" where the man who fell from the Magazine wall is laid out. The twelve customers are there, along with Hosty's crowd, the two girls, the three soldiers, and, strangest of all, J. B. Dunlop (a Viconian tire, W. B. Yeats, and J. W. Dunne, the authority on serial time). "Afeerd he was a gunner," but popping his corks and drinking his whisky, they shout, "*Thieve le Roué!*" Newspapers—from the "ourish times" to "Munster's Herald"—have sent reporters. Next, A.L.P. prepares the Eucharist, "his beers o'ryely, sopped down by his pani's annagolorum" (*panis angelorum*), which she has baked to help the mourners "salvage their herobit of him." The consumed god, "lying high . . . in all dimensions," surrounded by the "cummulium of scents," is wept by the nine orders of angels: "chilidrin and serafim, poors and personalities, venturous, drones and dominators, ancients and auldancients" (Cherubim, Seraphim, Powers, Principalities, Virtues, Thrones, Dominations, Angels, and Archangels, together with members of the family and assorted Dubliners). "Reduced to nothing," the great corpus awaits "a rouseruction of his bogey" (497.4–499.3). Meanwhile the Mass for the Dead proceeds ("Rockuiem . . . eyis" —*Requiem aeternam donna eis, Domine, et lux perpetua luceat eis*) through all the dancing and keening: "Lung lift the keying!" But some of the keening for the king—"Tschitt! Mergue!" for example—is less than solemn; for there's lots of fun at Finnegan's wake (499.4–14). But who exactly is the king they keen? He may be incestuous old "adipose rex," who answered the riddle of the Sphinx (475.3–4). But "Finnk. Fime. Fudd?" (Did you think me dead?) proves the fallen giant Finnegan himself (499.16–18).

Yawn's account of the wake, dismissed by the critical four as a tissue of lies, is certified, says Yawn, by what is "buried ofsins . . . insidesofme." From what is inside him, something like the "static babel" of a radio emerges, as much to Yawn's confusion as to that of his tormentors. "Whoishe linking in? . . . Whoishe?" asks Yawn. "Whu's within?" ask the four men.

What emerges is a bloody conflict of Gael against Gall and a hunt, followed by "Christ [peace] in our irish times" and other journals. Peace brings lovers: Tristan and Isolde, Swift and Stella. We know now who she is and who's within: either "Brinabride" Isolde or "Pipette" Stella. The four men, having tuned in, get the message as well as we. This page (500), a sequence of motifs, from Wagnerian "Bayroyt" perhaps, is constructed like a poem—"The Love Song of J. Alfred Prufrock," say; though Joyce would not have liked to hear that said. Let us say, then, that this page is a musical arrangement, as intricate and agreeable as the Sirens episode of *Ulysses*.

"SILENCE" (cf. parenthetical "Silent," 14.6) may indicate a considerable pause in the verbal process or the end of a cycle; but, if the second, what cycle, why here? Resuming as a theatrical production, the sounding of a deep, and a wireless or telephone call, the interrogation switches to the landscape and weather of a "particular lukesummer night" in Luke's Dublin, where bonfires (cf. "Baalfire's night," 13.36) light the affairs of "our lord of the heights nigh our lady of the valley." The moon, says Yawn, was shining through A.L.P.'s wintry fog on H.C.E. falling for the two girls "at their parkiest": "Hail many fell of greats! Horey morey smother of fog!" Turning from "Miss Somer's nice dream," says a questioner, let us examine more attentively the dump, that kitchen-midden of "broken pottery and ancient vegetables," at once Eden, where the "illassorted first couple first met," and the Park, where the three soldiers observed Earwicker and the two girls: "Trickspissers vill be pairsecluded" (501.7–503.29).

In this dump, whether Paradise or Park, grows the everlasting ashtree (Yggdrasill) or elm, which, says Yawn—as if Jack—is our "beingstalk," both tree of life and, as "tunc" suggests, the cross: "quickenbole and crossbones." Taking a "bard's highview" of "eggdrazzle," Yawn finds it crowded with birds (including Mark's wren) and apples. Both male and female—the form masculine, the gender feminine—this great tree shelters the three soldiers and the two girls: "burstall boys with their underhand leadpencils climbing to her crotch for the origin of spices and charlotte darlings with silk blue askmes chattering in [Darwinian] dissent to them." On the branches of this family tree are the holly and ivy of Christmas and the snake and fig leaves of the fall. And so from "germination" to "gemination," from "Ond's [Evil's] outset till Odd's end," this bird-infested "plantitude," whether watered with "tears such as angels weep" or "rocked of agues," has flourished: "nobirdy aviar soar anywing to eagle it!" "Encircle him circuly. Evovae!" (*Evoe* is the whoopee of Bacchantes.) In a word, it is our "Upfellbowm" (rise, fall, and *Apfelbaum,* 503.30–505.29).

Thinking only of Adam's sin, which, even if a *felix culpa,* has the "brimsts of fussforus" about it and which brought with it "the wittold, the frausch and the dibble—e.g., Bloom, Molly, and Blazes—the sour inquisitors turn now to fallen H.C.E., "the foerst of our treefellers [Adam and the three soldiers]." Yes, adds Yawn, "and, in the absence of any soberiquiet [name]," the "fanest of our truefalluses" (Christ? 505.32–506.18). Take the stand, say those judges; consider yourself a witness in our court, and tell us about the man who, drinking "Anna Lynsha's Pekoe with milk and whisky," builds "messuages" and, after closing time in the pub, drinks all the leavings, "the coat on him skinside out" (cf. 35.13). "Is it that fellow?" asks Yawn. His name is not "Toucher 'Thom,' " as you seem to think, though, "Pequeen ourselves," like any peeping Tom, he "bopeeped" at the two girls while Yawn was peeping at him. The "cloever spilling" (clavier playing and clover watering) of those girls, if attentively "liszted" to, suggests "bach" (506.19–508.36). Yawn and his four judges are in agreement here. Echoes of the Prankquean (508.26–28), the shooting of the Russian General (509.6–510.8), and the twenty-nine girls "haliodraping" around their "sunflower"—like the twenty lovesick maidens around Bunthorne-Wilde—lead to another review of the wake, the *Wake,* and the Wellington museum (510.13–36): "Whiskway and mortem!" The Norwegian Captain, the tailor's daughter, the Cad and Fox Goodman, Stella, Mutt and Jute, and the Prankquean again crowd the *Wake*: "the hoax that joke bilked" (511.1–36). The "tiroirs" of H.C.E.'s Stella are drawers in two senses, in the second of which the *tiroirs,* like those in human furniture by Dali, are "secretairslidingdraws" (511.27–30). The conference centers now on the marriage of H.C.E. and A.L.P. (512–14): The "park is gracer than the hole, says she." Nevertheless she loves her sailor-explorer, who, on shore now, keeps a pub, the "Toot and Come-Inn" (Tutankhamen) by the bridge. Here "Siriusly and selenely," like star and moon, the happy pair prospers behind the shutter. Twins are born: Shaun, his father in part—*ex ungue leonem* (from the claw you can deduce the lion)—and Shem, the Cad, always dancing the "polcat." What is Isabel made of? "Trists and thranes" and other goodies. The four men and the twelve were present at the marriage feast in "Eccles's hostel." What is the groom's name and what his address? asks an inquisitor. "i..'. .o..l." (Finn Mac-Cool), says Yawn (514.17–18). A marriage announcement and the advertisement of a money-lender—the two are not unconnected—follow (514.22–31). Did H.C.E. say anything important: "Nnn ttt wrd?" "Dmn ttt thg," says Yawn, "Sangnifying nothing." This "secret speech . . . obviously disemvowelled" is no more difficult than the rest of the "process verbal" (515.2–15).

As "eyewitless" and the Mister Bones of a minstrel show, Yawn answers questions about the "epic struggle" of father and son—a struggle not unlike that of the Ondt and the Gracehoper (515.21–516.2) or, as the opening sentence of *A Portrait* implies, of Stephen and his father. This "angelic warfare" involves the rebellion of Lucifer—the "luciferant" (35.11) Cad with his "pocket browning" or revolver. (Cubs, pups, and whelps imply the youth of this antagonist.) Father is "mardred" (murdered and martyred) as the clock strikes twelve or thereabouts, time of the rising son and of Leverhulme's "sunlife" soap. Mutt and Jute, Hosty, Buckley, and the "fender" observe the Miltonic struggle. Does the Cad's victory mean the "finnish" of the "revalvered" old man? Nothing of the kind. Finnish means Phoenix. After Vico's pure and pious war come peace and rebuilding. "Thanksbeer to Balbus," the great engineer and publican (516–18). "Vary finny," says Luke.

"A while back," he continues, while you were discussing the weather with Mark (501–02), you told the "grand jurors" it was raining. An inspired friend (A.L.P.), says Yawn, telling me rain was predicted, also told me about Earwicker's walk in Phoenix Park, where he seems to have met not only the Cad with a pipe, the two girls, and the three soldiers but the Four Masters (519.14–520.21). Nothing about these encounters is clear. Still less the consequent dispute among the Masters (520.22–522.4). Matthew, Mark, and John seem united, "three to one," against Luke, the "august one" (521.31–33). But "Johnny" (521.10) could be either John or Yawn or the two together. In whichever capacity, John denies that he has received anything for his evidence—not even a free drink of whisky or porter. To add to our difficulties, "Power," the "tristy minstrel," seems a confusion of Luke, the Dubliner, with Yawn. What is "yur right name now?" is the question (521.21–22) or where are we at, at all? Such shifting, merging, and uncertainty could mean Joyce's success in capturing the air of dream.

It is a relief after this to get back to what, if anything, happened in the Park, where the "fender" faced "a choice of two serious charges, as skirts were divided on the subject." And, adds Yawn, "bushes have eyes. . . . Buggered if I know" which of the two charges of "moral turpitude" I would choose if the choice were mine (522.7–19): "Are you to have all the pleasure quizzing . . . me?" A pretty "third degree witness!" says a quizzer; you have all the symptoms of H.C.E.'s "homosexual catheis of empathy. . . . Get yourself psychoanolised!" "I," says Yawn, as Joyce is said to have said to Jung, "can psoakoonaloose myself" (522.25–36). As a sample of what is "inside of me talking to myself," Yawn brings Sylvia Silence back (61.1–11; 523.1–4). Responding to a call for explanation and "rebus" or concrete example, he gives his questioners a long, incoherent account of Hosty, Frisky Shorty, the girls in the Park, fishy Mr. Coppinger (cf. 55.18) and all the little fishes of his family. Despite his "early bisectualism," Coppinger, *"Our Human Conger Eel,"* has been fertile enough. Another Hosty,

Yawn composes another ballad about H.C.E., the big fish the four fishermen are trying to catch. Fish? Rather Finn MacCool or a Danish invader sailing up the washerwomen's Liffey. Landing him is a matter of his landing (523.19–526.10).

It must be getting plain now—as I must say again—that the *Wake,* like life itself, repeats the same old things again and again. Their endless variations are funny sometimes, sometimes instructive, tiresome sometimes, sometimes poetic. The reappearance of the washerwomen—"Among the shivering sedges so? . . . Besides the bubblye waters of. . . . And tell me now" (526.5–11)—is poetic entirely. The reappearance of the three Grenadiers as British "anglers or angelers" is an instructive variation on an old theme (526.11–15). However funny, the four inquisitors are tiresome or, as the French would say, *marrant.* The very word, *marrant* means funny and boring.

At this point—if, indeed, there are points around here—"Cruachan" asks "Walker John" to do his "patmost" (526.18–20). Cruachan, seat of the kings of Connaught, must be John, the apostle; and Johnny Walker, the spirituous postman, must be John of Patmos, from whom we may expect a revelation. It may be, says Yawn of Patmost, that H.C.E. larked in the "furry glans with two stripping baremaids," but there was another girl who was "always mad gone" (like Maud Gonne) on that "most broadcussed man." This girl, lost in admiration of the me-ness of herself, was always looking at "her bachspilled likeness in the brook." So summoned from yawning depths, Isabel—the Revelation we have been expecting from Patmos—has her watery say through Yawn's watering mouth: "Woman will water the wild world over" (526.20–33).

"Nircississies," says this daughter of a great mother, "are as the doaters of inversion." Like "Secilas through their laughing classes" (or Alices inverted, like Narcissus, in a mirror), "Ys" and her image in the *Bach* are "poolermates in laker life" (526.34–527.2). Her loving words, addressed to the mirror she sits at, recall those of Gerty MacDowell—or, better, the exchanges between Daddy Browning and Peaches (65) or Shaun-

Swift and Stella (143–48). "Listenest, meme mearest!" says the
doting girl, fearlessly; for, as Benjamin Franklin almost said, a
girl in love with herself need fear no lovers.

Her "dare all grandpassia . . . geesing . . . at Strip Teasy"
is incestuous H.C.E. as Daddy Browning, the "old geeser who
calls on his skirt" (65.5–6). But Isabel is safe from his "wick-
red" designs; for, in her mirror or out, she has "two of everything up to boyproof knicks." Whatever the passing excitement
of her "little pom," she has remained, like the Blessed Virgin of
the litany, a "taper of ivory . . . hoops of gold." "It's meemly
us two," she says to her beloved in the mirror, "meme, idoll.
. . . How me adores eatsother simply (Mon ishebeau! Ma
reinebelle!)." So encouraged, she looks forward to marriage—
with herself apparently—in the chapel, "bloss as oranged," music
by "Mindelsinn," and all the proper ceremony: "Kyrielle elation
. . . Sing to us, sing to us, sing to us." Lying now "with warm
lisp" on the bank of the Tolka, her *Bach,* she and her image are
Swift's unmolested "hister" and "esster" (527.3–528.13).

What is this "Languishing hysteria?" asks an impatient inquisitor, "Is dads the thing in such or are tits the that?" Is the
girl of this "poseproem" (a prose poem reversed in a mirror),
Alice "through alluring glass?" "Herself in apparition with herself," is she the Virgin of the Annunciation: "Consuelas to
Sonias may?" (528.14–25)

Since this impatient critic rebukes Mark ("Moonster . . .
lion's shire"), John ("Connacht"), and Luke ("the leinstrel
boy"), he must be Matthew, who, properly enraged by nonsense, demands a more aggressive approach to the problem. Instead of remaining senile incompetents, we must become the
"bright young chaps" of President Roosevelt's "brandnew brain-
trust." So improved, we may be able to solve the matter of the
girls, "Misses Mirtha and Merry, the two [Swiftian] dreeper's
assistents," and the "three tailors"—or the whole family of that
"fancydress nordic" in his "wellingtons." Call constable "Sickerson" (Joe) to the microphone (528.27–530.22). Over a
radio "Hookup" (Yawn's voice) Joe contributes two verses in
Danish from Ibsen about a torpedo (*"torpid dough"*) and

Noah's ark (530.23–24). Enigmatic in the immediate context, these verses, reminding us of Ibsen's "Bigmesser" (530.32) or Master Builder, prepare us for the coming of H.C.E., builder of cities. Before his emergence, however, Kate, summoned in her turn and unwilling to be outdone by Joe, speaks through Yawn's mouth: "She's deep, that one"—deep inside Yawn, but not quite so deep as H.C.E.

Kate's "farternoiser" concerns H.C.E., "Ouhr Former who erred in having . . . gibbous disday our darling breed." What that man needs, Kate says, is confession, the "boob's indulligence," and the psalm or salmon book sanctioned by the Council of Trent. She used to massage his back on the kitchen table, in the intervals of cooking, until he looked at her with "lovensoft eyebulbs." Dancing at his wake and lifting her "juppettes," she showed her "hams" (530.36–531.26).

Enough of this broadcast—all this "finicking about Finnegan and fiddling with his faddles." It is about time to hear from H.C.E. Finn himself, the gigantic sinner "under shriving sheet. . . . Arise, sir ghostus!" (531.27–532.5)

Arising from the darkest deeps of Yawn, now host to a ghost, Earwicker has his say through filial lips. In a way, like Stephen Dedalus before him (*Ulysses*, 18), Yawn "himself is the ghost of his own father." Getting essential Yawn, the four analysts have got what they have been after. What Earwicker-in-Yawn has to say is divided into three parts. The first of these is not unlike the uncalled-for defense of his virtue when accosted by the Cad (36) or his boastful apology in the pub (363–67). The third is his praise of A.L.P. The second, a simple boast and most important of the three, affirms his importance as creator: founder of a family and builder of cities—the "Bygmester" of Chapter I (4–6) and the Jaun-Earwicker of Chapter XIV (446–48): "I'm not half Norawain for nothing" (452.36). Ibsen, architect of a doll's house, suitably attends the apology and boast of the Master Builder in the present chapter. As the names of rivers adorn Chapter VIII, and the names of battles the dubious triumph of Willingdone, so here the names of cities or their parts—from Belgrade to Belgravia, from Manhattan's Little Church Around the Corner to the Bronx. But Dublin—every city as Earwicker is everyman—is central. Hence the references to *Ulysses*, the book of this city. The rebuilding of cities follows the destruction of war as the building of cities proves the happiness of the happy fall and the humanity of the human age. "Things fall," says Yeats, and those who "build them again are gay."

The gaiety of the Master Builder's boast, transfiguring all the dread of cities with their dopes, rioters, and muggers, is that of Joyce, builder of another kind. The London of T. S. Eliot, like the Paris of Baudelaire, is a kind of hell. Shelley's hell is "a city much like London." Not so Dublin, which, whatever its paralysis and dirt, was dear to Joyce, a city man entirely. Building and rebuilding—even their often discreditable results—are gaiety's occasion. Being the Master Builder of Dublin or of the *Wake* is fun.

"Amtsadam" (532.6), the first word of Earwicker's monologue, is a fitting introduction to what follows. Amsterdam is a city; *amts* has to do, in German, with office-holding and Earwicker is a magistrate (7.23); Adam is the creative, happy faller. "Amtsadam," then, means creator and magistrate of a city. Both "Pontofacts massimust" and "Shitric Shilkanbeard," one of Dublin's Danish builders, Earwicker shares, as his stutter shows, Adam's guilt. Hence the insistence of this "cleanliving man" on his virtue in affairs with women: with his "halfwife"— his "verawife . . . nieceless to say"—with the two girls, and the twenty-nine "heliotrope ayelips," the floral yes-girls. "What spurt!" says he, "I kickkick keenly love" my Tennysonian-Chaucerian "dreams of faire women." "Mannequins Passe" (cf. 17.2), not only a matter of mannequins pissing in the Park, is a fountain in the city of Brussels (532.6–533.3).

To prove fidelity to his "wholewife," Earwicker summons witnesses. An Episcopalian chaplain can testify, Earwicker says, to his "clean charactering, even when detected in the dark." Indeed, there is no place like his home, not even John Howard Payne's or Ibsen's "duckyheim." To the applause of Mark, Matthew, Luke, and John, with Moody and Sankey, Gregorian chanters, and Johannes Bach calling the tune, Earwicker is always singing "Home Sweet Home" (533.13–23). The domestic songster easily modulates into a radio—"I am amp amp amplify"—broadcasting from Homeland a market report: "Holmstock unsteaden. . . . Big Butter Boost!" "Anew York gustoms. Kyow! Tak," with which he concludes his broadcast, includes New Year's, New York, Tokyo in reverse, and Danish thanks—out of Ibsen perhaps (533.30–534.2).

Resuming his defense, Earwicker finds no evidence to support the libels about his conduct in Phoenix or Gramercy Park, especially the "currish" accusations of the "caca cad," that "outcast mastiff" (Thomas Aquinas, the Dominican dog of God: "san Tommaso Mastino," *Ulysses,* 637), Mr. "Shames"-Shem, who should be ashamed of himself for his "Ibscenest" nonsense. Jarl "von Hunarig" hopes never to see that "spiking Duyvil" (New York) in "Nova Tara" (Dublin) again (534.7–535.21).

Is that you, "Whitehed?" ask the four old men. (Whitehead is Finn MacCool, Whitehead, the tailor, and white hat.) Speaking from his "profundust" (*De Profundis*), "Old Whitehowth," another O.W., says, "Pity poor Haveth Childers Everywhere." That, say the four, holding a séance now, must be a "disincarnated spirit, called Sebastion" (Melmoth), with "messuages" from the "deadported." The occult "indiejestings" of this "tonguer of baubble" suggest Oscar Wilde, whose "prisonce" (presence in prison) is affirmed by the Mozartian "zober. . . . flautish" voices of boys—bare, ruined choirboys maybe. "Poor Felix Culapert," a "foenix culprit" with open arse in the manner of Italy—*culo aperto.* May bells in the steeples of "ould reekeries" (Edinburgh), the "krumlin," and the "aroundisements" of Paris ring the old sinner out and, like the bells of *Sechseläuten,* ring in the new. (535.22–536.27. "Krumlin" combines the Kremlin with Crumlin, a district of Dublin.)

Undismayed by the critical asides of his four "jurats," Earwicker resumes his apology, swearing before God—"O rhyme us! Haar Faagher. . . ." (*Oremus!* Our Father. . . .)—that he has bared the twin sides of his past. Wilde? More like Parnell. Those in "gladshouses" (Gladstone's glasshouses) should Pigott no stones at the lover of Kitty O'Shea. "The elephant's house is his castle" (E.H.C., a shop for raincoats in Dublin, and a district and pub in London). Because of the "miscisprinks" of the Prankquean and the attempts to convert and baptize him under the auspices of Laurence O'Toole and two other patrons (the three soldiers), he has undertaken "to discontinue entyrely all practices." As for the allegations about Kate: he never did "cophetuise milady's maid." (King Cophetua married a beggar girl.) As for the two girls from "Fleshshambles" Street (Handel's Dublin): am I "their covin guardient" in London? "I would not know to contact such gretched . . . suistersees." As for the caddish three soldiers and their "shrubbery trick" in the Park: I swear by that great menhir, the Wellington Monument (cf. 36.18–25), that "this that is and that this is." ("Deucollion" thrice, the soldiers combine Deucalion, who repeopled the world after the flood, Duke alien or Wellington, and two cullions: testicles and rascals.) I swear by "Shopkeeper, A.G." (Shakespeare and Company, where *Ulysses* was published) that, however "spitefired" and "perplagued," I have done my best (536.28–539.15).

When, a Danish invader, I came over the sea to Dublin to establish my pub, the "brixtol," I found the place a "bog," made it a walled city, and civilized it under Henry II and Henry VIII with "famine . . . Englisch sweat and oppedemics." As tourists may learn from guidebooks, my Dublin is a pleasant place. The four men agree. Visit Drumcondra (a district of Dublin), they urge in four languages (539.16–540.12).

All rests on me, says H.C.E., "your sleeping giant" (cf. 6.33–35; 7.28–32), lying across country from Howth, my head, to the "mortification that's my fate"—the Magazine, feet, twins, and the scandal in the Park. A great builder, like Ibsen and Shakespeare, I have built a modern city: "where the bus stops there shop I." In my Dublin, as its motto shows, "Obeyance from the townsmen spills felixity by the toun." There is no more crime, no more disease. All is tranquil: milord, playing an innocent game of hide and seek, seeks milady in Hyde Park or the Mall. Looking at my works, like God in the Vulgate Genesis or Stephen on the beach (*Ulysses,* 49), I have found them "waldy

bonums" (*valde bona*). I have raised domes and skyscrapers
(cf. 4.35–36; 446–47). Filling in the Sloblands, I have made
Fairview Park. I have constructed a zoo and laid pipes for water
so that any citizen can enjoy a good cup of tea: "the coupe that's
cheyned for noon inebriates." I built a factory for Jacob's biscuits and Esau's pottage. Like Blazes Boylan, "I jaunted on my
jingelbrett." The Dublin Metropolitan Police guard my sons and
daughters—all the "foeburghers, helots and zelots." The "whites
of the bunkers' eyes" and "bringem young" prove my establishment a new world. Of course I have received "omominous letters . . . about my monumentalness" (540.13–543.21). But
two pages of advertisements for rooms (543–45)—Joyce's im-
provements upon Earwicker's claims?—prove the horrors beneath Dublin's respectability to be as brown as those of "The
Boarding House" and even funnier.

In his capacity of king, Earwicker granted a charter to the city
of "Tolbris" (Bristol) as Henry II granted Dublin to the city of
Bristol by a charter, sealed and signed "Enwreak us wrecks,"
Henricus Rex, who, by this charter of 1173, wrecks the city he
chartered in 1171 (545.13–23).

From "my siege of my mighty I was parciful of my subject,"
even those "bleakmealers" the two "pumpadears" and the three
"drummers." Ignoring these and their "tattled tall tales of me," I
established courts, hospitals, and graveyards. ("Sheridan's
Circle" must be Sheridan Square in New York, and "Lenfant" is
clearly Pierre L'Enfant, who planned Washington.) Whatever
my name, I have a coat of arms: two girls as crest, "flappant,
devoiled of their habiliments"; as boss an insect of the order of
coleoptera; in the lower field "a terce of lanciers"; with the
motto *"Hery Crass Evohodie"* (Here, tomorrow, today, and
Evoe or whoopee!). I deserve this for "my virtus of creation"
and will so deserve till daybreak. "Thus be hek" till closing time,
in any time, please. The chorus of oldsters, counting a Viconian
four, seems to approve (545.24–546.28).

The third part of the city-maker's monologue, repeating the
matter of Chapter VIII from another point of view, begins with
praise of "Fulvia Fluvia," his golden river-girl, broadcast from

the radio of Yawn's mouth. Had she flowed uphill in search of lovers, the rascals might have deceived her. As it is, Earwicker alone—he thinks—made love to his "waif" and "spoiled her undines." "Foxrogues" (Foxrock, near Dublin) and "pellmell" (Pall Mall) imply that we are still in the city where these undines were bought and soiled. The quartet provides a chorus to Earwicker's hymn of praise (546.29–547.12).

The pontifex, arching her stream with bridges, led it overland from the hills to the city, along Riverside Drive in New York, the Embankment in London, to Ringsend in Dublin, where, raising his trident, he caused Homer's "polyfizzyboisterous" seas to retire. He "knew" his "baresark bride"—with trident, and "with all my bawdy did I her whorship." They were one, "malestream in shegulf." Danish words, suited to old Dublin, affirm the permanence of their marriage (547.14–36).

Ships crowd the harbor of Annie Laurie, "who expoused that havenliness to beachalured ankerrides . . . in trinity huts they met my dame" (Trinity House, which controls shipping, in London, and "At Trinity Church I Met My Doom," cf. 102.03). "Hochsized" to this harboring girl, Earwicker provided her with clothing, "wispywaspy frocks" and "trancepearances" from Pim's and other shops. Old Dublin became the new Dublin of Georgia (cf. 3.7–8), when he sat down with the "little crither of my hearth" or, like Sir Noah Guinness, exposed his "bargeness" (548–49). The applauding quartet, singing of Stephen's Green, College Green, and the S.S. *Paudraic* in the harbor, seems sure that domestic Earwicker is not a bum entirely.

Far from being one, he provided "potted fleshmeats"—Plumtree's Potted Meat, no doubt, as provided by Boylan—and cosmetics for a girl who, like Solomon's Sheba, was "brown but combly." Combly? He gave her a comb "to teaze her tussy out." As he and his combed darling enjoyed life in Dublin's Mansion House, the "framous latenesses, oilclothed . . . and allpointed"—paintings of former lord mayors, Dick Whittington and Peter Stuyvesant among them—watched from the walls. "All admired her in camises," which, if Earwicker were "our pantocreator" (God and maker of panties), would be "tights for the gods." She also wore "littleritt reddinghats" when riding in Rotten Row. When at home, she used the privy he built for her "to be squatquit in most convenience" (550.4–551.27).

As for their city, he established universities and a democratic government, appropriate to the human age, in which many were polled, few chosen. He built churches. Indeed, as "Blabus was razing his wall," so H.C.E., a greater builder, was raising his— razing it, too, as the ambiguous comment of the choral quartet implies (551.28–552.34): "Hoke! Hoke! Hoke! Hoke!"

Anyway, whether *hoch* or hokum is implied, Earwicker, another Joyce with another Nora, tried to inscribe the alphabet on her virgin page. For her likelier delight he constructed Coney Island, at least five of the seven wonders of the world, Phoenix Park, the "bowery," and many other fair boulevards: the North and South Circular Roads. Westmoreland Street, Westland Row, and Sydney Parade, where Mrs. Sinico met her train (553.1–31). For these streets and Anna's pleasure, he provided rickshaws, tilburys, sedan chairs, and "turnintaxis" (cf. 5.32).

Terminal Matthew, Mark, Luke, and John may imply "Bless the bed I lie upon," the bed of the next chapter, where, indeed, they serve as observant bedposts. Nothing like these four for getting where the action—or inaction—is. But in each place and time, like Earwicker himself, they are different. Here and now, incompetent analysts; there and then, nostalgic sentimentalists; but always, like any historians, peepers.

479.13–14   The "twelves" could be the twelve men, but it seems likelier that they are the two Woolfs, Virginia and Leonard, who, as directors of the Hogarth Press, turned *Ulysses* down on grounds of indelicacy. In Joyce's manuscript Virginia Woolf found, to her dismay, a dog that pees, a man who farts. That day she read no more. Lucky she never looked into the *Wake*.

481.4   "Mithyphallic" seems a distortion of Rimbaud's "Ithyphalliques" ("Le Coeur Volé").

481.14–15 "Morning de Heights . . . rambling under-
groands," the first considerable reference to cities
in this chapter, seems to be Morningside Heights
on the subway in New York, mixed with volcanic
H.C.E. of Dublin. Cf. "morningrise was encam-
passed of mushroofs" (543.12–13), which brings
in the campus and surroundings of Columbia University. The S.S. *Columbia* (548.2) is anchored in
Dublin harbor. Odd that Joyce should have guessed
Columbia's future in Joycean studies: Campbell,
Robinson, Halper, Ryf, Sullivan, and many more.

482.31 "Prouts," "the bells of scandal" (483.6), and
"blarneying" (483.16) identify this authority on
the *Wake* as Mark of Munster. Father Prout of Cork
wrote "The Bells of Shandon," and Blarney Castle
is near Cork. The "easter" neatness and reappearance of "Borsaiolini's house of hatcraft" (483.10–
11) seems a reference to Joyce, who, always celebrating Easter, wore Borsalino hats. "Leap, pard!"
(483.14) seems Mr. Bloom, the black leopard or
panther (Christ) of *Ulysses*. The pard leaps at
Easter.

483.22 "Kalblionized" refers to two beasts of the "star-
menagerie" (476.25–26) of Revelation, 4:7. The
beasts associated with the four apostles appear
throughout this chapter, e.g., Mark's lion, 494.19,
528.30; Metcalfe Luke's ox, calf or bull, 476.26,
522.2,15; John's eagle, 482.15, 493.4. Matthew's
man, probably Yawn, is everywhere. John is also
associated with the lamb, e.g., 486.1.

484.36 "Eggs squawfish . . . marecurious" seems corrupt
alchemical Latin: *Ex quovis ligno fit mercurius?*
"Quovis" or anywhere, if there at all, is strangely
displaced.

485.5 "Yod" (cf. "Yad," 605.4) is the tenth letter of the
Hebrew alphabet as lambda ("lambdad," 486.1) is
the tenth letter of the Greek alphabet. Ten is the

number of God and H.C.E., both dads (261.23–24). "Moy Bog" (485.6) is My God in Russian.

492.22 "Achmed Borumborad" is Dr. Achmet Borumborad from Sir Jonah Barrington's *Personal Sketches* of eighteenth-century Dublin. Since Borumborad maintained a bathhouse in Dublin, he suits the watery context (492.24–27). Passing as a Turk, he was really an Irishman named Joyce. Barrington is mentioned in *Ulysses* (241). Bloom's lemon soap, used in a Turkish-looking bathhouse, is called Barrington's soap (*Ulysses,* 672). Bloom's Mrs. Yelverton Barry (*Ulysses,* 465) owes her name to Barry Yelverton in Barrington's reminiscences.

497.2–3 "Your exagmination . . . of a warping process" became the title of the first book on the *Wake: Our Exagmination Round His Factification for Incamination of Work in Progress* (Paris, Shakespeare and Company, 1929) by Samuel Beckett and company.

502.10 "Galumphantes" is an elephantine distortion of Lewis Carroll's "galumphing" from "Jabberwocky." Cf. "Lewd's carol" (501.36) and "Dodgson" (482.1). Carroll's interest in little girls provides a parallel to H.C.E.'s; but H.C.E., like Swift, was interested more in bigger girls.

505.16–17 "Trees like angels weeping" is a distortion of Milton's "Tears such as angels weep" (*Paradise Lost,* I, 620), quoted in *Ulysses,* 184. Earlier in the *Wake* (230.25) this line, plainly a favorite, becomes "such as engines weep."

511.21–22 "Mien swart hairy" is Danish for My dark gentleman. Cf. "dog meansort herring" (186.32) and "mind uncle Hare" (466.29–30), German for My dark gentleman, and Mutt's "women blown monk sewer" (16.4–5), French for My blond gentleman. Some Scandinavian invaders were dark, others blond.

517.33–35   "A triduum before Our Larry's own day." The
eleventh day of the eleventh month is three days
before the feast of St. Laurence O'Toole, Novem-
ber 14. Cf. "larry's night" (519.5). "Hog and
minne" (519.4) is Hogmanay or New Year's Eve.

521.13–15   "Jones' lame or Jamesy's gait" include, in a hob-
bling way, John Jameson, John's Lane, where
Power is distilled (at the corner of Thomas Street),
and James's Gate, where Guinness is brewed.
"Bushmillah" (Bushmill), the whisky of Ulster
(cf. "ulcers," 521.25), refers to Matthew here.
"Power" (521.22,24), one of Dublin's two whis-
kies, refers to Luke of Leinster, "leinconnmuns"
(521.28).

530.10–11   "Saint Patrick's Lavatory," not only St. Patrick's
Purgatory, is the convenience in the park behind
St. Patrick's Cathedral. Far from the Shelbourne
on occasion, I have found this convenience conve-
nient—so too the "greenhouse" on the Quay and
the more commodious one under Tom Moore's
statue near Trinity College, both celebrated in
Ulysses. A fourth, made use of by Mrs. Bloom
(*Ulysses*, 753), I have had no use for.

533.15–23   These seven or eight lines are a pretty mixture. In
the context of music (John Howard Payne, Moody
and Sankey, and J. S. Bach—from Do to Aw)
and home (Payne's "Home Sweet Home," Ibsen's
"cagehaused duckyheim," and marriage at Gretna
Green), the four old men become a domestic
quartet, singing "fourposter" (cf. Chapter XVI)
tunes of a fishy sort to a "sycamode [cf. 384.1]
euphonium." Where are those "whapping
oldsteirs"—big oldsters from Wapping Old Stairs
near the market for "tunies" in London—those
Frankfurters, number one, two, three, four? Mark
is "Murkiss"; Matthew is "Gregorio" (a Gregorian
chanter and "Matt Gregory," 384.10–11); John,

last of the four, is "Johannes far in back" or Johann
Bach. Luke, a little more difficult to identify, is
attended to by "Castrucci" or Castruccio, the
tyrant of Lucca, to whom Machiavelli devoted a
short biography. To Joyce's mind, which moved in
mysterious ways, Lucca suggested Luke.

535.34–35 "Haveth Childers Everywhere" provided the title
for this section of the *Wake* (532–54) when it was
printed separately in 1930, in a limited edition.

540.22–25 A catalogue of Ibsen's plays: *Peer Gynt, Caesar
and Galilean, The Lady from the Sea, Hedda
Gabler, Ghosts, When We Dead Awaken, Pillars
of Society, Rosmersholm. A Doll's House* ("duckyheim") has appeared earlier (533.18), and *The
Enemy of the People* ("folksfiendship") will appear later (542.18). The Master Builder ("Bigmesser," 530.32) presides over this section of the
Wake. In 1936 (*Letters,* III, 390) Joyce had a
poor opinion of Ibsen, the hero of his youth.

545.13–23 In this passage Joyce is parodying Henry II's sec-
ond charter (1173), the text of which I owe to
Patrick Henchy, Director of the National Library,
Dublin:

"Henricus Dei gratia. . . . Know ye, that I
have given, granted, and by my charter confirmed
to my subjects of Bristol my city of Dublin to inhabit. Wherefore I will and firmly command that
they do inhabit it, and hold it of me and of my
heirs, well and in peace, freely and quietly, fully
and amply, and honourably, with all the liberties
and free customs which the men of Bristol have at
Bristol, and through my whole land."

Earwicker's pub, sometimes called the Bristol,
may owe this name not only to the Bridge Inn
across the Liffey from the Mullingar but to the
City of Bristol or the Dublin of Henricus Rex.

552.29–30 "Chillybombom and forty bonnets," not only Ali

Baba and the Forty Thieves, is also, according to
Nathan Halper, a reference to Rebecca West and
the three bonnets she bought while meditating her
attack on *Ulysses* (*Strange Necessity*, New York,
1928, pp. 45–46). Cf. "a wife with folty barnets"
(20.27–28) and "three barnets" (141.14). Since
"barnets" is also Danish for children, Rebecca
West is associated with the Prankquean, who
plagued Earwicker as much as Rebecca West
plagued Joyce.

CHAPTER XVI · 555-90

AFTER the progress of Shaun through three Viconian ages, an age of renewal centering on H.C.E. and A.L.P. seems odder than it is. Shaun may be renewal's embodiment but, as we saw at the end of Chapter XV, H.C.E. is his center. In Chapter XVI Shaun, in a way, is still turning his insides out. Goaty Earwicker turned his "overgoat . . . sheepside out" (35.13). When sheepy Shaun, a turncoat in his turn, turns his undergoat out, we agree that renewal is overdue. It is the business of a *ricorso* to stir things up. What is more, we can expect the *ricorso* of Part III, the human age, to be more human—if this adjective is comparable—than the *ricorso* of Part I, the divine age. Though references to Genesis establish the presence of the divine age in the human *ricorso* of Chapter XVI, the unquiet desperation of this chapter—if you take a dim view of humanity—is human entirely. Earwicker's claims at the end of Chapter XV call for the reality of the chapter before us.

This chapter is Joyce's third major bedroom scene, each of which is more discouraging at first glance than at second. The first, at the Gresham Hotel, reveals Gabriel Conroy's incapacity, yet there is hope; for the snow that falls on all the living and the dead will melt tomorrow or the next day and flow into the Liffey. The second, at 7 Eccles Street, reveals Bloom's incapacity, yet there is hope: another day for Bloom, Molly's "melonsmellonous" capacity, and her final "yes." Whatever the ignominy of the third bedroom scene, at the Mullingar or Bristol, the cock crows at the end and—oh, yes—a sequence of yeses (from "Yes?" at the beginning, to "O yes! O yes!" as dawn approaches,

555.4, 585.26) prepares for the "Oyesesyeses!" (604.22) of
the following chapter. Seeing his horrors plain, Joyce, a yes-
man, accepted with equanimity what he transfigured with gaiety.
This funny chapter is one of the most serious. "I am not leer-
ing," says Mark's H.C.E. (570.24–25), "I am highly sheshe
sherious."

D. H. Lawrence, an authority on bedrooms—but a greater
authority on boys in the bushes—disliked Joyce's gaiety in matters so "sherious." On looking into *Finnegans Wake,* Lawrence
saw, as we have seen, nothing but "deliberate journalistic dirty-
mindedness." On looking into *Lady Chatterley's Lover,* Joyce saw
nothing but "the usual sloppy English." Lawrence and Joyce
were as incompatible as Shaun and Shem. But by no means
Shem alone, Joyce, at his best, is the union of Shem and Shaun
(473)—the union of incompatibles that Bruno celebrated in his
motto: *"In tristitia hilaris hilaritate tristis."* We cannot expect
everyone to find the compatibility of incompatibles compatible.

Chapter XVI takes up the story of Earwicker's night from
where it was suspended, for the intrusions of Tristan and Shaun,
at the end of Chapter XI. Rory O'Connor Earwicker, after
drinking the dregs, "came acrash a crupper" and "just slumped
to throne" as Kate came down with a candle (382). To bring
his fall and her inspection back to mind the scene recurs with
variations at the beginning of Chapter XVI (556–57). Evidently she gets the drunk upstairs to bed, where, however incapable, he tries to please his wife. A drunk is an imperfect lover.
Besides, Anne Lynch's lover, unluckier than Lady Chatterley's,
is distracted by the crying of a child in the next room. But father
and mother, such as they are, are doing their best again, such as
it is. That there are children in other rooms—Lawrence would
have been dismayed—shows that the best these lovers can do
was good enough once—or, to be accurate, twice.

Problem: is this bedroom scene an interruption of the dream
or part of it? Is Earwicker—if he is the dreamer—dreaming that
A.L.P. gets up to comfort a child or, waking from the dream,
does he encounter reality for a minute or two before going to

sleep again and dreaming the dawn in? My guess is that all in this chapter is part of the dream. Were there a temporary waking, the techniques of dream, constant throughout the chapter, would have to yield for a page or two to the techniques of waking. "Durk [*durch* and dark] the thicket of slumbwhere" (580.15), Earwicker is still riding his "nightmare"—that "couchmare" (*cauchemar* is nightmare in French; 576.28, 583.9), who, were the dream suspended, would be A.L.P. no more (*Alp* is nightmare in German) but plain Mrs. Porter, Coppinger—or Joyce maybe. If the dreamer, dreaming of being a publican in Chapelizod, were to wake up, he might find himself in bed, in Paris, with Mrs. Joyce, far from Chapelizod and environs.

That the four old men are around throughout the chapter, confirms my guess. What would they be doing—and "when-abouts" would they be at all—outside a dream? These four "seneschals" (566.8), who have served as Earwicker's judges, Tristan's historians, and Yawn's inquisitors, are now observant bedposts: "kinderwardens" around the "twinsbed . . . at their pussycorners" (555.3–11. Cf. "fourposter," 533.16; 598.22–23), peeping and listening again. Telling the gospel truth about what goes on in the bedroom, they tell it in gospel order: Matt's view first (559.22); Mark's second (564.2); Luke's third (582.30); and John's a poor fourth (590.23). These peepers also report the peeping of the twins, no less concerned with parental endeavors. For all this peeping Earwicker and the three soldiers have provided example. While father peeped at his two girls in the Park, those soldiers peeped at him—and "toms will till" (196.22).

Motifs, bringing old meanings along and taking new meanings from context, are suitable. The reappearing trial in court becomes a "bed of trial" (558.26). Tea, commonly domestic, acquires amorous additions. Washerwomen and reversals suit a *ricorso*. Games, frequent in the *Wake,* become the game of love, an application that Lawrence, despite his gamekeeper, would have abhorred. Wellington's reappearance may imply a victory no better than Pyrrhic. We are familiar with the working of motifs. Worthier of our notice now is what Joyce calls "a complex matter of pure form" (581.29–30).

Not narrative in structure—for there is little to tell—this chapter is an arrangement, closer to music, poetry, the cinema, and dream than the three simpler chapters that precede it. Chapter XVI is a sequence of matters, put side by side without apparent connection, that differ, one from another, in feeling, rhythm, diction, sense, and tone. That Joyce had the movements of a musical composition in mind is suggested by reference to two of his favorites, the Elizabethan lutanists William Bird (556.17–18) and John Dowland (570.3). Chapter XVI also brings to mind the structure of the long modern poem—*The Bridge,* for example—where matters alien to one another in rhythm, shape, and tone are juxtaposed without transitional device. These juxtapositions, not unlike the placing of elements in a seventeenth-century conceit, result in what Dr. Johnson called a *"discordia concors"*—a concordant discord or, to turn from poetry to the movies, what Sergei Eisenstein called "montage," the interaction of two things. That Joyce had the movies in mind is proved by many references: "moving pictures" and "shadow shows" (565.6, 14); "Closeup" and "Footage" (559.19, 31); "sound-picture" (570.14); and "leer" (567.5), a reversal of reel. It is not by accident that he called the *Wake* his "allnights newsery-reel" (489.35). As for dream: dreams, like newsreels and modern poems, lack logical or narrative coherence.

Let us look at the opening pages of Chapter XVI. After an introductory passage on the four old men, we suddenly find ourselves, without transition or explanation, in a poem or song about Isabel (556). Next, a passage, differing entirely in key, rhythm, diction, and tone, on H.C.E. and Kate in the pub (556–57). Next, a passage of a different sort on Earwicker's trial by jury (557–58). Then, a short interlude on the twenty-nine girls, followed closely by the first of the bedroom scenes (558). Little wonder after this dazzling sequence that someone asks: "Where are we at all? and whenabouts in the name of space?" (558.33) But we have a ready answer: At the movies, we are reading a long modern poem while listening to music in a dream.

Our "soundpicture"—or, better, our concert of arts—begins, appropriately, in a fog. (Compare the "freakfog" that opens Chapter III, 48.2, and the "fogbow" that opens Chapter XIII, 403.6.) Groping through the fog of sleep to find "whenabouts" we are (555), we find the four Viconian watchmen, "esker, newcsle, saggard, crumlin," and their donkey. These familiars cannot detain us now, nor can the twins over whom they watch, Kevin-Shaun, the eater, and Jerry-Shem, the drinker. But the next scene of the "nat by night" newsreel demands a pause.

A vision of Isabel (556)—spelt Isobel to introduce a female o perhaps—as the saint, nun, nurse, and merry widow she dreams of being, reveals the girl to them, you, us, and me, her admirers. Another Gerty MacDowell, she is also a "peach" for Daddy Browning and Tristan's Iseult la Belle. But that "Saint-ette Isabelle" (556.7) is *sans tête* or dumb as usual, is confirmed by the prettiness of the passage—a nasty prettiness that compli-cates Joyce's attitude toward his daughter, of whom Isabel, in part at least, is a projection. Love seems balanced by contempt. The rhythm of this song to Isabel, recalling songs to A.L.P. (e.g., 7.1–3, 25–27), is based, says Joyce in a letter (III, 138), on William Bird's "Woods so Wild" (see 556.17–18). Isabel at her mirror (527) is comparable.

The sudden shift from this prettiness to H.C.E., drunk on the floor of his pub (556–57), is surprising—and surprise, says T. S. Eliot, is a literary value. There, having drained his dregs, all "the leavethings from allpurgers' night," the publican lies. Thinking the noise of his fall a knocking at the door by the man from Schweppes (Shem), the postman (Shaun), or some other "fender" (cf. 65.35; 67; 70; 381–82), Kate comes down with a candle to find her boss honeymoon-naked on the sawdust with his "clookey in his fisstball." This one-handled engine is both more and less than the "cluekey to a worldroom beyond the roomwhorled" (100.29), but the "pious eyebulbs" of Earwicker on his back are almost the "lovensoft eyebulbs" (531.8) of Ear-wicker getting his back rubbed by Kate on the kitchen table. Kate's "tocher of davy's, tocher of ivileagh" (557.10–11), indicating pious astonishment, is from the Litany of the Blessed Virgin ("Tower of David, Tower of Ivory") mixed, as the occasion demands, with Lord Iveagh, brewer of Guinness.

In the courtroom now—another surprise—the twelve jurors, identified by a host of words ending in -tion, try Earwicker again for his nameless crime in the Park with the two girls and the three soldiers (557–58). Though, in a way, the "pest of the park" is as estimable as Adam Findlater, grocer, these jurors, according to "Nolans Volans" (cf. 93.1), find Earwicker guilty. At his previous trial, in Chapter IV, the four judges, more lenient than these twelve—at once jurors and patrons of the pub—had let the accused off "scotfree."

Now, in a bedroom scene—a scenario with stage directions— H.C.E. is discovered with A.L.P. Their "first position of harmony," according to Matt, is interrupted by the "cry off" of a waking child. Father, with "beastly expression . . . exhibits rage." Mother, exhibiting fear, hops out of bed, gets a lamp, and like the queen of a game of chess, moves down the hall to see what the matter is (558.26–560.6). The "old humburgh" (at once humbug and phallic hat) is disappointed, but his Homburg may "pawn up a fine head of porter" yet. Porter, brewed by Lord Iveagh, with the help of Lord Ardilaun, accounts for the name, at the moment, of the publican. This "bally builder" (bally is Gaelic, city) is Mr. Porter now and our "messmother" is Mrs. Porter, a pair who "care for nothing except everything that is allporterous" (560.7–36). He, like Bluebeard-Bloom and Finnegan at his wake, is "bloombiered." She is "booty with the bedst."

The scene shifts to the bedrooms of the "little Porter babes," the Corsican brothers in one room, Nuvoletta-Isabel (cf. 157.8) in the other. All heliotropic flowers attend her; and her mirror (cf. 526–27), replacing the Angelus, shows this "handmade . . . herword in flesh." The "Rosepetalletted sounds" of this second hymn to Isabel, as sweet maybe as those of the first, are maybe a little peachier. The twins in the next room are at once "foetal" maggots, waiting to be born, teething infants, and adolescents. Kevin, as we know, is "Father Quinn again," Dean

Swift, and Tristan, who will be off to "Amorica" (cf. 3.5) one day to get a "cashy job." Jerry, the "Jehu" (cf. 53.8), whose cry disturbed his parents, has "bespilled himself from his founding-pen"—has wet the bed, that is, and written chamber-pot music, a "book of craven images." Byron, Blake, and Le Fanu (563.12–21) applaud this "bleak" (ink in Danish) exercise—a kind of "anemone's letter." May Jacob and Esau, Ondt and Gracehoper ("Formio and Cigalette") preside over these boys until, united and reversed, they become "kerryjevin" (561.1–563.36). The witness, whose "I see" lends credibility to his evidence, must be peeping Matthew.

Mark's evidence reveals the bedded couple in "a second position of discordance." The "male entail," partly masking the "femecovert," becomes, from Mark's point of view, the landscape of Phoenix Park, which a central road "bisexes." The "cheeks" on either side of the road disclose "gentlemen's seats" and an "amiably tufted" plantation, which, when observed with "snaked's eyes," takes its place in "a tree story," as familiar as that of Adam and Eve. Yet there is a difference. The "bodom fundus" of the Park, like that of Wilde, is "open to the public till night at late," especially to "pederestrians." Worthy of note is a Wagnerian hollow—a vale hollow that "guttergloomering" on "woodensdays," gives "wankyrious thoughts" to members of the Metropolitan Police (564.1–565.8). "Mark well," says Mark, "what I say."

The woman, out of bed, comforts the crying child; for Mark, according to apostolic custom, repeats with variation what Matthew saw, Luke will see, and unsynoptic John will tell. You were only dreaming, says mother to crying child. The terrible black-panther father you were dreaming of is only "in your imagination." Your dreams were only "shadow shows." There may be "Thunner in the eire," but there is no terrible thunderer in this part of Eire. Here there is only a publican whose "thoroughbass grossman's bigness" calls for pidgin English, the language of such business—calls too, apparently, for Russian and Esperanto ("muy malinchily malchick" and *"Malbone dormas"*). Go back to sleep, for "morning nears" (565.13–32). If the "bad bold" father is only in Shem's imagination, Shem could be the dreamer of the *Wake*. But my vote still goes to Earwicker-Joyce, a union of Shem and his opposite. Shem alone, equal to *Chamber Music*, could never have dreamed the *Wake*.

An advertisement for the pub, a good place to stop on your way to the sulphur springs at Lucan, follows mother's comforting. The sleeping accommodations here are ample enough to hold all the people of the *Wake*: "Soakersoon" Joe, Kate, the twelve jurors, the twenty-eight girls, Isabella, and the twins, "daulphin and deevlin," who are "without to see" what they can of father and mother, at work again in bed, "without to be seen of them." Do not fail to see, says Mark, echoing A.L.P.'s Esperanto, the *"Maldelikato"* work in progress, and see that you do not fail (565.33–566.27). The first part of his exhortation, addressed to the peeping twins, seems as unnecessary as the second part, addressed to working Earwicker, is necessary; for that imperfect lover fears he cannot emulate the Wellington Monument, a considerable erection in the Park. (The "buntingcap of so a pinky on the point," suitable for "glover's greetings," may be obtained, elsewhere, at any apothecary's.) A fox hunt, girls on bicycles, and soldiers on tricycles or in troikas are more encouraging than "those puny farting little solitires" of a motorcycle built for one. The emergence of fallen Humpty Dumpty is even less encouraging. One can imagine the reaction of the woman whose "meekname mocktitles her Nan Nan Nanetta." But, whatever the nickname of her husband, "He shall come . . . who can doubt it?" The fox hunter, like other taxpayers, is sure at least of "illcome faxes" (566.28–567.34).

Success is promised by the breaking out of an Irish flag, "a rancher [orange], a fullvide [white], a veridust [green]," the "annamation of evabusies, the livlianess of her laughings, such as a plurity of bells," and the "autonement" of the twins, who, once fighting like York and Lancaster, Guelph and Ghibelline, are united in peeping now. H.C.E. enjoys a vision of triumph. "Nanny's Big Billy," his "hod hoisted" again, like waking Finnegan's, rides on Wellington's "Caubeenhauben" to be knighted by the king: "Arise, sir Pompkey Dompkey!" The former Humpty Dumpty, put together again—not by the king's horses or his men but by the king himself, responds to the accolade by reading a prepared speech: "alfi byrni gamman dealter etcera zezera eacla treacla kaptor lomdom noo"—a speech which, though in Greek, is not unlike Bloom's speech in Hebrew on a similar occasion (*Ulysses*, 487). The celebration of Earwicker's triumph has only started. Applauding ladies wave from balconies, and from all the steeples bells ring wildly out—from St. Laurence O'Toole's, the Gardiner Street church, and Bloom's church in Westland Row. A feast with "fuddlers free" is spread for "Old Finncoole"—"For we're all jollygame fellhellows which nobottle can deny!" The best actors, Tyrone Power and the Fays among them, appear in the best plays, "two genitalmen of Veruno," for example, and *All for Love*. And fireworks too. "Some wholetime in hot town tonight!" It is almost as jolly as a wake, which, in a way, it is (567.36–570.13).

Calling for another "soundpicture," Mark wonders how Mr. Pornter, Sir Pournter or Lord Pournterfamilias, whoever he is, is getting along. Plainly, the man is father Abraham, his wife, Sarah. The addition of one and one, yielding neither two nor marital one, yields, in this case, "one ought ought one" (cf. 261.23–24) or 1001, renewal's number. This hopeful union, recorded in runes cut in the trees of the Park, is not unlike that of Tristan and Iseult, "triste to death" and "kissabelle"—or, as "tantrist" implies, the reversal of this amorous pair (570.14–571.18).

Before taking "saarasplace" in bed with Mr. "Pouringtoher"—after her excursion down the hall—A.L.P., less Sarah now than Saar, sits on the chamber pot. "Listen! I am doing it," she says, and, lisping "privily," tells H.C.E. that all is well with the children. Though "bosomfoes," the twins may be digging a grave for their parents, and the girl may be planning to replace the washerwomen by the elm and stone, the three are quiet now (571.17–572.17). Cf. 21.2–3.

The synopsis or abstract of a play, suddenly here, is shocking by position and substance. This mishmash of incest, buggery, incestuous buggery, and, if possible, worse, is as intricate as a Restoration play and nastier than anything by a declining, or even a falling, Roman. The characters, who take their names from the Imperial City, are all the people of the *Wake,* and the scene of this Roman shocker is Chapelizod. Honophrius is H.C.E., Anita is A.L.P., Eugenius and Jeremias are the twins, and Felicia is Isabel—all "consanguineous to the lowest degree." Magravius seems H.C.E. in another capacity. Fortissa (Kate), Mauritius (Joe), seven rainbow girls, the four old men, the twelve customers, and Father Michael (from the letter) complicate "unnatural coits." All that has been latent in the familial complex comes to light here, as if from all the couches of Vienna, with all the help of Greece. The clarity of this abstract, emerging from the darkness of dream around it, insures the effect. Recoiling in horror from man's humanity to man, we laugh; for this amorous confusion is an example of what Ruskin, a better definer than Webster, called the grotesque, a kind of art, he said, that combines the frightful and the funny. A gargoyle on a tower of Notre Dame—the northern one by preference—is another example, less frightful and funny, however, because less human. Mankind in the abstract, as this abstract concretely proves, was Joyce's improper study (572.19–573.32).

From psychiatry of a sort we proceed to a sort of law, the one as discouraging as the other. "Wadding," an authority on "nullity" (573.26–27), has prepared us for an "umbrella history." (The umbrellas of *Ulysses,* 405—like brown macintoshes—are contraceptives.) In the court room where this history unfolds, we hear the case of Tangos, Ltd., a foreign firm selling "certain proprietary articles," versus Pango, a rival concern. The matter in dispute is a "cheque." Tangos and Pango are also the churches of Rome and England, which, like their cheque of "a good washable pink," check fertility. (All this recalls the handling of fertility and contraception in "Oxen of the Sun.") Judge Jeremy Doyle (Shem), citing rabbity Warren and Barren, instructs a jury of twelve Doyles. Ann Doyle or "Coppinger's doll," the bouncing witness, who, as bearer and endorser of rubber checks, speaks from experience, gives evidence in "corrubberation." The jury disagrees. Citing "Hal Kilbride" (Henry VIII), the judge dismisses the case (573.35–576.9).

After a brief return to the bed of trial, comes a long prayer to God, the Master of Master Builders, for "our forced payrents . . . big Maester Finnykin" and his little "couchmare" or the "solomn one and shebby." May he "dishcover her," and, however crumpled, may they "recoup themselves" on whatever road they follow: the road to Mandalay, the road to Arthur's Seat in Edinburgh, Unter den Linden, or Cheapside in London. Forgive their mortal sins as you forgive their "peccadilly." "To bed" and "On to bed" that begin and interrupt this prayer, suggesting Samuel Pepys's "And so to bed," may imply our peeping (576.10–577.36).

Questions now about the bedded pair. Is this man for whom we pray Tom, Dick or Harry, Finn MacCool or the Dane who keeps this hotel? And who this woman with the lamp: "Donauwatter," a Viennese washerwoman with British Sunlight Soap, a "peahen" or a tea-girl? Where are they going? If down the way they went up, "ease their fall"; for, our general parents, "they met and mated and bedded and buckled and got and gave . . . and bequeathed us their ills." They built our cities and turned our coats. May the dawn that brings "Finnegan, to sin again," light their way. Proverbial language fits this appendix to our prayer (576.3–580.22).

Mark's monologue, the longest and most coherent part of this chapter of incoherent parts—a coherence, that is, of the incoherent—modulates now from prayer for H.C.E. to his defense. It may be, says Mark, that this man, who leads a "doublin existents" (578.14), is worried by his "ambling limfy peepingpartner" (A.L.P.)—at once "slave of the ring" and rubber of the lamp. It may be that he has been slandered by Hosty's ballad and the gossip of the twelve customers on their way home from Finn MacCool's pub, yet the publican is as great a builder as Jack who built the house that Jack built. But for H.C.E. there

would be no cities with "Heinz cans everywhere." Surely, the
man who put them there is worth more than "a cornerwall
fark"—a fart for Mark of Cornwall (580.23–581.14).

Mark—not that one but this one—is heartily sorry, he con-
fesses, that the four apostles, "matinmarked for looking on," are
peeping now as the "trivials" (the three soldiers) once peeped
from their "bivouac" (the two girls): "I'm sorry to say I saw."
The man we peep at near the Wellington monolith is a "mono-
myth," who, abiding our inspection and outlasting it, is at once
one and another: "one not all the selfsame butstillone . . .
with a little difference" (581.15–36).

Whatever we say about our father, he begot us and for this
service deserves a vote of thanks. Let the tricolor ("greenmould
upon mildew over jaundice") wave over Dublin while "shame,
humbug and profit," his local descendants—as well as Noah's
sons and the three soldiers—praise "enver a man" (everyman in
Danish). His wife must share our praise. Whether or not we like
our parents, they are as necessary as the laws of Bruno ("sem-
peridentity . . . peasemeal upon variables") and Vico (a "meg-
aron of returningties, whirled without end to end"). While
"shysweet" Anna rests, "Humpfrey, champion emir, holds his
own" (582.1–27).

Luke looks at the "third position of concord" from the
front. So viewed, the female, apparently sitting on the male,
hides him a little. Metaphors of the Kingstown and Dalkey tramline and a horse race—the man "jovial on his bucky brown
nightmare" or vice versa at the moment—disclose the recreation
of "pairamere" (*père-mère*), going "a gallop, a gallop." No
wonder Swift foresaw "Bigrob dignagging his lylyputtana" (*put-
tana* is Italian for strumpet). Anna's lamp—like Mrs. Bloom's
—casts shadows enough on the blind for a man in the street to
"see the coming event" or a policeman as he "peels peering by."
Earwicker, the "robberer," is wearing his "waxened capapee."
(Dublin must have at least one Protestant or agnostic phar-
macy.) Anna has become her lamp; for Earwicker, now lamp-
wicker, has his "wick-in-her." Love is a game, something like

cricket, but "faster, faster" (582.28–588.4). As they play, like "shantyqueer" with the literate "hen [of] the doran's," the cock of the morning, announcing success, crows the dawn in: "Cocorico!"

The increase in population that Malthus (585.11) feared has been prevented by a strainbearing "prevenient . . . detachably replaceable." Give thanks for this and for a grateful partner: "dankyshin. . . . mercy, good shot!" Their "annastomoses," like any anastomosis, is a union of one anatomical vessel with another of another system—Anna, for example, with Moses. Enough of metaphor from biology, Bible, racing, and cricket. Enough of lamp and wick, of cock and hen. Now we are in parliament, sitting as a court: "O yes! O yes! Withdraw your member. Closure. The chamber stands abjourned" (585.7–27). Now, having put the kettle on, we expect a cup of tea you could trot a mouse on, but: "You never wet the tea!" (585.30–31. Cf. "tay is wet," 12.16) Some have taken this remark, whether Luke's or Anna's, to mean Earwicker's failure as a lover. Nothing of the kind. The cock has crowed—strange that the strongest of verbs should be a weak verb now—and in this Malthusian context failure to wet the family tea means no more than the prevention of fertility by a Malthusian rubber that Theodore Purefoy, mightiest progenitor of them all, had no use for.

There are rules for patrons of this pub. Do not disturb your neighbor; for "Others are as tired of themselves as you are." "Pubchat" and smutty talk in the bar are strictly prohibited. "Look before behind before" you disrobe. Do not throw water from the window or leave your "glove" in the bed; for Kate, the chambermaid, will tell "Omama," the two "laundresses" will gossip on the banks of the river and the two "maggies" in the Park. Pay your bill and, if you must make love, see that your "rent is open to be foreclosed or aback in your arrears." After all, this is "a homelet not a hothel" (585.34–586.18).

All is dark and quiet in the household now. Should "patrolman Seekersenn" (Joe), making his rounds, look up at the window, he would see no light, hear no sound—"siccar of inket goodsforetombed ereshiningem" (a mixture of English, Danish, and German that, according to Dounia Christiani, means: make certain of no goddamned appearances, 586.20–587.2).

Having peeped (587.3–5), the twins discuss the man they have peeped at. The "Hiss!" that begins Shaun's remarks and echoes through them all the way to "Triss. . . . Trem" and beyond (588.29–35) seems that of the snake—snake of the fall and snake of gossip. It is true, says Shaun, that piratical H.C.E., meeting the three soldiers in the snug of a pub—or at the "drolleries puntomine" of the *Wake,* doffed his white hat and treated them to Woodbine cigarettes and Cadbury's chocolates; but, as "Honeysuckler" (A.L.P.) knows, he is actually "Fred Watkins" (Tommy Atkins), one of the three—we "privates" are the others—he is treating so politely. He has "sinnerettes" to confess: the affair of those "two legglegels in blooms" and the soldiers three. Were those who "trespass against" him "forgiving up their . . . trespasses?" The Lord's Prayer suits one who, after all, is our father and "burgomaster." Though "Freda" (A.L.P.) complains that, when with Fred, she found it difficult to "keep her flouncies off" the "wetmenots," and to bare "her fiefighs fore him" after the "cad came back," she enjoyed a joyous bottle or two (587.5–588.14). Mr. Black-and-Tan Atkins is himself alone. There is "Noel like him" for holly and ivy. His "flumenbomb"—"Number two coming!"—has always preceded A.L.P.'s rain—"number one, in deep humidity!" Izzy is as busy as her tree-sterne. What "joy with a shandy" (584.12–34).

The holly-and-ivy man freed the "two pretty mistletots, ribboned to a tree," peopled the earth, and "forged himself ahead like a blazing urbanorb." In the cities the "Finner" founded, he became "our hugest commercial emporialist." If he fell humbly, he rose cheaply—and "the band played on" (588.35–589.19).

As Adam, the farmer-publican, he changed his "seven days license" and lost it. But as Noah, when "a main chanced to burst and misflooded his fortunes," he packed "two of a feather" into the ark—"in wading room only." As Moses, he received "the slate for accounts" from his keeper. As Jesus, he was "crossbugled" by the three buglers. Later on, "two hussites" (Luther and

Calvin) broke his laws, but the last straw was an "explosium of his distilleries" that dumped him on his "bankrump"—the fall in the pub. A "chameleon," the man assumes all the "true false-heaven colours" of the rainbow. Now "Mista Chimepiece," asked the time by some cad with a revolver, knows his "reign-bolt's shot" (589.20–590.12).

Shem, the "Jimmy d'Arcy" or "Jimmy MacCawthelock" to whom Shaun has addressed this estimate of father, agrees; for, according to the prayer, father made all "on earn as in hiving." He agrees that, as Noah, H.C.E. was the "formast" of the ark. But the "sweetish" man, greater than that, is "our all honoured christmastyde easteredman" (590.13–22) or Jesus-H.C.E. Himself.

John's view of the "fourth position of solution" is brief. The happy pair lies together, apart. The "Begum . . . blesses her bliss for to feel her funnyman's functions." The "Nebob" is just "worked out." Dawn is coming, and Vico's "Rounds" go round and round as always.

562.18; 563.19	Matthew's "I see" echoes the "I see" of Professor MacHugh (*Ulysses,* 144–50), who echoes Matthew during Stephen's *"Parable of the Plums."* In the gospel of Matthew (13:10–16) Jesus says that He speaks in parables to try his hearers, who, hearing, do not hear, seeing, do not see, "neither do they understand." Matthew the peeper here and MacHugh there, seeing without seeing or perceiving, are not unlike us, who, hearing Joyce's parables without seeing, see them without hearing.
563.20–21	Gipsy Devereux and Lilias are from Le Fanu's *House by the Churchyard.* I have already noticed other characters from this novel: Ezekiel Irons (27.23), Dangerfield, Fireworker O'Flaherty, Nutter, Castlemallard, Archer, Sturk (80.8–10). To these we

may add Moggy (79.30, 176.4) and Glascock
(Kevin Sullivan's favorite), who appears as
"Glassarse" (27.1). Also from Le Fanu these
houses: the Brass Castle, the Tyled House,
and Ballyfermot (183.5, 246.4–5). Not only
Joyce's elm and stone but his personified
Liffey may owe something to Le Fanu. "Look
at the river," says Devereux to Lilias (in
Chapter XXIV), "—is not it feminine? it's
sad and it's merry, musical and sparkling—
and oh, so deep! Always changing, yet still the
same."

567.22   "Brigadier-general Nolan." Cf. "half a league
wrongwards" (567.3). More than Bruno,
this Nolan is Captain Nolan, who ordered the
Light Brigade to charge "wrongwards."

568.9   The "autonement" of Shem and Shaun is not
unlike the "atonement" or at-onement of
Stephen and Bloom (*Ulysses,* 729). Atonement, communion, consubstantial, and coincidence, key words of *Ulysses,* mean more or
less what D. H. Lawrence meant by "together-
ness" in *Lady Chatterley's Lover.* Note "co-
coincidences" (*FW,* 597.1) which mixes
Bloom's cocoa or communion with his coincidences.

569.28–29   "Ithalians" in connection with "Moll
Pamelas" must refer to the cast of characters
in Richardson's *Sir Charles Grandison:* "Men,
Women, Italians." "Boyplay" is a byplay on
Synge's *Playboy,* and "bouchicaulture" (569.-
34–35) is one of many references in the *Wake*
to Dion Boucicault, e.g., "dyinboosycough"
(95.8). "My name is novel [Norval]" (569.-
35–36) is from John Home's *Douglas.*

583.34–584.17   This amorous game of cricket includes the
names of cricketers (Tyldesley, Studd, Stod-

dart, Abel, and W. G. Grace, greatest of all,
who appears several times in the *Wake*) and
technical terms (googly, bail, wicket, stump,
lob, leg, and test match). Somewhere in the
Wake—unfortunately the reference in Hart's
Concordance is inaccurate—Joyce uses
"LBW" or "leg before wicket." Cf. "Leg-
before-Wicked" (434.10). Other games of
cricket: 25.35–36, 337.1–3. Games of all
kinds abound in the *Wake,* e.g., chess (559.-
30–560.12), poker (261.F1,F4), bridge
(286.11–18). A game of football proceeds
through Joyce's battle of Waterloo. These
games are metaphors for conflict, connection
(bridge, for example) or making love—for
example, poker.

584.4 "Pigeony linguish." The motif of pidgin English, a language of commerce, is commonly
associated with Earwicker-Shaun and the
"chink in his conscience" (486.11): 28.3,24–
25, 41.12–13, 52.24–25, 82.12–14, 130.35,
240.24–26, 247.23–25, 257.7–8, 285.6–8,
299.29, 303.30–32, 311.26–27, 322.6,12,25,
325.14, 338.25–32, 339.22, 347.25–26, 374.-
35, 426.16–17, 485.29–36, 565.21–23,
608.19–20, 609.36. The debate of Patrick
and the Druid (611.5–612.36) is at once the
climax, end, and, since the Druid is Shem,
extension of the motif.

584.27 "Cocorico," the cockcrow that resounds
through the following paragraph, seems indebted to T. S. Eliot's "Co co rico" (*Waste
Land,* line 392). Eliot is commonly associated
with Shaun, who, as Haun (471.35) is *Hahn*
or cock, and who, in the next chapter (595.-
30) will be cock of the morning—Humphrey
Earwicker's Cock.

585.20   "The dapplegray dawn" as a horse suggests
          G. M. Hopkins' "Windhover," where the
          "dapple-dawn-drawn Falcon" introduces two
          horses, that of the Chevalier and a plow horse.
          Hopkins is named in connection with "falcon-
          plumes" (26.2,10). There is also a reference
          to sprung rhythm (293.L2). Since Hopkins
          was teaching Greek at Joyce's college when
          Joyce was a child, his interest in the poet is
          not surprising.

585.31   Failure to "wet the tea" is introduced by
          "Three for two will do for me and he for thee
          and she for you" (584.10–11) or "Tea for
          Two," the song of marriage. At the Prank-
          quean's party "they all drank free" (23.7–8)
          —drinks on the house and tea. A.L.P. is
          "Anne Lynch," a brand of tea: "Houseanna.
          Tea is the Highest" (406.27–28). Usually
          associated with home, family, marriage, and
          urine, tea is associated now with making love.
          Consider Mr. Bloom's "family tea" (Ulysses,
          71), his failure to get tea from Tom Kernan,
          and the missing "t" in his "high grade ha."

586.24–25 "Twentylot . . . do little ones," another of
          Joyce's excursions into family arithmetic,
          seems to include the twenty-eight girls
          ("twentylot"), the Earwicker family and
          H.C.E. ("a fiver"), Isabel and the twins ("a
          fee [fay?] and do little ones"), the two girls
          and the three soldiers ("the deuce or roamer's
          numbers"). To "multapluss" these numbers
          is beyond my capacity. Pretty good at words,
          I am pretty bad at numbers and a number of
          things.

587.32   "Beardall," the bearded father, in connection
          with "Freda" (588.2) may be H.C.E. and
          A.L.P. as Frieda and D. H. Lawrence, who,

not only bearded, was a Beardsall on his mother's side. "Bush" (588.2) suggests both the boy in the bush ("lost in the bush, boy?" 112.3) and the man behind the bush. Consider "Larry's on the focse" (382.21–22), a reference perhaps to *Lady Chatterley's Lover,* to which Chapter XVI may be Joyce's realistic rejoinder.

PART FOUR

CHAPTER XVII · 593-628

W HEN in the course of secular events we have enjoyed a *ricorso*—as we have in Chapter XVI—we expect another divine age. In Chapter XVII the divine abounds. There are saints, a druid, Easter, the Phoenix, the sun rising over Stonehenge, and, at last, a mystical union with our Father: "Prayfulness! Prayfulness!" (601.29) But, whatever this abundance, Chapter XVII must be taken as another *ricorso*. As the first chapter of the *Wake* is at once a divine age and a general introduction, so the last chapter is a general conclusion and a *ricorso* —the general *ricorso* of the *Wake* with its four Viconian ages— to stir things up before we go back to the first page to begin again. That the human age, shown by passages of abstract language, is still around is to be expected in what concludes the human *Wake*. What we have here, then, is a divine *ricorso*, as human as getting up in the morning to eat breakfast—our daily "Eatster" (623.8)—before facing another day that, we hope, in spite of our bitter judgment, will be "a newera's day" (623.7) and not more of the same thing. Finnegan may be "Finn, again!" (628.14), but will he be any steadier on that ladder?

In structure, Chapter XVII follows the principles of montage —the abrupt collocation of disparate matters that we noticed in Chapter XVI. But the montage of Chapter XVII is less like that of Chapter XVI than that of Chapter I. A general conclusion and a general introduction, parallel in function, demand parallel methods. Here, as in the first chapter, the collocation of matters is softened now and again by transitional passages, lacking entirely in Chapter XVI. Like Chapter I, Chapter XVII has an

intricate introduction. After this, in place of the tour of Waterloo, comes a saint's life. A discursive interlude separates this
holiness from the secular debate of Muta and Juva which, however different in substance and character from that of Mutt and
Jute, echoes it more or less. The exchange of Muta and Juva is
followed abruptly by that of Patrick and the druid. A philosophical interlude prepares us for another letter from A.L.P. that
modulates easily into her final monologue. Her last words, recalling in a way those of Mrs. Bloom, replace the address to the
dead that concludes Chapter I.

"Yes," the great female word—here as in Mrs. Bloom's monologue—suits the promise of renewal. Isis is back to make a
"newman" of her dead husband. The washerwomen apply their
soap again to the dirty wash in the river of regeneration, whether
Nile or Liffey. Buckley and the Cad, having attended to the old
man, attend the new now or, ganging up, become him. The four
old men are around again, inspecting. The letter promises renewal of litter by letters; for the word of the beginning is the
word of the end, and all, first or last, proceeds from the word.

Sanctus! Sanctus! Sanctus! (Holy! Holy! Holy!) is a good
way to begin a chapter of resurrection and waking up. Establishing holiness, *Sanctus,* from long association, also establishes the
presence of Shaun, the Son—that "lightbreakfastbringer"
(473.23–24)—who, crucified at the end of Chapter XIV, rises
like the sun now; for it is day at last and today is Easter. The
rising Son is the new Earwicker, risen after his fall, or Finnagain, rising at his wake, or anyone waking after sleep: "Array!
Surrection. Eireweeker. . . . O rally" (593.2–3). "Eireweeker," more than Earwicker alone, is the Irish rising of
1916, during Easter week. "O rally," more than Persse O'Reilly,
is The O'Reilly, killed at the Post Office in the Easter rising, and
"Sonne feine" (593.8), more than the rising Son, is Sinn Fein.
The Phoenix is rising from his pyre (593.4). The "now orther"
(593.11) is Tennyson's King Arthur, who, since "the old order
changeth," returns with the new. Since the "smog" of sleep is
dissipating, it is time to call all "daynes" who are down "to
dawn." News of the new "leader," who has doomed old

"husky," is spread by Tass, Reuters, and other news agencies (593.6). The publican, once humiliated by Hosty's ballad and the gossip of the twelve customers (-tion), now "baalad out of his humuluation" (593.13–19), will reopen his bar: "genghis is ghoon for you." Guinness as usual (cf. 16.31–32); Genghis is a Khan; a khan is a pub; and Genghis Khan comes from the East.

Matters of the East, both Near and Far, crowd this chapter. Egypt, India, China, Japan are here, along with their creeds and languages: Moslemism, Hinduism, and Buddhism, Sanskrit, pidgin English, and Nippon English. Here to serve no occult purpose, these oriental matters are here to assist the sun, which, after all, rises in the East. Complex no doubt, Joyce was almost never deep. (When oriental matters detained Lawrence, they served an occult purpose; for Lawrence was deep and almost always simple.) Nor was Joyce transcendental. The hand emerging from a cloud with a chart (593.19), serving no high purpose, is the hand of a gargoyle or a decoration on time's map.

The Near East first (593.20–24): Egypt and the Book of the Dead suggest as usual death and resurrection from "the domnatory of Defmut" (deaf-dumb, Mutt-Jute, tum-fed?). Resurrection after death is a reversal. When examined by the dawn's reversing light, "Nuahs . . . Mehs . . . Pu Nuseht," gods from the Book of the Dead, become Shaun, Shem, and The Sun Up; and "tohp," reversed, becomes phot or light. "Heliotropolis" (594.8–9), Heliopolis, the sunny Egyptian city of the Phoenix, becomes H.C.E.'s Dublin, with its three castles, the city of Tim Healy.

An invocation to the sun and the reviving word—a Sanskrit word—brings us back to Arthur, Tintagel, Morgan le Fay, and the arm in samite rising from the lake ("kal"). "Dimdom done" from the Lord's Prayer leads to "light kindling light," a thought from Newman for a "newman" (594.1–8; 596.36). The return of Arcturus (Arthur and a sun) will unite "kithagain with kinagain."

It is time to get up, wash behind the ears, and light the fire for breakfast. The "dawnfire" lights our kitchen—"clarify" begins at home—as it once lit that "great circle of the macroliths" at holy Stonehenge (cf. "Woodenhenge," 596.13). "Dane the Great" (dog-god, Earwicker), "Gallus," the cock, and "Sassqueehenna," his rivery hen, prepare to cook "chantermale," who, like the Phoenix, will rise from his pot—rise like H. C. E. Finnegan from his wake, where sailor and tailor dance the "turnkeyed trot" around "Henge Ceolleges, Exmooth," the alleged corpse (594.9–595.2). Lift Shaun's "deathbone" (193.29) and the quick quake. But lift Shem's "lifewand" (195.5) and "the dombs spake! Whake?"

From the Hill of Howth and Lambay Island to Knock Gate, near Chapelizod in the Park, the sleeping giant lies across the "langscape"—a long landscape of language—while his daughter-wife thinks of twenty-nine ways to say good-by and hope to see you soon. It's a long, long way to Tipperary and as long a way to "Newirgland's premier" or Shaun, whose food is all the counties of Ireland, or most of them. Our "mudden research" in "crom lech," Wellington museum, and dump discovers "the deep deep deeps of Deepereras"—Shaun's Tipperary dispensation. Kate's "tup. . . . Tep. . . . Top," replacing her "tip," attend our tour of dump, museum, and tomb. It may be that we have put "chantermale" in the pot, but "Conk a dook he'll do." He will arise from the pot to crow again; and, like the Dook of Wellington, conked and consigned to the museum, he will be up again and at 'em. "Svap," the Sanskrit verb for sleep, is balanced by "nachasach," an afterthing from the land of the rising sun (595.3–33). So let the "sap" sleep till they take down the shutter from his shop. "The friarbird," at once the firebird and the united brothers, will fix him up.

The "natural child" is H.C.E, new and old, who, in a catalogue of his natural variety, appears to be "quite a big bug" yet, yet "a sort of heaps" from the "lemoronage" dump. He is a thundering "dunderfunder," St. Patrick, and, when returning from the burial demanded by "Banba" (Ireland), he is "fincarnate." "Risurging into chrest," he is our "pesternost," founder of our city and all the "subs of dub." The "sousenugh" (a soused Sassenach) keeps our pub—blessed be the barrel—where he has encouraged "wiles with warmen and sogns." As "atman," the "fabulafigured" man is the Hindu oversoul. Yet he has responded to the "gygantogyres" of Yeats and of "Jambud-vispa Vipra," a Hindu incarnation of Vico. In short, like Jonathan himself, he is "synthetical, swift" (595.34–596.33).

"By the antar of Yasas" (attar of roses and yeses), this "Loughlin" (Dane) from "Fingal" has become, during the night, a "newman." Do you mean to say we have been having "a sound night's sleep"—to the sound of the *Wake?* Yes. And now that the thousand-and-one nights are over, and over the last pages of the "bokes of tomb, dyke and hollow" (the Book of the Dead and the three soldiers), it is time to "rolywholyover." Consider universal process. Our lives are but "the one substrance of a streamsbecoming . . . totalled . . . and teldtold" in the *Wake* in "tittletell tattle." According to the creator (Joyce and God) "in whose words were the beginnings," there are two sides to any question, "the yest and the ist" (West-East, past-present) or "feeling aslip and wauking up," conflict and the peace of bed and breakfast—all, as Vico says, a dream "perhapsing under lucksloop," or, as Bruno says, a kind of "swigswag systomy dystomy" which everybody "anywhere at all doze" (does, sleeps, knows). "Why? Such me." Anyway the *Wake* is about over; for "every talk has his stay" and every dream comes to an end, "howpsadrowsay" (596.34–597.23).

The sleeper awakes to a future of "maybe mahamayability." (*Maha* is great and *maya* is the manifested world of Hindus.) The "torporature" is right for "humid nature." Have you "eaden fruit" in Eden or "snakked mid a fish" (received the Eucharist in gossipy Dublin)? We are waking from "a dromo of todos" (a twin or running dream of all), of every person, place or thing, everywhere. Noctambules, we have ambled through the night towards "the Nil"—at once nothing and the river of renewal—with Victoria Nyanza (a lake) and Albert Nothing (A.L.P. and H.C.E. Cf. 558.27–28; 600.12–13). The night was long but it has gone and "the is coming to come"—the "the" that ends the book perhaps. Good-by to "ghastern," the ghosts of yesterday, and hello to "morgning." There is hope; for "Padma" (the Buddhist lotus) or Isabel, "this flower that bells," attends the hour of rising. Whatever our doom or whatever the writing on the wall ("Tickle, tickle"), "Lotus spray." Let us give thanks (Danish *tak*) that the West end has met the "Ind" (the East end, 597.24–598.16) at last.

There is something "supernoctural" about H.C.E., whatever you call him—the Eucharist or *Hoc Corpus Enim*, for example. "Panpan and vinvin" (*panis*, Latin bread; *vin*, wine), if reversed, may be the "vanvan and pinpin" in your Tamil tamale— no more than bread and wine. Whatever "Mildew, murk, leak and yarn" saw in the bedroom, and whatever the last sounds from the multilingual *Wake,* our "camparative accoustomology" (598.17–26), "Old yeasterloaves may be a stale as a stub."

Whatever the troubles of time—then, now, was, is, shall be "in tense continuant"—dawn has come to the city of "Ysat Loka" (Chapelizod) where our "hugibum," our "weewee mother," her children and servants will enjoy a "madamanvantora"—a *mahamanvantara* (Hindu great manifestation, *Ulysses,* 40) of madam and man (598.28–599.2).

The time for tay is the time of day. But, as the Cad asked, "Whithr a clonk?" Vico has the answer Earwicker lacked. First a divine age when our Father "that arred in Himmal" made Adam, who named the animals, and thunder started the cycle of marriage, burial, and *ricorso* or divine providence. It is Vico's time; and, according to his laws, society, taking shape, finds adjustment. But enough of Viconian morphology. There's a pub in the town. There's a dump or museum ("Tip") in the Park, and, besides Vico, there is Bruno of Nola (599.3–24).

Where? As abstract language proves, we are in the human age. By its light we can review the whole foggy "pantomime," to which little can be added. Now we can see that its allegorical protagonists, the old man of the sea and the old woman of the sky, are really Father Time and Mother Space, who, on the stage of "this drury world of ours . . . boil their kettle with their crutch" (599.25–600.4).

"Innalavia" (Anna Livia of the pub) is a *poule* or "pool," between the deltas of the fishpond and the arrow, or a river, "minnyhahing" like Hiawatha's, piddling under the "poddlebridges in a passabed," the regenerating "river of lives." When we "lave" (wash) in her or leave her, it is "alve and vale"—*ave et vale*. Nin and Funn live in "Cleethabala," the mixed-up city of "Libnud," founded by "an accorsaired race" of Danish rovers, where Albert, seeking Victoria Nyanza, found a "Fall" —a "Caughterect." Caught in the act, like Adam, he earned his bread with the sweat of his plow. But this harrowing story—as inconsequential as any dream—has a redeeming side. His *culpa* was *felix:* "Goodspeed the blow!" His Eve is the white tree of life ("Vitalba"), an "alomdree," from or on which "little white bloomkins"—at once children and drawers—depend. Near the tree is a stone, Patrick's "shame rock." Maybe H.C.E. is Shaun's stone, but this stony yogi—treestone entirely—is also Shem's tree, "his oakey doaked with frondest leoves." As for pools, lakes, and loughs: there are Lake Leman and Lake Erie, "that greyt lack" where Isis and Ashtoreth, goddesses of fertility, rule their orbal city, making all on earth as it is in heaven (600.5–601.9).

Now the twenty-nine girls of February—fifteens plus fourteens, "a lunary with last a lone"—hail heavenly Kevin with song, dance, and flowers, as they did in Chapter IX. Holier now, they represent the churches of Dublin: "S. Gardenia's" (the Gardiner Street church, attended by the flower of Dublin), "S. Eddaminiva's" (Adam and Eve's), and "S. Loellisotoells" (St. Laurence O'Toole's and the church of Swift's two girls). Twenty-six churches seem insufficient for twenty-eight—or, with Isabel, twenty-nine—girls; but if we count Adam and Eve's and the church of Swift's girls as two apiece, there are twenty-eight churches, and we can rest easy, all worries spent. While the tongues of the maidens acclaim Kevin, we "Ascend . . . and shrine"—arise and shine, out of bed and ready for breakfast. Kate is in the kitchen, cooking. A new world is before us: Australia or New Zealand. New Zealand seems new enough, but since Z is the last letter and A the first, "Newer Aland" is newer. If "smark" enough, you must conclude that Z is to A as the last half sentence of the *Wake* is to the first. "One seekings." Of the "leeward" and "windward" brothers it is "flowerfleckled" Kevin

the girls single out as "someone imparticular who will somewherise for the whole"—the new H.C.E., rising in place of the
old, and, like him, at once particular and "imparticular"
(601.10–602.8) or as general as the Russian General and as
worthy to be shot at by another son.

The introductory conclusion or conclusive introduction that
detains us—concluding the book, that is, and introducing this
chapter—is passing now into a saint's life, that of St. Kevin
of Glendalough, valley of the two lakes. A transitional passage, linking preface with hagiology, celebrates "Coemghen"
(Caoimhgin is Gaelic for Kevin). This holy boy, a "woodtoo-
gooder" and a rolling "tun" (barrel and stone, that gathers no
"must") is the "son." "Roga," whose voice is silent in his presence, may be a reversal of *agora* or Old Mother Space, combined with questioning *rogo,* both the skeptical market place and
A.L.P. The ass of the four old men is there along with a reporter
from the *Durban Gazette,* who, from the new world of South
Africa, finds the "latterman" agreeable: "may he live for
river!" The "Saturnights pomps" is the wake of old father Saturn, Saturday night in his pub, and the *Saturday Evening Post,*
as much a product of the new world as Dutch Schultz, "per-
humps." Headlines from the newspaper and shots from newsreels expose old perhumpsing Humphrey while the latterman,
his successor, making his rounds for "geese and peeas and oats"
(G.P.O. or General Post Office and food), encounters a "merry-
foule of maidens." Traces of bacon and eggs from breakfast on
the lips of the "sunsoonshine" fail to impair his smile. "Shoen!
. . . Shoon the Puzt!" shout the twenty-nine adoring girls,
"Bring us this days our maily bag!" What "an ovenly odour"
from his daily bread and butter! If Shem is a baker and Shaun is
a butterman, Kevin is a composite of Shem and Shaun, as
closely united now as bread and butter. The "hydes of march [in
Hyde Park]. . . . Heard you the crime," a "pipe," and Fox
Goodman confirm the Cad's presence in this replacement of father. Shem's presence—probably recessive—in the mixture does
not keep those "heliotrollops," whether *fille, Frau* or Danish

pige, from hailing sonny boy, who, like his father, favors all the girls, "dubbledecoys" in particular (602.9–603.33).

Through a stained glass window the rising sun lights Coemghem's saintly legend. Confusing "Heremonheber" (united twins) with Jerry, even "Roga's voice" commends him. It is still too early in the morning for the malt house of "Malthus" (cf. 585.11) to be open "for hourly rincers' mess" (early risers' Mass and hourly drinking in the pub). The door of the pub is closed, but "Besoakers loiter on" (soaks loitering later on). It is even too early for the Angelus (6 A.M.): "the engine of the load with haled morries [lorries] full of crates." It is too early for the first tram to take the place of night's "milk train" on the milky way. So there is time for a brief life from "aubrey" of our saint: *"Hagiographice canat Ecclesia"*—the church hymns the new H.C.E., the "who is who is," our patron saint (603.34–604.21). "That's what's that . . . what."

"Oyesesyeses!" proclaims the new H.C.E., opening his court with the last words of courted Mrs. Bloom, "I yam as I yam." Swift, the hero of *Exiles,* and God, announcing "I am what I am," preceded this divine yam—a yam, like Mr. Bloom's Irish potato, is from the New World—this nitrogen in the air of the Irish free state, this Canadian "Habitant" of the Thousand Islands, this Mediterranean with Western and Eastern approaches (604.22–26).

So announced, the life of St. Kevin of Glendalough (604–06) proceeds under the holiest auspices. The nine orders of angels attend him: seraphs, cherubs, thrones, dominations, virtues, powers, principalities, archangels, and angels—or eight of them at least; for I have been unable to track dominations down. All seven of the sacraments are there: baptism, confirmation, the Eucharist, penance, extreme unction, holy orders, and matrimony. All seven of the orders of the church: priest, deacon, subdeacon, acolyte, exorcist, lector, doorkeeper—and bishop, sometimes considered the eighth, immediately follows Kevin's brief life. All—angels and clerics alike—follow the seven canonical hours: matins-lauds, prime, tierce, sext, nones, vespers, compline. The steps toward beatification proceed from venerable to blessed to saint, either doctor or anchorite, whether under Ambrosian or Gregorian dispensation, in ecclesiastical colors proper to the season: gold, red, violet, and sable. Some of the cardinal virtues—fortitude, for example—are around, but none of the deadly sins. Tracking these elements down in this agreeable arrangement—one of the most agreeable in the *Wake* —will give you pleasure, as much pleasure, I hope—and hope is a cardinal virtue—as it has given me.

Shaun assumed the habit of a monk in Chapter XV (483.32– 35). Now, as Kevin, he acts according to old habit. Briefly, Aubrey's brief life of St. Kevin is this or—if one transposes his singular life into the plural—his "miracles, death and life are these." After espousing the true cross, "invented" by St. Helen, Kevin proceeded under angelic guidance to Glendalough, near Tom Moore's "meeting waters" at Avoca in County Wicklow. (These meeting waters, the rivers "Yssia and Essia," are as swift—and Swiftian—as the waters of the girls in the Park.) Kevin took along his "portable *altare cum balneo*," a bathtubaltar, like one of Crashaw's "portable and compendious oceans." Lauding the blessed Trinity with *Sanctus, Sanctus, Sanctus* ("the triune trishagion"), Kevin made for the more navigable of the two lakes at Glendalough, where, following the precedent of Yeats at Lough Gill, he rafted his portable bathtubaltar to a "lake Ysle" in the "enysled lakelet." On his lake isle of Glendalough, like Yeats on Innisfree, Kevin built him a "honeybeehivehut" (605.17–24), then dug a hole that he filled with water. Having filled his bathtubaltar with water, he placed his tub in his water hole and in his tub he sat—in water surrounded by water on an island surrounded by water, concentrically. So disposed, "Saint Kevin Hydrophilos," as water-loving as Mr. Bloom (*Ulysses*, 671), and enjoying the first sacrament like a Baptist, meditated the regeneration of man by water—what A.L.P. commonly attends to (605.4–606.12). "Yee," not only what he said on sitting down in cold water, is Mrs. Bloom's terminal "yes" and H.C.E.'s preliminary "Yad" (cf. "Yod," 485.5, the tenth letter of the Hebrew alphabet). "Messy messy" and "douche

douche" (605.2) are important words of this tale of a bathtub. Since "mishe mishe" is what Shem says and "tauftauf" what Shaun says (3.9–10), St. Kevin, the regenerated H.C.E. and another Yeats (a father figure), must be a union of Shem and Shaun. Shaun alone, unable to read the letter he carries, could not have followed the great example of Yeats.

Between this aquatic play and the following interlude are two exclamations (606.13): "Bisships, bevel to rock's rite! Sarver buoy, extinguish!" Bishops suit the context of deacon, priest, and saint. The Mass—rite of Peter, the rock—is over and the server, a boy from the parish, puts the candles out. But bishops bevelling to the right-hand rook suggest chess, checking the king perhaps or mating him. And "Bisships" or two ships suggest the navigation of twins, two ships passing the night in the *Wake*, coming by the aid of a "buoy" to port now. Whatever the entire meaning of these exclamations, the interlude concerns old H.C.E., his sin, fall, and wake: "Nuotabene." After these his waking up.

The "three Benns" (Irish mountains and Hebrew sons) seem to be the three peeping soldiers. The "fairypair," not the two girls this time, are, as *"O ferax cupla!"* shows, H.C.E. and A.L.P. in the Bristol, the hen coop by the trolly track. They are something "to right hume about." But if you scribbled a letter about H.C.E., the "arky paper" (a Danish sheet of paper from Noah's ark), the penmarks on it, and the "style, stink and [Christlike] stigmataphoron" would prove him "one sum in the same person." The "Panniquanne" with her "peequuliar talonts" is A.L.P. as the mannequin of Brussels (17.2) and the Prankquean, making her wit, with a clean pair of heels. Her "fancy claddaghs" are rings from Galway and clothes. H.C.E., like St. Kevin, combines "tofatufa" and "Missas in Massas" (tauftauf-mishe mishe, with the two girls and A.L.P. *en masse* or at Mass). Great sinning means good sons on the "socerdatal tree" of the "MacCowell family," the family of "wise head" (white head is Finn MacCool). "Teak off that wise head!" echoes the story of the tailor and sailor: "Take off thatch whitehat" (322.1–8. Cf. 623.9). Jacob, the Cad with the pipe, and

Esau, with his lentil-pottage, let father know it is the "hours of changeover," both theirs and his—time to take that white hat off. (The hat, as we know from the battle of Willingdone and Lipoleum, is a sign of authority.) Shem's first riddle of "the anniverse" (170.4–5), exposing a "Sham," becomes: "when is a nam nought a nam?" Reversal of man, uncertainty about name ("nam"), and "Watch" prove this the hour of "changeover." "Four horolodgeries," the four old timekeepers, call time now for old "Champelysied." It is time for him "to seek the shades of his retirement." Indeed, it is time for a wake, where all the girls of Chapelizod "tear around and tease their partners"; it's lots of fun at Finnegan's wake. And it's high time for high tea—Tetley's tea. Jostling another dancer at the wake, someone begs another's pardon (606.14–607.22).

The wake is over. The "regn of durknass" is recessing. "Solsking," the sun, is coming up. The "Boergemester," builder and mayor—that Grand Old Man, another Gladstone—is glad to leave the fog of Isolde with no mark on him. "Heave mensy upponnus!"—Lord have mercy and set the table (*mensa*) for breakfast (607.24–36). In the "vague of visibilities, mark you. . . . Uncle Arth," you have suffered, like the Draper himself, from the slanders of "the two drawpers assisters and the three droopers assessors." Constable "Sigerson," taking your blood pressure, was as bad. The quartet from Chapter XV (e.g., 547, 550), questioning "Mister Ireland? And a live?" more or less agrees (608.1–15).

Father is waking from his dream of mother in the "harms" of "meassurers soon and soon," his twin sons, those so-and-sos, messieurs taking his measure. The voice of Anna is calling him down for tea, "the brew with the foochoor in it." What did he see in that dream? "Nyets," he says, "I dhink I sawn to remumb or sumbsuch." Maybe, the sleepy mumbler adds, I saw a "traylogged" thing (a delta) and an "acutebacked quadrangle" (the *Wake*). But the "week of wakes is out and over"—over and out. Earwicker, the "wick weak" of Anna's lamp (583.31), is waking as the "Phoenican [Finnegan the Phoenix] wakes" and rises from his Asiatic ashes ("Ashias"). We are passing from the

Wake to the wide-awake world (608.16–35). At sunrise, every man is a "newman" and, in a way, a son.

Dreaming on at sunrise—a more deliberate phenomenon at Chapelizod than elsewhere—we dream that we are waking from an agreeable dream of touring "the no placelike no timelike absolent" (or the *Wake*) in our gearless, clutchless car (cf. calling all cars, 593.2). In the placeless, timeless scenery of this dream opposites mingle: little Welsh people ("pettyvaughan") with big Irish people ("magnumoore"), lighthaired "mersscenary blookers" with darkskinned "pigttetails" (three soldiers, two Danish girls), who, like Wilde's fox hunters, seem "unprobables in their poor suit of the improssable" or H.C.E. Present at this hunt are the four old men, to whom "maru" lends a Japanese air, and their ass. Also present are the three flower-fruit girls, old "Rosina" Kate, Anna, and Isabel, three hens "ricocoursing" like cocks crowing at a *ricorso*. Their home is the pub with about a dozen branches for all twelve patrons. These pubs will open when the rising sun of Japan gives "to every seeable a hue and to every hearable a cry" (E.H.C.) and to every place a time. Meanwhile, we await "Hymn"—Earwicker-Shaun, Patrick, or the sun (609.1–23).

The dialogue of Mutt and Jeff or *Muta* (change) and *Juva* (youth), centering on "Hymn," proceeds in a mixture of pig Latin and pidgin English, with a little Nipponese added for good measure. Nevertheless, their dialogue, like the rest of the *Wake,* is basically English.

Muta and *Juva* notice smoke rising from Earwicker's house, where Kate, no doubt, is making breakfast. "Dies is Dorminus master," says *Juva: Deus est dominus noster* as day is the lord of sleep with all its *tenebrae.* (Explaining this in a letter, I, 406, Joyce says that the Book of the Dead, which he has in mind, is also called Chapters of the Coming-forth by Day.) *Muta's* "Diminussed aster," echoing *dominus noster,* adds the fading morning star, by whose light he seems to see a "wolk in process" —a procession of folk, a folk-process, and *Work in Progress* or the *Wake.* Yes, says *Juva,* this crowd is H.C.E. from the land of the chrysanthemum, shouting *banzai* while "moveyovering"

the battlefield of Cabra, not far from Clontarf. (*Muta's* pidgin
English is no worse than *Juva's* Japanese, and no better.) A
field of battle recalls the Russian General and Buckley who,
"fundementially" disgusted by the "whorse proceedings" of the
General, shot him. But General H.C.E., having fallen from the
Magazine wall ("Fing Fing!"), now rises "from undernearth the
[Wellington] memorialorum." May Vico's lightning ("Fulgi-
tudo"), says *Muta,* strike Earwicker's "Rhedonum." (Far from
clear, this word may include Latin *rhaeda* or *raeda,* a four-
wheeled carriage, or Rhea, the mother goddess, and her
domum.) Vico's lightning starts the cycle that ends, as Dublin's
motto indicates, with the building of cities. But Earwicker
is a divided man. You can bet your bottom dollar every
"dime," says *Juva,* that Earwicker has bet "half his crown" on
Buckley and the other half on the "Eurasian Generalissimo." Is
he, then, "paridicynical?"—cynical about parricide and paradise? "Ut vivat volumen," *Juva* replies, "sic pereat pouradosus!"
(That the book may live, let paradise be lost, as Yeats says in
"The Choice.") Plainly the twins have been discussing *Finnegans
Wake* and perfection of the work that an artist must abandon
hope of heaven for. Talk of betting, drinking, wenching, and
Vico's "Piabelle et Purabelle" leads to *Muta's* reflection, according to Bruno, on "diversity" and "appeasement." That the quarreling twins have become one at last is proved by their cordial
agreement. Lend me your "hordwanderbaffle" (Danish hot
water bottle), says *Muta.* Here it is, says *Juva;* may it be your
"wormingpen." Terminal "Shoot" must mean that Buckley—or
the twins as one *bouchal*—has shot the Russian General again.
How different *Muta* and *Juva* in the last chapter from Mutt and
Jute in the first. No communication there. Here, getting along as
famously as W. S. Gilbert's twins, they too could sing: "Together we stand as one individual" (609.24–610.33).

Talk of betting accounts for a brief visit to the race track
(610.34–611.2). In the "Grand Natural" sweepstakes "Velivi-
sion" is victor, "Peredos Last"—commercial eye, that is, defeats
Miltonic ear by a neck. Wee Winny Widger, from Chapter II
(39.11), is back to give tips on the human race: "Two draws"

are the two girls in drawers; "Heliotrope" is Isabel; "Three ties" are the three soldiers. "Jocky the Ropper" and "Jake the Rape" are the twins. "Paddrock and bookley chat," an admirable transition, looks back to the chat of *Muta* and *Juva* about Buckley, a good shot, and forward to that of rocky Patrick and booky Berkeley. But elements in the dialogue of *Muta* and *Juva*— Buckley, Leary, and "druidful"—have anticipated this transition; and, says Joyce (*Letters*, I, 406), *Juva's* "Dies is Dorminus master," a better anticipation, shows what's the matter with Berkeley.

If Berkeley-Balkelly-Buckley is Shem and if Patrick is Shaun, the twins are now as disunited as, when *Muta* and *Juva*, they were united. Certainly Berkeley is the artist and Patrick the practical man. If Berkeley is Buckley in the sense of united *bouchal*, Patrick must be the Russian General, who, reversing the story, shoots Buckley. The "Thud" (612.36) of fallen Buckley is parallel to the "Shoot" (610.33) that fells the General. Whoever these antagonists, they resume the pidgin English and Nippon English of *Muta* and *Juva;* and, according to Joyce (*Letters*, I, 406), this debate continues "the defence and indictment" of the *Wake,* defense by Berkeley, the artist, and indictment by Patrick, the general public. "Thud" marks the artist's defeat by society. This passage, as obscure as anything in the *Wake,* is one of the first parts Joyce wrote—in 1923, along with the simpler stories of Rory O'Connor and Tristan (*Letters*, I, 202–05; III, 79).

"Tunc" (611.4), recalling the *Tunc* page of the Book of Kells (on the crucifixion), may imply the crucifixion of the artist. That Berkeley, the artist, speaks pidgin English, the language of Oriental commerce, seems odd until we reflect that, to the public, the *Wake* sounds like pidgin English. Berkeley, the Irish "archdruid," like Mutt in Chapter I, confronts a foreign invader, this time Patrick, the archbishop. Brilliant in his rainbow robes, the druid tells Patrick, the "niggerblonker," dressed in pragmatic black and white, a thing or two about epiphany. The veil of illusion, says Berkeley, hides the "hueful panepiphanal" world of Lord Joss from vulgar eyes; for each object in the "heupanepi" world, absorbing six of the seven colors of solar light, reflects the obvious seventh. To the heuristic "seer," however, the absorbed colors are apparent. Looking within and below appearance, he sees the thing in itself, the "sextuple gloria" retained "inside" the object that Patrick with his simple eye misses or ignores. Take High King Leary for example. You see his red head. But to the eye of insight, the color is green. To the "throughsighty" seer, what you think his "sixcoloured" worsteds and his saffron kilt, are as green as spinach. Whatever the outer colors of his other belongings, to the man of vision they are as green as cabbage, parsley, and olives. In short, whatever an Irishman wears outside, inside he is wearing the green. Green, the Irishman's epiphany, must be detected and fixed by the Irish artist. "Hump cumps Ebblybally" (H.C.E. as a Dubliner—from the bally of Eblana) has the essential green of King Leary perhaps, or perhaps, as a Danish invader, he is Patrick's equivalent. Resolving this ambiguity would tax an Empson (611.4–612.15).

At this point ("Punc") Patrick, ignoring subtleties, makes his *Punkt*—Punc for Tunc. A "shiroskuro blackinwhitepaddynger" (*dynger* is Danish for dump), he disposes of the "Irismans ruinboon" and the "possible viriditude of the [sage-green] sager" by the "probable eruberuption [red] of the saint." Disposing of these as Alexander disposed of the Gordian knot, Patrick kneels before the three-sided "Balenoarch" (a whale of a God) and hails Him as "the sound sense sympol in a weedwayedwold of the firethere the sun in his halo cast." The Blessed Trinity, the Thing in Itself, is the true inwardness of all things; and the light of day, whatever its septuple ingredients, is one. In this light things are what they seem. Forced to acknowledge truth, Berkeley falls, defeated (612.16–36).

Before making his point, Patrick wipes himself with his "shammyrag" (shamrock) as the Russian General wiped himself with turf from the old sod (612.24–25). Accepting the point (612.34–36), Berkeley "throw his seven" (discarding his seven colors, took a crap), but, apparently, failed to wipe "His Ards" (arse and art). Defeated by the Prankquean, Jarl van Hoother "ordurd" (23.4), and Hosty's ballad (44.19–21) is Cambronne's *merde.* Who is the Russian General now—Patrick or Berkeley—and who the creative defecator? Empson absent, we resign ourselves, as negatively capable as Keats, to ambiguity— of the seventh type perhaps or the eighth.

"Good safe firelamp!" (Ireland and the light of day) shout the applauding "heliots," all the sun-loving helots of Ireland: *Per dominum nostrum, Jesum christum, filium tuum.* "Taaw- haar?" All the heliots—"Sants and sogs, cabs and cobs"—agree that Berkeley's tar water, a thing of black night, is gone for- ever. It is daylight now. "Dies," as *Juva* said, "is Dorminus mas- ter." Our Feast of Tabernacles (cf. "Sukkot," 612.15) demands lights. "Trancefixureashone" (Shaun transfigured?) and Shem's "Shamwork" shed equal light now that "every crisscouple" is "crosscomplimentary" in the "farbiger pancosmos." "Gud- struce," more than God's truth, is creative peace after the "trampatrampatramp" of a civil war. Nothing has been added to our closed system, nothing subtracted from it. "Only is order othered" now that saint and sage have had their say and found appeasement in the land of "laurens" O'Toole. *"Fuitfiat"* is a reversal of God's "Fiatfuit" (17.32) in the Vulgate Genesis (613.1–16).

An interlude, separating the conclusion of these associated debates from A.L.P.'s letter, stirs old things up again: darkness, breakfast, fall, renewal, the *Wake,* and Vico's process. Amenti, the underworld of the Book of the Dead, is gloomy; but among the "skullhullows and charnelcysts" of this "weedwastewol- dwevild" (cf. "weedwayedwold," 612.29), a sort of wasteland, plants are sprouting, insects fertilizing. A cup of tea for break- fast and "Ralph the Retriever" (H.C.E.) and "thea," goddess of tea (A.L.P.), will be as "spickspan as a rainbow." As above, so below: a bowl of tea will move the bowel (613.17–26).

From tea to toast: Here's to "Health, chalce, endnessnesses- sity!" May H.C.E.'s "likkypuggers," little pigs in a poke (cf. "little pukers," 250.11), arrive! Vico's thunder and lightning prove "optimominous"; for morning and evening of the new day —a lovely day for mirages—will bury the orchard of man's dis- obedience if, like Adam, that "toilermaster," you "make good that breachsuit" of fig leaves and get yourself up to kill. "Jas-minia" (A.L.P.) must adjust herself to the prospect of one, two or three women: "Monogynes . . . Diander. . . . grazeheifer, ethel or bonding"—Kate the last of these. All the "horod-ities" (children) will be coming back from Anna's washhouse, "Ormepierre [elm-stone] Lodge," rinsed, starched, and clean again from the "lathering" in "mournenslaund," the sad laundry of morning. As with water, so with fire. "Habit reburns" like a Viconian Phoenix. The nation, too, will be reborn, whatever the old betrayals: "If you sell me," said Parnell, "get my price" (613.27–614.18).

What has happened in the *Wake?* How does it end? (Maybe the four old men ask these questions.) If we forget, the *Wake* "will remember itself." Every side, gesture, and word in this "perusiveness" will bring it back to mind. "Have we cherished expectations" with H.C.E.? The "plainplanned liffeyism assem-blements" (P.L.A.) will satisfy them; for "dim delty Deva" is dear dirty Dublin's goddess of the delta (614.19–26). What matter anyway if we remember or forget?

The *Wake,* as Mamalujo knows, is a "millwheeling vicoci-clometer, a tetradomational" construction, built like Yeats's "gazebo" or a machine with "clappercoupling smeltingworks ex-progressive process," known to Vico as "eggburst, eggblend, eggburial and hatch-as-hatch can" (religion, marriage, burial, and *ricorso*) or, according to Bruno, a dialectical process of "decomposition" and "recombination" in which the "heroti-cisms, catastrophes and eccentricities" of H.C.E. are "transmit-ted by the ancient legacy of the past [A.L.P.] . . . letter from litter." The course of history, whether flowery peace or war's inhumanity, reveals the same old "adomic structure" of H.C.E., our atomic Adam, "as highly charged with electrons as hopaz-ards can effective it." When the cock crows, you may be sure of breakfast—"as sure as herself pits hen to paper and there's scribings scrawled on eggs" (614.27–615.10).

"Letter from litter" and the hen lead us from this philosophi-cal rumination about the *Wake* to another state of the teastained letter, the *Wake*'s epitome. As we may have suspected all along,

Finnegans Wake is about *Finnegans Wake,* less the history of everyman, everywhere, at every time than a commentary on this history of that history. Taking from this moderate exaggeration what you can, forget the rest and read the letter, which, like one of Nora's, is eloquently incoherent. But so, after all, is Mrs. Bloom's monologue. Joyce's opinion of woman was at once high and low, higher than mine, for example, and lower. Such depths and heights of insight make us agree on the whole with Jung (*Letters,* III, 253), who, after reading *Ulysses,* said, only "the devil's grandmother knows so much about the real psychology of a woman. I didn't."

A.L.P.'s new letter, sent this time from "Dirtdump" or dear dirty Dublin and the dump in the Park, is addressed to "Dear. . . . Reverend. . . . majesty" or H.C.E., to whose defense and praise she devotes her ramblings. Nursery tales—"jerk of the beamstark," "goldylocks," and "handsel for gertles," for example—and popular songs, "the brinks of the wobblish," show her simplicity. Milton's "twohangled warpon" and "paladays last" show the literacy that letters require. (Even Mrs. Bloom, no writer of letters, had heard of Rabelais and Byron.) "Denighted of this light's time," says A.L.P., she has been denighted and delighted by the *Wake;* but she resents the insinuations of those snakes, sneakers, and muckraking "Mucksrats" who, ignorant of the "honorary tenth commendmant," have bared "full sweetness against a nighboor's wiles" (cf. 14.25–27). Let these "slimes"—the two girls and the three soldiers—"forget him their trespasses" (615.12–36).

Persse O'Reilly, Huckleberry Finn MacCool, or whatever you call him is about to get up after having been downed by the Cad with the pipe, the two girls, and the three "pestituting" soldiers. But, "unperceable to haily, icy and missilethroes," that "coerogenal hun" (a union of H.C.E., the Hun, with A.L.P., the hen; *hun* is Danish for she) is "balladproof." Getting up, he will enjoy sausage and tea for breakfast. With a prayer to St. Laurence O'Toole, "we now must close." It may be as far from closing time for letter as for pub, but anyway, 111 or 1001 blessings in closing (616.1–617.5).

H.C.E., she continues, is the "direst of housebonds," yet the MacCool brothers, those "bucket Toolers" (cf. 5.3–4), have conspired against him, like the Cad, in the Phoenix "pork martyrs." But these "timsons," who have killed Tim-H.C.E., have "changed their characticuls [Caractacus and arses] during their blackout." A little music "ought to weke him to make up" at his "grand fooneral," which will be attended by the twenty-eight girls, the twelve customers, and the four "moracles" (617.7–26).

When young, A.L.P. had auburn hair, a shape, and a "cubarola glide" on Wonderland Road. Her mirror tells her she has changed. Moreover, the Cad has gone off with "the pope's wife" (cf. 38.9). What "Sully," the bootmaker, has to do with these affairs is beyond me (617.30–618.34); and incoherence alone justifies the instrusion of Adam Findlater, "our grocerest churcher" with his Christmas parcel. But her "polite conversation," straight from Swift, is that of a river talking in "the rhythms in me amphybed."

While she has flowed in her valley, "hampty damp" has occupied "the himp of holth" (Hill of Howth). "We've lived in two worlds." It is time now, however, for "herewaker" (German *Erwecker?* Cf. "uhrweckers," 615.16, Danish alarmclocks) to arise, "erect, confident and heroic" (E.C.H.). Whatever his reversals and "his real namesame," his "wee one woos." Her P.S. qualifies acceptance of life with Earwicker. Fed up with "nonsery reams," aware that the "rigs" of the Ritz are rags, she is worn out (618.35–619.19).

If, forgetting montage, we resume the metaphor of music, A.L.P.'s terminal monologue (619–28) is the *Wake*'s coda, different in rhythm and key from her letter and the recitative that precedes it. Like Mrs. Bloom's terminal monologue in function, A.L.P.'s coda is unlike it in feeling, tone, and center. Mrs. Bloom circles around four fleshly points. A.L.P., taking a mazy course from Chapelizod to Dublin Bay, flows through memories of her family to acceptance of age and death. Mrs. Bloom's monologue, saying "yes" to life, is at once funny and serious. A.L.P.'s, despite gaiety of language, is serious alone—pathetic, and charged with sentiment that evades the embarrassing sentimentality of *Giacomo Joyce*. An odd conclusion for a book so gay; but maybe Joyce, saying "I am highly sheshe sherious" (570.25), meant what he said. Indeed, serious gaiety was his customary way of accosting life and death. Like Mrs. Bloom, the old lady says "yes," but her acceptance of our general lot is qualified, at times, by impatience and disenchantment. Centered on Earwicker and her children, as Mrs. Bloom on Bloom, she sees through them as Mrs. Bloom through Bloom. A.L.P. has lived, is tired. Not altogether discouraged, she takes what we get. Her voice is the voice of Joyce, transposed to be sure, and uncommonly "sheshe sherious," saying all he had to say about living and dying—as movingly on the final page as on the final page of "The Dead."

"I am leafy speafing," says A.L.P. "Leafy" is both the Liffey, river of life, arched by trees at Chapelizod and Island Bridge, and "only a leaf" on the family tree of life. "Lsp. . . . Lpf" are leaf-and-Liffey talk, which, so introduced, continues in rhythms at once choppy and flowing, like the river in "that wind as if out of norewere" (626.4). Her "goolden wending," from leafy Chapelizod through the city to the sea, is celebrated on a "soft morning"—a rainy day. "Folty and folty all the nights have falled" like Noah's rain (619.20–24).

Her disorderly flow, bearing all the flotsam of the *Wake* and no little of its jetsam, demands ordering if, following without imitating her course, one must speak of what she speaks of. She talks like an old woman in a chair. I, an old man in mine, talking like a professor, must reduce her "traumscrapt" (623.36) to categories for my "little pukers." Better, of course, to take her as she flows through eddies and backwaters without categorical interference.

Regressing to a second childhood, the old lady still talks under the spell of "old mutthergoosip" (623.3–4) and her "nonsery reams"—fewer rhymes, however, than tales. Among these are Old King Cole, Babes in the Wood, Goody Twoshoes, Puss in Boots, Little Red Ridinghood, Cinderella, Ali Baba, *Robinson Crusoe* and *Uncle Tom's Cabin*.

Recapitulating themes, as a coda should, her coda touches on

the following in no discernable sequence: 1. Buckley and the
Russian General (620.4). "Rosensharonals" mixes the General
with the two girls as roses of Sharon. 2. The washerwomen with
"dirty clothes to publish"—washing dirty linen, of the twins,
this time, in public (620.18–23). 3. "Pearse orations" to "gap-
ers" (620.24) confronts Persse O'Reilly with the three soldiers.
4. King Arthur, Arthur Guinness, Mark of Cornwall, and Isaac's
sons (621.7–20). "Send Arctur guiddus" unites Sir Arthur Guinness with King Arthur, a guiding star, and a saint. 5. Finnegan
falling with his hod from the scaffold (621.28–29) becomes Finn
MacCool, the Salmon of Wisdom (625.16), and "white hat"
(623.9) or blond Finn and Whitehead, the tailor, who recurs
with the sailor (624.27–30; 626.9–15). 6. The hunt with Earwicker as fox (622.25–623.3). 7. Grace O'Malley, Howth Castle, "vom Hungerig," and the Prankquean (623.10–17). 8.
Swift's Struldbrugs and Houyhnhnms (623.23–24) are followed
by Hester, Esther, Cadenus, and *A Tale of a Tub* (624.25–27).
9. Ibsen's *Peer Gynt* and "bigmaster. . . . soleness," scaling
his tower of Babel and falling, like Humpty Dumpty, from it
(624.9–13). 10. The hen's letter, by "traumscrapt" from Boston, is combined with letters of the alphabet and Pigott's forgery: "heth hith ences" (623.31–624.4). 11. "On limpidy
marge I've made me hoom" (624.15)—"At Trinity Church I
met my doom"—connects this coda with that of Chapter IV
(102–03). Other motifs recur, but eleven seems a sufficient
number—suitable too for a *ricorso*.

All the motifs are connected, more or less, with H.C.E., who
at the beginning of her monologue is a Wonderful Old Boy
(624.23), in the middle a "Cooloosus" (625.22), near the end
a "bumpkin" (627.23), and at the end the terrible sea. For her,
as for us all, Earwicker is a queer mixture. He has a "great
poet" in him—his Shem side no doubt—a side, she says, that
"bored me to slump" (619.31–33), as Joyce's Shem side bored
Nora. The "contrairy" twins, as different as North from South,
says A.L.P., are "you all over," when their external becomes his
internal, division. "No peace at all" in him, with him, or with his
separated constituents, who are liable to change in a "twinngling

of an aye" (620.12–18). As various as divided, H.C.E. reminds her of "wonderdecker" (Vanderdecken, the Flying Dutchman), Sinbad the Sailor, Patrick Sarsfield (Earl of Lucan), and Wellington, the Iron Duke (620.6–9).

As for the rest of her family: worry over the quarreling twins made Earwicker long for a girl: "Your wish was mewill." Though Isabel, when she came, had little "matcher's wit," she had "perts of speech" more agreeable to H.C.E. than to her mother. Isabel was to Earwicker what "he," a union of the twins, was to A.L.P. "Let besoms be bosuns," recalling "bisons is bisons" (16.29), enlarges it with the besom proper to a girl (620.26–621.1). These little "cuppinjars" of the Coppinger family (621.15), like the Prankquean's "porterpease," are a "lintil pea" and a "cara weeseed" (625.23–24).

Little wonder that, feeling "the weight of old fletch" (621.33), she needs a new girdle (621.18). But desperate though her particular situation is, the general situation is hopeful: the Phoenix will flame out through her children and "the book of the depth" is closed. The Cad's "Pax Goodmens" (peace on earth to men of good will), ringing out twelve o'clock from Le Fanu's "church by the hearseyard," announces a beginning as well as an end (621.1–3,34–35). Twelve o'clock is also the hour when Cinderella's carriage becomes a "bumpkin" (627.22–23) and when, summoned by Bow bells, Dick Whittington turns back to rebuild "Londub" (625.35–36). Finnegan, who at his wake seems done for, will be "Finn, again!" (628.14), glad to have been "waked." As for me, she says, "I'll begin again in a jiffey" (625.32–33) when, maybe, the birds of dawn and sterner men of letters begin their "treestirm shindy" (621.36).

Though A.L.P. is "near to faint away. Into the deeps," memories of life with Earwicker—a tower of strength to one so "wea" —ease her passage: those days when he followed a "pining child round the sluppery table with a forkful of fat" and those no less domestic days when he "shootst throbbst into me mouth" (cf. 396.2; 493.5–10,28). At this point one may be tempted to say with Mulligan's Dowden (*Ulysses,* 204) that "life ran very high in those days"; but it may be that, resorting to metaphor, she means the meeting of the river at Island Bridge with the uprushing tide: "Where you meet I." Either way, her frightening Earwicker came "darkly roaring," with flashing eyes, to "fan me cooly" or "perce me rawly. . . . till delth to uspart" (626.1–32). There is no happier example of Dublin talk.

Now, however, it is time to go; for Earwicker has changed again. Dual as usual, he is not only the terrible sea to which she flows—the paternal sea—but the young "sonhusband," who, replacing the old man, will take a new wife, "a daughterwife from the hills. . . . swimming in my hindmoist" to replace old A.L.P. In brief, Shaun-H.C.E. and Nuvoletta-Isabel-A.L.P. will take the place of their parents. Nuvoletta? After the river enters the sea, the sun sucks water up into a cloud which, according to cyclical necessity, will drop a tear into the river (159.10–18), and so for river and ever. "Let her rain now if she likes," says A.L.P., "for my time is come." All may be a "Tobe-continued's tale" (626.18), but, dying now, I am "Loonely [as the moon] in my loneness" (627.1–34).

"I am passing out. O bitter ending!" (627.34) begins a page that has few rivals in the works of Joyce. This page, last of the book and, in a sense, his last—is one of his best poems, all of which are in prose. Passing out to her "cold mad feary father" with his "therrble prongs"—H.C.E. as a kind of Neptune before becoming "Finn, again"—she becomes a child: "Far [Danish father] calls." "Mememormee!" the memory (Greek *mneme?*) of what is past, is also the promise or the hope—shared by every dying animal—of more me to come. "The keys to. Given! A way" (cf. "the keys of me heart," 626.30–31) are the keys to heaven, the given away, and the given or whatever is. ("What will be," says Isis-A.L.P., "Is Is," 620.32.) Five indefinite articles precede definite "the": what is given or what in "The Man on the Dump" Wallace Stevens calls "The the." A.L.P.'s final "the" is equivalent to Mrs. Bloom's final "yes." Both are words of acceptance. But "the," the last word, goes with "riverrun," the first. "The riverrun," more than the end and beginning of the *Wake,* includes all betwixt and between.

593.1   "Sandhyas! Sandhyas! Sandhyas!" a motif associated with Shaun and T. S. Eliot, whose Sanskrit
"Shantih shantih shantih" amused Joyce. In his
parody of *The Waste Land* (*Letters,* I, 231) Joyce
renders this as *"Shan't we? Shan't we? Shan't we?"*
Eliot's "Da" (Sanskrit give, *Waste Land,* line 400)
reappears in the *Wake* as "Dah!" (594.2) or, by
reversal, Had. Cf. "Vah!" (594.1) or Hav. Campbell and Robinson have identified many of the
Sanskrit words in Chapter XVII.

593.13   "The leader." Cf. "through strength towards joy-
ance" (598.24–25); "fearer" (604.28); and
"douche" (605.2), which connect Shaun with the
Nazis and Fascists.

594.10–13 Leverhulme's Sunlight Soap. Cf. Pear's Soap
(593.9): "Good morning, have you used Pear's
Soap?" Here "Piers aube" (dawn for Persse O'-
Reilly) is connected with Patrick Pearse, who led
the Easter rising. Cf. Mr. Bloom's lemon "soap-
sun" (*Ulysses,* 440). Soap and washing, as in
Chapter VIII, imply renewal.

595.10–17 The counties of Ireland as Shaun's food: Cork,
Limerick, Waterford, Wexford, Louth, Kildare,
Leitrim, Kerry, Carlow, Leix, Offaly, Donegal,
Clare, Galway, Longford, Monaghan, Fermanagh,
Cavan, Antrim, Armagh, Roscommon, Sligo,
Meath, Westmeath, Mayo ("kilalooly")—twenty-
five out of the thirty-two counties, but there must
be others that escape me.

595.33   "Syd." Cf. "Tom" (597.30) and "Tim" (598.27).
Syd and Tom, from *Tom Sawyer,* are the twins
here. Tim is Tim Finnegan or H.C.E. Together,
Syd, Tom, and Tim are the three soldiers.

597.31–32 "Excelsius . . . torporature" refers to Anders
Celsius, the Swedish astronomer, who invented the
Centigrade thermometer.

601.3   "Tasyam kuru salilakriyamu" contains two Japanese words: *kuru*, to come, and *yamu*, to cease. The rest, I am assured by Setsuko Ohara, is not Japanese. Indeed, the whole sentence, including the apparent Japanese, Miss Ohara tells me, is Telugu (a language of India) for: You should deal fairly with her or do her justice—advice to H.C.E. on dealing with A.L.P. *Tasyam* is by or to her; *kuru* is do; *salila* is good; *kriyamu* is act.

603.12–15   "Shay for shee . . . nakeshift" refers to Parnell, escaping in his nightshirt from Kitty O'Shea's bedroom (cf. 388.3). "G.M.P." seems to combine Member of Parliament with General Medical Practitioner. "Shay for shee and sloo for slee" is "Tea for Two" in its sexual capacity. "His hydes of march" connects Parnell with Caesar and Earwicker, accosted by the Cad.

605.15–17   "Centripetally . . . ventrifugal" may allude to the union of centripetal Bloom and centrifugal Stephen, *Ulysses,* 703.

605.24   "Fortitude," a cardinal virtue. Had I lacked it, I could not have come through the *Wake*. Had I not lacked prudence, another cardinal virtue, I would not have started coming.

609.9   The "Ass" of the four old men, by what Mr. Bloom would call coincidence, is Danish *as* or god. God is one of the aspects of Stephen Dedalus.

615.2–5   "Since the days of Plooney" is another parody of Edgar Quinet on the permanence of flowers. Cf. 14.35–15.11; 236.19–32; 281.4–13.

619.27–29   "Terce . . . sixt . . . none" recall St. Kevin's canonical hours. If, playing with these numbers, you add them (3 plus 6 plus 0), you get 9, a "norvena" or novena.

623.36   "Maston, Boss" is a reversal of Boston, Mass. Cf. "ech" (623.9) and "Conal O'Daniel" (625.12). Reversals are to be expected in a *ricorso*—at other times too.

625.6–8   *"Cadmillersfolly, Bellevenue, Wellcrom"* is *Cead mile failte,* Gaelic for 100,000 welcomes. Cf. "Cead mealy faulty rices" (16.34–35). *"Bellevenue"* adds welcome in French, and *"Wellcrom,"* a reversal of Cromwell (H.C.E.), in English. The Cad's folly seems involved. "Villities valleties" is the vanity of vanities of cities and valleys. "Murphies" could be a reference to Samuel Beckett and "Spendlove" to Oliver Gogarty, who, in *Mourning Became Mrs. Spendlove,* wrote about Joyce—though dates may rule the latter possibility out.

625.26–27   "Eblana. . . . sama sitta." *Sama sitta* is Estonian for same shit. Dublin (Eblana) is the same city and the same shit. Joyce's opinion of Dublin had not changed much since *Dubliners.*

BIBLIOGRAPHY

Atherton, James S., *The Books at the Wake,* London, Faber & Faber, 1959.

Beckett, Samuel, Stuart Gilbert, Eugene Jolas, *et al., Our Exagmination,* Paris, Shakespeare and Company, 1929. Reprinted as *An Exagmination.*

Benstock, Bernard, *Joyce-again's Wake, An Analysis of Finnegans Wake,* Seattle, University of Washington Press, 1965.

Bonheim, Helmut, *A Lexicon of the German in Finnegans Wake,* Berkeley, University of California Press, 1967.

Campbell, Joseph and Henry Morton Robinson, *A Skeleton Key to Finnegans Wake,* New York, Harcourt, Brace, 1944.

Christiani, Dounia, *Scandinavian Elements in Finnegans Wake,* Evanston, Northwestern University Press, 1965.

Ellmann, Richard, *James Joyce,* New York, Oxford University Press, 1959.

Glasheen, Adaline, *A Second Census of Finnegans Wake,* Evanston, Northwestern University Press, 1963.

Halper, Nathan, "The 'Most Eyeful Hoyth' of *Finnegans Wake,*" *New Republic,* CXXIV (May 7, 1951).

—————— "James Joyce and the Russian General," *Partisan Review,* XVII (July, 1951).

—————— "Joyce and Eliot: a Tale of Shem and Shaun," *The Nation,* CC (May 31, 1965).

—————— "The Date of Earwicker's Dream," *Twelve and a Tilly,* London, Faber & Faber, 1966.

Hart, Clive, *A Concordance to Finnegans Wake,* Minneapolis, University of Minnesota Press, 1963.

———— *Structure and Motif in Finnegans Wake*, Evanston, Northwestern University Press, 1962.

———— *Twelve and a Tilly*, edited by Clive Hart and Jack P. Dalton, London, Faber & Faber, 1966.

———— *A Wake Newslitter*, edited by Clive Hart and Fritz Senn. Periodical since 1962.

Hayman, David, *A First-Draft Version of Finnegans Wake*, Austin, University of Texas Press, 1962.

Higginson, Fred H., *Anna Livia Plurabelle: the Making of a Chapter*, Minneapolis, University of Minnesota Press, 1960.

Hodgart, M. J. C. and Mabel P. Worthington, *Song in the Works of James Joyce*, New York, Columbia University Press, 1959.

Joyce, James, *Letters:* Vol. I, edited by Stuart Gilbert; Vols. II and III, edited by Richard Ellmann, New York, Viking, 1966.

Litz, Walton, *The Art of James Joyce*, London, Oxford University Press, 1961.

Moseley, Virginia, *Joyce and the Bible*, Dekalb, Northern Illinois University Press, 1967.

O Hehir, Brendan, *A Gaelic Lexicon for Finnegans Wake*, Berkeley, University of California Press, 1967.

Tindall, W. Y., *The Joyce Country*, University Park, Pennsylvania State University Press, 1960. Photographs of Chapelizod, the Liffey, Earwicker's pub, the Magazine, the Wellington Monument, Adam and Eve's, the Vico Road, Howth, Kevin's Glendalough.

Wilson, Edmund, "The Dream of H. C. Earwicker," *The Wound and the Bow*, New York, Houghton, Mifflin, 1941.

SELECTIVE INDEX

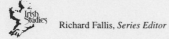 Richard Fallis, *Series Editor*

Irish Studies presents a wide range of books interpreting important aspects of Irish life and culture to scholarly and general audiences. The richness and complexity of the Irish experience, past and present, deserve broad understanding and careful analysis. For this reason, an important purpose of the series is to offer a forum to scholars interested in Ireland, its history, and culture. Irish literature is a special concern in the series, but works from the perspectives of the fine arts, history, and the social sciences are also welcome, as are studies that take multidisciplinary approaches.

Selected titles in the series include: